INTERNET MARKETING

DRYDEN *is*

A Harcourt Higher Learning Company

Now you will find The Dryden Press'
distinguished innovation, leadership, and
support under a different name . . . a new
brand that continues our unsurpassed
quality, service, and commitment to
education.

We are combining the strengths of our
college imprints into one worldwide
brand: Harcourt

Our mission is to make learning
accessible to anyone, anywhere,
anytime—reinforcing our commitment
to lifelong learning.

We are now Harcourt College Publishers.
Ask for us by name.

One Company
"Where Learning
Comes to Life."

www.harcourtcollege.com
www.harcourt.com

INTERNET MARKETING

JAGDISH N. SHETH
EMORY UNIVERSITY

ABDOLREZA ESHGHI
BENTLEY COLLEGE

BALAJI C. KRISHNAN
UNIVERSITY OF MEMPHIS

HARCOURT COLLEGE PUBLISHERS

Fort Worth   Philadelphia   San Diego   New York   Orlando   Austin   San Antonio
Toronto   Montreal   London   Sydney   Tokyo

Publisher........................ **Mike Roche**
Acquisitions Editor........ **Bill Schoof**
Market Strategist........... **Beverly Dunn**
Developmental Editor... **Bobbie Bochenko**
Project Editor................ **G. Parrish Glover**
Art Director.................. **Garry Harman**
Production Manager...... **Suzie Wurzer**

Cover design: Johnny Rutledge

ISBN: 0-03-032133-6
Library of Congress Catalog Card Number: 00-105690

Address for Domestic Orders
Harcourt, Inc., 6277 Sea Harbor Drive, Orlando, FL 32887-6777
800-782-4479

Address for International Orders
International Customer Service
Harcourt, Inc., 6277 Sea Harbor Drive, Orlando, FL 32887-6777
407-345-3800
(fax) 407-345-4060
(e-mail) hbintl@harcourt.com

Address for Editorial Correspondence
Harcourt College Publishers, 301 Commerce Street, Suite 3700, Fort Worth, TX 76102

Web Site Address
http://www.harcourtcollege.com

Printed in the United States of America

0 1 2 3 4 5 6 7 8 9   039   9 8 7 6 5 4 3 2 1

To Rehna R. Sheth, my first granddaughter, who is a New Millennium Baby and has her own Web site

- Jagdish Sheth

To my mother Azadeh Eshghi

- Abdolreza Eshghi

To my wife Radha and my parents

- Balaji Krishnan

⬤PREFACE

No other business function is as radically transformed as the marketing function as a consequence of the rapid and universal acceptance of the Internet as a medium of information and communication. As an integrated medium for product/service information (Web pages), interactive communication (e-mail), and market transactions (electronic commerce), the Internet is making more impact on marketing practice than the invention of the printing press during the industrial revolution or the emergence of radio and television in the last century.

This textbook, consisting of thought-provoking articles, (and supplemented by a Web-based and periodically updated annotated bibliography and other supplemented material) is designed to serve four purposes.

First, it is designed to serve as a textbook for new elective courses in marketing such as Web Marketing, Electronic Commerce, and Information Age Marketing that currently improvise using ad hoc and topical readings mostly from the popular press.

Second, it is designed as a supplement to the core MBA courses in marketing management where the existing textbooks lag behind a rapidly-emerging knowledge base on the Internet and its impact on marketing.

Third, it is designed as an introductory marketing book for a number of new courses such as MS in Information Technology Management or MS in E-Commerce. Typically, such courses have a broad scope and have an introductory marketing course to update non-business majors with the latest concepts in e-marketing.

Finally, the textbook is designed to serve as a theme for the capstone marketing course in most advanced undergraduate programs. Currently, this capstone course is taught either with the use of a computer simulation game or by the case method for integrating core and electric courses in marketing. The textbook focuses on exploring how the Internet can be used to both improve marketing efficiency (cost reduction) and marketing effectiveness (customer loyalty). It includes articles written by leading scholars on how the Internet is transforming each marketing function (market research, product development, managing intermediaries, advertising & promotion, customer service, and sales force management) in ways that will make it more efficient and effective.

It took us at least two years to develop the complementary Web-centric annotated bibliography and other sources of information. We would like to acknowledge research support provided by Nauzar Vimadalal and our own institutions. We are especially thankful to Bentley College for allowing us to link our textbook directly to their Information Age Portal that updates infor mation pertinent to marketing.

We would also thank our book team at Harcourt College Publishers: Bill Schoof, Acquisitions Editor; Bobbie Bochenko, Developmental Editor; Beverly Dunn, Marketing Manager; Parrish Glover, Project Editor; Suzie Wurzer, Production Manager; Garry Harman, Art Director; and Lisa Kelley, Manufacturing Manager for providing excellent support to this project.

Lastly we would like to thank the business professionals and writers who contributed provocative readings and cutting-edge research to this project. It is enthusiasm and creativity like yours that will propel business into the new century.

About the Authors

Dr. Jagdish N. Sheth is the Charles H. Kellstadt Professor of Marketing in the Goizueta Business School and the founder of the Center for Relationship Marketing (CRM) at Emory University. Prior to his present position, he was the Robert E. Brooker Professor of Marketing at the University of Southern California and the founder of the Center for Telecommunications Management (CTM); the Walter H. Stellner Distinguished Professor of Marketing at the University of Illinois; on the faculty of Columbia University as well as the Massachusetts Institute of Technology. Dr. Sheth is nationally and internationally known for his scholarly contributions in Marketing, Customer Satisfaction, Global Competition, and Strategic Thinking. He is on the editorial boards of at least a dozen scholarly journals in marketing, international business and quantitative methods, as well as Series Editor of Research in Marketing (JAI Press). Dr. Shethís research interests have shifted from consumer psychology, attitude research and multivariate methods to marketing theory, global strategy and relationship marketing.

Abdolreza Eshghi is Associate Professor of Marketing and the Director of the Master of Science in Information Age Marketing at Bentley College. Dr. Eshghi received his Ph.D. from the University of Illinois and teaches marketing strategy, international marketing and database marketing.

Balaji C. Krishnan received his Ph.D. in Business Administration from Louisiana State University, in 1998. His research interests are in the area of pricing and price promotions, cross cultural research, and consumer behavior in computer enabled environmentalist. He has been teaching a course called ìMarketing on the Internet,î since 1996. He is currently the facilitator for the E-Commerce area of the Institute for Managing Emerging Technology in Memphis. He has published in the Journal of Consumer Affairs and Journal of Public Policy and Marketing. He is also on the editorial board of the Journal of Business Research.

TABLE OF CONTENTS

INTERNET MARKETING

Introduction

A profound shift in the economy is underway—the industrial age economy is rapidly giving way to the Internet age economy. Just as the transformation from the agricultural era to the industrial age fundamentally changed how we organized and managed economic activity, the transformation to the Internet age economy is precipitating discontinuities in the business landscape on a scale and a speed never imagined until just a few years ago.

In the agricultural era, land was the critical resource for wealth creation. Indeed, groups, communities, and nations who controlled large tracts of land and developed the appropriate tools and technologies (hand tools, tractors, ploughs, combines, mining equipment, etc.) for its utilization, survived and prospered. Land gradually lost its significance in wealth creation as the industrial revolution picked up steam. In the industrial age, capital emerged as the primary driver of economic growth and prosperity. And so, for much of this era, wealth creation revolved around effective utilization of capital, facilitated by the appropriate tools, technologies, and institutions (banks, checks, stocks and shares, etc.).

At the dawn of the 21st century, we are once again witnessing a monumental societal transformation in human history. The revolution in information technology, spurred by digital electronics, has propelled "information" to the position of the most critical factor in wealth creation. While information has always played an important role throughout the history of mankind, not until recent years was it possible to create, collect, store, process, and distribute information on a massive scale at such low cost. The industrial age was the age of information dictatorship in which the content and flow of information was monopolized by a few in power (large businesses and government), while the powerless masses (small businesses and customers) suffered at the mercy of those in power.

The digital revolution is empowering the masses by democratizing information. It is dismantling the old regime and replacing it with a new one—the "network economy,"[1] an economy in which everyone is connected to everyone else—people to people, firms to firms, firms to customers, and customers to firms in a more or less level playing field. This "explosion in connectivity"[2] has been made possible by advent of the Internet.

The Internet

The birth and growth of the Internet, a network of computers that spans the globe, is linked to four major developments. The Internet was first created in the late 60s and early 70s when the U.S. Department of Defense began a series of experiments to link the Department's main computers and imposed rules for information exchange on all users. The real growth of the Internet, however, came in 1985 after the National Science Foundation connected six supercomputer centers with a high speed "backbone" that allowed the scientists to move digitized data across the network using a simple system known as electronic mail (e-mail). Since e-mail messages are digitized, they can be transmitted at high speed and much lower cost than the telephone or ordinary mail. Since 1985, the number of host computers that make up the Internet has doubled every year, a trend that is likely to continue in the foreseeable future.

The second major development came in 1989 when Tim Berners-Lee at the University of Geneva, Switzerland, developed a set of rules governing a library of files (text, pictures, sound, or video) stored on the computers that make up the Internet. This is referred to as the World Wide Web because any one file can contain pathways to many other files stored on the network. Therefore, the content of a file is accessible, regardless of where it may be physically stored in the world, through any other file. Tim Berners-Lee's home page provides more details on the evolution and the future direction of the World Wide Web.[3]

The third major development—the introduction of *image capable* browsers—occurred in 1993. Pioneered by Mosaic, these software products allow personal computer users to browse easily from one file to another on the Internet. The widespread availability of the browsers in 1994 transformed the Internet from a way to run computers from a distance to a two-way global information super-highway.

The phenomenal increase in demand for multimedia transmission of information over the Internet has made *broadband access* the next critical phase in the evolution of the Internet as a commercial medium. Telephone lines have proven to be extremely inadequate for handling large amount of data at high speed. As a result, telephone and cable television companies are scrambling, through mergers and acquisitions, to build new transmission capacities. But this is only a part of a more fundamental restructuring of the information technology industry currently underway.[4]

Cross-Industry Consolidation

Historically, firms within the information industry invested their resources to create core capabilities around a single form of information, such as voice, text, image, data, and video. For example, telecommunication companies focused on voice, while publishing companies specialized in text form of information. Furthermore, companies within each industry vertically integrated to provide a full-range of capabilities from creation and collection to display and storage to processing and distribution of a given information form.

The explosion in connectivity and the consequent pressure to provide broadband access has forced a realignment within the information industry. The wave of corporate mergers and acquisitions in recent years clearly demonstrates that leading players are reorganizing themselves along the lines of information function or capability. At the same time, there appears to be a tendency toward horizontal integration across diverse forms of information. For example, the recent merger of CBS and Viacom brought together companies in the entertainment (video), broadcast (voice), television (image), and publishing (text) industries. We believe that ultimately three broad industry groups will emerge from this reorganization. Firms within the *digital content* group will focus on creating core capabilities in content across diverse forms of information. Players within the *digital appliances* group will primarily engage in the manufacture of a wide variety of communication devices. And finally, companies in *the digital networks* will focus on processing and distribution of different forms of information. Further, companies in each group may align themselves with companies in other groups by way of equity participation or joint ventures.

Information Technology as a Strategic Resource

The foregoing discussion clearly demonstrates that the information technology revolution is fundamentally reshaping the business landscape for firms within the information-intensive industries. At the same time, we are witnessing a profound change in the role of information technology within the organization in general. We believe information technology is increasingly assuming a strategic role in a wide range of industries from high tech to high touch, from consumer to industrial to services. Four distinct forces drive the strategic importance of information technology: a) intense competition, b) globalization, c) organizational change, and d) technology revolution. We will now discuss why and how each force is enhancing the strategic importance of information technology.

Intense Competition

In much of the developed world, most dominant industries of the industrial age are at a mature stage of the life cycle. Characterized by slow or no growth and excess capacity, firms are locked in fierce market share battles with their competitors. Examples of market share battles can be found in virtually every industry ranging from steel and metal to automobile and appliance to mainframe computing. Forward-looking and innovative companies are increasingly utilizing information technology to gain a competitive advantage over their rivals. We have identified at least four ways companies use information technology to gain an edge in the marketplace.

First, information technology is helping companies to automate the *Front Office* and the *Back Office* in an attempt to reduce operating costs. For example, many functions and tasks such as billing, logistics, inventory management, sales, customer service, etc. can be automated at substantial savings. Second, information technology can improve product or service quality by providing quality assurance, minimizing errors per unit of activity. Perhaps the best example of this is the scanner technology. The Universal Product Code (UPC) provides superior quality assurance in many industries ranging from retail (merchandise handling) to airlines (baggage handling).

Third, companies are using information technology to provide value-added services to differentiate their offerings. For example, FedEx has used information technology not only to enhance the reliability of its service, but also to enable its customers to monitor the status of their package on-line via the Internet. Finally, information technology can be used for competitive intelligence. The best example here is the Sabre system developed by American Airlines. Since every airline has to deposit its schedule and fares, it gives American Airlines insights into competitors' schedules and fares.

Globalization

Globalization drives the information technology revolution as much as it is driven by it. There are at least two ways in which globalization helps proliferation of information technology around the globe. First, increased exposure and awareness through global mass media fuels diffusion of information technology. Millions of people see and want access to the latest technologies available in the western world. The Internet is now available, though on a limited scale, in the remotest corners of the world. Second, globalization of business creates a lucrative market for vendors of information technology to expand their offerings to meet the communication needs of multinational corporations around the world. For example, two leading telecommunications companies in the world, AT&T and British Telecom, recently announced formation of a strategic alliance, to be called Advance, to meet the needs of their multinational corporate clients for wireless communications. The objective of the alliance is to offer trans-Atlantic roaming using a single handset while allowing users to keep their phone numbers when travelling in different countries. The alliance would globalize what is now a country-by-country market for mobile communications.[5]

We can also think of at least two ways in which information technology diffusion has fueled globalization of business. First, it has made the playing field even for smaller companies who did not otherwise stand a chance to participate in the global economy. Second, information technology has virtually removed two major obstacles in cross-cultural communications—distance and time-zone differences.

Organizational Change

The third major force for increasing the importance of information technology is corporate reorganization. First, as competition has intensified in mature industries, companies have taken steps to increase operational efficiencies while improving effectiveness. For example, middle management layers have been either consolidated or eliminated all together creating flatter organizations. Instead, companies have opted to invest in information technology.

Second, the wave of mergers and acquisitions in the 80s and the 90s has set off a massive organizational change as merged companies have attempted to consolidate and merge their respective information technologies, raising the strategic importance of information technology within the organization. Third, protection of corporate tangible and intangible assets has become a top management concern as cases of industrial espionage and crises have proliferated in recent years. It is believed that with adequate information technologies it is possible to prevent, contain, or at least quickly respond to such corporate crises.

Finally, faced with hyper-competition in mature markets, many corporations have adopted a market-driven approach. When such a shift occurs, the value chain and flow of operations changes significantly. For example, manufacturing is less driven by availability of parts and components and more by market demand. A truly market-driven operation requires an efficient and integrated information system that links otherwise separate functions of market research, database management, customer order entry, customer service, etc. In short, enterprise-wide integration of functional level decision support systems has shifted information technology to a centralized strategic function at the highest level of the organization.

Information Technology Revolution

While the first three forces create the need, information technology revolution is the enabling force increasing the strategic importance of information technology. Three forces have fueled rapid commercialization of very innovative information technologies.

First, we have witnessed extremely sharp *experience curves* in information technology industries resulting in an explosion of computing power at incredibly low costs. A desktop computer has more computing power these days than the Apollo 7 spacecraft only two decades ago. This phenomenon has made a wide array of information technologies affordable to millions of small businesses and households. Clearly, Moore's Law once again explains similar cost reductions in fiber optics, switching systems, and digital devices.

Second, information technology capabilities such as processing, memory, switching, and intelligence have become *distributed* over time. This has eliminated the need for a centralized location (e.g., the mainframe CPU) to house these capabilities. Instead, these capabilities have been distributed at the end user level. Consequently, we have seen an explosion in connectivity through local area networks, wide area networks, metro area networks, and global networks to afford multiple end users processing, storing, and switching capabilities.

Finally, information technologies are increasingly integrated. It is now possible to transmit, store, process, and distribute different forms of information on a single integrated technology. Cisco Systems CEO John Chambers's vision of a "New World Network"[6] that will seamlessly blend the technology of the Internet with high-speed optical fibers, cable, and wireless systems to carry text, voice, video, and data everywhere seems to be nearing reality sooner than expected.

In short, the net impact of the information technology revolution is a fundamental transformation of the enterprise from a collection of fragmented functional divisions operating on the basis of lagged data to a fully integrated entity acting in real time. In other words, the *Connected Enterprise* has emerged from the ruins of functional and time silos.

Internet Marketing

What is the meaning of Internet marketing and how is it different from conventional marketing? Marketing as a corporate function focuses on satisfying customers' current and future needs through mutually beneficial exchanges. While the fundamental premise of marketing remains the same, the Internet age has prompted a radical examination of how marketing's basic mission is carried out. In this regard, we believe three fundamental paradigm shifts are taking place. First, implementation of the *marketing concept* in industrial age was embedded in certain assumptions that are no longer valid in the Internet age. In the industrial age, marketers initiated and controlled the exchange process, whereas Internet age customers increasingly initiate and control the exchange—"customers define what information they need, what offering they are interested in, and what price they are willing to pay." In other words, Internet age marketing is the age of "reverse marketing."[7]

Second, the standards by which marketing's performance is evaluated have shifted to a higher plateau. Customers demand high quality products at affordable prices and faster and better service. Accordingly, the traditional trade-off between effectiveness and efficiency is no longer relevant. The Internet age marketer is expected to satisfy customers' current and future needs effectively and efficiently—*effective efficiency*—by facilitating mutually beneficial exchanges. Third, marketing exchanges no longer revolve around a single transaction in a given point in time. Forward-looking enterprises are increasingly shifting their focus from narrowly defined product-market categories to the totality of customers' experiences in "market spaces."[8] A "market space" is where "customers are locked not just into products but into the entire system" and where firms can provide "a whole lot of value-added services" as a mechanism to gain a sustainable competitive advantage over their rivals. For example, GE not only manufactures and sells aircraft engines, but also sells to Southwest Airlines "*Power by the Hour*," a service that involves electronically monitoring engine performance in flight and tracking all maintenance and repair data. Similarly, Goodyear Tire & Rubber offers its customers like Navistar International Transportation Corporation and Mitsubishi Motor Corporation not just tires, but entire wheel assemblies, painted and ready for just-in-time use. Incidentally, these assemblies may or may not include Goodyear's tires, depending on customers' specifications.[9]

Automation and Integration of Marketing Functions

There is very little doubt that the information technology revolution is radically transforming the marketing function on a scale unimaginable just a decade ago. The transformation is taking shape along two dimensions: (a) *automation* of a wide range of *back and front office* marketing functions, and (b) *integration* of marketing functions across the enterprise and the supply chain. We elaborate on these points below.

The advent of the *intranets*, has spawned extensive *automation* of marketing functions increasing marketing efficiency. More and more marketing functions ranging from market research to product design to sales, to customer service are getting automated. However, *back office* operations such as order processing, fulfillment, logistics, and inventory management typically are among the first functions to be automated. We believe two factors drive back office automation through the Intranets. First, such functions tend to be quantifiable and repeatable. For example, "the sales and service processes are not that difficult to map out and quantify. We start with a number of prospects; push them through the pipeline; and out the bottom of the funnel comes a certain dependable quantity of new sales."[10] Second, many companies have been able to increase marketing productivity markedly by automating *back office* functions. For example, Panasonic generated more than five times the typical direct mail response rate at $78,000 lower than they thought would be necessary with the help of a campaign management tool.[11] Wal-Mart, curator of the world's largest commercial data warehouse, uses powerful analytical tools to analyze the market basket of its shoppers to increase the efficiency of product assortment planning, store layouts, and better understand product-to-product affinities. Utilizing powerful analytical tools, Wal-Mart is able to create new information about relationships between different products, between consumers and products, and between products and prices. At this capacity, Wal-Mart's data warehouse is better termed a " 'knowledge colony' that spans all corporate databases and it's dynamic; it can continue to expand."[12]

Additional cost savings and efficiencies can be realized when the firm connects its internal databases and systems with those of the companies within the supply chain through the *Extranets.* Such systems expedite material and information flows, improving efficiency, customer service, and ultimately customer satisfaction. Major corporations are making heavy investments in automation of supply chain. For example, GE has invested millions of dollars in setting up an IT-based service center complete with 17 system engineers and experts in artificial intelligence, and data collection focusing on remote monitoring and diagnostics of customer equipment to maintaining and upgrading non-GE equipment.[13]

While significant gains can be realized through cost cutting, rationalization, and automation, a single-minded focus on efficiency improvement alone will not guarantee a sustainable competitive advantage and future growth. Evidence is mounting that without a holistic view of customer relationships, automation of marketing functions can "create islands of disparate information that are inaccessible to the organization as a whole."[14] Indeed, lack of enterprise-wide integration can actually lead to customer frustration and dissatisfaction stifling future growth. Powerful forces are further fueling a tremendous growth in enterprise-wide integration of marketing functions. Due to falling barriers to entry, commoditization of products in many sectors, and shortening of product life cycles, price has become the primary purchasing criteria in many markets. As a result, brand loyalty and customer loyalty have become vanishing breeds making market "churn" endemic.[15] Therefore, forward-looking companies are increasingly integrating all customer "touch points" into an enterprise-wide customer relationship management (CRM) as the vehicle to focus on profitable relationships. It is recognized that it may be necessary to "fire a customer" if other attempts to turn the relationship into a profitable one fails.[16]

Therefore, CRM is emerging as one of the hottest areas in integration of marketing functions. Leading suppliers of marketing automation tools are broadening their product portfolios to integrate a wide range of "front office" functions. For example, Siebel Systems, the leading supplier of sales force automation software, has acquired Scopus Technology, a call center company. Similarly, Clarify and Vantage, both pioneers in the call center market, have moved into broader CRM through mergers and acquisitions.[17] The first generation of CRM tools were designed to integrate a number of technologies, including database mining, campaign management tools, and call center systems. More recently, however, a new breed of marketing automation has been introduced—*Marketing Optimization*—designed to create a "marketing platform that enables closed-loop planning, budgeting, implementation and analysis . . . integrating sales force automation, CRM, order entry, and other initiatives."[18]

The journey along the automation and integration dimensions does not end with the CRM or *marketing optimization*. While these systems permit marketers to make good on a long-held promise "to customize goods or services for individual customers in high volumes and at relatively low costs,"[19] developments in information technology hold out yet another promise. And that is the promise of *interactive marketing*. Interactive marketing is the ability (a) to address an individual, (b) to gather and remember the response of that individual, and (c) to address the individual once more in a way that takes into account his or her unique response."[20] Such interactivity is possible when the enterprise-wide CRM is linked to the supply chain and its collaborators. Pioneers such as Amazon.com, eTrade, Dell, and Cisco have ushered in the era of interactive marketing where the marketing exchange process from information gathering to advertising and communication to order taking to delivery and customer service are highly automated and integrated across the enterprise and the supply chain. These pioneering efforts have led the "brick and mortar" companies such as Barnes and Noble and Home Depot to consider their own interactive marketing and e-business strategies. At Home Depot, for example, the entire process of purchasing a new kitchen from kitchen design to ordering new cabinets and appliances to delivery and installation are seamlessly automated and highly integrated across the enterprise and the supply chain through the company Intranet and the World Wide Web.

In summary, at the dawn of the Internet age we stand witness to an enormous societal transformation that is impacting every aspect of human society. The impact of the Internet will likely be even more dramatic than the impact of other technologies since the industrial revolution due to its incredible speed precipitating change. Moreover, the Internet is much more universal than the technologies of the industrial age. Societies who never caught up with the industrial revolution are catching up very quickly with the digital revolution.

In the marketing domain, the impact of the digital revolution has been more profound than any other business discipline. Marketing functions are becoming increasingly automated and integrated leading to a significant improvement in efficiency and effectiveness of marketing resources. This has prompted a fundamental re-examination of marketing theories, concepts, and practices. This book of readings is dedicated to bring the cutting-edge thinking and practices that is shaping marketing in the 21st century.

Notes

1. Kevin Kelly, "New Rules for the New Economy," *Wired*, September 1997.
2. Philip Evans and Thomas Wurster, "Strategy and the Economics of Information," *Harvard Business Review*, September–October 1997.
3. http://www.w3.org/People/Berners-Lee/1996/ppf.html
4. For a more detailed account of the evolution of the Internet see Ambar Machfoedy and Matti Aistrich, "Note on Marketing on the World Wide Web," Harvard Business School Publishing, 1996.
5. Seth Schiesel, "AT&T and British Telecom Plan Global Wireless Link," *New York Times*, September 17, 1999.
6. *Business Week*, September 13, 1999.
7. Sawhney and Kotler.
8. Sandra Vandermerwe, "Increasing Returns: Competing for Customers in the Global Market," *Journal of World Business*, winter 1997, pp. 333–50.

9. Julia King, "IT Moves Manufacturers beyond Core Products," *Computerworld*, September 28, 1998.

10. Don Peppers and Martha Rogers, "Smart Marketing," *Sales and Marketing Management*, September 1998, p. 32.

11. Don Peppers and Martha Rogers, "Marketing's New Direction," *Sales and Marketing Management*, March 1999, p. 48.

12. Denise Zimmerman, "Wal-Mart Set to Dig Deeper into its Data Warehouse," *Supermarket News*, March 10, 1997, p. 69.

13. Julia King, "IT Moves Manufacturing Beyond Core Products," *Computerworld*, September 28, 1998.

14. Anne Fischer Lent, "Automating the World of Business," *Sales and Marketing Management*, May 1997, p. 2A.

15. Paul Taylor, "The Customer is King in the Digital Marketplace," *The Financial Times*, February 3, 1999.

16. Dale Renner, Global Managing Partner, Anderson Consulting, quoted in Paul Taylor, op-cit.

17. Paul Taylor, *Financial Times*, February 3, 1999.

18. *PR Newswire*, September 1, 1999.

19. James Gilmore and B. Joseph Pine II, "The Four Faces of Customization," *Harvard Business Review*, January-February 1997, pp. 91–101.

20. John Deighton, "The Future of Interactive Marketing," *Harvard Business Review*, November-December 1996, pp. 4–16.

I

Internet Age and Marketing

Kelly, Kevin (1997), "New Rules for the New Economy," *Wired Magazine*, Vol. 5 (September).
http://www.wired.com/wired/archive/5.09/newrules_pr.html.

Glazer, Rashi (1991), "Marketing in an Information-Intensive Environment: Strategic Implications of Knowledge as an Asset," *Journal of Marketing*, 55, October, 1–19.

Hoffman, Donna and Thomas P. Novak (1997), "A New Marketing Paradigm for Electronic Commerce," *The Information Society*, 13, 1, 43–54.

Sheth, Jagdish N. and Rajendra S. Sisodia (1997), "Consumer Behavior in the Future," in *Electronic Marketing and the Consumer*, Robert A. Peterson, eds. Thousand Oaks, CA: Sage Publications, 17–38.

Quelch, John A. and Lisa R. Klein (1996), "The Internet and International Marketing," *Sloan Management Review*, 37 (spring), 60–75.

I

Internet Age and Marketing

Introduction

This Readings Book is an attempt to bring attention to four areas of knowledge and learning appropriate for marketing students. First, what are the foundations of Internet age marketing? The papers selected in this area are by eminent thinkers who suggest marketing as a discipline, function, and organization may change forever with the emergence of the Internet age. For example, marketing may be less of an annual expense and more of an asset to be invested, maintained, and rebuilt similar to what we do in factory production. Similarly, marketing may not be an isolated function or department but may be integrated in the company in its strategy, operations and supply chain management.

Articles in Part I examine the impact of digital revolution on marketing. The first article by Kevin Kelly, *New Rules for the New Economy*, sets the stage by identifying the differences between the industrial age economy and the "Network Economy." He argues that the Network Economy is governed by rules that revolve around several axes. First, wealth in the new economy flows directly from innovation, not optimization; that is, wealth is not gained by perfecting the known, but by imperfectly seizing the unknown. Second, the ideal environment for cultivating the unknown is to nurture the supreme agility and nimbleness of networks. Third, the domestication of the unknown inevitably means abandoning the highly successful known—undoing the perfected. Fourth, in the thickening web of the Network economy, the cycle of "find, nurture, destroy" happens faster and more intensely than ever before. Based on these underlying principles, the author further identifies a set of twelve rules that govern the Network economy.

Rashi Glazer in *Marketing in an Information-Intensive Environment: Strategic Implications of Knowledge as an Asset* presents a framework for thinking about the impact of information and IT on marketing. The focus is on the concept of "information" or "knowledge" as both an asset to be managed and a variable to be researched. The author presents a series of propositions examining the consequences of increasing information intensity for some key components of firm strategy and organizational structure. Four main hypotheses emerge from the framework: 1) the traditional notions of market attractiveness may no longer be appropriate; 2) the traditional choices between strategic options may no longer be meaningful; 3) competitive advantage is achieved through managing a firm's set of exchanges or relations; 4) organizational structures and information-processing styles are changing to adapt to the new strategies and reflect the concurrent breakdown of the boundaries among a firm's departments and between the firm and the outside world. The concepts discussed are illustrated with a description of the transaction-based information systems that are being implemented in a variety of firms in pursuit of competitive advantage.

In the third article, *A New Marketing Paradigm for Electronic Commerce*, Hoffman and Novak argue that the World Wide Web possesses unique characteristics that distinguish it in important ways from traditional commercial communications environments. Because the Web presents a fundamentally different environment for marketing activities than traditional media, conventional marketing activities are becoming transformed, as they are often difficult to implement in their present form. The authors discuss the idea that these changes portend an evolution in the "marketing concept" and argue that in order for marketing efforts to be successful in this new medium, a new business paradigm is required. In this new approach, the marketing function must be reconstructed to facilitate electronic commerce in the emerging electronic society underlying the Web.

In a futuristic article, *Consumer Behavior in the Future*, Sheth and Sisodia discuss the convergence that is likely to take place in the area of digital electronic technology best borne out by the merger of Time Warner and AOL. They discuss both the supply side (represented by technology evolution) as well as the demand side (represented by lifestyle changes and demographics) forces that drive a number of trends such as disintermediation and reintermediation of the distribution channel, personalization leading to mass customization, shopping on demand, consumers as co-producers, greater value consciousness (of money, time and effort), blurring between consumer and business markets, power shift from marketers to consumers, the automation of consumption, and the concept of personal marketplace.

In the last reading in this part, *The Internet and International Marketing*, Quelch and Klein examine the impact of the Internet on global markets and new product development, the advantages of an intranet for large corporations, and the need for foreign government support and cooperation. While the Internet offers many benefits to both existing multinational corporations (MNC) and start-up companies, the challenges of an inadequate technological infrastructure, concerned policymakers, and existing distribution and organization structures all seem formidable. The authors argue that a major challenge for international marketers is achieving a balance between the new medium's ability to be customized and the desire to retain coherence, control, and consistency as they go to markets worldwide.

1

New Rules for the New Economy

Twelve dependable principles for thriving in a turbulent world

BY KEVIN KELLY

The Digital Revolution gets all the headlines these days. But turning slowly beneath the fast-forward turbulence, steadily driving the gyrating cycles of cool technogadgets and gotta-haves, is a much more profound revolution—the Network Economy.

This emerging new economy represents a tectonic upheaval in our commonwealth, a social shift that reorders our lives more than mere hardware or software ever can. It has its own distinct opportunities and its own new rules. Those who play by the new rules will prosper; those who ignore them will not.

The advent of the new economy was first noticed as far back as 1969, when Peter Drucker perceived the arrival of knowledge workers. The new economy is often referred to as the Information Economy, because of information's superior role (rather than material resources or capital) in creating wealth.

I prefer the term Network Economy, because *information* isn't enough to explain the discontinuities we see. We have been awash in a steadily increasing tide of information for the past century. Many successful knowledge businesses have been built on information capital, but only recently has a total reconfiguration of information itself shifted the whole economy.

The grand irony of our times is that the era of computers is over. All the major consequences of stand-alone computers have already taken place. Computers have speeded up our lives a bit, and that's it.

In contrast, all the most promising technologies making their debut now are chiefly due to communication between computers—that is, to connections rather than to computations. And since communication is the basis of culture, fiddling at this level is indeed momentous.

And fiddle we do. The technology we first invented to crunch spreadsheets has been hijacked to connect our isolated selves instead. Information's critical rearrangement is the widespread, relentless act of connecting everything to everything else. We

Kevin Kelly is *Wired*'s executive editor.

are now engaged in a grand scheme to augment, amplify, enhance, and extend the relationships and communications between all beings and all objects. That is why the Network Economy is a big deal.

The new rules governing this global restructuring revolve around several axes. First, wealth in this new regime flows directly from innovation, not optimization; that is, wealth is not gained by perfecting the known, but by imperfectly seizing the unknown. Second, the ideal environment for cultivating the unknown is to nurture the supreme agility and nimbleness of networks. Third, the domestication of the unknown inevitably means abandoning the highly successful known—undoing the perfected. And last, in the thickening web of the Network Economy, the cycle of "find, nurture, destroy" happens faster and more intensely than ever before.

The Network Economy is not the end of history. Given the rate of change, this economic arrangement may not endure more than a generation or two. Once networks have saturated every space in our lives, an entirely new set of rules will take hold. Take these principles, then, as rules of thumb for the interim.

1 The Law of Connection
Embrace dumb power

The Network Economy is fed by the deep resonance of two stellar bangs: the collapsing microcosm of chips and the exploding telecosm of connections. These sudden shifts are tearing the old laws of wealth apart and preparing territory for the emerging economy.

As the size of silicon chips shrinks to the microscopic, their costs shrink to the microscopic as well. They become cheap and tiny enough to slip into every—and the key word here is every—object we make. The notion that all doors in a building should contain a computer chip seemed ludicrous 10 years ago, but now there is hardly a hotel door without a blinking, beeping chip. Soon, if National Semiconductor gets its way, every FedEx package will be stamped with a disposable silicon flake that smartly tracks the contents. If an ephemeral package can have a chip, so can your chair, each book, a new coat, a basketball. Thin slices of plastic known as smart cards hold a throwaway chip smart enough to be your banker. Soon, all manufactured objects, from tennis shoes to hammers to lamp shades to cans of soup, will have embedded in them a tiny sliver of thought. And why not?

The world is populated by 200 million computers. Andy Grove of Intel happily estimates that we'll see 500 million of these by 2002. Yet the number of noncomputer chips now pulsating in the world is 6 billion! They are already embedded in your car and stereo and rice cooker. Because they can be stamped out fast and cheap, like candy gumdrops, these chips are known in the industry as "jelly beans." And we are in the dawn of a jelly bean explosion: there'll be 10 billion grains of working silicon by 2005, a billion not long after. Someday each of them may be as smart as an ant, dissolved into our habitat.

As we implant a billion specks of our thought into everything we make, we are also connecting them up. Stationary objects are wired together. The nonstationary rest—that is, most manufactured objects—will be linked by infrared and radio, creating a wireless web vastly larger than the wired web. It is not necessary that each connected object transmit much data. A tiny chip plastered inside a water tank on an Australian ranch transmits only the telegraphic message of whether it is full or not. A chip on the horn of each steer beams out his pure location, nothing more: "I'm here, I'm here." The chip in the gate at the end of the road communicates only when it was last opened: "Tuesday."

The glory of these connected crumbs is that they don't need to be artificially intelligent. Instead, they work on the dumb power of a few bits linked together. Dumb power is what you get when you network dumb nodes into a smart web. It's what our brains do with dumb neurons and what the Internet did with dumb personal computers. A PC is the conceptual equivalent of a single neuron housed in a plastic case. When linked by the telecosm into a neural network, these dumb PC nodes created that fabulous intelligence called the World Wide Web. It works in other domains: dumb parts, properly connected, yield smart results.

A trillion dumb chips connected into a hive mind is the hardware. The software that runs through it is the Network Economy. A planet of hyperlinked chips emits a ceaseless flow of small messages, cascading into the most nimble waves of sensibility. Every farm moisture sensor shoots up data, every weather satellite beams down digitized images, every cash register spits out bit streams, every hospital monitor trickles out numbers, every Web site tallies attention, every vehicle transmits its location code; all of this is sent swirling into the web. That tide of signals is the net.

The net is not just humans typing at each other on AOL, although that is part of it too and will be as long as seducing the romantic and flaming the idiotic are enjoyable. Rather, the net is the collective interaction spun off by a trillion objects and living beings, linked together through air and glass.

This is the net that begets the Network Economy. According to MCI, the total volume of voice traffic on global phone systems will be superseded by the total volume of data traffic in three years. We're already on the way to an expanded economy full of new participants: agents, bots, objects, and machines, as well as several billion more humans. We won't wait for AI to make intelligent systems; we'll do it with the dumb power of ubiquitous computing and pervasive connections.

The whole shebang won't happen tomorrow, but the trajectory is clear. We are connecting all to all. Every step we take that banks on cheap, rampant, and universal connection is a step in the right direction. Furthermore, the surest way to advance massive connectionism is to exploit decentralized forces—to link the distributed bottom. How do you make a better bridge? Let the parts talk to each other. How do you improve lettuce farming? Let the soil speak to the farmer's tractors. How do you make aircraft safe? Let the airplanes communicate among themselves and pick their own flight paths.

In the Network Economy, embrace dumb power.

2 The Law of Plentitude
More gives more

Curious things happen when you connect all to all. Mathematicians have proven that the sum of a network increases as the square of the number of members. In other words, as the number of nodes in a network increases arithmetically, the value of the network increases exponentially. Adding a few more members can dramatically increase the value for all members.

Consider the first modern fax machine that rolled off the conveyor belt around 1965. Despite millions of dollars spent on its R&D, it was worth nothing. Zero. The second fax machine to roll off immediately made the first one worth something. There was someone to fax to. Because fax machines are linked into a network, each additional fax machine sliding down the chute increases the value of all the fax machines operating before it.

So strong is this network value that anyone purchasing a fax machine becomes an evangelist for the fax network. "Do you have a fax?" fax owners ask you. "You should get one." Why? Your purchase increases the worth of their machine. And once you join the network, you'll begin to ask others, "Do you have a fax (or email, or Acrobat software, etc)?" Each additional account you can persuade onto the network substantially increases the value of your account.

When you go to Office Depot to buy a fax machine, you are not just buying a US$200 box. You are purchasing for $200 the entire network of all other fax machines and the connections between them—a value far greater than the cost of all the separate machines.

The fax effect suggests that the more plentiful things become, the more valuable they become. But this notion directly contradicts two of the most fundamental axioms we attribute to the industrial age.

First hoary axiom: Value came from scarcity; diamonds, gold, oil, and college degrees were precious because they were scarce.

Second hoary axiom: When things were made plentiful, they became devalued; carpets no longer indicated status when they could be woven by the thousands on machines.

The logic of the network flips these industrial lessons upside down. In a Network Economy, value is derived from plentitude, just as a fax machine's value increases in ubiquity. Power comes from abundance. Copies (even physical copies) are cheap. Therefore, let them proliferate.

Instead, what is valuable is the scattered relationships—sparked by the copies—that become tangled up in the network itself. And the relationships rocket upward in value as the parts increase in number even slightly. Windows NT, fax machines, TCP/IP, GIF images, RealAudio—all born deep in the Network Economy—adhere to this logic. But so do metric wrenches, triple-A batteries, and other devices that rely on universal standards; the more common they are, the more it pays you to stick to that standard.

In the future, cotton shirts, bottles of vitamins, chain saws, and the rest of the industrial objects in the world will also obey the law of plentitude as the cost of producing an additional copy of them falls steeply, while the value of the network that invents, manufactures, and distributes them increases.

In the Network Economy, scarcity is overwhelmed by shrinking marginal costs. Where the expense of churning out another copy becomes trivial (and this is happening in more than software), the value of standards and the network booms.

In the Network Economy, more gives more.

3 The Law of Exponential Value
Success is nonlinear

The chart of Microsoft's cornucopia of profits is a revealing graph because it mirrors several other plots of rising stars in the Network Economy. During its first 10 years, Microsoft's profits were negligible. Its profits rose above the background noise only around 1985. But once they began to rise, they exploded.

Federal Express experienced a similar trajectory: years of minuscule profit increases, slowly ramping up to an invisible threshold, and then surging skyward in a blast sometime during the early 1980s.

The penetration of fax machines likewise follows a tale of a 20-year overnight success. Two decades of marginal success, then, during the mid-1980s, the number of fax machines quietly crosses the point of no return—and the next thing you know, they are irreversibly everywhere.

The archetypical illustration of a success explosion in a Network Economy is the Internet itself. As any old-time nethead will be quick to lecture you, the Internet was a lonely (but thrilling!) cultural backwater for two decades before it hit the media radar. A graph of the number of Internet hosts worldwide, starting in the 1960s, hardly creeps above the bottom line. Then, around 1991, the global tally of hosts suddenly mushrooms, exponentially arcing up to take over the world.

Each of these curves (I owe Net Gain author, John Hagel credit for these four examples) is a classic template of exponential growth, compounding in a nonlinear way. Biologists know about exponential growth; such curves are almost the definition of a biological system. That's one reason the Network Economy is often described more accurately in biological terms. Indeed, if the Web feels like a frontier, it's because for the first time in history we are witnessing biological growth in technological systems.

At the same time, each of the above examples is a classic model of the Network Economy. The compounded successes of Microsoft, FedEx, fax machines, and the Internet all hinge on the prime law of networks: value explodes exponentially with membership, while this value explosion sucks in yet more members. The virtuous circle inflates until all potential members are joined.

The subtle point from these examples, however, is that this explosion did not ignite until approximately the late 1980s. Something happened then. That something was the dual big bangs of jelly bean chips and collapsing telco charges. It became feasible—that is, dirt cheap—to exchange data almost anywhere, anytime. The net, the grand net, began to nucleate. Network power followed.

Now that we've entered the realm where virtuous circles can unfurl overnight successes in a biological way, a cautionary tale is in order. One day, along the beach, tiny red algae blooms into a vast red tide. Then, a few weeks later, just when the red mat seems indelible, it vanishes. Lemmings boom and disappear. The same biological forces that amplify populations can mute them. The same forces that feed on each other to amplify network presences into powerful overnight standards can also work in reverse to unravel them in a blink. Small beginnings can lead to large results, while large disturbances have only small effects.

In the Network Economy, success is nonlinear.

4 The Law of Tipping Points
Significance precedes momentum

There is yet one more lesson to take from these primeval cases of the Network Economy. And here, another biological insight will be handy. In retrospect, one can see from these expo-curves that a point exists where the momentum was so overwhelming that success became a runaway event. Success became infectious, so to speak, and spread pervasively to the extent that it became difficult for the uninfected to avoid succumbing. (How long can you hold out not having a phone?)

In epidemiology, the point at which a disease has infected enough hosts that the infection moves from local illness to raging epidemic can be thought of as the tipping point. The contagion's momentum has tipped from pushing uphill against all odds to rolling downhill with all odds behind it. In biology, the tipping points of fatal diseases are fairly high, but in technology, they seem to trigger at much lower percentages of victims or members.

There has always been a tipping point in any business, industrial or network, after which success feeds upon itself. However, the low fixed costs, insignificant marginal costs, and rapid distribution that we find in the Network Economy depress tipping points below the levels of industrial times; it is as if the new bugs are more contagious—and more potent. Smaller initial pools can lead to runaway dominance.

Lower tipping points, in turn, mean that the threshold of significance—the period before the tipping point during which a movement, growth, or innovation must be taken seriously—is also dramatically lower than it was during the industrial age. Detecting events while they are beneath this threshold is essential.

Major US retailers refused to pay attention to TV home-shopping networks during the 1980s because the number of people watching and buying from them was initially so small and marginalized that it did not meet the established level of retail significance. Instead of heeding the new subtle threshold of network economics, the retailers waited until the alarm of the tipping point sounded, which meant, by definition, that it was too late for them to cash in.

In the past, an innovation's momentum indicated significance. Now, in the network environment, significance precedes momentum.

Biologists tell a parable of the lily leaf, which doubles in size every day. The day before it completely covers the pond, the water is only half covered, and the day before that, only a quarter covered, and the day before that, only a measly eighth. So, while the lily grows imperceptibly all summer long, only in the last week of the cycle would most bystanders notice its "sudden" appearance. But by then, it is far past the tipping point.

The Network Economy is a lily pond. The Web, as one example, is a leaf doubling in size every six months. MUDs and MOOs, Teledesic phones, wireless data ports, collaborative bots, and remote solid state sensors are also leaves in the network lily pond. Right now, they are just itsy-bitsy lily cells merrily festering at the beginning of a hot network summer.

In the Network Economy, significance precedes momentum.

5 The Law of Increasing Returns
Make virtuous circles

The prime law of networking is known as the law of increasing returns. Value explodes with membership, and the value explosion sucks in more members, compounding the result. An old saying puts it more succinctly: Them that's got shall get.

We see this effect in the way areas such as Silicon Valley grow; each new successful start-up attracts other start-ups, which in turn attract more capital and skills and yet more start-ups. (Silicon Valley and other high tech industrial regions are themselves tightly coupled networks of talent, resources, and opportunities.)

The law of increasing returns is far more than the textbook notion of economies of scale. In the old rules, Henry Ford leveraged his success in selling cars to devise more efficient methods of production. This enabled Ford to sell his cars more cheaply, which created larger sales, which fueled more innovation and even better production methods, sending his company to the top. While the law of increasing returns and the economies of scale both rely on positive feedback loops, the former is propelled by the amazing potency of net power, and the latter isn't. First, industrial economies of scale increase value linearly, while the prime law increases value exponentially—the difference between a piggy bank and compounded interest.

Second, and more important, industrial economies of scale stem from the herculean efforts of a single organization to outpace the competition by creating value for less. The expertise (and advantage) developed by the leading company is its alone. By contrast, networked increasing returns are created and shared by the entire network. Many agents, users, and competitors together create the network's value. Although the gains of increasing returns may be reaped unequally by one organization over another, the value of the gains resides in the greater web of relationships.

Huge amounts of cash may pour toward network winners such as Cisco or Oracle or Microsoft, but the supersaturated matrix of increasing returns woven through their companies would continue to expand into the net even if those particular companies should disappear.

Likewise, the increasing returns we see in Silicon Valley are not dependent on any particular company's success. As AnnaLee Saxenian, author of Regional Advantage, notes, Silicon Valley has in effect become one large, distributed company. "People joke that you can change jobs without changing car pools," Saxenian told Washington Post reporter Elizabeth Corcoran. "Some say they wake up thinking they work for Silicon Valley. Their loyalty is more to advancing technology or to the region than it is to any individual firm."

One can take this trend further. We are headed into an era when both workers and consumers will feel more loyalty to a network than to any ordinary firm. The great innovation of Silicon Valley is not the wowie-zowie hardware and software it has invented, but the social organization of its companies and, most important, the networked architecture of the region itself—the tangled web of former jobs, intimate colleagues, information leakage from one firm to the next, rapid company life cycles, and agile email culture. This social web, suffused into the warm hardware of jelly bean chips and copper neurons, creates a true Network Economy.

The nature of the law of increasing returns favors the early. The initial parameters and conventions that give a network its very power quickly freeze into unalterable standards. The solidifying standards of a network are both its blessing and its curse— a blessing because from the de facto collective agreement flows the unleashed power of increasing returns, and a curse because those who own or control the standard are disproportionately rewarded.

But the Network Economy doesn't allow one without the other. Microsoft's billions are tolerated because so many others in the Network Economy have made their collective billions on the advantages of Microsoft's increasing-returns standards.

In a Network Economy, life is tricky for consumers, who must decide which early protocol to support. Withdrawing later from the wrong network of relationships is painful—but not as painful as companies who bet their whole lives on the wrong one. Nonetheless, guessing wrong about conventions is still better than ignoring network dynamics altogether. There is no future for hermetically sealed closed systems in the Network Economy. The more dimensions accessible to member input and creation, the more increasing returns can animate the network, the more the system will feed on itself and prosper. The less it allows these, the more it will be bypassed.

The Network Economy rewards schemes that allow decentralized creation and punishes those that don't. An automobile maker in the industrial age maintains control over all aspects of the car's parts and construction. An automobile maker in the Network Economy will establish a web of standards and outsourced suppliers, encouraging the web itself to invent the car, seeding the system with knowledge it gives away, engaging as many participants as broadly as possible, in order to create a virtuous loop where every member's success is shared and leveraged by all.

In the Network Economy, make virtuous circles.

6 The Law of Inverse Pricing
Anticipate the cheap

One curious aspect of the Network Economy would astound a citizen living in 1897: The very best gets cheaper each year. This rule of thumb is so ingrained in our contemporary lifestyle that we bank on it without marveling at it. But marvel we should, because this paradox is a major engine of the new economy.

Through most of the industrial age, consumers experienced slight improvements in quality for slight increases in price. But the arrival of the microprocessor flipped the price equation. In the information age, consumers quickly came to count on drastically superior quality for less price over time. The price and quality curves diverge so dramatically that it sometimes seems as if the better something is, the cheaper it will cost.

Computer chips launched this inversion, as Ted Lewis, author of *The Friction Free Economy*, points out. Engineers used the supreme virtues of computers to directly and indirectly create the next improved version of computers. By compounding our learning in this fashion, we got more out of less material. So potent is compounding chip power that everything it touches—cars, clothes, food—falls under its spell. Indirectly amplified learning by shrinking chips enabled just-in-time production systems and the outsourcing of very high tech manufacturing to low-wage labor—both of which lowered the prices of goods still further.

Today, shrinking chip meets exploding net. Just as we leveraged compounded learning in creating the microprocessor, we are leveraging the same multiplying loops in creating the global communications web. We use the supreme virtues of networked communications to directly and indirectly create better versions of networked communications.

Almost from their birth in 1971, microprocessors have lived in the realm of inverted pricing. Now, telecommunications is about to experience the same kind of plunges that microprocessor chips take—halving in price, or doubling in power, every 18 months—but even more drastically. The chip's pricing flip was called Moore's Law. The net's flip is called Gilder's Law, for George Gilder, a radical technotheorist who forecasts that for the foreseeable future (the next 25 years), the total bandwidth of communication systems will triple every 12 months.

The conjunction of escalating communication power with shrinking size of jelly bean nodes at collapsing prices leads Gilder to speak of bandwidth becoming free. What he means is that the price per bit transmitted slides down an asymptotic curve toward the free. An asymptotic curve is like Zero's tortoise: with each step forward, the tortoise gets closer to the limit but never actually reaches it. An asymptotic price curve falls toward the free without ever touching it, but its trajectory closely paralleling the free is what becomes important.

In the Network Economy, bandwidth is not the only thing headed this way. Mips-per-dollar calculations head toward the free. Transaction costs dive toward the free. Information itself—headlines and stock quotes—plunges toward the free. Indeed, all items that can be copied, both tangible and intangible, adhere to the law of inverted pricing and become cheaper as they improve. While it is true that automobiles will never be free, the cost per mile will dip toward the free. It is the function per dollar that continues to drop.

For consumers, this is heaven. For those hoping to make a buck, this will be a cruel world. Prices will eventually settle down near the free (gulp!), but quality is completely open-ended at the top. For instance, all-you-can-use telephone service someday will be essentially free, but its quality can only continue to ascend, just to keep competitive.

So how will the telcos—and others—make enough money for profit, R&D, and system maintenance? By expanding what we consider a telephone to be. Over time, any invented product is on a one-way trip over the cliff of inverted pricing and down the curve toward the free. As the Network Economy catches up to all manufactured items, they will all slide down this chute more rapidly than ever. Our job, then, is to create new things to send down the slide—in short, to invent items faster than they are commoditized.

This is easier to do in a network-based economy because the criss-crossing of ideas, the hyperlinking of relationships, the agility of alliances, and the nimble quickness of creating new nodes all support the constant generation of new goods and services where none were before.

And, by the way, the appetite for more things is insatiable. Each new invention placed in the economy creates the opportunity and desire for two more. While plain old telephone service is headed toward the free, I now have three phone lines just for my machines and will someday have a data "line" for every object in my house. More important, managing these lines, the data they transmit, the messages to me, the storage thereof, the need for mobility, all enlarge what I think of as a phone and what I will pay a premium for.

In the Network Economy, you can count on the best getting cheaper; as it does, it opens a space around it for something new that is dear. Anticipate the cheap.

7 The Law of Generosity
Follow the free

If services become more valuable the more plentiful they are (Law #2), and if they cost less the better and the more valuable they become (Law #6), then the extension of this logic says that the most valuable things of all should be those that are given away.

Microsoft gives away its Web browser, Internet Explorer. Qualcomm, which produces Eudora, the standard email program, is given away as freeware in order to sell upgraded versions. Some 1 million copies of McAfee's antivirus software are distributed free each month. And, of course, Sun passed Java out gratis, sending its stock up and launching a mini-industry of Java app developers.

Can you imagine a young executive in the 1940s telling the board that his latest idea is to give away the first 40 million copies of his only product? (It's what Netscape did 50 years later.) He would not have lasted a New York minute.

But now, giving away the store for free is an applauded, level-headed strategy that banks on the network's new rules. Because compounding network knowledge inverts prices, the marginal cost of an additional copy (intangible or tangible) is near zero. Because value appreciates in proportion to abundance, a flood of copies increases the value of all the copies. Because the more value the copies accrue, the more desirable they become, the spread of the product becomes self-fulfilling. Once the product's worth and indispensability is established, the company sells auxiliary services or upgrades, enabling it to continue its generosity and maintaining this marvelous circle.

One could argue that this frightening dynamic works only with software, since the marginal cost of an additional copy is already near zero. That would misread the universality of the inverted price. Made-with-atoms hardware is also following this force when networked. Cellular phones are given away to sell their services. We can expect to see direct-TV dishes—or any object with which the advantages of being plugged in exceed the diminishing cost of replicating the object—given away for the same reasons.

The natural question is how companies are to survive in a world of generosity. Three points will help.

First, think of "free" as a design goal for pricing. There is a drive toward the free—the asymptotic free—that, even if not reached, makes the system behave as if it does. A very small flat rate may have the same effects as flat-out free.

Second, while one product is free, this usually positions other services to be valuable. Thus, Sun gives Java away to help sell servers and Netscape hands out consumer browsers to help sell commercial server software.

Third, and most important, following the free is a way to rehearse a service's or a good's eventual fall to free. You structure your business as if the thing that you are creating is free in anticipation of where its price is going. Thus, while Sega game consoles are not free to consumers, they are sold as loss leaders to accelerate their eventual destiny as something that will be given away in a Network Economy.

Another way to view this effect is in terms of attention. The only factor becoming scarce in a world of abundance is human attention. Each human has an absolute limit of only 24 hours per day to provide attention to the millions of innovations and opportunities thrown up by the economy. Giving stuff away garners human attention, or mind share, which then leads to market share.

Following the free also works in the other direction. If one way to increase product value is to make products free, then many things now without cost hide great value. We can anticipate wealth by following the free.

In the Web's early days, the first indexes to this uncharted territory were written by students and given away. The indexes helped humans focus their attention on a few sites out of thousands and helped draw attention to the sites, so webmasters aided the indexers' efforts. By being available free, indexes became ubiquitous. Their ubiquity quickly led to explosive stock values for the indexers and enabled other Web services to flourish.

So what is free now that may later lead to extreme value? Where today is generosity preceding wealth? A short list of online candidates would be digesters, guides, cataloguers, FAQs, remote live cameras, Web splashes, and numerous bots. Free for now, each of these will someday have profitable companies built around them. These marginal functions now are not fringe; remember, for instance, that in the industrial age Readers Digest is the world's most widely read magazine, that TV Guide is more profitable than the three major networks it guides viewers to, and that the Encyclopaedia Britannica began as a compendium of articles by amateurs—not too dissimilar from FAQs.

But the migration from ad hoc use to commercialization cannot be rushed. One of the law of generosity's corollaries is that value in the Network Economy requires a protocommercial stage. Again, wealth feeds off ubiquity, and ubiquity usually mandates some level of sharing. The early Internet and the early Web sported amazingly robust gift economies; goods and services were swapped, shared generously, or donated outright—actually, this was the sole way to acquire things online. Idealistic as this attitude was, it was the only sane way to launch a commercial economy in the emerging space. The flaw that science fiction ace William Gibson found in the Web—its capacity to waste tremendous amounts of time—was in fact, as Gibson further noted, its saving grace. In a Network Economy, innovations must first be seeded into the inefficiencies of the gift economy to later sprout in the commercial economy's efficiencies.

It's a rare (and foolish) software outfit these days that does not introduce its wares into the free economy as a beta version in some fashion. Fifty years ago, the notion of releasing a product unfinished—with the intention that the public would help complete it—would have been considered either cowardly, cheap, or inept. But in the new regime, this precommercial stage is brave, prudent, and vital.

In the Network Economy, follow the free.

8 The Law of the Allegiance
Feed the web first

The distinguishing characteristic of networks is that they have no clear center and no clear outer boundaries. The vital distinction between the self (us) and the nonself (them)—once exemplified by the allegiance of the industrial-era organization man—becomes less meaningful in a Network Economy. The only "inside" now is whether you are on the network or off. Individual allegiance moves away from organizations and toward networks and network platforms. (Are you Windows or Mac?)

Thus, we see fierce enthusiasm from consumers for open architectures. Users are voting for maximizing the value of the network itself. Companies have to play this way, too. As consultant John Hagel argues, a company's primary focus in a networked world shifts from maximizing the firm's value to maximizing the value of the infrastructure whole. For instance, game companies will devote as much energy promoting the platform—the tangle of users, developers, hardware manufactures, etc.—as they do to their product. Unless their web thrives, they die.

The net is a possibility factory, churning out novel opportunities by the diskful. But unless this explosion is harnessed, it will drown the unprepared. What the computer industry calls "standards" is an attempt to tame the debilitating abundance of competing possibilities. Standards strengthen a network; their constraints solidify a pathway, allowing innovation and evolution to accelerate. So central is the need to tame the choice of possibilities that organizations must make the common standard their first allegiance. Companies positioned at the gateway to a standard will reap the largest rewards. But as a company prospers, so do those in its web.

A network is like a country. In both, the surest route to raising one's own prosperity is raising the system's prosperity. The one clear effect of the industrial age is that the prosperity individuals achieve is more closely related to their nation's prosperity than to their own efforts.

The net is like a country, but with three important differences:

1. No geographical or temporal boundaries exist—relations flow 24 by 7 by 365.

2. Relations in the Network Economy are more tightly coupled, more intense, more persistent, and more intimate in many ways than those in a country.

3. Multiple overlapping networks exist, with multiple overlapping allegiances.

Yet, in every network, the rule is the same. For maximum prosperity, feed the web first.

9 The Law of Devolution
Let go at the top

The tightly linked nature of any economy, but especially the Network Economy's ultraconnected constitution, makes it behave ecologically. The fate of individual organizations is not dependent entirely on their own merits, but also on the fate of their neighbors, their allies, their competitors, and, of course, on that of the immediate environment.

Some biomes in nature are shy of opportunities for life. In the Arctic there are only a couple of styles of living, and a species had better get good at one of them. Other biomes are chock full of opportunities, and those possibilities are in constant flux, appearing and retreating in biological time as species jockey toward maximum adaptability.

The rich, interactive, and highly plastic shape of the Network Economy resembles a biome seething with action. New niches pop up constantly and go away as fast. Competitors sprout beneath you and then gobble your spot up. One day you are king of the mountain, and the next day there is no mountain at all.

Biologists describe the struggle of an organism to adapt in this biome as a long climb uphill, where uphill means greater adaptation. In this visualization, an organism that is maximally adapted to the times is situated on a peak. It is easy to imagine a commercial organization substituted for the organism. A company expends great effort to move its butt uphill, or to evolve its product so that it is sitting on top, where it is maximally adapted to the consumer environment.

All organizations (profit and nonprofit alike) face two problems as they attempt to find their peak of optimal fit. Both are amplified by a Network Economy in which turbulence is the norm.

First, unlike the industrial arc's relatively simple environment, where it was fairly clear what an optimal product looked like and where on the slow-moving horizon a company should place itself, it is increasingly difficult in the Network Economy to discern what hills are highest and what summits are false.

Big and small companies alike can relate to this problem. It's unclear whether one should strive to be the world's best hard disc manufacturer when the mountain beneath that particular peak may not be there in a few years. An organization can cheer itself silly on its way to becoming the world's expert on a dead-end technology. In biology's phrasing, it gets stuck on a local peak.

The harsh news is that getting stuck is a certainty in the new economy. Sooner, rather than later, a product will be eclipsed at its prime. While one product is at its peak, another will move the mountain by changing the rules.

There is only one way out. The organism must devolve. In order to go from one high peak to another, it must go downhill first and cross a valley before climbing uphill again. It must reverse itself and become less adapted, less fit, less optimal.

This brings us to the second problem. Organizations, like living beings, are hardwired to optimize what they know and to not throw success away. Companies find devolving a) unthinkable and b) impossible. There is simply no room in the enterprise for the concept of letting go—let alone the skill to let go—of something that is working, and trudge downhill toward chaos.

And it will be chaotic and dangerous down below. The definition of lower adaptivity is that you are closer to extinction. Finding the next peak is suddenly the next life-or-death assignment. But there is no alternative (that we know of) to leaving behind perfectly good products, expensively developed technology, and wonderful brands and heading down to trouble in order to ascend again in hope. In the future, this forced march will become routine.

The biological nature of this era means that the sudden disintegration of established domains will be as certain as the sudden appearance of the new. Therefore, there can be no expertise in innovation unless there is also expertise in demolishing the ensconced.

In the Network Economy, the ability to relinquish a product or occupation or industry at its peak will be priceless. Let go at the top.

10 The Law of Displacement
The net wins

Many observers have noted the gradual displacement in our economy of materials by information. Automobiles weigh less than they once did and perform better. The missing materials have been substituted with nearly weightless high tech know-how in the form of plastics and composite fiber materials. This displacement of mass with bits will continue in the Network Economy.

Whereas once the unique dynamics of the software and computer industry (increasing returns, following the free, etc.) were seen as special cases within the larger "real" economy of steel, oil, automobiles, and farms, the dynamics of networks will continue to displace the old economic dynamics until network behavior becomes the entire economy.

For example, take the new logic of cars as outlined by energy visionary Amory Lovins. What could be more industrial-age than automobiles? However, chips and networks can displace the industrial age in cars, too. Most of the energy a car consumes is used to move the car itself, not the passenger. So, if the car's body and engine can be diminished in size, less power is needed to move the car, meaning the engine can be made yet smaller, which means that the car can be smaller yet, and so on down the similar slide of compounded value that microprocessors followed. That's because smart materials—stuff that requires increasing knowledge to invent and make—are shrinking the steel.

Detroit and Japan have designed concept cars built out of ultralightweight composite fiber material weighing about 1,000 pounds, powered by hybrid-electric motors. They take away the mass of radiator, axle, and drive shaft by substituting networked chips. Just as embedding chips in brakes made them safer, these lightweight cars will be wired with network intelligence to make them safer: a crash will inflate the intelligence of multiple air bags—think smart bubblepak.

The accumulated effect of this substitution of knowledge for material in automobiles is a hypercar that will be safer than today's car, yet can cross the continental US on one tank of fuel.

Already, the typical car boasts more computing power than your typical desktop PC, but what the hypercar promises, says Lovins, is not wheels with lots of chips, but a chip with wheels. A car can rightly be view as headed toward becoming a solid state module. And it will drive on a road system increasingly wired as a decentralized electronic network obeying the Network Economy's laws.

Once we see cars as chips with wheels, it's easier to imagine airplanes as chips with wings, farms as chips with soil, houses as chips with inhabitants. Yes, they will have mass, but that mass will be subjugated by the overwhelming amount of knowledge and information flowing through it, and, in economic terms, these objects will behave as if they had no mass at all. In that way, they migrate to the Network Economy.

Nicholas "Atoms-to-Bits" Negroponte guesstimates that the Network Economy will reach $1 trillion by 2000. What this figure doesn't represent is the scale of the economic world that is moving onto the Internet—that grand net of interconnected objects—as the Network Economy infiltrates cars and traffic and steel and corn. Even if all cars aren't sold online right away, the way cars are designed, manufactured, built, and operated will depend on network logic and chip power.

The question "How big will online commerce be?" will have diminishing relevance, because all commerce is jumping onto the Internet. The distinctions between the Network Economy and the industrial economy will fade to the difference of animated versus inert. If money and information flow through something, then it's part of the Network Economy.

In the Network Economy, the net wins. All transactions and objects will tend to obey network logic.

11 The Law of Churn
Seek sustainable disequilibrium

In the industrial perspective, the economy was a machine that was to be tweaked to optimal efficiency, and, once finely tuned, maintained in productive harmony. Companies or industries especially productive of jobs or goods had to be protected and cherished at all costs, as if these firms were rare watches in a glass case.

As networks have permeated our world, the economy has come to resemble an ecology of organisms, interlinked and coevolving, constantly in flux, deeply tangled, ever expanding at its edges. As we know from recent ecological studies, no balance exists in nature; rather, as evolution proceeds, there is perpetual disruption as new species displace old, as natural biomes shift in their makeup, and as organisms and environments transform each other. So it is with the network perspective: companies come and go quickly, careers are patchworks of vocations, industries are indefinite groupings of fluctuating firms.

Change is no stranger to the industrial economy or the embryonic information economy; Alvin Toffler coined the term future shock in 1970 as the sane response of humans to accelerating change. But the Network Economy has moved from change to churn.

Change, even in its toxic form, is rapid difference. Churn, on the other hand, is more like the Hindu god Shiva, a creative force of destruction and genesis. Churn topples the incumbent and creates a platform ideal for more innovation and birth. It is "compounded rebirth." And this genesis hovers on the edge of chaos.

Donald Hicks of the University of Texas studied the half-life of Texan businesses for the past 22 years and found that their longevity has dropped by half since 1970. That's change. But Austin, the city in Texas that has the shortest expected life spans for new businesses, also has the fastest-growing number of jobs and the highest wages. That's churn.

Hicks told his sponsors in Texas that "the vast majority of the employers and employment on which Texans will depend in the year 2026—or even 2006—do not yet exist." In order to produce 3 million new jobs by 2020, 15 million new jobs must be created in all, because of churn. "Rather than considering jobs as a fixed sum to be protected and augmented, Hicks argued, the state should focus on encouraging economic churning—on continually re-creating the state's economy," writes Jerry Useem in Inc., a small-business magazine that featured Hicks's report. Ironically, only by promoting churn can long-term stability be achieved.

This notion of constant churn is familiar to ecologists and those who manage large networks. The sustained vitality of a complex network requires that the net keep provoking itself out of balance. If the system settles into harmony and equilibrium, it will eventually stagnate and die.

Innovation is a disruption; constant innovation is perpetual disruption. This seems to be the goal of a well-made network: to sustain a perpetual disequilibrium. As economists (such as Paul Romer and Brian Arthur) begin to study the Network Economy, they see that it, too, operates by poising itself on the edge of constant chaos. In this chaotic churn is life-giving renewal and growth.

The difference between chaos and the edge of chaos is subtle. Apple Computer, in its attempt to seek persistent disequilibrium and stay innovative, may have leaned too far off-balance and unraveled toward extinction. Or, if its luck holds, after a near-death experience in devolution it may be burrowing toward a new mountain to climb.

The dark side of churn in the Network Economy is that the new economy builds on the constant extinction of individual companies as they're outpaced or morphed into yet newer companies in new fields. Industries and occupations also experience this churn. Even a sequence of rapid job changes for workers—let alone lifetime employment—is on its way out. Instead, careers—if that is the word for them—will increasingly resemble networks of multiple and simultaneous commitments with a constant churn of new skills and outmoded roles.

Networks are turbulent and uncertain. The prospect of constantly tearing down what is now working will make future shock seem tame. We, of course, will challenge the need to undo established successes, but we'll also find exhausting the constant, fierce birthing of so much that is new. The Network Economy is so primed to generate self-making newness that we may find this ceaseless tide of birth a type of violence.

Nonetheless, in the coming churn, the industrial age's titans will fall. In a poetic sense, the prime task of the Network Economy is to destroy—company by company, industry by industry—the industrial economy. While it undoes industry at its peak, it weaves a larger web of new, more agile, more tightly linked organizations between its spaces.

Effective churning will be an art. In any case, promoting stability, defending productivity, and protecting success can only prolong the misery. When in doubt, churn. In the Network Economy, seek sustainable disequilibrium.

12 The Law of Inefficiencies
Don't solve problems

In the end, what does this Network Economy bring us?

Economists once thought that the coming age would bring supreme productivity. But, in a paradox, increasing technology has not led to measurable increases in productivity.

This is because productivity is exactly the wrong thing to care about. The only ones who should worry about productivity are robots. And, in fact, the one area of the economy that does show a rise in productivity has been the US and Japanese manufacturing sectors, which have seen about a 3 to 5 percent annual increase throughout the 1980s and into the 1990s. This is exactly where you want to find productivity. But we don't see productivity gains in the misnamed catch-all category, the service industry—and why would we? Is a Hollywood movie company that produces longer movies per dollar more productive than one that produces shorter movies?

The problem with trying to measure productivity is that it measures only how well people can do the wrong jobs. Any job that can be measured for productivity probably should be eliminated.

Peter Drucker has noted that in the industrial age, the task for each worker was to discover how to do his job better; that's productivity. But in the Network Economy, where machines do most of the inhumane work of manufacturing, the task for each worker is not "how to do this job right" but "what is the right job to do?" In the coming era, doing the exactly right next thing is far more "productive" than doing the same thing better. But how can one easily measure this vital sense of exploration and discovery? It will be invisible to productivity benchmarks.

Wasting time and being inefficient are the way to discovery. The Web is being run by 20-year-olds because they can afford to waste the 50 hours it takes to become proficient in exploring the Web. While 40-year-old boomers can't take a vacation without thinking how they'll justify the trip as being productive in some sense, the young can follow hunches and create seemingly mindless novelties on the Web without worrying about whether they are being efficient. Out of these inefficient tinkerings will come the future.

In the Network Economy, productivity is not our bottleneck. Our ability to solve our social and economic problems will be limited primarily by our lack of imagination in seizing opportunities, rather than trying to optimize solutions. In the words of Peter Drucker, as echoed recently by George Gilder, "Don't solve problems, seek opportunities." When you are solving problems, you are investing in your weaknesses; when you are seeking opportunities, you are banking on the network. The wonderful news about the Network Economy is that it plays right into human strengths. Repetition, sequels, copies, and automation all tend toward the free, while the innovative, original, and imaginative all soar in value.

Our minds will at first be bound by old rules of economic growth and productivity. Listening to the network can unloose them. In the Network Economy, don't solve problems, seek opportunities.

2

Marketing in an Information-Intensive Environment: Strategic Implications of Knowledge as an Asset

RASHI GLAZER

The author presents a framework for thinking about the impact of information and information technology on marketing. The focus is on the concept of "information" or "knowledge" as both an asset to be managed and a variable to be researched. After developing a particular operationalization of the value of information in marketing contexts, which can be used to describe firms in terms of their relative levels of "information intensity," the author presents a series of propositions examining the consequences of increasing information intensity for some key components of firm strategy and organizational structure. The concepts discussed are illustrated with a description of the transaction-based information systems that are being implemented in a variety of firms in pursuit of competitive advantage.

Among the most interesting and publicized business stories in recent years are the following.

- Federal Express's COSMOS customer service system tracks every movement of every package in the network (through hand-held computers carried by all employees who handle packages). It has become the basis for the firm's continuing ability to differentiate itself in an increasingly competitive market. The company is now providing customers with terminals and/or software so that they can tie into the system directly—in effect enabling Federal Express to *manage* its own shipping department, thus creating huge customer switching costs.

Rashi Glazer is Assistant Professor and Northern Telecom Scholar, Walter A. Haas School of Business, University of California, Berkeley. The article has benefited from discussions with Noel Capon, Stephan Haeckel of IBM, and Frederick Webster, and from the comments of members of the Marketing Science Institute's Steering Group on Information Technology. The support of the Marketing Science Institute is gratefully acknowledged.

- American Airlines' SABRE reservation system, in addition to its well-documented role in retail travel agencies, is the basis of both the firm's successful frequent-flier program and its ability to implement "yield-management" or flexible and dynamic pricing. The system has now been extended to in-house corporate travel departments and helps organizations *manage* their travel and entertainment operations.

- McKesson, the pharmaceutical wholesaler, implemented its pioneering ECONOMOST system by placing terminals in drugstores and tying them into McKesson's central computer. Originally designed to expedite order processing and control inventory, the system rejuvenated the wholesale drug distribution industry (not coincidentally resulting in the elimination of dozens of competitors). McKesson is now effectively *managing* retail drugstores for its clients by selling back to them summaries of information collected daily.

- Inland Steel, whose interactive computer network with its customers began as an attempt to keep customers informed of the status of their orders, now provides a wide range of value-added services, from billing and funds transfer to consulting on technical product specifications. The system effectively enables the firm to differentiate itself in a mature "commodity" product category by helping customers to *manage* their own operations.

These examples, though notable, are but representative of what is fast emerging as a major development in the evolution of business strategy. In all cases, the organization first put in place an information technology infrastructure and then went *beyond the technology* to view the management of *"information" itself* as an asset to gain competitive advantage.

A central theme of this generation has been the onset of the "information age," in which information or knowledge replaces matter and energy as the primary resource of society (Bell 1973). Notions of an "information economy," a "postindustrial" society, or a "knowledge revolution" have been reflected in the work of observers in many fields for several years. Surprisingly, however, despite the wealth of evidence that "information" and information technology are rapidly transforming almost all phases of economic and business activity, relatively little formal attention has been paid to the effects of the transformation on marketing theory and practice. (An important exception is the book *Marketing in an Electronic Age*, edited by Buzzell 1985, and the Harvard conference on which it is based.)

This article presents a framework for thinking about the impact of the changing information environment on marketing. The objectives are (1) to develop a conceptual measure of the *value of information* in a marketing context and (2) to propose several strategic and organizational implications that follow from the measure developed and the subsequent ability to describe a firm as more or less *information intensive*. Thus, an organized structure is suggested for integrating—in a form useful to marketing academicians and practitioners—several of the myriad of information-related issues that are either being treated indirectly and in isolation or ignored altogether in the absence of a common meeting-ground.

The article is not intended to be comprehensive, but suggests a few central themes that can be used to stimulate further discussion and research. In the absence to date of a significant body of empirical work in the area by academicians, most of what is known about the changing information environment and marketing comes from the rapidly accumulating evidence (often reported in popular management books—Drucker 1980; Peters 1987; etc.) documenting corporations' experience with the phenomenon. In general, aside from some salient examples that illustrate key points, such evidence is not reviewed here. (For a detailed summary of applications of information technology in marketing through 1986, see Farley and McCann 1988.)

A theoretical rationale for the explicit formal consideration of information and information technology by marketing scholars and managers is rooted in the generally accepted definition of marketing as the set of activities involved in the facilitation of *exchange* (e.g., Bagozzi 1975; Kotler and Levy 1969). As goods and services move along the value-added chain (Porter 1985) from supplier to firm to distributor to consumer, increasingly a major component of exchange is the exchange of information. In that sense, the value-added chain can be viewed as a communications channel. One of the most dramatic developments in recent times has been technology's role in significantly expanding the capacity of the channel to store, process, and transmit information.

The effects of this expansion in channel capacity, typically the result of the adoption of computer and telecommunications technology, generally involve:

1. An increase in the *speed* with which information is transmitted.

2. An increase in the *amount* of information that can be stored and processed in a given unit of time.

3. As a consequence of 1 and 2 and perhaps most important, the creation of new types or *patterns* of information organization, so that quantitative changes 1 and 2 are giving rise to qualitative changes as well.

Increases in the speed and amount of processing are functions of technology, but the emergence of new ways of "packaging" or organizing information suggests the importance of considering *information itself*, above and beyond the technology, as the key variable for analysis.

These developments have taken place in society at large as well as within individual enterprises. The theme of this article is that the business paradigms predominating today—which are revealed through firm strategies and organizational structures—are functions of an older, more capacity-constrained information environment. As that environment changes, so too do the paradigms, strategies, and structures that evolved with it. In particular, two major trends can be identified.

• The emergence of knowledge or information itself as an *asset* in its own right, often with significant marketplace value.

• The blurring of current boundaries and the (potentially radical) redefinition of traditional conceptual categories—between the firm and the outside world as well as within the firm itself.

After a brief discussion of some issues surrounding attempts to measure an information construct, one particular conceptual framework is described for the valuation of information in a marketing context. Next, the notion of "information intensity" is introduced and a series of specific propositions is presented for the effect of increasing information intensity on marketing strategy and organizational structure. Finally, many of the ideas advanced are illustrated with a description of the emerging transaction-based information systems.

A Framework for Valuing Information

Conceptual Background

"Information" can be defined as data that have been organized or given *structure*—that is, placed in *context*—and thus endowed with *meaning*.[1,2] In keeping with the theme developed here, within marketing this "context" (and thus the meaning of "information") can be seen to be a function of information's role in facilitating exchange. At the same time, for economic users of information such as the firm, the meaning of a piece of information is clearly related to the measure of its *value* (e.g., Cherry 1966). One of the objectives of this article is to suggest a conceptual framework for measuring the *value* of information so that an otherwise abstract concept can be made more operational and thus prove useful for marketing academicians and practitioners as a guide to future research in the area. "Conceptual" is stressed here because practical implementation of the proposed measurement system may be difficult in many applications in the absence of more general changes in organizations' accounting and evaluation systems.[3]

Traditional attempts at measuring the value of information have been inherently problematic, for clearly the construct is context-dependent and multidimensional. The formal or quantitative definition and measure of information (Shannon and Weaver 1949) as that which reduces uncertainty or changes an individual's degree of belief (probability distribution) about the world has not provided the foundation for a practical measurement system in most applications, despite the fact that it appears to reflect our intuitive understanding of the proper role of information. As several observers have noted, the mathematical definition of information ignores any consideration of content, so that two "signals" that reduce uncertainty by the same amount (and are therefore formally equivalent) may have vastly different meanings to the receiver (Arrow 1974; Garner 1962). Consequently, though measurement of any given stock of information in purely mathematical communication theoretic terms is straightforward, its use has been limited because measures of the meaning of the information to the relative agents are ignored.

Attempts to measure the value of information and information technology have proceeded from a number of directions. At the macro level, several researchers (Machlup 1962; Porat 1974) have estimated the relative proportion of gross national product devoted to an information or knowledge "sector." Clearly, this proportion (relative to the sectors of manufacturing, agriculture, and even traditional services) has been growing dramatically in the last two decades. Within this perspective, the challenge is how to account both for economywide nonhardware information technology resources and for the knowledge-related activities of individual businesses whose primary focus is not the sale of information products.

From the level of the firm, the focus to date has been on how to develop appropriate measures of investment in information technology, an area with which an increasing number of organizations are grappling as pressures mount to justify the growing rate of expenditures. Work in this area primarily involves attempts to identify the improvements in *performance* resulting from the incremental technology-related investment (Parker and Benson 1988).

The real issue, however, is the need to go beyond the technology *per se* and to consider the "output" of the technology—the *information itself*—as an important variable for analysis. From this perspective, information technology is seen as the mechanism behind, or *enabler* for, the phenomenal growth in the production and distribution of information. Hence, the concern here is somewhat different from that in recent work emphasizing the competitive advantage of information systems as "strategic weapons" (Parsons 1983; Wiseman 1985) or the particular ways in which information technology affects the "tools of the trade" in marketing (e.g., Buzzell 1985).

Consideration of an information or knowledge "theory of value" (Bell 1973; Haeckel 1985) begins with an appreciation of the peculiar attributes of information as a "commodity." The typical economic good has such properties as divisibility, appropriability ("either I have it or you have it"), scarcity, and decreasing returns to use. In contrast, information as a commodity differs from the typical good in that it (1) is not easily divisible or appropriable, (2) is not inherently scarce (though it is often perishable), and (3) may not exhibit decreasing returns to use, but often in fact increases in value the more it is used (Porat 1976; Stiglitz 1975). Furthermore, unlike other commodities, which are nonrenewable and (with few exceptions) depletable, information is (4) essentially self-regenerative or "feeds on itself" (Huber 1984), so that the identification of a new piece of knowledge immediately creates both the demand and conditions for production of subsequent pieces.[4] These attributes of information are the basis for the valuation process developed here.

A Measure of the Value of Information

There are many components to a completely thorough valuation of a firm's information assets (or the sum total of "what it knows"). As suggested, the concern in this article is with information that is processed to facilitate exchange within the value-added chain—(1) *downstream*, between firm and consumers (including marketing channels), (2) *upstream*, between firm and supplier, and (3) *within* the firm itself, to facilitate operations. The unit of analysis used is the *transaction*. Typically, the term refers to the exchange, say between firm and consumer, of goods or services for money. However, beyond the exchange of goods for money, information also is exchanged. From the perspective of the firm, this information is assumed to be deposited in a "memory store"—for example, in the form of a record of the transaction itself, or additional data about the consumer involved in the transaction, or the conditions in which the exchange took place (Figure 1).

The following discussion focuses on the stored information's role in facilitating future transactions. Consider first the downstream transactions between firm and consumers. Three value components can be identified.

| FIGURE 1 | VALUE OF TRANSACTION-BASED INFORMATION |

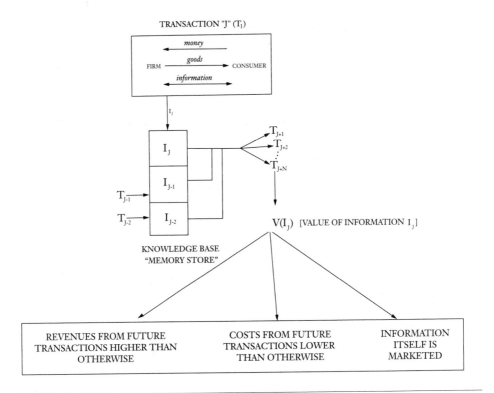

1. Given the information, revenues from subsequent transactions are greater than they otherwise would be (either because the number of future transactions is increased, e.g., through the ability to sell additional units or complementary products, or as a result of the ability to command higher prices from future transactions, e.g., as a result of the ability to provide customized service).

2. Given the information, costs of subsequent transactions are lower than they otherwise would be (e.g., through more efficient communications programs or more economical distribution arrangements—inventory, delivery, etc.).

3. The information itself is marketed (e.g., sold to other firms).

Though implementation of the proposed measures may be problematic for many firms—particularly the estimation of the changes in revenues and costs resulting from having collected and processed information—in theory the exercise is no different from many others involving forecasts of the response functions associated with other marketing variables, such as in using decision calculus models (Little 1970). Furthermore, as depicted in Figure 1, revenues and costs from subsequent transactions are obviously functions of information collected from many previous transactions and so it may be difficult in practice to assess the value of any single piece of information. This point is consistent with the notion that "meaningful" information results from the grouping of otherwise discrete items of data into an organized structure or pattern. Hence, the challenge for organizations that want to adopt formal information-measurement procedures is the identification of the relevant patterns or the appropriate level at which to aggregate individual items of information.

The total value of the cumulative information associated with the transactions between the firm and its customers can be designated V_i^c. Similarly, one can identify V_i^s, the value of the information associated with the upstream transactions between the firm and its suppliers (where the role of the information is to reduce the costs of the factor inputs that go into the firm's products and services), and V_i^f, the value of information associated with exchanges *within* the firm (where the goal is generally the reduction of production/operations costs).

The three measures of the value of information associated with different types of transactions—V_i^c, V_i^s, and V_i^f—can be aggregated to give $V(I) = V_i^c + V_i^s + V_i^f$, the total value of the firm's information. (The Appendix outlines a more formal treatment of the proposed valuation procedure).

Note that the focus here is on the valuation of *information* and not on the technology. However, as the formal analysis in the Appendix suggests, if information technology is a fixed cost, which is allocated across the number of items of information collected and processed (as indeed is the purpose of investment in information technology), the role of the technology in the valuation process becomes negligible *as long as opportunities are present for it to be used in processing a sufficiently high volume of information*. The function of a valuation framework that is oriented toward the *information itself* is to ensure that the firm has the incentive to identify such opportunities.

The Information Intensiveness Continuum

The variable $V(I)$ forms the basis for a measure of a firm's *information intensity*. In practice, depending on the particular application (e.g., when two firms are being compared on their levels of information intensity), it may be useful to normalize $V(I)$ by firm profits (giving $V(I)/\Pi(F)$), revenues (giving $V(I)/R(F)$), or overall assets (giving $V(I)/A(F)$). Thus, firm A is more information intensive than firm B if, say, $V(I_A)/\Pi(F_A) > V(I_B)/\Pi(F_B)$.

More generally, a firm is information intensive to the degree that its products and operations are based on the information collected and processed as part of exchanges along the value-added chain. Whereas traditional products and operations are relatively static, information-intensive products and operations *change* as new data from the environment become incorporated into them. Though all three components—V_i^c, V_i^s, and V_i^f—contribute to the overall level of a firm's information intensity, of particular interest from a marketing perspective is the role of V_i^c, the value of information associated with exchanges between the firm and its customers.

An important development in many firms is the extent to which an informational or knowledge component is becoming an increasingly large part of the "product" or offering itself. As noted, several factors contribute to the measure V_i^c—increased revenues from future transactions, reduced costs, and the sale of the information itself. It is useful to think in terms of an *information intensiveness continuum*, the levels of which represent the various types of information associated with products. A firm's product offerings can be placed along the continuum on the basis of the extent to which these different factors form the basis for their "value added."[5]

The focus here is on the typical organization's products and goes beyond the more obvious situations of firms that are primarily in the information/knowledge business (publishing, software, etc.). A second important source of "information value added," which is related to but conceptually distinct from the current emphasis, is the degree to which "knowledge" components such as microprocessors are an increasingly large part of most traditionally "dumb" products, reflecting the general trend toward substituting information for matter/energy and capital/labor.

At one extreme of the continuum are offerings that are information independent—products whose features are the same regardless of the information exchanged as part of the firm's transactions with customers. Most traditional products as well as standardized services (e.g., McDonald's) would fit into this category.

Next along the continuum is information that is not part of the offering *per se*, but is critical to the marketing effort. This represents the well-known concept of a product as fundamentally providing a solution to a customer's problem and is an established part of marketing theory. From a practical perspective, information of this type is usually associated with the selling effort, particularly in industrial buying situations (e.g., providing the results of technical experiments).

At an intermediate point on the continuum is information collected and processed that allows for the provision of customized offerings. In general, products that evolve rapidly in response to customer feedback (even if at the segment as opposed to individual-consumer level) would also fit into this category. Thus, many products in high technology industries, which often rely on "value-added resellers," are information intensive in this sense (above and beyond the obvious fact that such products also change rapidly as a result of technological advances). A notable illustration of the phenomenon in a traditionally "low tech" industry is found in Matsushita/Panasonic's bicycle division in Japan, which collects detailed computerized data from a customer at the point of purchase (bicycle store) and uses the information to "custom-build" any one of several hundred thousand models. Historically, "customization" has always depended on the collection of information (indeed, it is the traditional basis for the definition of "service"), but the example underscores how information processed from transactions can have value even in traditional manufacturing contexts.

At yet another point along the continuum is information or knowledge that is actually part of the offering (or "bundle"), but is secondary to the main product (and is sometimes treated as a "loss leader"). Providing an electronic inventory system to sell hospital supplies (e.g., American Hospital Supply) would fit into this category. In this case, information collected and processed is clearly critical to the offering, but is not deemed to have independent market value in its own right.

Finally, at the other end of the continuum is information that may have been useful *initially* in marketing the offering (or is perhaps a byproduct of the initial marketing effort), but later becomes a marketable product itself—often with potential to eclipse the original product in revenues and/or profits. The most dramatic examples of this trend are airline reservations systems (e.g., American Airlines' SABRE), as well as other so-called *transaction-based information systems* and many financial services (i.e., information once provided as part of the rationale for selling money that is now sold on its own, with banks such as Citicorp and Australia's Westpac in the vanguard).

Along the continuum, the underlying dynamic is a shift from information as a support for the classical (usually physically based) notion of a product or service toward information as a wealth-generating asset in its own right. A product offering is farther along the continuum the more its "value added" is a function of information collected and processed from transactions. In terms of the formal valuation framework, as one moves along the continuum, product offerings are based initially on information's role in reducing costs and increasing revenues from future transactions and later on the sale of the information itself. At a given point of time, the firm is likely to have stocks of information assets—and product offerings based on them—at various places along the continuum. As noted in the Appendix, V_i^c is the cumulative effect of the profits (value added) resulting from aggregating these separate stocks of information assets.

At the same time, the more a given stock of information (e.g., knowledge about a customer segment's purchase behavior patterns) is seen as delivering one particular source of value (e.g., by lowering the costs of reaching a target segment), its meaning to the firm is likely to go beyond its original function and it comes to provide other sources of value (e.g., next by enabling the firm to provide a customized offering to that segment and ultimately by acquiring sale value to other firms). Indeed, one of the most important implications of the notion of an information intensiveness continuum is that the various components of "information value" are not independent. Rather, the successful implementation of "earlier" uses sets the stage for "later" applications. In this important sense, and unlike most traditional economic commodities, information appreciates in overall value the more it is used. Thus, a firm is information intensive—increasing V_i^c and, by extension, $V(I)$—not only if it has many separate stocks of information assets (and hence products) spread along the range of the continuum, but also to the degree that its information assets (and products) are concentrated at the "later" points of the continuum.

Strategic and Structural Implications of Information Intensity

The notion of *information intensity* provides an operationalization that can be used as the basis for a series of hypotheses about the effects of the changing information environment on business activity. The measure of a firm's information intensity is given by $V(I)$, typically normalized by a measure such as profits or revenues (e.g., to adjust for firm size), to give, say, $V(I)/\Pi(F)$—in which case a firm is said to be more information intensive than another if a greater proportion of its profits can be attributed to information assets.[6] In the following discussion, $V(I)^*$ is defined as the normalized value of a firm's information (the measure of its information intensity) without specification of the particular basis for the normalization.

As suggested, considerable evidence supports the general proposition that the economy as a whole is becoming more information intensive and that this trend will continue dramatically for the foreseeable future. Among the theoretical arguments used to justify the proposition are (1) the apparently inevitable substitution of information/knowledge for capital and labor combined with (2) the inherently nonscarce and seemingly unlimited (or, at most, channel-capacity-limited) renewable and regenerative aspects of information/knowledge in comparison with most other commodities, which are at best scarce, nonrenewable, and usually depletable.

However, the emphasis here is on the consequences of increasing information intensity on individual firms. A *primitive assumption* is that the typical firm (i.e., not just one in the "information business") is becoming more information intensive or, within the system outlined, that V(I)* is positive. This hypothesis warrants formal empirical validation, but it appears to have sufficient face validity and a growing body of anecdotal evidence for its support.

The focus of attention then shifts to a comparison of the consequences of increasing information intensiveness on the specific strategic and structural variables of concern to marketing scholars and practitioners. The overall theme of this article is that the greater the information intensity of a firm (i.e., as V(I)* increases), the more the effects of the expansion in channel capacity and the attributes of the information "commodity" will come to reshape the reigning business paradigm. In particular, it is suggested that, whereas traditional physical-based commodities (which are appropriable, scarce, and have decreasing returns to use) lead to concerns with boundaries, ownership, and allocation, *information* (which is nonappropriable, nonscarce, and has increasing returns to use) *results in the breaking down of boundaries and leads to issues of access, sharing, and creating opportunities for use.*

In the next sections, a series of specific, interrelated propositions are offered about some of the consequences of increasing information intensity on the two key dimensions along which strategy is conducted—*market attractiveness* and *competitive position* (e.g., Abell and Hammond 1979; Kerin et al. 1990)—as well as on some associated issues in *organizational structure*. In each case, the variable of interest is hypothesized to be a function of increasing information intensity, V(I)*.

Market Attractiveness

The first dimension along which strategy traditionally has been developed is *market attractiveness*. It is often defined in terms of the product life cycle and operationalized as market growth rate (as in the Boston Consulting Group portfolio; Day 1977), though more generally it is a function of the overall structure characterizing the industry in which the firm competes (Porter 1980). Regardless of which perspective is adopted, both rely on the presence of stable and predictable information flows and the assumption of generally accepted and agreed-upon levels of knowledge among all relevant participants in a market. The rapid expansion in channel capacity is rendering obsolete the premise of a stable information environment, resulting in the widespread predictions of increased *turbulence* popularized by many observers (Drucker 1980; Peters 1987; Toffler 1970). Turbulence can be defined in terms of more events per unit of time—which naturally leads to destabilization and unpredictability—and is a direct consequence of proliferating information technology and an expansion in the overall stock of knowledge (Huber 1984). The reason is that (1) because the value of much information is time-sensitive, there is increasing pressure to use information quickly, and (2) because the value of information increases with use, there is an incentive to use more of it.

A basic premise of strategic thought is that turbulent markets are inherently less attractive, and therefore a general consequence of a firm's becoming more information intensive is that, at least by *conventional* criteria, its markets will be seen to be less attractive. In the following subsections, more specific propositions are advanced that expand on this general hypothesis.

Product Life Cycle.   The first proposition concerns the relation between increasing information intensity and product life cycles.

> P_1: The greater the information intensity of a firm, the shorter are its products' life cycles.

As suggested previously, a major characteristic of an information-intensive firm is that the value added of its products is a function of information collected and processed from transactions. The proposition is a consequence of two factors. First, the economywide proliferation of information technology means that more information about new products in general is being communicated more quickly, thus speeding the diffusion process. Though information technology is one of the forces leading to the phenomenon of shorter life cycles across *all* product classes (Capon and Glazer 1987), the most dramatic effects are associated with products well along the information-intensiveness continuum because they benefit the most from advances in rapid information processing.[7]

Second, and more profound, the proposition follows directly from the notion of an information-intensive product as one that changes as new data from the environment are incorporated into it. Indeed, to the extent that a product is far along the information-intensiveness continuum, it becomes both more necessary and easier change the offering. It is more necessary to the degree that knowledge is self-regenerative or "feeds on itself" (and thus a piece of knowledge immediately creates the demand for a new piece of knowledge) and because information is often time-sensitive. At the same time, it is easier because the process essentially involves adding some new information/knowledge and can typically be carried out at much lower costs than corresponding matter- or energy-based changes. The result is a more rapid evolution in the basic product form and a shift in emphasis toward successive *generations* of the product, with the life cycle of any one generation or "version" (including, perhaps, individual "brands") assuming less importance.

Thus, the life cycles of products of many high technology industries have shortened dramatically, not only as the result of rapid advances in their underlying technology, but also because they change frequently in response to market information or customer feedback (which is often incorporated into the product's value added through OEMs, value-added resellers, or other marketing intermediaries). Perhaps the most dramatic examples of the phenomenon, however, have been in transaction-based financial services—where new products are continually being introduced, only to mature rapidly and decline, and are followed by the birth of other new products.

Industry Definition/Product-Market Boundaries. The widely used industry-structure framework developed by Porter (1980) identifies the degree of rivalry among current industry participants, the threat of new entrants, and buyer/supplier power as the determinants of market attractiveness. An attractive industry is assumed to be one in which the firms (1) do not compete too vigorously because there are well-established rules of conduct, (2) have been able to erect stable barriers to entry against new firms as well as substitute technologies, and (3) have a reasonable degree of bargaining power with their customers and suppliers. An implicit prerequisite for these conditions to hold is *meaningful boundaries* that identify who is and is not currently in the industry and define the respective roles of firm, supplier, and customer. The changing information environment is having a profound influence on each one of these assumptions, particularly the premise of meaningful industry boundaries and well-defined roles for economic agents.

At a fundamental level, as product offerings become more information intensive, the relative proportion of matter and energy decreases. Yet, it is the matter- and energy-based characteristics of products that have been used traditionally to distinguish one product class from another and that, by extension, have been the basis for industry definitions. (The same situation holds for most services, which typically are still tied to an underlying physical-based material.) However, in the absence of a new basis for industry definitions, as the information intensiveness of a firm increases, its products begin to compete more with the products of other firms in other industries (Capon and Glazer 1987; Porter and Millar 1985).[8] Hence:

> **P₂:** The greater the information intensity of a firm, the more the traditional product-market boundaries shift such that the firm increasingly faces new sources of competition from firms in historically noncompetitive industries, particularly if those firms are also information intensive.

The emergence of the "super-industry"—combining telecommunications, computers, financial services, and retailing into what is essentially an *information industry*—is perhaps the most obvious and dramatic example of this phenomenon. Firms once as diverse as AT&T, IBM, Merrill Lynch, Citicorp, and Sears find that they are now in direct competition, often with essentially the same products, not as the result of diversification but of the rather natural extension and redefinition of their traditional product lines and marketing activities. This development reflects the fact that many of those firms' products have evolved to the point where significant proportions of their value added are no longer based on their historically "unique product *features*," but rather on the information exchanged as part of customer transactions—much of which cuts across traditional product lines.

An important question for future research is: What—if anything—will replace the traditional product-oriented basis of industry definition in an information-intensive economy? One possibility is that the current concept of "an industry" will lose much of its empirical import, as firms find that they are competing in wider and more diverse arenas, for shorter time intervals, and it becomes increasingly difficult to identify with regularity any one particular group of firms as "the competition." An alternative view is that the presence of more numerous and diverse competitors is part of the transition toward a well-established information economy and that, when "things settle down," firms will once again organize into more homogeneous groupings, or industries, each specialized in the type of information products or services they deliver. Knowledge specialization is indeed an inherent feature of an information economy (Drucker 1988); the latter development, however, may rely heavily on the assumptions of "things settling down" and of a decline in the rate of increase in channel capacity expansion and information or knowledge production. By most accounts, such a decline is not expected in the near future (Huber 1984). Furthermore, because information is typically nonscarce and nonappropriable, sustaining competitive advantage for meaningful periods of time through product differentiation in information-intensive firms is difficult.[9] A third view, then, which follows from the perspective developed here and is essentially a corollary to P_2, is embodied in the following proposition.

P_3: The greater the information intensity of a firm, the more its management tends to define its "industry" (and hence its competitors) in terms of market or customer characteristics as opposed to product characteristics.

Here, "product characteristics" refers to product features or attributes that are fixed and independent of the customer, whereas "market" or "customer" characteristics are attributes of consumers (demographic characteristics, buying behavior, etc.) that cut across product lines. Ideally, it is the *interaction* between the two sets of characteristics that is important (and is the basis for most segmentation schemes). The proposition does not imply that product characteristics are ignored, only that there is a dramatic shift in emphasis. Indeed, for the newly competing firms such as Merrill Lynch, Sears, and AT&T, what gives *strategic continuity* to the emerging businesses in which they participate is the apparent belief that the basis for differential advantage does not lie in products but in the relationships cultivated with a particular set of consumers or markets. As is discussed shortly, these relationships are rooted in the nature of the information flows established between the firm and its customers. The notions of the customer as the firm's primary asset (Levitt 1983) and the market rather than the product as the locus of competition have been at the core of marketing theory for some time, but in practice they have yet to form the foundation for industry definitions (which are still based on such factors as SIC codes). This situation may now be changing, though it remains to be seen whether consumers will respond to the new initiatives in the form of increased loyalty.

Buyer/Supplier Power. Relative industry attractiveness is also being questioned in terms of other traditionally predictable components of industry structure: buyer and supplier power (Frazier 1983; Porter 1980; Stern and Reve 1981). "Knowledge is power" is a well-established social principle, and a major determinant of marketing power has always been the levels of information possessed by agents. Increases in information-processing capacity throughout the value-added chain are changing the patterns of what buyers and suppliers, respectively, "know" in given situations—often (as information is nonappropriable) in the direction of equalization—thus altering both the dynamics and terms of negotiation. In the short run and in any given situation, depending on the context (and in particular on who "knew more" originally), the balance of power might shift in the direction of buyers *or* sellers, in either case leading to dislocations in industry structure and influencing relative industry attractiveness (Porter and Millar 1985). However, in the long term, if increasing information intensity brings new competitors into an industry (P_2) with products that have shorter life cycles (P_1), and if firms tend to define their competition in terms of markets rather than products (P_3), customers will presumably have more options and lower switching costs. Hence:

P_4: The greater the information intensity of a firm, the more the relative power between the firm and its buyers shifts in favor of the buyers.

At the same time, to the extent that the firm is successful in differentiating itself in terms of the types of information products/services it offers (a development that, as noted, may be difficult to sustain), the shift in power in favor of buyers may be neutralized. Indeed, in general, it may be difficult to predict the specific effect of increasing information intensity on buyer/seller relations because of the presence of countervailing forces.

An important example of the problem concerns the changing nature of relations between the firm and its marketing intermediaries or distribution channels—where fundamental shifts are taking place in the respective roles of agents along the value-added chain. As much as anything else, marketing channels have been communications channels, whose role it is to transmit and process information along with (physical) goods. Thus, as product offerings become increasingly information intensive, the traditional "supporting" services performed by the channel (i.e., the provision of information) are becoming primary carriers of value in their own right. The situation is magnified to the extent that relationships with consumers (a function of information flows) assume more importance and it is the distributor who is closer to the customer and has been responsible for customer communication. These developments favor a shift in power toward distribution channels and away from the firm. The successes of the pharmaceutical wholesaler McKesson (which has now become the major force in the industry, with significantly greater power than the manufacturers) and of WalMart in retailing are examples of this trend.

However, at the same time, the very changes in information technology and ensuing expanded communications channel capacity that have resulted in increasing information intensity are also eliminating the need for the lengthy distribution structures that have historically characterized most industries. Even for physically based goods, advances in transportation and materials handling, above and beyond those in communications technology, have made it possible (and necessary, where time sensitivity is an issue) for firms to bypass layers of intermediaries. For information-intensive offerings (which are often time sensitive), the ability of firms to sell directly to their customers is increased dramatically, thus favoring a shift in power toward the firm and away from the downstream channel. American Airlines' SABRE system enables the firm to deal directly with in-house corporate travel departments (and, increasingly, consumers in their homes), thus bypassing traditional travel agents.

It may be an empirical question as to which of the two contrasting views of the overall effect of the changing information environment on marketing channel relationships is likely to prevail. However, at least in the short run, *both* scenarios point to the breakdown of traditional roles and the emergence of a *new source of competition* for the firm from players (i.e., channel members) that have typically been its partners and customers. In any given context, which of the two views prevails is likely to depend on other situational variables; but in general, if there is a "winning" hypothesis, it is likely to favor the agent—firm or distributor—that is first able to develop and then *manage* the information networks that are increasingly at the basis of product value added. In the long run, the key question is whether this new source of extended rivalry (Porter 1980) will remain a permanent feature of industry structure or whether it is a transitory phase to be replaced by a renewed recognition of firm-channel interdependence, though one based on different principles than apply today.

Competitive Position

The changing nature of channel relationships is an example of the degree to which increases in information intensiveness are changing the stable and predictable "rules of the game" that serve to define industry structure. In the most general sense, as industry structures change, the degree of competition or level of rivalry among both current and new players intensifies. In a more turbulent environment, this is true by definition, but it is important to identify the mechanism through which it occurs— that is, because all firms in a redefined industry must learn to compete against players that bring diverse sets of experience to the arena, competition is increasingly not only about products and markets, but over whose rules of the game should be followed (Buaron 1981). In the past, these rules were hidden and thus implicitly agreed upon or taken for granted. Now, in many cases the changing information environment has made them visible and they are being challenged.

Because the rules of the game specify the dimensions of competition, the issue is magnified to the extent that information/knowledge is displacing the traditional, and generally accepted, factors of capital and labor as the basis for competitive activity. As noted, one effect is that the offerings of firms competing in previously disparate product categories are beginning to look more similar and the product itself, as classically defined, may be less a source of sustainable differential advantage. If so, then the question becomes: What will form the basis for competitive strategic advantage in the future?

The second dimension of strategic thinking is the relative *competitive position* of the firms in a market. Whereas the "market attractiveness" axis of the "strategic grid" is designed to capture environmental variables that the firm takes as given or are beyond its control, "competitive position" is a function of the particular set of actions and strategic direction *chosen* by the firm in light of its overall situation analysis. Traditionally, the choice of competitive position is between broad market-share leadership (typically, by becoming the high volume/low cost producer) and a narrow market follower status (through "differentiation" and "focus" on a target segment or niche). As is true for market attractiveness, an increasingly information-intensive environment is forcing a reevaluation of some of the fundamental assumptions behind the traditional choice of competitive position and suggests the emergence of a new basis for achieving competitive advantage.

Market-Share Versus Differentiation Strategies. In contrasting so-called leader-follower or market-share and differentiation approaches, it is first useful to see how the various sources of information value as outlined previously (V_i^c, V_i^s, and V_i^f) are critical to the success of each strategy. The viability of the high volume/low cost approach is rooted in the notion of the experience curve (Boston Consulting Group 1968), which in a fundamental sense represents the formal inclusion of information or knowledge into the production function (Arrow 1962). The economic rationale for gaining the benefits of accumulated experience is that the average cost of producing subsequent units of a product is reduced as know-how (i.e., information) becomes a relatively higher component of the value added associated with the product. Though a variety of factors combine to drive costs down, many of them can be attributed to what are defined here as V_i^s, or the value of the information associated with the transactions between the firm and its suppliers (resulting in lower factor input costs), and V_i^f, the intrafirm exchanges of information (which result in generally reduced operating costs).

In contrast to the high volume/low cost strategy, the differentiation/focus approach relies less on accumulated experience (or knowledge) with the product (or the manufacturing of the product) than it does on accumulated *experience with the consumer.* Niche strategies depend, first, on the ability to gain accurate and increasingly detailed information about specific target groups or segments and, next, on the capacity to process that information quickly and accurately. Thus, in terms of the framework outlined here, the success of these strategies appears to be linked most closely to V_i^c, the value of the information associated with the exchanges between the firm and its markets.

The implication of the preceding discussion is that, in the context of competitive strategy, firms typically have traded-off two *types* of information value—product experience/knowledge (V_i^f and V_i^s) for market/experience knowledge (V_i^c). This tradeoff reflects the prevailing view of market-share and differentiation strategies as polar opposites on the continuum of strategic options, because volume/cost leadership is assumed to be incompatible with the ability to serve the idiosyncratic needs of specific and diverse segments. The tradeoff is embodied further in the contrasting strategic objectives and associated time frames of long-run market share versus short-run profitability for, respectively, the high volume/low cost and differentiation approaches.

As noted previously, a proposed effect of increasing information intensiveness is shorter product life cycles. The market-share approach—which often depends on experience effects and early investment in fixed capacity in anticipation of future volume, and allows for longer payback periods and greater margins of error between periods—is based on the management of product-market growth and often relies on sufficiently long life-cycle growth rates. Furthermore, as a consequence of information technology, factor inputs (including knowledge or information) are becoming equalized across firms more quickly and there is a greater degree of industrywide shared experience. Consequently, sustaining cost leadership in manufacturing alone is increasingly difficult. The situation is magnified for products well along the information-intensiveness continuum, where manufacturing value added is correspondingly less important.

However, the initial impression that increasing information intensity seems to be biased against market share and in favor of differentiation/profitability may be misleading. Rather, one of the most profound implications of information-processing technology for strategic thinking is the realization that the *traditional strategic tradeoff may be obsolete.* The advent of "programmable automation" methods (Hayes and Jaikumar 1988) such as flexible manufacturing—in which hardware-intensive processes are replaced by software-intensive ones, or information is substituted for capital and labor—has enabled firms in a wide range of industries to retain the benefits of scale and production experience without sacrificing the ability to customize offerings for specific target groups (e.g., Matsushita bicycles in Japan).

In a similar vein, with expanded information-processing channel capacity, *flexible marketing* systems are being developed—for example, retail scanner data collection systems, geodemographic and psychographic (e.g., zip-code-based) targeting techniques, and related technologies, along with modular distribution or advertising methods (such as the increasing practice of using different voice-overs accompanying a single visual platform in television advertising). These structures are designed to capture cost-saving procedures without the rigid standardization that inhibits adaptation to changing environmental conditions and have dramatically increased the precision with which marketers can facilitate the exchange process.

The role of flexible marketing assumes even greater importance to the extent that manufacturing and product-related factors are becoming less important in the overall value-added calculation. Indeed, as discussed, for information-intensive offerings, the classically defined "product" component of the marketing mix is giving way to other classically defined marketing-mix elements used to communicate information about the product (distribution, advertising, salesforce, etc.) as the primary carrier of value added. Hence:

P_5: The greater the information intensity of the firm, (a) the more the reliance on flexible marketing systems—that is, the greater the degree of managerial discretion about the nonproduct elements of the marketing mix, primarily those involved with communications activities (distribution, advertising, salesforce) and (b) the greater the importance of nonproduct marketing-mix elements in contributing to overall value added.

In the limit, as nonproduct factors assume less importance, the once-meaningful distinction or boundary between the product itself and the distribution and communication activities used to *support* the product may be losing its theoretical as well as empirical import (Ray 1985). More generally, however, the essence of the preceding argument is that increasing information intensity enables the firm to focus *at the same time* on gaining product and marketing knowledge/experience. As shown in Figure 2,

FIGURE 2	STRATEGIC OPTIONS AND SOURCES OF KNOWLEDGE

MARKET INFORMATION/KNOWLEDGE
(V_i^c)

		LOW	HIGH
	LOW	FOLLOWER I	DIFFERENTIATION: NICHE OR TARGET MARKETING II
PRODUCT INFORMATION KNOWLEDGE $(V_i^S V_i^F)$	**HIGH**	COST/VOLUME LEADERSHIP; EXPERIENCE EFFECTS III	FLEXIBLE MANUFACTURING AND MARKETING IV

the strategic options open to firms as a function of knowledge can be summarized in a 2 × 2 matrix, where the dimensions are product information/knowledge (V_i^f and V_i^s) and market information/knowledge (V_i^c), each of which can be either at a (relatively) low or high level. Though historically firms have chosen to compete in *either* cell II or III, the demands of the changing information environment may lead firms increasingly to excell on *both* dimensions and compete in the lower right corner. More formally:

P6: The more information intensive the firm, the greater the degree to which competitive position is defined less in terms of a choice between high volume/low cost market-share leadership and narrow/differentiation strategies and more in terms of to the ability *to combine simultaneously* both approaches.

As a corollary:

P7: The more information intensive the firm, the greater the degree to which longer term market share and shorter term profitability are seen as compatible strategic objectives.

Sources of Competitive Advantage: Customer Relations. The information-intensive environment described here is characterized by (1) the breakdown in boundaries between traditional strategic options and the dissolution of the conventional criterion for defining competitive position, (2) the decline of the classical "product" as a basis for differentiation, (3) the changing nature of buyer/supplier power, and (4) the need for flexibility in manufacturing and marketing decision making. In such a climate, the key question becomes: What is the source of long-run sustainable competitive advantage? One answer that emerges from the current analysis suggests that the source is the *management of the overall set of relations between the firm and its environment* or, equivalently, because these relations are developed through the *pattern of exchanges* in which the firm is involved, the source is the management of the firm's information-processing system. This general goal is achieved through several separate but interdependent strategic initiatives.

P_8: The greater the information intensity of the firm, the more the strategic objective becomes maximizing the number of transactions with the same (loyal) customers through the sale of an increasingly wide and diverse array of products and services (from the firm).

The rationale for this hypothesis is rooted both in the tendency toward shorter product life cycles (P_1) and in the proposed movement toward industry definition in terms of market rather than product characteristics (P_3) and the balance-of-power shift in favor of buyers over suppliers (P_5). At the same time, the ability of flexible manufacturing and marketing systems to deliver customized offerings at low cost means that the firm has the potential to "be many more things to many more people." Consequently, historical industry boundaries are dissolving and firms realize that they can compete effectively in previously ignored or "foreign" businesses. (Firms as diverse as Coca-Cola, Disney, and Citicorp have been leaders in this ability; they capitalize on their relationships with customers—or consumer franchise—to sell a range of products and services beyond their initial corporate missions or areas of immediate production expertise). From a marketing perspective, the real question facing these firms is: How far can the corporate franchise be extended and how deep are the company's overall customer relationships or goodwill? In other words, how effectively has the firm managed its communications and flow of information?

Relations with Channels and Competitors. A key feature of the changing information environment is hypothesized to be a dramatic increase in the overall level of competition and the emergence of new sources of competition for the firm—including agents, such as channel members, who have typically been its partners. It is proposed that, to neutralize this trend, marketing strategy in information-intensive firms will not be confined to the goal of getting and keeping end-user customers, but will extend to efforts aimed at promoting long-term relationships or forging sustainable strategic alliances. To the extent that a firm is successful in such efforts with another member in the value-added chain, the firm reduces the risk of a former partner such as a distributor becoming a direct competitor while also creating powerful barriers to entry by other, more traditional competitors that want to use the same channels.

At the same time, the turbulence resulting from shorter product life cycles (P_1) and the shifting product-market boundaries (P_2) or industry definitions (P_3) is also leading the firm to seek strategic alliances, joint ventures, and general partnerships with a wide array of businesses, not just other members along the value chain. In other contexts, of course, many of these players are a firm's traditional competitors. For example, Miles and Snow (1986) describe the emergence of "dynamic networks," or confederations of organizations that band together to achieve mutual objectives by combining different sets of skills required by a situation. Such networks are a growing phenomenon in industries that are generally R&D- or technology-driven (Harrigan 1986), but are particularly important in information-intensive industries. The reason is that *the value of a given stock of information/knowledge is maximized to the extent that opportunities are identified for it to be used as often and as quickly as possible.* Hence:

P₉: The more information intensive the firm, the greater the degree to which it is involved in strategic alliances.

The movement toward a concern with partnerships (whether with other members of the value chain or with traditional competitors) potentially is one of the most dramatic consequences of the changing information environment—a shift in thinking away from the "extended rivalry" (Porter 1980) and competitive game-theoretic perspective that dominates current thinking in favor an *extended cooperation* framework that increasingly reflects the actual attitudes of firms toward their channels (Anderson, Lodish, and Weitz 1987; Webster 1976) or their traditional competitors (Harrigan 1986).

This phenomenon appears to be happening in spite of—or perhaps because of—a climate in which the overall level of competition is hypothesized to be greater. In such an environment, however, though there may be more competitors, the specific locus of competition becomes more difficult to identify as the spread of the "commodity" of interest (information) proliferates. Information is ultimately nonappropriable and is most valuable when shared (increasingly, as quickly as possible), because each partner brings something (additional knowledge) to the situation. It is rare that a party cannot benefit from the specialized knowledge added by the others (at least within a time frame during which the information is still relevant). The resulting framework is one of *interdependence* (Herriott 1988; Huber 1984) in which the nature of competition changes—away from a focus on "beating the other guy" and toward concerns with being excluded from the general information-processing network and being denied the opportunity to participate in *adding value to the given stock of available knowledge.* Consequently, the following proposition is a corollary of P₉.

P₁₀: The more information intensive the firm, despite an increase in the overall level of competition, the greater the extent to which managerial attention is focused less on competitive strategy (i.e., directed at a specific group of competitors) and more on cooperative strategy.

Organizational Structure

The focus on managing the set of relations or information exchanged between the firm and its environment leads directly to a more general consideration of the consequences of increasing information intensity for organizational structure. Issues associated with the notion of "the firm as an information processor" have either explicitly or implicitly engaged the attention of many economists and organizational theorists from several perspectives (e.g., Arrow 1974; Galbraith 1977; Lawrence and Lorsch 1967; March and Simon 1958; Marschak and Radner 1972; Williamson 1975). Though a complete discussion of this topic is well beyond the scope of this article, the concerns associated with increasing information intensiveness and organizational structure should be of interest to marketing scholars and professionals for three reasons.

1. The boundary between the firm and the outside world is dissolving and marketing has historically been responsible for managing many of the relationships across that boundary.

2. The boundary between marketing and other divisions is also dissolving, leading to the possibility that the traditional notion of marketing as a distinct functional area within the firm is being rendered obsolete.

3. The *process* or "style" by which marketing decisions are made is changing.

In this section, some propositions about the impact of information on issues of organizational structure are discussed briefly. (The effects of information technology in altering the day-to-day patterns of work or skills required in marketing departments are not addressed explicitly. For a general review of these issues, see Walton and Lawrence 1985.)

Inter- and Intraorganizational Boundaries.   A major consequence of the increases in information flows resulting from expanded channel capacity is that the boundary (in a functional, if not yet formal, sense) differentiating what is inside the firm from what is outside is becoming considerably less clear. The most obvious examples of the phenomenon are the notion of the strategic alliance and the extended concept of "dynamic networks" or confederations of organizations that band together to achieve mutual objectives. The full implication of these developments is a major subject for future research, but it is apparent that current definitions of the "firm," as well as conceptions of the relations between the firm and both its value-added partners and competitors, are likely to undergo considerable reformulation.

Perhaps the most significant implication of these developments for marketing pertains to the breakdown in the boundary separating the "traditional firm" from the "traditional consumer." Today, this breakdown is manifest through such forms as the transaction-based information systems linking firms to their customers and in the emerging phenomenon of truly interactive home shopping (Batra and Glazer 1989; Talarzyk 1989). However, though the initial rationale for these systems is the delivery of better and more efficient service from firm *to* consumer, once the information infrastructure is established, the mechanism is available for rapid and continual *two-way* communication. When this capability is coupled with flexible manufacturing systems, and given the hypothesized trends toward shorter product life-cycles (P_1) and increased buyer power (P_5), the conditions are in place for a radical shift in the role of the firm—from being the *provider* of goods and services to being a *partner* in the *creation* of goods and services. Hence:

P_{11}: The more information intensive the firm, the greater the degree to which its customers *participate* in product design/creation, resulting in the breakdown in the formal distinctions between "producer" and "consumer."

Of perhaps more short-term concern is the role of marketing (or of any single functional area) in relation to other departments within the organization. It is vital to appreciate that the traditional organizational structure (e.g., Miles and Snow 1978) is a legacy of an era in which the technologies for communication and information processing were noticeably slower and more capacity-constrained than they are today. Thus, the historical firm is one that *moves* "products" through a series of separate departments, from R&D, through production, to marketing, and then to sales (with a second group of separate support functions: accounting, finance, human resources, etc.)—the entire operation coordinated by a central administration with ultimate responsibility for the whole.

Given an environment in which both the volume and speed of information have increased exponentially, several commentators, reflecting what many firms are already implementing, have discussed the need for organizations to move away from the hierarchical centralized structure toward a "flatter," more decentralized form—where decision making is vested with individuals who are closer to *and have greater knowledge about* the customer and the competitor markets in which the firm operates (Capon and Glazer 1987; Drucker 1988; Mintzberg 1979). This shift in structure has two implications: meaningful (i.e., bottom-line) responsibility becomes *shared* throughout the firm, but at the same time so does the "ownership" of specific functional skills previously residing within a single department.

The latter development results from the fact that the linear step-by-step approach to tasks that now characterizes corporate problem solving is ill-equipped to cope with the turbulence—reflected in phenomena such as shorter product life cycles (P_1) and the emergence of new and surprising sources of competition (P_2)—that is hypothesized to characterize information-intensive firms. This situation is familiar to any manager who has waited for another department in the firm to "get back to him," only to find that, by the time it does, the customer has gone elsewhere. Apparently what is needed is not managers who know a lot about marketing (*or* finance *or* production) and little about anything else, but managers who know a lot about a particular set of customers (and *enough* about marketing *and* finance *and* production) and hence enable the firm to serve those customers' needs before the competitors do. The profile of the manager of the future remains an important topic for future research, but it is argued here that information-intensive firms are already undergoing a breakdown in the traditional structures regulating who within the firm is responsible for what function (e.g., Webster 1988). More specifically:

P_{12a}: The more information intensive the firm, the greater the degree to which the marketing department is involved in activities traditionally associated with other functional areas.

P_{12b}: The more information intensive the firm, the greater the degree to which other functional areas are involved in activities traditionally associated with marketing.

Style of Information Processing. Finally, an important implication of P_{12} is that, though the traditional focus of the impact of information technology on firm structure has been on hierarchical and centralized versus flat and decentralized forms, a related yet potentially more useful distinction might be that between *sequential* and *parallel* modes of information processing.

In this regard, a useful (and not coincidental) metaphor is suggested. In the contemporary theory of the firm as an information processor, the firm resembles the typical digital computer (rooted in the so-called von Neumann architecture) with its linear/sequential orientation and localized, spatially separate memory stores; different departments within the firm have their own areas of expertise, which are drawn upon in turn as needed to advance the common goal. In contrast, the changing environment seems to demand structures reflecting the emerging parallel associative-memory or distributed-storage computers. Such structures rely on shared processing—whereby different units have access to and operate on the same information—to achieve significant gains in output and efficiency over the older structures. From the standpoint of the firm, such processing implies the presence of cross-functional or interdepartmental (from the traditional perspective) "decision groups" or teams that come together for the explicit purpose of developing and marketing products, but whose members do not claim ownership or control over specific stores of information. Hence, as basically a corollary to P_{12}:

P_{13}: The more information intensive the firm, the greater the reliance on decision groups or teams and the parallel, rather than sequential, processing of information.

In general, the discussion of organizational structure suggests that the new modes of information processing implied by the changing environment are exactly as required for the hypothesized evolution in strategic thinking outlined previously. The notion that firm strategy and structure evolve together is a central theme of most organizational theorists (Chandler 1962; Miles and Snow 1978). However, one of the effects of proliferating information technology and increasing information intensity may be the realization of the depth to which both current strategy *and* structure are but two aspects of the same phenomenon.

It is becoming apparent that both the historical ability to form strategy and the specific types of strategies employed have been functions of a particular information-processing framework, as are the organizational structures that have evolved around it. Though firms have chosen different strategies, they traditionally have shared a common structure. In the future, firms that change their structure and style of information processing will implicitly be adopting a new set of strategic principles. In that sense, the new structure will be the new strategy.

Transaction-Based Information Systems

Among the primary mechanisms through which firms have been implementing most of the propositions advanced are the transaction-based information systems (TBIS). Those structures, though still in the early stages of their evolution, represent the most visible manifestation to date of firms' attempts to achieve high levels of V(I) or information intensity. The firms cited in this article (Federal Express, American Airlines, McKesson, Inland Steel, Matsushita, Citicorp, etc.) provide notable examples of TBIS at various stages in their evolution. The Matsushita and Inland Steel cases are particularly important because they represent firms that are developing information-intensive strategies in typical manufacturing environments that are not traditionally transaction rich.

When fully integrated, the TBIS networks (which are at the basis of what has recently been described as "relationship marketing" or "frequency marketing") process and communicate information about every transaction between the point of purchase (whether it is at a retail location or, eventually, in the home), the distributor, the firm, and perhaps even the firm's suppliers. The salient points in the various examples cited are how information is turned into an asset and how the value of the asset (e.g., in terms of the valuation methodology and the information-intensiveness continuum) is leveraged by creating opportunities for its *continued use*—so that present items of information or knowledge are continually being processed into new packages or patterns (i.e., moved along the continuum), through combination with other previously stored items of information, to be exchanged. Within this framework, the goal of the TBIS member is to ensure that it participates in, and in some sense is compensated for, each transaction or information-processing "occasion." Thus, the overall strategic objective of the TBIS firm appears to be (as formally described in P_8) the maximization of transactions—or opportunities for exchange—with its various constituencies.

The entire TBIS channel can be described as a sophisticated information-processing "organism," whose efficiency and effectiveness (in a competitive sense) improve through *experience*. In that way, the TBIS embodies the emerging strategy for how to gain competitive advantage in information-intensive environments, despite the inherent inappropriability and indivisibility of information as a commodity and the ease with which it is distributed throughout the market (so that "what one person knows, everybody else soon knows").

Thus, though it may be difficult for the firm to extract significant value from any single stock of information/knowledge considered in isolation, a sustainable position can be achieved through participation in the *management* of an ongoing information system where the processing of a *cumulative and dynamic knowledge base* becomes a viable source of value added. At the same time, the bonds (or, equivalently, the switching costs) resulting from the shared processing experience created among the members of the TBIS (e.g., a firm and its distributors) can create a strong "informational barrier to entry" against other organizations that might want to access the same knowledge base. In this respect, the TBIS represents an attempt to reinstitute a set of boundaries between a group of agents and the rest of the environment in markets where information is rendering many boundaries essentially obsolete. The objective is to leverage the value of the information asset by creating a network *within which* it can easily be produced and distributed, while simultaneously excluding others from gaining the same level of access to it and achieving the same degree of processing effectiveness and efficiency. In terms of information technology, the relationship between the technical infrastructure embodied in the TBIS and the value-added chain is thus a reciprocal one: the purpose of the TBIS is to strengthen the chain, but ongoing and long-term relations among channel members are necessary to realize the returns from investment in a TBIS.

Though the TBIS has been developed largely in relation to value-added chains, the same principles can apply to strategic alliances—that is, to partnerships with organizations that are often a firm's competitors. The focus of strategic alliances, to date, has been relatively short term in the sense that firms come together for well-defined purposes with the expectation that they will part company after their objectives have been realized. However, to the extent that the alliance is transaction-based, so that the information processed can become the foundation for a continued series of *future* transactions, strategic alliances may evolve into long-term partnerships.

In this respect, the TBIS also is the embodiment of at least one rationale for the continued presence of the *large firm* in the business climate of the future. One implication of much of the preceding discussion is that not only are many of the traditional advantages of size being neutralized (e.g., scale/experience applied to manufacturing in light of long product life cycles), but that, indeed, rapid expansion in the general store of information inherently leads to confederations of smaller, interdependent, knowledge-specialized units. In such an environment, the large organization is at best unnecessary and at worst an impediment to progress (Peters 1987)—unless it can be the foundation for "informational economies of scale" (Wilson 1975). The TBIS provides that foundation by shifting the focus away from the inevitable rise in individual specialized pockets of knowledge and smaller decision-making units and toward the *management* of the larger network that will *coordinate*—and thus be compensated for the value it adds to—the information flows upon which decisions are made.

Conclusion

The argument is made that the technology-induced expansion in information-processing capacity has led to the emergence of information/knowledge as an asset to be managed and that, in turn, the inherent characteristics of the information "commodity" are having a profound impact on a wide range of strategic and structural variables of interest to both scholars and practitioners. Table 1 summarizes the specific propositions advanced and also suggests the high level of interdependence among the individual propositions and the degree to which they are often corollaries of each other. In general, four principal hypotheses emerge from the framework presented.

1. The traditional notions of market attractiveness may no longer be appropriate.

2. The traditional choices between strategic options may no longer be meaningful.

3. Competitive advantage is achieved through management of the set of exchanges or relations (i.e., the information system) with which the firm is involved.

4. Organizational structures and information-processing styles are changing to adapt to the new strategies and reflect the concurrent breakdown in boundaries between the firm and the outside world and among individual departments within the firm.

TABLE 1	SUMMARY OF PROPOSITIONS AND MAJOR CONCEPTUAL ARGUMENTS IN THEIR SUPPORT[a]

Proposition	Conceptual Support
Market Attractiveness	
P1 Shorter product life cycles	Follows from proliferation of information technology; definition of information-intensiveness continuum; self-regenerative attribute of information "commodity"
P2 Shifts in product market boundaries; new sources of competition	Follows from increasing information in product value added (displacing matter and energy)
P3 Industry definitions based on markets rather than products	Corollary to P_2; nonappropriability attribute of information as a "commodity"
P4 Buyer/supplier power shift in favor of buyers	Follows from P_1, P_2, and P_3
Competitive Position	
P5 Increased marketing mix discretion; importance on non-product-mix elements	Flexible marketing systems; information displacing matter and energy in product value added
P6 Breakdown in distinction between market share and differentiation strategies	Flexible marketing and manufacturing systems; information replacing capital and labor
P7 Compatibility between profitability and market share strategic objectives	Corollary to P_6
P8 Focus on maximizing transactions with same customers	Follows from P_1, P_3, and P_5; flexible manufacturing and marketing systems
P9 Focus on strategic alliances	Follows from P_1 and P_3; increasing returns-to-use attribute of information as a "commodity"
P10 Focus on cooperative as opposed to competitive strategy	Corollary to P_9; increasing returns-to-use attribute of information as a "commodity"
Organizational Structure	
P11 Breakdown in distinction between firm and consumer; customers participate in design and creation of products	Definition of information-intensiveness continuum; two-way transaction-based information systems; flexible manufacturing and marketing
P12 Breakdown in distinction between marketing and other departments in firm	Follows from P_1 and P_3; increasing returns-to-use and nonappropriability attributes of information
P13 Parallel rather than sequential processing of information; decision teams	Corollary to P_{12}

[a] In all cases, the phenomenon identified in the proposition is hypothesized to be a function of increasing information intensity at the level of the firm $(V(I)^*)$.

A major focus of the discussion is the identification of an important unifying theme, above and beyond the impact of information on specific strategic or structural factors. Thus, regardless of the level at which the analysis takes place, the most striking effect observed is the blurring of traditional categorical distinctions or the questioning of conceptual definitions that have been taken for granted—between the firm and the outside world, within the firm between marketing and other departments, and within marketing between the generic marketing strategies and among the various marketing decisions.

As noted at the outset, the evidence for the ideas developed, though mounting, remains largely anecdotal in the absence of a rigorous systematic empirical study. Consequently, the propositions discussed are intended as a series of researchable hypotheses and a main implication of the article is that a research effort is needed to test them. A major goal of the article is to offer a framework within which the specific topics can be addressed—most notably, the development of a conceptualization for the measurement of the value of the information/knowledge asset and the associated notion of information intensity. This goal appears to be a prerequisite to further efforts at documenting the consequences of the changing information environment for the various strategic and structural variables of interest. It is likely that systematic research efforts to understand how information and information technology are changing both business theory and practice have been frustrated to date by the lack of meaningful progress in the measurement and valuation areas.

Clearly, a range of topics is introduced and space limitations preclude a full and detailed elaboration of each proposition. Future research in the area should involve more thorough exploration of the individual hypotheses presented, as well as others that are not introduced—in particular, those pertaining to the role of the marketing mix and the changing nature of consumer decision making.[10] At the same time, it is the very pervasiveness of the phenomena that argues for the plausibility of the current treatment. This point is particularly important to the extent that other explanations can be offered for the areas investigated and, because so many things are changing at once, it is impossible to trace the causal chain precisely. Thus, this article suggests that it is the recognition of the overall *pattern* of the consequences following from increasing information intensity—above and beyond the correctness of any one hypothesis—that is important and that, in the end, the construct of "information" itself may be one way to impose meaning on a host of otherwise seemingly unrelated data.

Finally, to the extent that the propositions presented here are supported, the overall implication for the field of marketing is significant, if perhaps controversial. Among the most important conclusions of the current discussion is the realization that a focus on customer markets is the ultimate source of competitive success and, at the same time, such focus must become the goal of the entire organization. "Marketing" has always been simultaneously a way of thinking or philosophy of problem-solving and a set of activities associated with a specific function (the "marketing department"). Both as a philosophy and as a function, marketing competes with other philosophies and other functions. If the changing information environment succeeds in transforming business activity along the lines suggested here, marketing as philosophy would appear to have triumphed even as its activities have become too important to be left to the marketing function.

APPENDIX

The following brief description provides a more formal treatment of the general information valuation procedure presented in the article.

Formally, if T_j is the jth transaction, let $r(T_j)$ and $c(T_j)$ be the revenue and cost functions respectively and $r(T_{j+1}/I_j)$ and $c(T_{j+1}/I_j)$ be the respective revenue and cost functions associated with the j + 1 transaction *given* I_j (the information stored from the jth transaction). Furthermore, let $r(I_j)$ and $c(I_j)$ be the revenues and costs associated with the *sale* of information collected from the jth transaction and $c(IT)/j$ be the allocated fixed costs of the information technology used to collect and process I_j. Let $\Pi() = r() - c()$ be the profit function. Then the *value of information* I_j is given by

$$v(I_j) = \Sigma\Pi(T_{j+n}/I_j) + \Pi(I_j)$$
$$= \Sigma[r(T_{j+n}/I_j) - r(T_{j+n})] - \Sigma[c(T_{j+n}) - c(T_{j+n}/I_j)] + [r(I_j) - c(I_j)] - c(IT)/j,$$

where $\Sigma[r(T_{j+n}/I_j) - r(T_{j+n})]$ are the incremental revenues from (n) future transactions as a result of the information from the jth transaction and $\Sigma[c(T_{j+n}) - c(T_{j+n}/I_j)]$ are the reduced costs of future transactions as a result of the information from the jth transaction. If revenues are greater and costs lower from future transactions than they otherwise would be, given information from transaction j, then $r(T_{j+n}/I_j) > r(T_{j+n})$ and $c(T_{j+n}/I_j) < c(T_{j+n})$. Thus, the value of information I_j is measured by the sum of (1) profits from future transactions that are a function of information collected along with transaction j and (2) profits from the sale of the information itself. Similarly, the value of information associated with transaction j + 1 is $v(I_{j+1}) = \Sigma\Pi(T_{j+1+n}/I_{j+1}) + \Pi(I_{j+1})$. The total value of the cumulative information associated with the transactions between the firm and its customers is $V_i^c = v(I_j) + v(I_{j+1}) + \ldots v(I_{j+n})$.

Analogous measures can be constructed for the value of the information associated with the upstream transactions between the firm and its suppliers and for the value of information associated with exchanges *within* the firm. Thus, for the former, if T_k is the kth transaction between the firm and its suppliers and I_k the information associated with the kth transaction, then $v(I_k) = \Sigma[c(T_{k+m}) - c(T_{k+m}/I_k)] - c(IT/k)$ is the value of information I_k (e.g., a reduction in the cost of the factor inputs of the firm's products). The total value of the cumulative information associated with the transactions between the firm and its suppliers is $V_i^s = v(I_k) + v(I_{k+1}) + \ldots v(I_{k+m})$.

Similarly, though it may be extremely difficult to identify and measure in practice, we can label T_1 as an intrafirm transaction and I_1 as the information associated with the transaction, resulting in $v(I_j) = \Sigma[c(T_{j+p}) - c(T_{j+p}/I_j)] - c(IT/l)$, the value of information I_j. The total value of the cumulative information associated with intrafirm transactions is given by $V_i^f = v(I_j) + v(I_{j+1}) + \ldots v(I_{i+p})$.

The three measures of the value of information associated with different types of transactions—V_i^c, V_i^s, V_i^f—can be aggregated to give $V(I) = V_i^c + V_i^s + V_i^f$, the total value of information processed by the firm.

Reprinted with permission from the Journal of Marketing, *published by the American Marketing Assoociation, Glazer, Rashi. October 1991/Vol, 55, pp. 1–19.*

Endnotes

1. Here, "meaning" denotes the organization of a set of otherwise independent symbols into a "pattern" that maps into an external referent system—one outside the system, or language, from which the symbols are drawn (e.g., Garner 1962). Information that has been codified *further* is sometimes used in defining "knowledge" (e.g., Machlup and Mansfield 1983), particularly where one wants to distinguish information from knowledge. In this article, such a distinction is not be made.

2. Though the definition of "information" given is familiar within the literature, the notion of exactly what constitutes "information" is by no means clear. An excellent example of the problem is found in the seminal work *The Study of Information: Interdisciplinary Messages*, edited by Machlup and Mansfield (1983), which brings together the views of 40 distinguished scholars in many fields on the study of "information," yet carefully avoids the adoption of a single, unifying definition of the construct.

3. An important example is the nonprofit industry consortium Computer Aided Manufacturing-International's (CAM-I) attempt to change conventional cost accounting methods and quantify investments in quality, flexibility, turnaround time, and other intangible or "information"-related constructs (*Business Week* 1988).

4. The demand for new information may be constrained by *human* information-processing limitations (e.g., Simon 1978), regardless of the increases in channel capacity of information technology. Limitations in human information processing is a major theme in decision-making research.

5. Porter and Millar (1985) describe a related "information-intensiveness" matrix. Haeckel (1985) develops a classification scheme in which the application of information moves from an "experimental" stage, through an "efficiency/convenience" stage (doing the same things at less cost), through an "effectiveness" stage (in which old problems are addressed in new ways), to a "previously unthinkable" stage (representing truly innovative uses). Little (1987) describes a similar evolutionary pattern in which information (1) displaces labor, (2) improves conventional services, (3) enhances aspects of marketing to change their character, and (4) creates new forms and services.

6. One potential problem with normalizing by profits is that, as V(I) increases, so too may Π(F). However, the relevant issue may be whether V(I) and Π(F) increase at the same rate. One of the general hypotheses of this article is that, on average, V(I) is increasing at a faster rate than Π(F).

7. More generally, industries characterized by high degrees of technological change of any kind face shorter product life cycles (Capon and Glazer 1987; Qualls, Olshavsky, and Michaels 1981).

8. Shifts in product-market boundaries are also a function of increases in globalization and deregulation, both of which have been influenced by advances in information technology.

9. To the extent that the contemporary political/legal climate supports stronger intellectual property rights, firms may be able to achieve product differentiation through information appropriability.

References

Abell, Derek F. and John S. Hammond (1979), *Strategic Market Planning: Problems and Analytical Approaches.* Englewood Cliffs, NJ: Prentice-Hall, Inc.

Anderson, Erin, Leonard M. Lodish, and Barton A. Weitz (1987), "Resource Allocation Behavior in Conventional Channels," *Journal of Marketing Research*, 24 (February), 85–97.

Arrow, Kenneth J. (1962), "The Economic Implications of Learning by Doing," *Review of Economic Studies*, 29 (June), 155–73.

——— (1974), *The Limits of Organization.* New York: W. W. Norton and Company.

Bagozzi, Richard P. (1975), "Marketing as Exchange," *Journal of Marketing*, 39 (October), 32–9.

Batra, Rajeev and Rashi Glazer, eds. (1989), *Cable TV Advertising: In Search of the Right Formula.* Westport, CT: Greenwood Press.

Bell, Daniel (1973), *The Coming of Post-Industrial Society.* New York: Basic Books, Inc.

Boston Consulting Group (1968), *Perspectives on Experience.* Boston: Boston Consulting Group.

Buaron, Roberto (1981), "New-Game Strategies," *The McKinsey Quarterly* (Spring), 24–40.

Business Week (1988), "The Productivity Paradox" (June 6), 100–14.

Buzzell, Robert, ed. (1985), *Marketing in an Electronic Age.* Cambridge, MA: Harvard University Press.

Capon, Noel and Rashi Glazer (1987), "Marketing and Technology: A Strategic Coalignment," *Journal of Marketing*, 51 (July), 1–14.

Chandler, Alfred D., Jr. (1962), *Strategy and Structure: Chapters in the History of the Industrial Enterprise.* Cambridge, MA: MIT Press.

Cherry, Collin (1966), *On Human Communication.* Cambridge, MA: MIT Press.

Day, George (1977), "Diagnosing the Product Portfolio," *Journal of Marketing*, 41 (April), 29–38.

Drucker, Peter F. (1959), "Long Range Planning," *Management Science*, 5 (April), 230–45.

——— (1980), *Managing in Turbulent Times.* New York: Harper & Row Publishers, Inc.

——— (1988), "The Coming of the New Organization," *Harvard Business Review*, 88 (January–February), 45–53.

Farley, John and John McCann (1988), "What Is 'News' on Information Technology in Marketing." Cambridge MA: Marketing Science Institute.

Frazier, Gary (1983), "On the Measurement of Interfirm Power in Channels of Distribution," *Journal of Marketing Research*, 20 (May), 158–66.

Galbraith, J. (1977), *Organization Design.* Reading, MA: Addison-Wesley Publishing Company.

Garner, Wendell R. (1962), *Uncertainty and Structure as Psychological Concepts.* New York: John Wiley & Sons, Inc.

Glazer, Rashi (1989), "Marketing and the Changing Information Environment: Implications for Strategy, Structure, and the Marketing Mix," Report #89–108. Cambridge, MA: Marketing Science Institute.

Haeckel, Stephan H. (1985), "Strategies for Marketing the New Technologies: Commentary," in *Marketing in an Electronic Age*, Robert Buzzell, ed. Cambridge, MA: Harvard University Press.

Harrigan, Kathryn R. (1986), *Managing for Joint Venture Success.* Lexington, MA: Lexington Books.

Hayes, Robert H. and Ramchandran Jaikumar (1988), "Manufacturing's Crisis: New Technologies, Obsolete Organizations," *Harvard Business Review*, 88 (September–October), 77–85.

Herriott, Scott R. (1988), "Types of Cooperation and the Theory of Strategy," Working Paper Series No. 88-1, Department of Management Sciences, University of Iowa.

Huber, George P. (1984), "The Nature and Design of Post-Industrial Organizations," *Management Science*, 30(8), 928–51.

Kerin, Roger A., Vijay Mahajan, and P. Rajan Varadarajan (1990), *Contemporary Perspectives on Strategic Market Planning.* Boston: Allyn and Bacon, Inc.

Kotler, Philip and Sidney J. Levy (1969), "Broadening the Concept of Marketing," *Journal of Marketing*, 33 (January), 10–15.

Lawrence, Paul R. and Jay W. Lorsch (1967), *Organization and Environment.* Boston: Harvard Business School.

Levitt, Theodore (1983), *The Marketing Imagination.* New York: The Free Press.

Little, John D. C. (1970), "Models and Managers: The Concept of a Decision Calculus," *Management Science*, 16(8), 466–85.

——— (1987), "Information Technology in Marketing," MIT working paper.

Machlup, F. (1962), *The Production and Distribution of Knowledge in the United States.* Princeton, NJ: Princeton University Press.

——— and Una Mansfield (1983), *The Study of Information: Interdisciplinary Messages.* New York: John Wiley & Sons, Inc.

March, James and Herbert Simon (1958), *Organizations.* New York: John Wiley & Sons, Inc.

Marschak, Jacob and Roy Radner (1972), *Economic Theory of Teams.* New Haven, CT: Yale University Press.

Miles, Raymond E. and Charles C. Snow (1978), *Organizational Strategy, Structure and Process.* New York: McGraw-Hill Book Company.

——— and ——— (1986), "Network Organizations: New Concepts for New Forms," *California Management Review*, 28 (Spring), 62–73.

Mintzberg, Henry (1979), *The Structuring of Organizations.* Englewood Cliffs, NJ: Prentice-Hall, Inc.

Parker, Marilyn M. and Robert J. Benson (1988), *Information Economics: Linking Business Performance to Information Technology.* Englewood Cliffs, NJ: Prentice-Hall, Inc.

Parsons, Gregory L. (1983), "Information Technology: A New Competitive Weapon," *Sloan Management Review* (Fall), 3–14.

Peters, Thomas J. (1987), *Thriving on Chaos: Handbook for a Managerial Revolution*. New York: Alfred A. Knopf, Inc.

Porat, Marc U. (1974), "Defining an Information Sector in the U.S. Economy," Institution for Communication Research, Stanford University.

——— (1976), "The Information Economy and the Economics of Information: A Literature Survey," Program in Information Technology and Telecommunications Center for Interdisciplinary Research, Stanford University.

Porter, Michael E. (1980), *Competitive Strategy: Techniques for Analyzing Industries and Competitors*. New York: The Free Press.

——— (1985), *Competitive Advantage: Creating and Sustaining Superior Performance*. New York: The Free Press.

——— and Victor E. Millar (1985), "How Information Technology Gives You Competitive Advantage," *Harvard Business Review*, 85 (July–August), 149–60.

Qualls, William, Richard W. Olshavsky, and Ronald E. Michaels (1981), "Shortening of the PLC—An Empirical Test," *Journal of Marketing*, 45 (Fall), 76–80.

Ray, Michael L. (1985), "An Even More Powerful Consumer?" in *Marketing in an Electronic Age*, Robert Buzzell, ed. Cambridge, MA: Harvard University Press.

Shannon, Claude and Warren Weaver (1949), *The Mathematical Theory of Communication*. Urbana, IL: The University of Illinois Press.

Simon, Herbert (1978), "Rationality as Product and Process of Thought," *American Economic Review*, 68, 1–16.

Stern, Louis and Torger Reve (1981), "Distribution Channels as Political Economies: A Framework of Comparative Analysis," *Journal of Marketing*, 44 (Summer), 52–64.

Stiglitz, Joseph E. (1975), "Information and Economic Analysis," IMSSS Technical Report #155, Stanford University.

Talarzyk, W. Wayne (1989), "In-Home Shopping: Impact of Television Shopping Programs," in *Cable TV Advertising: In Search of the Right Formula*, Rajeev Batra and Rashi Glazer, eds. Westport, CT: Greenwood Press.

Toffler, Alvin (1970), *Future Shock*. New York: Random House, Inc.

Walton, Richard E. and Paul R. Lawrence, eds. (1985), *Human Resource Management: Trends and Challenges*. Cambridge, MA: Harvard University Press.

Webster, Frederick E., Jr. (1976), "The Role of the Industrial Distributor," *Journal of Marketing*, 40 (July), 10–16.

——— (1988), "Rediscovering the Marketing Concept," Report No. 88–100. Cambridge, MA: Marketing Science Institute.

Williamson, Oliver E. (1975), *Markets and Hierarchies: Analysis and Antitrust Implications*. New York: The Free Press.

Wilson, Robert (1975), "Informational Economies of Scale," *Bell Journal of Economics*, 6(1), 184–95.

Wiseman, Charles (1985), *Strategy and Computers: Information Systems as Competitive Weapons*. Homewood, IL: Dow Jones-Irwin.

3

A New Marketing Paradigm for Electronic Commerce

DONNA L. HOFFMAN
THOMAS P. NOVAK

The World Wide Web possesses unique characteristics which distinguish it in important ways from traditional commercial communications environments. Because the Web presents a fundamentally different environment for marketing activities than traditional media, conventional marketing activities are becoming transformed, as they are often difficult to implement in their present form. In this paper, we assert that these changes portend an evolution in the "marketing concept" and argue that in order for marketing efforts to be successful in this new medium, a new business paradigm is required in which the marketing function is reconstructed to facilitate electronic commerce in the emerging electronic society underlying the Web.

The World Wide Web is the first and current networked global implementation of a hypermedia computer-mediated environment (CME). As such, it allows users of the medium to provide and interactively access hypermedia content, and to communicate with each other. These unique forms of interactivity, "machine-interaction" and "personinteraction," respectively, have contributed to the rapid diffusion of the Web as a commercial medium in the last several years (Hoffman and Novak 1995).

The traditional marketing communications model for mass media (e.g. Lasswell 1948; Katz and Lazarsfeld 1955) holds that mass communication is a *one-to-many* process whereby a firm transmits content through a medium to a large group of consumers. The key feature underlying all models of mass media effects is that there is no interaction present between consumers and firms.

The new model underlying marketing communications in a hypermedia CME like the Web (Hoffman and Novak 1995) is a *many-to-many* mediated communications model in which consumers can interact with the medium, firms can provide content to the medium, and in the most radical departure from traditional marketing environments, *consumers* can provide commercially-oriented content to the medium. In this mediated model, the primary relationships are not between sender and receiver, but rather with the CME with which they interact. In this new model, information or content is not merely transmitted from a sender to a receiver, but instead, mediated environments are created by participants and then experienced.

The Transformation of Marketing Activities

An important consideration in the structural analysis of the Web as a media and marketing environment is that it possesses unique characteristics which distinguish it in important ways from traditional commercial environments. First, as we argued above, the Web is a virtual hypermedia environment incorporating interactivity with both people and computers. Thus, the Web is not a simulation of a real-world environment, but an alternative to real-world environments (see, for example, de Long 1995), where consumers may experience *telepresence* (Steuer 1992), the perception of being present in the mediated, rather than real-world, environment.

Second, within the virtual environment, both experiential (e.g. "netsurfing") and goal-directed (e.g. "online shopping") behaviors compete for consumers' attention. Third, consumer capability in the virtual environment, as well as challenges posed by the environment, introduce a competency issue which does not exist so fundamentally in the physical world. This competency issue involves flow, which is the "process of optimal experience" achieved when a motivated consumer perceives a balance between their skills and the challenges of their interaction with the CME (Csikszentmihalyi 1990). Flow is a central construct when considering consumer navigation on commercial Web sites (Hoffman and Novak 1995).

Because the World Wide Web presents a fundamentally different environment for marketing activities than traditional media, conventional marketing activities are being transformed, as they are often difficult to implement in their present form. This means that in many cases, these marketing activities have to be reconstructed in forms more appropriate for the new medium.

This process of transformation and reconstruction of marketing and communication activities in information-intensive environments has been noted by numerous researchers (e.g., Glazer 1991; Reid 1991; Blattberg, Glazer and Little 1994; Stewart and Ward 1994; Venkatesh, Sherry, & Firat 1993; van Raaij 1993). In order to maintain a virtual community on the Internet, Reid (1991), for example, has argued that users have had to deconstruct and reconstruct the nonverbal communication that exists in interpersonal communication by typing their feelings out in ascii and constructing a notational system to convey emotion (e.g. emoticons such as "smileys," as discussed in Reid 1991). In addition, the online medium has the potential to transform the individual's identity, resulting in a relative anonymity of users in these environments. In a marketing context, this hinders personal selling at the same time that it encourages negative word-of-mouth activity (i.e. brand or corporate "flaming").

Most important from a marketing perspective, however, is the manner in which the Web transforms the marketing function. For example, the many-to-many communication model turns traditional principles of mass media advertising (based on the one-to-many communication model) inside out, rendering application of advertising approaches which assume a passive, captive consumer difficult, if not impossible (Hoffman and Novak 1994). Thus, marketers must reconstruct advertising models for the interactive, many-to-many medium underlying the Web in which consumers actively choose whether or not to approach firms through their Web sites, and exercise unprecedented control over the management of the content they interact with. Informational and image "Internet presence sites" (Hoffman, Novak and Chatterjee 1995) provide examples of such new forms of Web-based advertising.

The Evolution of the Marketing Concept

Market orientation operationalizes the "marketing concept," in which firms attempt to uncover and satisfy customer needs at a profit, and refers to the "organization wide generation of market intelligence pertaining to current and future customer needs," along with the dissemination and responsiveness of the organization to such (Kohli and Jaworski, 1990). Kohli and Jaworski (1990) suggest that a market orientation will be more related to business performance under conditions of intense competition and unstable market preferences. Since these conditions, along with technological uncertainty, face and will continue to face firms developing new offerings in the Web for years to come, and since a market orientation can represent a significant competitive advantage for a firm in such cases, it follows that firms interested in Web-based business efforts adopt a market orientation.

Yet, surprisingly, as it is currently evolving, not enough is being done to include the consumer in the development of emerging media (Dennis & Pease 1994). Instead, developments are being driven largely by a one-to-many mass communication model that presumes the growth of a passive mass "audience" rather than heterogenous users seeking varied experiences. But in order to adopt a market orientation, firms must understand their customers and engage in consumer research. However, very little in the way of in-depth consumer research is currently being conducted, perhaps because in information intensive environments, the marketing function is often performed by other functional areas (Glazer 1991) that may not be as familiar with the marketing function as marketers.

The current technological and market turbulence of the Web represents more than mere technological evolution. Thus, we argue that successful Web marketing efforts will require an evolution in the marketing concept to where the firm not only attempts to discover and meet customer needs profitably, but also engages in marketing activities that contribute positively to the development of the emerging medium itself, by developing new paradigms for electronic commerce.

For example, consider a current practice that reflects traditional models. A well known difficulty from a business perspective is that most Web sites have been unable to induce visitors to register, especially when no payment is required to consume content. But if the firm does not know, at a minimum, the characteristics of those visiting its Web site, application of the marketing concept becomes challenging. One proposed solution is to centralize the registration process, collecting demographic and psychographic information from consumers for resale at both the within-site and across-site levels to Web sites interested in linking consumer navigation and transaction behavior with consumer marketing variables (Internet Profiles Corporation 1996).

But a new paradigm constructed from considering the Web as a many-to-many communications medium might suggest *decentralizing* the registration process so that the *consumer* retains ownership of his or her personal information and benefits by selling it to commercial Web sites who may desire it. Developing such a concept would not only facilitate registration, but also allow the consumer to participate in and benefit from the process.

In such cases, the role of marketing thus moves from "merely" satisfying customer needs to including an altruistic, cooperative goal of facilitating the development of the market itself, one that explicitly includes the consumer. This is consistent with a recent report by the National Academy of Sciences (U.S. Congress 1994): "In the new business environment, cooperation may prove more rewarding than competition, and information-sharing more fruitful than information control."

Several propositions from Glazer (1991) regarding information intensive marketing environments support our extended marketing concept. Specifically, information leads to "issues of access sharing, and creating opportunities for use." Greater involvement in strategic alliances is proposed to lead to an "extended cooperation framework." Further, in information-intensive environments such as the World Wide Web, attention will be focused less on competitive strategy and more on cooperative strategy.

Reconstructing Marketing for the New Media

To a large extent, many of the original structures that were constructed to facilitate electronic commerce on the Web were characteristic of a primitive, simple society, bound by "mechanical solidarity" (Durkheim 1933), with a common consciousness and internalized set of shared values. These shared (and originally largely anti-commercial) values arose largely from the original core group of Internet users, a relatively homogeneous group of students, academicians, and researchers. In large part, we believe these origins account for the unwillingness of consumers to register on Web sites and pay for content. However, as the Internet continues to evolve into a complex, heterogeneous virtual society, "organic solidarity" will develop from an increasing interdependence between people pursuing different goals. This produces an increasing division of labor, which will transform existing paradigms and require new rules of cooperation and competition to emerge.

Marketers should focus on playing an active role in the construction of new organic paradigms for facilitating commerce in the emerging electronic society underlying the Web, rather than infiltrating the existing primitive mechanical structures. Consider the nascent attempts by previously proprietary commercial online services to exercise control over both consumer access to the Web and the ability of consumers to provide content to the Web. Increasingly, the commercial online services are becoming consumer gateways to the Web and becoming more like user-friendly Internet Service Providers than closed, proprietary networks.

Yet, as these services reinvent their businesses in the context of many-to-many decentralized open networks, they are beginning to reshape themselves under a broadcast cable model in which a series of Web site selections will be offered to consumers as "channels" easily accessible by a simple point-and-click interface. Web sites not endorsed may be accessible, but would require knowledge of the URL; it would be less likely that consumers would seek out such content. In some cases, consumers may not even know additional content exists, let alone how to access it. Such attempts, following from the traditional one-to-many mass model of communication effects, obviously do take full advantage of the medium's unique features and hold enormous implications for how the Web will develop as a commercial medium. At the minimum, it implies the development of homogenized content that would appeal to a mass audience, with attendant negative implications for niche or small Web sites lacking mass audience appeal. This erroneous view of the Web as a traditional broadcast medium also largely explains the United States Justice Department's recent efforts to censor "indecent" content on the Internet (American Civil Liberties Union, et.al. v. Janet Reno 1996).

In contrast, the effective marketer will be actively constructing new models for marketing on the Web, based upon an increasingly diverse and complex virtual society. Such efforts will contribute to the establishment of organic solidarity within the heterogeneous market defined by segments of consumers and firms doing business on the Web.

It is still too soon to predict the form these efforts might take, even as the business models emerge (Hoffman, Novak, and Chatterjee 1995). Yet it seems clear that 1) steps to build the infrastructure for electronic commerce; 2) mechanisms that take advantage of the medium's unique features; and 3) attempts to develop stimulating and exciting content-rich sponsored environments, hold tremendous promise toward this goal.

Infrastructure for Electronic Commerce

In a recent report on Electronic Enterprises, the Office of Technology Assessment (U.S. Congress 1994) noted that "because exchange transactions will increasingly be carried out electronically and online, the network will in many instances serve as the market." While it has been said for traditional media that "the medium is the message" (McLuhan 1964), with the Web it is also true that "the medium is the market." The establishment of broadly-based, "integrated destination sites" (Hoffman, Novak, and Chatterjee 1995) like GNN (www.gnn.com), HotWired (www.hotwired.com), and Pathfinder (www.timeinc.com) support this observation and lead us to argue that as media increase in their interactive and navigational capabilities, they move from serving as communication and marketing channels to serving as markets.

Press (1993) speculates that the Internet as a marketplace has the potential to make markets more efficient. This is particularly so for the Web because it offers not only the opportunity to provide full information to consumers about goods and services, but lends itself to rich detail and specificity regarding such information, especially compared to traditional media. There is also greater probability of a well-informed consumer, since the consumer has greater control over the search process. Such control is likely to facilitate a highly developed form of, for example, price comparison shopping. Thus, compared to conventional markets, the cost of information should be lower and the information quality should be higher (and closer to "perfect"), leading to a higher degree of market efficiency (Stigler 1961). Therefore, the market represented by the Web also has the potential to be a more efficient market than conventional markets. (See, however, Schickele (1993) for an opposing view point.)

However, before this can occur, the infrastructure must be built. The current difficulty transmitting sensitive data, such as credit card numbers and the like, securely over the Internet is transforming traditional payment processes. Until secure systems are widely implemented on the Web, the lack of such represents a significant barrier to adoption of the Web for commercial transactions. Thus, new systems must be developed to permit virtual transactions directly over the network. These may take the form of "digital cash" (e.g. Medvinsky and Neuman 1993; Rose 1994) or credit card number encryption, allowing commercial transactions to take place directly rather than through parallel traditional channels such as 1-800 telephone numbers.

Equally important will be online dynamic content directories both within a site and across the Web. With over 21 *million* Web pages indexed by Digital Equipment Corporation's Alta Vista search index (www.altavista.digital.com) as of February 19, 1996, and the number growing daily, efficient ways to help consumers sort and search through the myriad of offerings available will be critical. Research in consumer decision making suggests that, in the absence of heuristics, decision effectiveness degrades in the presence of too much information (Keller and Staelin 1987; Keller and Staelin 1989; Meyer and Johnson 1988). Thus, the challenge for marketers will be to develop, in conjunction with consumers, rule-based systems for the organization of content that exploit the principles of network navigation and facilitate flow (see Hoffman and Novak 1995 for more discussion).

A Unique Medium

Chatterjee and Narasimhan (1994) observe that as a distribution channel, the Web possesses 1) extremely low entry and exit barriers for firms; 2) increasing irrelevance of distribution intermediaries; and 3) the capability to not only keep pace with market change, but accelerate it. Because the Web increases the power of the consumer and decreases the power of the firm, compared to traditional channels of distribution, the consumer and the firm approach "symmetrical power" and the best communication efforts are likely to be "collaborative" rather than "autonomous" (Mohr & Nevin 1990).

Glazer (1991) notes that in the presence of higher information intensity, channel power shifts in favor of consumers and a breakdown occurs in formal distinctions between producer and consumer. In the information intensive Web environment, the firm is no longer broadcasting a single communication to many consumers, but in effect tailoring its communications according to consumers' varied interests and needs. This is currently implemented through the unique process of network navigation in which the consumer chooses what information (if any) to receive from the firm. Thus, marketers must begin to examine the manner in which these more collaborative communication efforts should proceed.

These shifts in channel power hold important implications for consumer participation in the marketing process. For example, consumers may collaborate not only in idea generation and product design, but also in the marketing communication effort itself. This is because interactivity in the Web gives consumers much greater control of the message. Such control may manifest itself in startlingly new ways: for example, it is feasible for consumers interested in purchasing big-ticket durables such as cars or appliances to broadcast their interest and solicit open bids from different firms (Cutler 1990). Similarly, Digital has enjoyed success with their innovative program of making the Alpha AXP computer systems available to potential customers for "test drive" over the Web (Jarvenpaa and Ives 1994).

Such activities are possible because the process of network navigation in the Web is characterized by open access to information. The original motivation for developing an "internetwork" of computers, on which the Web is based, was to enable geographically dispersed computers representing diverse platforms to link and communicate so they could economically share costly resources (Hafner and Lyon 1996; Roberts 1988). The Internet thus developed in a rich and exciting atmosphere of intellectual curiosity fostered in an unconstrained and creative environment (Licklider 1988; Miya 1990).

The Question of Content

Marketers can utilize the opportunities for customer interaction inherent in the Web in numerous ways, including 1) the design of new products; 2) the development of product and marketing strategy, and 3) the innovation of content. The evolution of content on the Web is dependent upon not only the evolution of existing metaphors and communication codes from traditional media, but also new techniques and conventions inherent in the possibilities of the medium itself (Biocca 1992). One implication of this is that the content (and business models) that will make the Web commercially successful have likely not been invented yet, and may require more than a simple continuous innovation of existing content (Grossman 1994).

As evidence that a discontinuous evolution in content will be required to fuel the growth of the Web, witness the difficulties experienced in applying traditional content to the alternative new interactive multimedia, such as pay-per-view, video-on-demand, and interactive TV. Few applications have yet to meet with consumer acceptance in test markets, and even fewer have come online in any significant way (Schwartz 1994). To generate and evaluate "future content," the consumer must somehow be placed in a future frame-of-reference. Promising product development techniques include Information Acceleration (Urban, Weinberg & Hauser 1994; Hauser, Urban and Weinberg 1993), and virtual reality and role-playing "informances" approaches being developed at firms such as Interval Research Corporation (Kirkpatrick 1994).

Hoffman and Novak (1995) have argued that flow will lead to increased quality time in a hypermedia CME like the Web. Thus, content developers should seek to facilitate the flow experience, as it has numerous positive consequences. One important consideration is whether and at what point in the process consumers are likely to become bored (e.g. when network navigation is not sufficiently challenging) or anxious (e.g. when network navigation is too difficult), increasingly the likelihood of "site jumping."

Concluding Remarks

The limitations of relying on old paradigms become apparent when we consider the "more is better" logic implicit in current approaches to measuring consumer activity on sponsored content Web sites. Driven by traditional mass media models, "hit" and visit counting methods implicitly seek to achieve unstated mass audience levels, since in traditional media, "advertising effectiveness" is tied to ratings or circulation models where larger numbers are preferred. Yet in the Web, advertising effectiveness can be explicitly tied to customer response and the possibility exists of developing new measurement systems that capture the value of a single consumer's visit and subsequent response in new and innovative ways.

New bases for market segmentation will also be needed for Web-based marketing efforts because consumers vary in their ability to achieve flow. Research can determine the variables that relate to a consumer's propensity to enter the flow state and such information can be used to develop marketing efforts designed to maximize the chances of the consumer achieving flow. Since "repeat purchase," that is, repeat visits to a particular Web site, will be increased if the environment facilitates the flow state, the marketing objective on the first visit (i.e. "trial"), will be to provide for these flow opportunities.

Pricing strategy is also relevant here. Commercial online service pricing models are largely based upon connect time and usage charges. Such schemes have the effect of discouraging usage and, increasingly, consumers are demanding flat-rate pricing schemes. In the short run, flat-rate systems encourage consumer experimentation and system use (National Academy of Sciences 1994, Chapter 5). Continued use feeds demand because, as the anecdotal record shows, usage tends to be "addicting." This suggests that pricing algorithms that encourage browsing will encourage usage (Hawkins 1994). In the long-run, usage-based pricing may be more appropriate as the Web matures as a medium, one day becoming as ubiquitous as the telephone (National Academy of Sciences 1994, Chapter 5).

In sum, we have argued that the traditional one-to-many model, with its attendant implications and consequences for marketing theory and practice, has only limited utility in emerging many-to-many media like the World Wide Web, and that a new marketing paradigm is required for this communication medium. In this paradigm, new rules of cooperation and competition can emerge in which marketers focus on playing an active role in the construction of new standards and practices for facilitating commerce in the emerging electronic society underlying the Web.

The Web as both medium and market is more likely to be successful if it frees consumers from their traditionally passive role as receivers of marketing communications, gives them much greater control over the search for and acquisition of information relevant for consumer decision making, and allows them to become active participants in the marketing process. Firms have the opportunity to reap the benefits of this innovation in interactivity by being closer to the customer than ever before.

February 19, 1996. Paper submitted for the Special Issue on Electronic Commerce for The Information Society.

References

American Civil Liberties Union, et al., v. Janet Reno (1996), Civil Action No. 96-963. In the United States District Court for the Eastern District of Pennsylvania. Memorandum. Buckwalter, J. February 15.

Biocca, Frank (1992), "Communication Within Virtual Reality: Creating a Space for Research," *Journal of Communication*, 42(2), 5–22.

Blattberg, Robert C., Rashi Glazer, and John D.C. Little, eds. (1994), *The Marketing Information Revolution*, Boston: Harvard Business School Press.

Chatterjee, Patrali and Anand Narasimhan (1994), "The Web as a Distribution Channel," OwenDoctoral Seminar Paper. [colette.ogsm.vanderbilt.edu/seminar/patrali_anand_final/first.htm].

Csikszentlmihalyi, Mihaly (1990), *Flow: The Psychology of Optimal Experience*, New York: Harper and Row.

de Long, Brad (1995), "The Shock of the Virtual: How the Website of the U.C. Museum of Paleontology Feels More "Real" than the Museum Itself," essay posted to the apple-internet-users Usenet mailing list, July 31. [archived at econ158.berkeley.edu /theshockofthevirtual.html].

Cutler, B. (1990), "The Fifth Medium," *American Demograpnics*, 12(6), 24–29.

Dennis, Everett E. and Edward C. Pease (1994), "Preface," *Media Studies Journal*, 8(1), xi–xxiii.

Durkheim, Emile (1933), *The Division of Labor in Society*, "translated by George Simpson, New York: Free Press of Glencoe.

Glazer, Rashi (1991), "Marketing in an Information-Intensive Environment: Strategic Implications of Knowledge as an Asset," *Journal of Marketing*, 55(October) 1–19.

Grossman, Lawrence K. (1994), "Reflections on Life Along the Electronic Superhighway," *Media Studies Journal*, 8(1), 27–39.

Hafner, Katie and Matthew Lyon (1996), *When Wizards Stay Up Late: The Origins of the Internet*. Simon & Shuster.

Hauser, John R., Glen L. Urban, and Bruce D. Weinberg (1993), "How Consumers Allocate Their Time When Searching for Information," *Journal of Marketing Research*, 30(November) 452–466.

Hawkins, Donald T. (1994), "Electronic Advertising on Online Information sytem$," *Online*, 18 (2), 26–39.

Hoffman, Donna L. and Thomas P. Novak (1994), "Commercializing the Information Superhighway: Are We In For a Smooth Ride?" *The Owen Manager*, 15 (2), 2–7. [URL: http://colette.ogsm.vanderbilt.edu/smooth.ride.html].

Hoffman, Donna L. and Thomas P. Novak (1995), "Marketing in Hypermedia Computer-Mediated Environments: Conceptual Foundations," Project 2000 Working Paper No. 1. Owen Graduate School of Management, Vanderbilt University.

Hoffman, Donna L., Thomas P. Novak and Patrali Chatterjee (1995), "Commercial Scenarios for the Web: Opportunities and Challenges," *Journal of Computer-Mediated Communications*, Special Issue on Electronic Commerce, 1(3), shum.huji.ac.il/jcmc/vol1/issue3/ vol1no3.html.

Internet Profiles Corporation (1996), "About I/CODE: A Universal Registration System," www.ipro.com.

Jarvenpaa, Sirkka and Blake Ives (1994), "Digital Equipment Corporation: The Internet Company (A). CoxMIS Cases, Edwin L. Cox School of Business, Southern Methodist University. [http://www.cox.smu.edu/mis/cases/home.html].

Katz, E. and P.F. Lazarsfeld (1955), *Personal Influence*, Glencoe: Free Press.

Keller, Kevin Lane and Richard Staelin (1987), "Effects of Quality and Quantity of Information on Decision Effectiveness," *Journal of Consumer Research*, 14, 200–213.

Keller, Kevin Lane and Richard Staelin (1989), "Assessing Biases in Measuring Decision Effectiveness and Information Overload," *Journal of Consumer Research*, 15(4), March, 504–508.

Kirkpatrick, David (1994), "A Look Inside Allen's Think Tank: This Way to the I-Way," *Fortune*, July 11, 78–80.

Kohli, Ajay K. and Bernard J. Jaworski (1990), "Market Orientation: The Construct, Research Propositions, and Managerial Implications," *Journal of Marketing*, 54(April), 1–18.

Lasswell, H.D. (1948), "The Structure and Function of Communication in Society," in *The Communication of Ideas*, Bryson, ed., New York: harper and Brothers.

Licklider, J.C.R. (1988), "Some Reflections on Early History," in *A History of Personal Workstations*, Adele Goldberg (Ed.). NY.

McLuhan, Marshall (1964), *Understanding Media*, New York: McGraw-Hill.

Medvinsky, Gennady and B. Clifford Neuman (1993), "NetCash: A Design for Practical Electronic Currency on the Internet," *Proceedings of the First ACM Conference on Computer and Communications Security*, November [URL:ftp://gopher.econ.lsa.umich.edu/pub/Archive/netcash.ps.Z]

Meyer, Robert J. and Eric J. Johnson (1989), "Information Overload and the Non-robustness of Linear Models," A Comment on Keller and Staelin, *Journal of Consumer Research*, 15, 498–503.

Miya, Eugene (1990), "Re: Internet: The Origins," alt.folklore.computers, comp.misc, USENET News, October 16.

Mohr, Jakki and John R. Nevin (1990), "Communication Strategies in Marketing Channels: A Theoretical Perspective," *Journal of Marketing*, 54(October), 36–51.

National Academy of Sciences (1994), *Realizing the Information Future: The Internet and Beyond.* [URL:http//xerxes.nas.edu:70/1/nap/online/rtif].

Press, Larry (1993), "The Internet and interactive television," *Communications of the ACM*, 36(12), 19–23.

Reid, Elizabeth M. (1991), "Electropolis: Communication and Community on Internet Relay Chat," Honours Thesis, University of Melbourne, Department of History. [URL:gopher://wiretap.spies.com:70/00/Library/Cyber/electrop.txt].

Roberts, Larry (1988), "The ARPANET and Computer Networks," in *A History of Personal Workstations*, Adele Goldberg (Ed.). NY.

Rose, Chris (1994), "Burn Those Bank Notes - Digital Cash is Coming," *Power PC News*, 1 (10), July 22, Document no 3032. [http://power.globalnews.com/articles/v01i10.htm].

Schickele, Sandra (1993), "The Internet and the Market System: Externalities, Marginal Cost, and the Public Interest," Proceedings 1993 International Networking Conference. [URL:gopher://ietf.cnri.reston.va.us/11/isoc.and.ietf/inet/INET93/papers;document FAA .Schickele].

Schwartz, Evan I. (1994), "Fran-On-Demand," *Wired*, September, 60–62.

Steuer, Jonathan (1992), "Defining Virtual Reality: Dimensions Determining Telepresence," *Journal of Communication*, 42(4), 73–93.

Stigler, G. (1961), "The Economics of Information," *Journal of Political Economy*, 69, (June), 213–25.

Stewart, David W. and Scott Ward (1994), "Media Effects on Advertising," in *Media Effects, Advances in Theory and Research*, Jennings Bryand and Dolf Zillman, eds., Hillsdale, NJ: Lawrence Erlbaum Associates.

Urban, Glen, Bruce Weinberg and John R. Hauser (1994), "Premarket Forecasting of Really New Products," Working Paper, Massachusetts Institute of Technology.

U.S. Congress, Office of Technology Assesment, Electronic Enterprises: Looking to the Future, OTA-TCT-600 (Washington, DC: U.S. Government Printing Office, May 1994). [URL:ftp://otabbs.ota.gov/pub/elenter].

van Raaij, W. Fred (1993), "Postmodern consumption," *Journal of Economic Psychology*, 14, 541–563.

Venkatesh, Alladi, John F. Sherry, Jr., and A. Fuat Firat (1993), "Postmodernism and the Marketing Imaginary," *International Journal of Research in Marketing*, 10, 215–223.

4

Consumer Behavior in the Future

JAGDISH N. SHETH
RAJENDRA S. SISODIA

In the not-too-distant future, rapid advances in technology, escalating global competition, and rising consumer expectations for quality, speed of response, and customization will require companies to substantially rethink their business models. One thing is clear: the future will be substantially different from the present. Society went through dramatic change and upheaval as a result of the transition from the agricultural age to the industrial age; the transition to the information age will be accompanied by even greater change. That transition is well underway, but still remains in its early stages.

The emerging consensus about the future of today's various information industries is that they will converge because they are all increasingly based on digital electronic technology. The vision revolves around the presence of an interactive broadband digital "highway" terminating in very high resolution multimedia display terminals in consumers' homes and workplaces. The viewer would be in control of content scheduling and selection; information would not, for the most part, be "broadcast" (except for live events); rather, it would be stored in digital "video servers" to be viewed or downloaded on demand. For a detailed discussion of some of the characteristics of future "information malls," see Sheth and Sisodia (1993).

Today's World Wide Web (WWW) represents a crude approximation of the capabilities and functionality that are expected to be widely deployed by the middle of the next decade. It is serving as a very large test bed for companies and as a "training platform" for consumers to learn new modalities of interaction and consumption.

From the perspective of consumers, the primary impact of the deployment of such an infrastructure will be to ease the often severe time and place constraints that are currently placed on them. No longer will goods and services be offered primarily at the convenience of the seller; "anytime, anywhere" purchasing as well as consumption will become commonplace.

These impacts will become more acute as communication bandwidths rise exponentially and terminal equipment becomes simultaneously more powerful, sophisticated, easier to use, affordable, and portable (smarter, easier, cheaper and smaller). Once the appropriate hardware is in place and the telecommunications infrastructure has been established, an enormous range of services can be exchanged at nominal incremental cost, such as location-independent shopping and banking, computer-mediated education, and training, professional consultations, and various informational, entertainment, and leisure services. This combination of technologies is likely to become quite widespread in the United States by the year 2005, and in other advanced countries by 2010.

Changing consumer behavior will make it necessary for the marketing function to change dramatically as well. In fact, we believe that the marketing function will be at the center of change; marketing will become increasingly decentralized and fully integrated into business operations. Marketing and its institutions have a great deal to lose as well as many opportunities to make dramatic gains. We believe that successful marketing in this new environment will involve "monocasting" or "pointcasting" of communications, "mass customization" of all marketing mix elements, a high degree of customer involvement and control, and far greater integration between marketing and operations. There will be more efficient utilization of marketing resources, reduced customer alienation resulting from misapplied marketing stimuli, increased pressure to deliver greater value, and intense jostling for the loyalties of "desirable" customers. In this chapter, we present a framework for analyzing the types of changes we expect to see emerge in the future, speculate about the impacts of these changes on consumer behavior, and suggest how the marketing function will have to respond.

Forces Driving Changes in Consumer Behavior

Two major forces influence consumer behavior: evolving technology, and changing lifestyles and demographics. These are respectively described below.

Supply Side: Technology Evolution

Undoubtedly, the pace of technological evolution in recent years is having and will continue to have a great impact on the lives of consumers. Rudy Puryear, a senior information technology strategist at Andersen Consulting, describes the new age as the "age of less." Technology allows consumers to go shopping without going to the store (storeless); travel without a ticket (ticketless); work without going to an office (officeless), and so on. Three aspects of technology are of particular significance.

Production Technology. Breakthroughs in production technology, such as CAD-CAM, flexible manufacturing systems, and just-in-time production are affecting competitive marketing in a number of ways. For example, they are redefining the limits of quality, greatly increasing the level of affordability for many products, enabling a higher level of customization, and providing customers with a great deal of variety. Other significant technologies in this arena include photorealistic visualization, groupware (e.g., conferencing systems across design functions and across design, manufacturing and sales), virtual reality, design-for-manufacturability-and-assembly databases, component performance history databases, and 3-D physical modeling technologies such as stereolithography.

Distribution Technology.   Recent innovations in distribution technology include (1) computer-assisted logistics (CALS), (2) the refinement of scanner and other product identification and tracking technologies, (3) electronic data interchange (EDI), (4) point-of-sale (POS) terminals linked to vendors, (5) expert systems, (6) satellite-based locational systems, (7) automated retail and warehouse ordering, and (8) flow-through logistics. Benefits include (1) reduced damages, (2) reduced supplier and distributor wholesale inventories, (3) warehousing, transportation, administrative, and manufacturing efficiencies, (4) reduced "forward buying," (5) better market coverage, (6) fewer stockouts and distress sales, (7) more refined target marketing, and (8) faster response to market trends.

Technologies for Personal Use.   Technologies having the fastest gains in price-performance are those intended for personal rather than institutional use. Personal information devices have been riding and will continue to ride a steep experience curve based on the unique "economics of electronics." One of the fundamental properties of such technologies is their inverse economies of scale; the smaller the unit, the greater the price-performance. This is due to the fact that smaller units can be produced in mass quantities with very low (sometimes near-zero) variable costs. Large units, on the other hand, tend to be produced in small volumes and retain a significant proportion of variable costs. Thus, today's personal computers offer far more by way of "MIPS per dollar" than do today's mainframes or supercomputers; video games and other lower end consumer devices tend to offer even better price-performance than that.

Consumers will rely heavily on these technologies, while producers will rely on a mix of personal and institutionally oriented technologies. As the power and pervasiveness of the technologies at their command grow, consumers will be in the hitherto unique and unaccustomed position of controlling a far greater share of the information and communication flow between the buyer and seller than ever before. In other words, consumers can and will have more information about product providers in most cases than providers will have about consumers; far from being passive "targets" of marketing activity, consumers will dictate the timing and modality of communications, and they will determine the time and place of any resulting transaction.

Demand Side: Lifestyle and Demographic Changes

Broad demographic shifts are underway that are causing gradual but major changes in society. These macro-level changes have a major impact on individual consumer behavior.

Negative Growth Birth Rates and Rising Median Age in Developed Countries.
The birth rate in the United States has been falling for more than two decades. The decline in the birth rate began in 1965, when the arrival of "the pill" caused the fertility rate to fall by 30 percent in one year. The legalization of abortion a decade later caused another precipitous drop.

Wolfe (1996) described this phenomenon as "deyouthing—an historically unprecedented event going relatively unnoticed." During the 1990s, the number of adults under the age of 35 will decline by 8.3 million. This transition is having a major effect on consumption patterns. For example, as a result of deyouthing, the housing industry has shrunk dramatically; new housing starts have declined from 1.8 million per year in the 1970s to less than a million currently.

Other developed nations are experiencing even more severe effects from this trend because they tend to have much lower levels of immigration than the United States (more than 90 percent of the population growth in the United States between 1990 and 2050 will be due to immigration). Populations in most developed countries are actually shrinking. The trends for Japan are especially ominous. Between 1990 and 2030 alone, the number of Japanese under the age of 50 will decrease by some 24 million people, a net 26 percent loss of population. Birth rates in less developed countries by and large continue above the replacement level, although the overall trend is downward.

The differences in median ages across countries can be quite dramatic. The median age of adults in the United States is now 43 and will reach 50 in less than two decades. According to Wolfe (1996), the "psychological center of gravity" (PCG) is a five-year window around this median age of adults, or 38 to 48. He suggests that this PCG defines the primary tendencies of a culture; for the United States, this suggests that middle-age values and perspectives will increasingly come to dominate the national psyche. In particular, older consumers tend to respond more favorably to relationship marketing approaches than do younger consumers.

More Women in Workforce. Full-time working women now represent 56 percent of all women and will represent 65 percent by the year 2000. This has put tremendous pressure on the "traditional" family. The old model was that women would stop working when they decided to have kids. The new model is that most women MUST work if they want to have kids.

As a result of the loss of its anchor (i.e., a full-time homemaker), the family as a unit of social and consumption analysis is becoming obsolete. As single-person or dual-career households proliferate, the need to define a separate existence or space will result in highly individualistic lifestyles and behaviors, even within family units. We will increasingly have to look at individual behavior; family members exhibit more of a roommate lifestyle. This will increase the need for personalized attention to each household.

Also as a result of this trend, most households are now relatively time poor and money rich; any time marketers impose a time or place constraint, the market will react negatively. Time in particular will become the most precious commodity. As activities compete for time, consumers will redesign tasks that consume too much time and embrace time-saving and time-shifting technologies. They will demand hassle-free ("get it right the first time") service on demand.

Cooking in the home is quickly becoming a dying art; nobody does it anymore (almost). A third of our meals are eaten out now; this will rise to two-thirds. Of this remaining two-thirds, 50 percent are not cooked by us at all. The kitchen is increasingly the communication center of the house rather than the food center.

The increased numbers and visibility of women in the workplace have led to a gradual blurring of gender distinctions. For men, jewelry, cosmetics, personal care items, and plastic surgery are all growth markets.

Lifestyle, Income, and Ethnic Diversity. By 2000, only 55 percent of the U.S. population will be WASPs. Hispanics are the fastest growing group and will be the largest minority by that time. African Americans will remain at 12 percent, whereas the percentage of Asians will grow. California and Texas will become white-minority states.

As a result of the changing ethnic make-up of U.S. society, several changes are underway. In many sectors, neglected ethnic markets are becoming lead markets; for example, salsa and other Mexican sauces now sell more than ketchup. The local grocery store is now a world bazaar, something that requires extraordinary logistic systems. Increasing cultural diversity is leading to a clash of value systems: the Protestant work ethic versus other values. There are also increasing linguistic problems, especially in schools and the workplace.

Although we will still have a sizable middle class, there will be a sharp dichotomy between the rich and poor. A large percentage of the population will be affluent, and a sizable group will be below the official poverty level. The middle class will decline from 60 percent of the population in 1950 to 30 percent in 2000. The affluent class will go from 10 percent to 30 percent. As a result of such polarization, we will see simultaneous growth at the extremes: more and more premium products, and more economical ones as well. Products will also have to become more customized. Price ranges in product categories are getting ever wider; for example, in 1960 soups ranged from 19 cents to 59 cents per serving, whereas in 1990 they ranged from 39 cents to $4.00.

Other Demand-side Shifts

Numerous other demand-side shifts are taking place that will have enormous influence. Among them, five stand out.

Increase in Regional Differences. The population shift to the Sunbelt and to small towns, with their respective differences in climate, value structure, and even occupation, will widen the cultural differences in parts of the country. The United States is apt to more closely resemble Europe, where regions vary significantly in growth, employment, language, and consumption values.

Increased Stress. The blurring of traditional family roles, the increase in autonomy, older age, and the need to manage time all point toward a society that will have higher levels of stress, both at home and work. Stress, in turn, will generate productivity issues and behavioral problems, such as drug and alcohol abuse.

Greater Concern for Privacy. People will become more aware of their lack of privacy and potential loss of individual rights. As the social norms of a previously homogeneous society give way to pluralistic and diverse values, the legal rights of individuals will be emphasized.

Emphasis on Safety and Security. Concern for personal and public safety will rise sharply, partly because of the aging population and partly because of income redistribution. Additionally, as more people live alone, they will feel more vulnerable. Law enforcement will remain a major social issue.

Entrepreneurial Spirit. Opportunities created by exploding new technologies and the rise in niche markets will encourage personal entrepreneurship. As a result, small businesses will continue as the dominant component of societal change in terms of new business formation, employment growth, political power, regulatory policy, and personal wealth.

The Impact on Consumer Behavior

Already we can see that human behavior is changing rapidly as a result of the latest technological revolution: changes in marketplace behavior will naturally follow. As people start to change the way they work, communicate, and spend their leisure time, they will undoubtedly exert strong pressure on companies to change the way they do business with them. Accustomed to always being within electronic reach of their family and colleagues, they will chafe at marketers who demand adherence to rigidly defined modes of commerce. Used to instantaneous response to their requirements for information and entertainment, they will scarcely tolerate delays of weeks or months to receive a desired product. Being able to optimize their lifestyle factors more and more, they will shun clothing retailers who fail to meet their size or color requirements a third of the time. Capable of "doing more with less" with constantly improving technology, they will resent the high costs (primarily in time and effort) of acquiring the goods and services they need.

Clearly, future consumers will be dramatically different from past or even present consumers. They will be more demanding, more time-driven, more information intensive, and highly individualistic.

A combination of a ubiquitous broadband digital communications network and high-definition display terminals will further accelerate changes in consumer behavior. With targeted, interactive digital media in the future, advertisers will be able to "mass customize" their messages as well as allow for user interaction and input. Consumers are already migrating to direct marketing systems in huge numbers. With the deployment of advanced technologies, this trend will accelerate. When consumers can "walk" down a virtual grocery shopping aisle on their HDTV set and click on the products they want, huge numbers are bound to respond. This can be taken a step further; virtual reality linked to a broadband pipe creates "telepresence," so that users can actually "travel" to other places and experience different things.

Such elements of virtual reality will help, but will not be a prerequisite. One-way home shopping via television is already a large business; with much higher resolutions and more interactivity, it will take over a larger share of retailing's current domain. While enhancing convenience, such systems will also lead buyers to make more informed purchases. For one thing, buyers will gain immediate access to a variety of independent buying services, providing distributed expertise on demand. Because of interactive advertising, buyers will be much more active in seeking even marketer-provided information.

From Time-bound and Location-bound Marketing to Time-free and Location-free Marketing

Commerce today, for the most part, tends to be time and location bound. That is, transactions are constrained to occur at particular times and/or at particular locations. If the consumer is unable to transact at those times or those locations, the transaction either will not occur at all, or will occur between the consumer and another supplier. Even if the transaction does occur, that is, the consumer is able to comply with the time and place requirements set by the supplier, it will often force undesirable trade-offs on the consumer. In other words, the consumer may have no choice, and hence complies, but is left with a latent sense of dissatisfaction. Most consumers have numerous ways to spend that same time, and the location constraint imposes an additional burden on the time, effort, and expense of making oneself physically available to make the transaction.

As anyone who has lived through the past two decades can attest, time and place constraints are slowly giving way, under the pressure of increasingly hectic consumer lifestyles, heightened competition, and myriad enabling technologies. Behavioral barriers to the adoption of alternative modes of interacting, be they based on ingrained habits or perceived risks, have become increasingly porous.

We believe that this forward momentum will result in a positive feedback loop that will accelerate the rate of consumer migration toward alternative modes of transacting. Although no positive feedback loop can persist forever, we believe that a period of rapid, even explosive, growth lies ahead in this arena. It will subside only as a large majority of consumers have been converted to the new model of commerce. (See Figure 1.)

We are, then, in the midst of a sea-change from gravitational commerce, demarcated by its time and location constraints upon customers, to an era of digital commerce, which will be almost entirely free of those constraints. The future will see

---

| FIGURE 1 | **PAST AND FUTURE MODES OF MARKETING** |

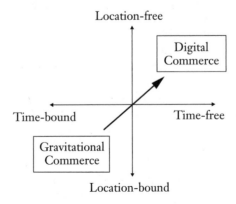

anytime, anywhere procurement coupled with anytime, anywhere consumption; more and more products and services will be purchased and consumed anytime, anywhere. Consumers will receive advertising and other forms of information "on demand."

The crucial importance of increased time and place utility is nowhere more evident than in the banking industry. Banks face a massive dislocation in the near future, as their vast and expensive time- and location-bound distribution networks (branches) become rapidly obsolete. Ironically, some banks are still building branches, while others are moving proactively to reconfigure their branch networks. For example, Wells Fargo announced in the fall of 1995 that it planned to move 72 percent of its existing branch network into in-store (supermarket) locations. Since in-store branches require only 20 to 25 percent of the cost of conventional branches, this represents a substantial cost saving, as well as a way to expand market coverage in terms of time as well as geography. The more major shift, of course, is the move toward home or remote banking. This trend, still in its early infancy, will take time and place utilities to much higher levels.

With regard to supermarket retailing, the impact of increased emphasis on time and place utilities will be even greater. Already, supermarkets can offer electronic ordering and home-delivery services for relatively low start-up costs. A recent survey indicates that more than 25 percent of supermarket chains offer home delivery, potentially reaching more than 40 percent of the population. A significant barrier to broader adoption of home shopping is the delivery charge, which runs from $7 to $10 an order. Survey research by Management Horizons shows significant consumer resistance to any delivery charge (*Supermarket News* 1996).

What is needed is a business model that is optimized for home shopping, rather than one in which the service is added on as an ancillary to traditional retailing. An analysis by Management Horizons indicates substantial savings can be made in operating a delivery depot compared to operating a supermarket. On a typical $100 order, home delivery will cost a typical supermarket operator an extra $10 to process, pick, check out, and deliver from the supermarket. A delivery depot can process and deliver the same order for about $10 to $12 less in total cost than the supermarket can.

To summarize, the future success of marketers will depend on their ability to deliver total customer convenience. This includes hassle-free search (advertising-on-demand), hassle-free acquisition (home delivery), hassle-free consumption (e.g., products with built-in expert systems to enable maximal value extraction), and hassle-free disposal.

Emerging Trends in Consumer Behavior

We foresee eight major trends in consumer behavior. These trends are listed in Figure 2; each is briefly discussed.

Disintermediation and Reintermediation

Current marketing practice depends heavily on the presence of multiple intermediaries between the producer and consumer. These intermediaries primarily add time and place utilities to the functional utility "engineered" into the offering by the producer. They provide broader and more convenient access to products for a wider range of customers.

| FIGURE 2 | EMERGING TRENDS IN CONSUMER BEHAVIOR |

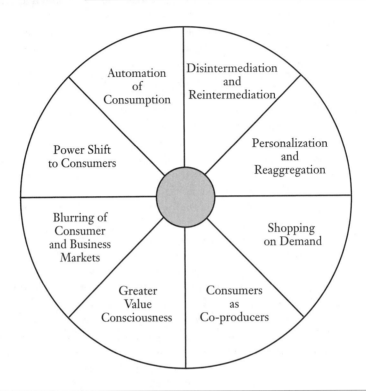

In addition to serving as essential conduits for getting products to the market, intermediaries have also served as informational conduits. Producers typically have little or no direct contact with end-user customers and must rely almost entirely on intermediaries for information pertaining to those customers. Likewise, intermediaries often play a role in directing and filtering information from producers that is intended for end users.

Building an adequate distribution channel is usually the biggest hurdle that a new entrant must face in establishing a foothold in a market; this is usually the slowest and most expensive part of the marketing mix to implement. Distribution channels add huge cost elements. For example, they may include multiple warehouses at the factory, wholesaler, retailer, and even consumer level.

As has already been well documented, the electronic world changes all that. Companies small and large are able to achieve a high level of accessibility almost immediately. Establishing a two-way information flow directly with end users is readily possible. The automation of numerous administrative tasks enables the company to serve huge numbers of customers efficiently and effectively. Innovations such as demand-driven marketing can dramatically lower systemwide inventory levels.

As a result, more and more companies are finding it possible to deal directly with more and more of their customers. In the process, they are putting enormous pressures on their intermediary (e.g., wholesaling and retailing) partners. This trend toward disintermediation is still in its early phases, and massive dislocations will occur as a result of it.

The trend will also cause major growth in the support services needed by companies that deal directly with larger numbers of customers. For example, growth in small package shipping will likely far exceed that in bulk shipments or the building of warehouse space.

Another consequence of this trend may well be what we call reintermediation. By this we mean that new categories of intermediaries will emerge to capture the value-creating opportunities that will undoubtedly be spawned by the confluence of new ways of interacting between consumers and producers. As with traditional intermediaries, these too will thrive on the basis of economic transfer principles; intermediaries that deliver greater value at lower cost will prosper.

Examples of new types of intermediaries may include rating services, automated ordering services, services based on consolidating numerous small orders from numerous consumers into more economically viable quantities, and so forth. Market specialists could emerge who would orchestrate the offerings of numerous suppliers around the specialized needs of a single customer.

Personalization: From Aggregation to Disaggregation and Reaggregation

The emergence of a relatively homogeneous mass market earlier in this century led to the development of various mass marketing approaches that continue to define and dominate the marketing function today. For some time now, we have recognized that the mass market is splintering (even atomizing) into ever smaller segments. Talk has even arisen in recent years of a so-called segment of one, and Stan Davis came up with the powerful oxymoron of "mass customization" as the way in which we will have to increasingly operate in the future.

Although we certainly agree with the broad premise of this argument, we believe some important caveats apply. First, customers are not always looking for customized products; they may be perfectly content in many cases with a well-designed standardized product. However, mass customization applies to more than the product; it should encompass all the appropriate elements of the marketing mix. Thus, the price, advertising message, and/or the distribution mode may be customized, even if the product is not.

Second, new forms of aggregation of demand will undoubtedly occur. In the past, these were driven entirely by producers. In the future, it will become increasingly facile for the aggregation to be driven by customers. For example, customers who individually purchase small quantities of a product will find it very easy to pool their purchases to enjoy better terms.

Shopping on Demand

As discussed earlier, consumer behavior in the future will increasingly feature shopping on demand and consumers will cease to be held hostage to the time and place constraints historically imposed on them by businesses. Shopping on demand will include anytime, anywhere procurement as well as anytime, anywhere consumption.

Consumers as Co-producers

In many facets of consumption, consumers will take on increasingly active roles. For example, they will become directly involved in designing and customizing the products they purchase. They will take over some of the support and service functions that are normally performed by companies; this trend is akin to the one toward self-service in retailing. For example, FedEx now allows its customers to track their own packages via the Internet, bypassing the customer service department altogether.

From Insourcing to Outsourcing. Somewhat paradoxically, we believe that as consumers take more control over certain commercial relationships, they will also relinquish a measure of control in other areas. This is not as contradictory as it might first appear; after all, consumers have a limited amount of time and effort that they are willing to expend, necessitating trade-offs. As a result of escalating time pressures and growing economic resources, consumers will begin to outsource household functions much more over time. The argument here is very similar to the one that drives outsourcing in the business context; specialist vendors will be used to deliver far better price-performance value than consumers can create in-house. In other words, the make-versus-buy question will increasingly be resolved in favor of buy. Many services (such as lawn care, house cleaning, and child care) are already outsourced to a significant degree. Many new areas will be added in the future. For example, household product needs may be outsourced to such firms as Proctor and Gamble, and in-home dining may be outsourced to restaurants that will deliver prepared food daily to the consumer's home.

Greater Value Consciousness

Although they have benefited in many ways as well, consumers have paid the price for marketing's extraordinary lack of productivity in the past. High advertising budgets, the proliferation of brands, runaway sales promotions, uneconomic levels of inventory build-up—all of these activities added costs way out of proportion to the value they created (which was, in many cases, negative).

As marketing reforms, customer expectations for value received will soar. Consumers will demand and receive more value in exchange for the four primary resources at their disposal: money, time, effort, and space.

Money. Consumers will expect to pay less for most products. They will willingly pay more, provided that the additional value offered exceeds the incremental price. Because of their recent experience with major product categories such as computers and consumer electronics, consumers have come to expect as a given the proposition that products get better and cheaper over time. We believe (and many economists concur) that an era of negative inflation will characterize many more product categories.

Time. For many consumers, especially those in two-income households, time is a more valuable currency than money. Many consumers will gladly make a trade-off, paying a higher price if they can save time in the process. Marketers must be extremely wary of placing heavy time demands on consumers.

Effort.   As life gets ever more complex in so many dimensions, consumers are looking for convenience and simplicity wherever they can find it.

Space.   Given a choice, consumers would rather not be forced to warehouse large quantities of products in their basements in order to benefit from lower prices. Heavy users should get the advantages of scale economy; however, they should not have to swallow huge lumps of inventory in order to do so.

Value buying will become paramount, as consumers become more value-conscious than ever. They will be better educated about offerings. Given the efficiency with which information will be shared between customers and between customers and companies, it will be almost impossible for companies to survive without delivering peak value. In contrast with the past, consumers will respond far more to innovation-based differentiation than to image-based differentiation.

Barriers to consumption will increasingly disappear as a result of the adoption of value-based marketing, more creative pricing approaches (leasing, metering), the separation of form from function, and the removal of artificial constraints. Given the right value equation, the limits to consumption will be revealed as being far less than were believed possible. It is now commonplace for households to have numerous radios, telephones, calculators, and even computers. Many consumers own three or more watches.

Greater competitive pressures on pricing, coupled with an enhanced ability to easily locate the best price, will be a fact of life in the new world. The impact of this will be threefold. First, successful manufacturers will increasingly seek to control their prices at retail to minimize what they view as destructive intrabrand price competition. Second, the primary drivers of profitability will be mostly on the cost side; companies with highly efficient production and marketing systems will prosper. Third, strong customer relationships will give companies an opportunity to broaden those relationships through the provision of an ever-expanding array of products and services. In essence, we believe that many successful producers of a product will become retailers of a multitude of other products for the same customer.

Blurring Between Consumer and Business Markets

The lines between the home and the workplace are rapidly blurring. More and more people work at least part-time in their homes, and a growing number of people undertake some of their personal tasks at the office. As this trend continues, many consumer decisions will become more like business decisions. Many technology applications traditionally seen as home based will be important to businesses as well. For example, video shopping has great potential in a business environment; an automobile mechanic will be able to see a picture before ordering a part. To see how to make repairs the worker has not done in a long time, he or she will be able to view a video clip.

This movement of home-based services to business and vice versa can already be observed. Typical home-bound applications such as television and VCRs are now "trickling up" into business applications. Telephone answering machines trickled up to businesses as voice mail. Business applications such as e-mail, the Internet, EDI, and accounting software are trickling down into the home market. Dual-purpose applications include video shopping, distance learning, travel planning, news on demand, legal/financial advice, information services/on-line databases, and so forth. Some applications will remain geared to the business or consumer market, although even here analogous applications may be developed.

Power Shift from Marketers to Consumers

Inevitably, increased competition and greater access to more powerful information tools will put greater power in the hands of savvy consumers. As a result, it is possible that buyers will increasingly be viewed as marketers and sellers as prospects in the marketplace. In any event, consumers will no longer be targets of marketing activity; they will be knowledgeable and demanding drivers of it.

Marketers will have to show far greater respect for consumers, who have increasingly become immune to marketing hype. Instead, they will demand content-rich information and demonstrable product innovations. Transactions will occur in the context of a complex relationship revolving around lifestyle issues. Customer managers will be charged explicitly with identifying, retaining, and growing profitable customer relationships.

Market activity will be driven almost entirely by buyer demand; marketing management will essentially become demand management: the task of influencing the level, timing, and composition of demand in a way that will help the organization achieve its objectives. Customer knowledge will truly become the cornerpiece of effective marketing, and that knowledge will become a highly valued corporate resource. By linking directly into production systems, consumers will effectively become producers; they will engage in self-service, self-design, and self-ordering and provisioning.

Consumers will be highly information-technology literate; they will therefore not be impressed by the mere use of such technology. They will be highly efficient at information searching and processing. Consumers can already conduct product research on-line, log onto bulletin boards and interact with other consumers, and provide and receive helpful hints about the product, its use, and acquisition. In this environment, "information invitations" may become common; companies will have to seek permission to present their case to consumers by inducing interest, unlike the message clutter that is rampant today.

As communication between marketers and customers becomes increasingly interactive, relationship marketing will become the rule rather than the exception. Buyers and sellers will interact in real time. Just-in-time marketing will replace the traditional just-in-case marketing. Time and place constraints on purchasing (and even consumption of many products and services) will become obsolete. The nearly instant gratification of customer needs will be common; thus, lead times of all kinds (e.g., for product development or between order placement and shipment) will have to shrink dramatically.

The Automation of Consumption

Consumers' time poverty and an abundance of information technology will lead to a greatly increased level of automated transactions with marketers. Akin to automatic replenishment as practiced in the business-to-business marketing arena today, such arrangements will become increasingly commonplace in the future. They may happen directly between consumers and manufacturers for larger purchases, and through intermediaries for smaller purchases. As discussed elsewhere, suppliers of large items or major services will have the opportunity to become the supplier of choice for an ever-widening array of goods and services (the concept of customer equity).

Other related concepts from the business marketing arena that will rapidly find analogs in the consumer marketing arena include vendor-managed inventory, supply chain management, electronic data interchange, customized pricing, and various forms of risk sharing (such as the revenue-sharing formulas offered by manufacturers of some infrastructure equipment such as telecommunications gear).

One important development will be that savvy consumers will increasingly demand that corporations share the benefits of cost cutting with them. Just as Wal-Mart demands that P&G lower its costs and then share the benefits with it, so too will customers with a high lifetime value demand and receive similar consideration. Smart companies will do this without being forced; they will proactively invest resources in those relationships with the greatest long-term value. Currently, investment in customers usually stops after they have become customers; spending on customer retention activity is much less than on acquisition. Further, loyal customers tend to subsidize those who are less loyal, as well as the acquisition of new ones. Overall, the economics of customer acquisition and retention will require and will receive much more understanding and attention than they do currently.

The Concept of a Personal Marketplace.   The Personal Marketplace (PM) is a hypothetical mechanism to make effective use of the vast amounts of consumer and transaction data generated today. It is a repository where participating companies prepare and market custom-tailored offerings directly to a consumer. These are categorized by product and/or service, as specified by the consumer. By selecting a particular category, the consumer alerts companies that he or she is a potential customer, and offers begin to flow in. The customer voluntarily provides as much customizing information as needed. Participating companies agree not to sell the data they collect outside the PM, and not to use it to market in any other channel.

The Impact of Changing Consumer Behavior on Marketing

As we (Sheth and Sisodia 1995a,b) previously pointed out, the marketing function is in the midst of a serious and escalating productivity crisis. For several decades the marketing function has consumed an ever-growing share of corporate expenditures while failing to deliver increased customer loyalty or greater profitability. The marketing tools and tactics that worked well in decades past are increasingly relics of an era that is rapidly fading.

Our discussion of changing consumer behavior suggests that the root cause of marketing's problems is behavioral. In other words, marketing today largely operates under the modalities of industrial-age commerce, while consumer behavior has changed and will continue to change rapidly and dramatically. Industrial-age marketing, coupled with information-age consumer behavior, creates a misalignment that renders much of what marketing does ineffectual and sometimes damaging.

It is not surprising, then, that marketing today is incredibly inefficient. For example, in 1996, $159 billion was spent on advertising in the United States alone, plus a nearly equal amount on sales promotions. This amounts to $1,250 per person per year, or $5,000 per year per four-member household. The advertising dollars buy an average of 1,600 exposures per day per person; only two percent of those result in positive recall.

Even direct marketing is highly inefficient; there are 254,000,000 Americans, but four billion names for rent. Direct marketing is regarded as successful when it is 98 percent wrong. It is viable only because trees continue to be cheap, and postal rates are still relatively low.

In addition to being inefficient, marketing is too often ineffective as well. Customer dissatisfaction runs high in many industries, and brand loyalty continues to erode. Most customers have become conditioned to being opportunistic and short-term oriented.

A full-blown productivity crisis now exists in marketing. Consequently, we can expect to see major budget cuts in marketing in coming years, as companies search for greater operating efficiency.

Interactive broadband communication systems have the potential to make the marketing function far more productive, mainly because they directly target the areas of communications and selling, which is where the bulk of marketing resources are expended. Both outbound communications (e.g., advertising, sales promotion, and personal selling) and inbound communications (e.g., ordering and customer service) will be impacted.

With such systems, companies will be able to integrate advertising, sales promotion, personal selling, and physical distribution to a far greater extent than is now possible. They will be able to achieve maximal market coverage with a relatively small amount of inventory, dramatically reducing costs in the process. Marketing efforts will be tailored for and targeted directly at the most responsive segments of the market. Companies will close the loop by making it almost effortless for customers to interact with them and with each other.

Firefly: Harnessing the Power of Word-of-mouth Marketing

An interesting example of how marketing can leverage emerging networking technology is a new service called Firefly. Firefly is one of the first commercial services to attempt to harness the power of peer recommendations or word-of-mouth marketing (Judge 1996). It (http://firefly.com) works by building detailed psychographic profiles of members, based on their answers to scores of questions. On the basis of this information, Firefly then identifies the individual's "psychographic neighbors" (other individuals who appear to have similar predispositions) and recommends products and services on the basis of what others have reported liking. The information is also used to pinpoint advertising messages to individuals. Although currently limited to music and movies, Firefly is planning to add mutual funds, restaurants, and books.

Going beyond facilitating transactions, Firefly also enables user-to-user communications, with communities based on shared interests. Corporate users of the service so far include Merrill Lynch, MCI, Dun & Bradstreet, Reuters, Yahoo, and ZD Net.

Importantly, Firefly has aggressively sought to maintain user privacy; it does not require users to provide real names and addresses unless they choose to. The company has gone so far as to hire Coopers & Lybrand to conduct audits twice a year to ensure that it is adequately safeguarding user privacy. Firefly's privacy policies have earned it plaudits from the Electronic Frontier Foundation, an entity that advocates privacy for Internet users.

How Marketing Must Respond

Paradoxically, marketing must simultaneously get smaller and bigger in the future. At the most successful marketing companies, there will be fewer full-time marketers than there are today. At the same time, the role of marketing will grow. Marketing will exert functional control over operations, customer service, and pricing to a far greater extent than it currently does. Many more employees will be considered part-time marketers. Marketing will evolve into the truly integrating business function it was always intended to be.

The ongoing information and communications revolution presents a once-in-a-lifetime opportunity for marketing to radically define its base operating models and configure them for maximum efficiency and effectiveness. Because this future is approaching at a much faster rate than previously envisioned, marketers must begin now to understand its dimensions and invest in developing the core capabilities that will be needed to succeed in the future. Marketing will have to do the following.

Become More Technology Savvy.   Marketing will have to develop a deep understanding of the drivers and trajectories of computing and communications technology. It will have to develop just-in-time capabilities in areas such as pricing and provisioning. Companies will have to learn to leverage visually interactive communications and refine on-line transaction processing systems. They will have to invest in sophisticated logistical capabilities aimed at serving individual consumers. They will have to become adept users and developers of expert systems and other forms of artificial intelligence technologies, such as voice recognition systems and intelligent agents. All of this will require a massive investment in the information technology platforms that are used in marketing.

Learn How to Retain Customer Loyalty.   Consumer behavior in the future, coupled with slow market growth rates, will make customer retention an even more important driver of profitability. Marketing's primary focus on customer acquisition will thus have to change to one based on relationship management.

Learn How to Become the Quarterback.   Marketing's ability to quarterback cross-functional teams organized around customer needs will be key in the future. This will require two levels of integration. First, the marketing function will have to integrate its own activities, which are performed today in semiautonomous "silos." Second, the marketing function will have to be linked and integrated with other business functions.

Practice Interactive, One-to-one Marketing. The ability to undertake direct, interactive marketing will be a critical element in future marketing success. This goes far beyond database marketing as currently practiced. The most important element will be to develop virtual empathy with consumers on a one-to-one basis. One-to-one interactions may take several forms: person-to-person (marketer interacts with customer), person-to-system (marketer interacts with customer's "agent"), system-to-person (marketer's "agent" interacts with customer), and system-to-system (marketer's agent interacts with customer's agent). All of these forms of interaction will be necessary in the future.

Agent Technology and Household Management Computers

Increasingly, company-consumer interaction will in fact be computer-computer interaction, as computers at either end take on the personalities of sellers and buyers. Although this may seem far-fetched today, consider the extent to which this is already widespread in the following commercial applications:

- Smart robots are used by travel agents to ferret out the best fares by using a variety of creative approaches.

- Numerous expert systems are being used by companies in areas ranging from the approval of credit applications to the fine tuning of blast furnaces to the prediction of photocopier failures.

- Automated trading systems (program trading) have been used by brokerage firms on Wall Street for many years.

With the blurring of boundaries between the workplace and the home (already there is talk of "home at work" along with "work at home"), we believe it is only a matter of time and appropriate marketing before such innovations are deployed in the mass market, where they will have a much greater impact.

Consider the possibility of a household management computer (HMC). An HMC could operate during off hours at night searching the globe for goods and services needed for the household. Although the search is based on specifications used in the past, these could be modified according to what the HMC may learn in the market. The HMC could operate in one of three ways. For commodities such as oil and heating, the HMC can make purchase decisions, place orders, schedule delivery, and authorize payment without further intervention by the consumer. For somewhat more complex decisions such as which styles of dress shirt to buy, the HMC may collect and store information. The consumer can review that information at a later time and make decisions. The information is verbally presented to the user, and verbal responses are also received by the computer. For more complex decisions requiring large amounts of information and significant financial outlays, the HMC gathers information, requests the delivery of electronic samples and other product information, and presents a recommendation on the basis of agreed-upon criteria.[1]

One possible innovation in the future might be "feel sites." These are locations where consumers can go to try on clothes, taste food, or sit on furniture before returning to the Internet to finalize a purchase decision.[2]

Marketing's Stranded Assets

A "stranded asset" is a sunk cost that may no longer provide economic value. For example, in the electric utility industry, many nuclear plants have become stranded assets; they were built at enormous cost but are no longer competitive with more efficient ways of generating electricity. Companies have little choice but to write off such assets and invest in newer ones (or to simply stop producing internally and rely on purchases from the market).

We believe that marketing has built up numerous potentially stranded assets. More and more, these relics of a fast-fading era will have to be replaced. If they are not replaced, they will represent a severe drag on the competitiveness of the firms that continue to own them. Examples of stranded assets include the following:

- Retailing space—banks and supermarkets will be increasingly replaced by home-based retailing; in the last decade, the average time spent at malls by consumers has declined dramatically, from 7 hours a month to only 2 1/2 hours.

- Warehousing space—manufacturers, wholesalers, retailers, consumers; replaced by virtual warehouses.

- Office space—there will be more space-independent working.

- Inflexible manufacturing plants—for example, GM has some plants that are capable of making only one particular type of pick-up truck.

- Outbound telemarketing setups—these have proven to be extraordinarily efficient at alienating large numbers of customers.

Certain capabilities will be in short supply and will thus be at a premium. Examples include small-order-size delivery systems (agile logistics), picking systems, and order-fulfillment experts.

Conclusion

Wehling (1996, p. 170), senior vice president of advertising at Proctor and Gamble, recently noted that

> Over the long term, marketers who remain unprepared for the sea-change we're about to experience won't survive. Marketers who understand the implications and get ahead of the curve will not only survive, they'll thrive. They'll emerge more competitive than ever and they'll build relationships with consumers that are deeper and more enduring than any we can create today.

A marketing revolution is only just beginning. We are now climbing onto a technological treadmill; companies that are not already on board may not be able to make up for lost ground. New entrants will base their business model on the starkly different economics of the information age. Consequently, these new entrants will create numerous stranded assets among traditional marketers.

The world is changing in major ways that few of us have begun to fathom. In particular, the world in which marketing exists is getting reshaped with great speed. The microprocessor forever changed the world of computing and nearly destroyed IBM. IBM was forced to change dramatically simply to survive. Analogous to IBM, marketing will die if it does not change.

There will undoubtedly be winners and losers in this process, as well as leaders and laggards. Those marketers who move proactively now to redefine the function and rewrite its value equations will position themselves for a bright future. If it is managed right, marketing may lose the battle but win the war. If it is not managed right, operations or customer services may drive the corporation—to the ultimate detriment of customers as well as shareholders.

Notes

1. Dwayne McCollum, MBA student, George Mason University.
2. Carol Diggs, MBA student, George Mason University.

5

The Internet and International Marketing

JOHN A. QUELCH

LISA R. KLEIN

Is the Internet just another marketing channel like direct mail or home shopping? Or will it revolutionize global marketing? Will large multinationals lose the advantages of size, while small start-ups leverage the technology and become big players internationally? The authors discuss the different opportunities and challenges that the Internet offers to large and small companies worldwide. They examine the impact on global markets and new product development, the advantages of an intranet for large corporations, and the need for foreign government support and cooperation.

The Internet promises to revolutionize the dynamics of international commerce and, like the telephone and fax machine, may be a major force in the democratization of capitalism. Small companies will be able to compete more easily in the global marketplace, and consumers in emerging markets, in particular, will benefit from the expanded range of products, services, and information to which the Internet will give them access. As a recent Forrester industry report explains, the Internet removes many barriers to communication with customers and employees by eliminating the obstacles created by geography, time zones, and location, creating a "frictionless" business environment.[1] Much of the current expansion in Internet use, accelerated by the emergence of the World Wide Web (WWW), is driven by marketing initiatives—providing products and product information to potential customers. However, in the future, many companies, especially those operating globally, will realize a much broader range of benefits from this medium's potential as both a communication and a transaction vehicle.

Currently, the Internet is mainly a U.S. phenomenon, due to the later start and historically slower growth of Internet access in other countries. More than half the Internet's nearly 7 million host computers are located in the United States, with the remainder spread across 100 other countries.[2] In 1995, 22 countries came on-line.[3] In 1994, there was wide variation in the number of Internet hosts per 1,000 people, ranging from more than 14 in Finland to fewer than 0.5 in South Korea (see Table 1).

John A. Quelch is Sebastian S. Kresge Professor of Marketing and Lisa R. Klein is a doctoral candidate in marketing at the Harvard Business School.

TABLE 1	INTERNATIONAL GROWTH OF THE INTERNET		
	Number of Hosts (January 1995)	**Hosts per 1,000 People**	**1995 Growth in Hosts (Annual Percentage)**
Finland	71,372	14.0	103%
United States	2,044,716	12.4	100
Australia	161,166	9.0	50
New Zealand	31,215	9.0	441
Sweden	77,594	8.8	83
Switzerland	51,512	7.8	40
Norway	49,725	7.7	57
Canada	186,722	7.0	96
Holland	89,227	6.0	98
Denmark	25,935	5.5	181
United Kingdom	241,191	4.0	112
Austria	29,705	3.8	92
Israel	13,251	3.0	96
Germany	207,717	2.5	77
Hong Kong	12,437	2.2	52
Belgium	18,699	2.0	125
France	93,041	1.8	68
Czech Republic	11,580	1.5	153
Japan	96,632	1.0	86
South Africa	27,040	<1.0	147
Spain	28,446	<1.0	141
Taiwan	14,618	<1.0	83
Italy	30,697	<1.0	80
South Korea	18,049	<1.0	101
Poland	11,477	<1.0	121

Source: C. Anderson. "The Accidental Superhighway," *The Economist*, 1 July 1995, p. S3. Survey by M. Lottor, Network Wizards, as summarized by The Internet Society, obtained from <http://www.isoc.org>.

With fewer non-U.S. businesses on line, fewer access nodes, higher telecommunications rates, and lower rates of personal computer ownership, consumer use of the Internet internationally is currently much lower than in the United States, where commercial on-line services like CompuServe and America Online (AOL) have also facilitated Internet use. But CompuServe and AOL have only recently begun to aggressively market their services in other countries. CompuServe first began global expansion in 1987 with entry into Japan through collaboration with Japanese partners.

The on-line service now boasts 500,000 subscribers outside the United States. AOL's attempts to establish Europe Online were delayed until late 1995 due to disagreements with its European-based partners. Although these commercial providers are now positioned for aggressive growth abroad, their slower than expected expansion has delayed consumer education about and adoption of the Internet.

Internet access in overseas markets now promises to grow rapidly as the on-line services expand and as regional and national governments and telecommunication companies become more interested (see Table 1). For example, China recently launched ChinaWeb, a Web site whose stated purpose is "To help China in her rapid transformation to an information society, and to promote business and commerce with China through the bridge of Internet."[4] As an emerging bellwether market, China's response to the Internet augurs well for its worldwide expansion. Some predict that the European market will fully open only when the telecommunications industry is deregulated in 1998, reducing phone charges for Internet usage and allowing the number of users to reach the critical mass necessary to spur the growth of European commercial Web sites.[5] However, these transitions will not occur overnight. Some national governments will doubtless try to limit their populations' access to the Internet, fearing the free flow of ideas and the importation of products purchased over the Internet at the expense of local sales taxes and custom duties.

Many international users of the Internet are similar to U.S. users. An on-line survey of more than 13,000 Internet users conducted by Georgia Tech's Graphics, Visualization, and Usability Center (GVU), from April through May 1995, counted 2,500 responses from other countries, primarily from English-speaking users. A comparison of the demographic profiles of foreign and domestic users uncovered few differences, with both audiences skewed toward college-educated white males in their early thirties, earning higher than average incomes and employed in the computer, education, and other professional fields.[6]

The long-term international growth of the Internet raises the opportunity for cross-border information flows and transactions. In 1995, transaction volume over the Web was estimated at more than $400 million, up from less than $20 million in 1994—more than 80 percent of which went to U.S. companies. Of the total sales, exports accounted for approximately 43 percent.[7] An informal poll of a dozen Web sites reveals that the internationally based audience comprises, on average, 20 percent of total traffic and transaction volume (see Table 2).

Current estimates predict that global transaction volume will reach more than $1 billion in 1996. However, transactions are concentrated in a limited number of product categories, even within the United States, due to: (1) the distinctive demographic profile of current Internet users;(2) the type of product information most easily presented electronically, given limitations in bandwidth; (3) trade regulations; and (4) transaction security concerns.

For example, products with generally low prices sell better. A recent survey of Internet shoppers reported that 64 percent of purchases were for software, books, music, hardware, and magazines.[8] The GVU survey revealed that on-line purchasers were much more likely to buy hardware and software priced at under $50 than over $50, with more than 60 percent citing transaction security concerns as the major deterrent. In addition, legal restrictions limit cross-border transactions; many software

| TABLE 2 | INTERNATIONAL AUDIENCES | | | | |

Company	Industry	Primary Audience	Secondary Audience	International Business	
				Percentage of Traffic	Percentage of Transactions
Software.net	Software	End customers	Suppliers	20%	30%
Wordsworth Books	Books	End customers	Publishers	25	25
CD Now	Music	End customers		20	20
Underground Music Archive	Music	End customers	Musicians	N/A	30
Zima	Liquor	End customers		6	N/A
CatalogSite	Catalogs	End customers	Catalog distributors	15	N/A
Individual Inc.	News service	Customers and subscribers	Advertisers, press, employees	25	25
3M	Diverse business products	Business market end customers and distributors	Consumer market end customers	20	N/A
OnSale	Auction house	Buyers and sellers		20	20
Consulting, Inc.	Consulting	Client and job seekers	Partners and employees	20	N/A
American Venture Capital Exchange	Venture capital	Entrepreneurs and investors		5	3
Building Industry Exchange	Information	Buyers and suppliers		30	N/A

Source: Personal interviews and e-mail correspondence with webmasters at each site conducted from December 1995 to January 1996. Based on sample week hit and transaction counts.

products cannot be sold internationally for security reasons due to their inclusion of encryption technologies. Likewise, exports of liquor are restricted. But these constraints will likely be overcome as Internet use diffuses and adopter profiles become more heterogeneous, as bandwidth and software capabilities expand, and as data security issues are resolved.

The purpose of this article is to explore how the Internet may change the rules of international marketing. Is the Internet potentially revolutionary or just another marketing channel like home shopping or direct mail? The answer depends on how much added value there is in Internet communications and transactions compared to existing alternatives. The value-added will vary across country markets and according to company type. Because distribution channels tend to be less developed, less direct, or less efficient in emerging markets than in the United States, the Internet may offer special opportunities in these markets. In addition, the differences in speed of, control over, and access to communication and distribution channels between the Internet and traditional media and distribution channels internationally will offer different mixes of opportunities and challenges to large multinational companies (MNCs) and to small businesses.

Types of Web Sites

A company's choice of evolutionary path depends on whether it is an established MNC or a start-up company created to do business solely on the Internet (see Figure 1). (Any company that establishes a site on the Internet automatically becomes a multinational company.) Existing MNCs tend to adopt the information-to-transaction model, whereas start-up companies tend to use the transaction-to-information model.

The MNC starts by offering information to address the needs of its existing customers. Federal Express's initial site, launched in November 1994, was a relatively small twelve-page site focusing on the package-tracking service previously available only to business with corporate accounts. Customer response to the service was much greater than expected, causing the company to expand its server capacity and the site itself to include information on the range of delivery options and downloadable desktop software to prepare packages for shipping and keeping records.[9] However, neither FedEx nor its competitor UPS yet offer on-line transactions so customers can arrange for package pick-up, delivery, or billing directly on the Web site.

3M's Web site gives information on a growing number of its nearly 60,000 products, news of innovations in its product markets, and directories of its worldwide operations, but has only recently begun offering items for sale. Currently, it offers a $15 mouse pad—and only within the United States.

Rockport, the shoe company, plans to launch a Web site in spring 1996, which will initially focus on giving existing and potential customers information on foot care and on its product line. The company plans to expand the site to provide links to its local retail outlets and eventually to collect and analyze individual purchase histories to help customers select future purchases. Only with this detailed amount of customer information and involvement does the company see on-line transactions as worthwhile.

On the other hand, simple economics require Internet start-ups to begin with transactions and then continue to use the medium to build a brand image, provide product support, and win repeat purchases. Companies such as Software.net and CD Now have followed this model. Software.net, an on-line software retailer, allows customers to purchase and download software directly from its Web site. This type of on-line distribution was the first of its kind; the company has since added a database of links to product reviews and software manufacturers and created product discussion bulletin boards to help customers choose software. CD Now is an on-line music store. Recent additions to this transactions-driven business include lengthy album and artist reviews, concert calendars, and new release notification.

| FIGURE 1 | EVOLUTIONARY PATHS OF A WEB SITE |

MCNS

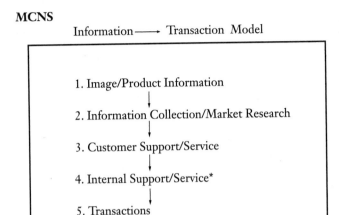

Information ⟶ Transaction Model

1. Image/Product Information
   ↓
2. Information Collection/Market Research
   ↓
3. Customer Support/Service
   ↓
4. Internal Support/Service*
   ↓
5. Transactions

Internet Start-ups

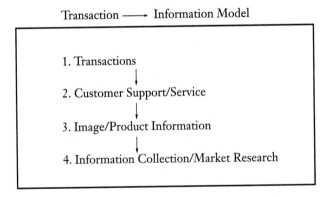

Transaction ⟶ Information Model

1. Transactions
   ↓
2. Customer Support/Service
   ↓
3. Image/Product Information
   ↓
4. Information Collection/Market Research

*Recently, the rapid growth in awareness of, and software and support for, such internal information networks or intranets makes it likely that this could be among the first stages for companies establishing a Web site in the future.

Whichever of the two business models a company pursues, the specific functions embodied in a Web site, whether targeted to internal or external users, need to generate revenue or reduce costs (see Figure 2). As an MNC or start-up develops its site to incorporate a broader range of functions, it needs to assess how the functions influence the global business model. For example, transaction capabilities can have both revenue-generation and cost-reduction potential, depending on whether the company is attracting new customers and sales or transferring existing sales to a more profitable

FIGURE 2	DRIVERS OF INTERNET BUSINESS MODELS

Primary Business Impact

	Cost Reduction	Revenue Generation
Internal	Technical, Legal and Administrative Support Database Management Internal Research **Company Information**	**Marketing and Sales Support/Information**
Customer Focus		
External	Customer Service **Transactions**	**Product Information** Promotions Database Development Market Research **Transactions**

medium. Similarly, providing information to internal and external audiences can increase revenues by facilitating incremental sales or increased margins. The dissemination of information via the Internet can also reduce costs by replacing communications through less cost-efficient channels.

Many companies are conducting international commerce on the Internet with this range of business models supporting several different types of Web sites. (For a simple framework categorizing these sites, see Figure 3.)

Quadrant 1

Quadrant 1 (in Figure 3) includes companies using the Web primarily as a communication tool to engage in one-way and two-way communications with a range of outside audiences, such as end users, intermediaries (e.g., dealerships, retail outlets), and suppliers (e.g., software developers). These companies provide customer services to the U.S. market and just happen to attract international traffic as well. The benefit to international consumers is merely the opportunity to access information and support faster, more cheaply, and more directly than existing communication systems like telephone, fax, mail, and direct mail can. For example, the Apple Computer Web site offers up-to-date detailed technical information, software updates, product specifications, and press releases to Macintosh users and developers. International customers can obtain information and product support that is often superior to or more timely than that available from channels in their domestic markets.

FIGURE 3	CATEGORIES OF WEB SITES

Web Site Content

	Information Support/Service Only	Transactions
Domestic	**1** Apple Computer Saturn Reebok CatalogSite	**2** Software.net Wordsworth Books Mr. Upgrade CD Now Godiva Chocolates LIGHTNING Instrumentation Yvonne's Weinkabinett
Global	**3** Building Industry Exchange Federal Express Sun Microsystems ChinaWeb Gateway to New Zealand Digital Equipment Corp. Eli Lilly & Co. British Airways Consulting Inc.	**4** TRADE'ex Underground Music Archive American Venture Capital Exchange Online BookStore CapEx

Audience Focus

Site Description	Location	Industry
3M	United States	Diverse business products
American Venture Capital Exchange	United States	Venture capital
Apple Computer	United States	Computer hardware, software
British Airways	United Kingdom	Airline
Building Industry Exchange	United States	Construction
CapEx	Germany	Venture capital
Catalog Site	United States	Mail-order catalogs
CD Now	United States	Music
ChinaWeb	China	Information
Consulting Inc.	United States	Information
Digital Equipment Corp.	United States	Computer hardware
Eli Lilly & Co.	United States	Pharmaceuticals
Federal Express	United States	Package delivery
Gateway to New Zealand	New Zealand	Information
Godiva Chocolates	United States	Food
LIGHTNING Instrumentation	Switzerland	Networking equipment
Mr. Upgrade	United States	Computer repair
Online BookStore	United States	Books
Reebok	United States	Footwear
Saturn	United States	Automobiles
Software.net	United States	Computer software
Sun Microsystems	United States	Computer hardware, software
TRADE'ex	United States	Computer equipment
Underground Music Archive	United States	Music
Wordsworth Books	United States	Books
Yvonne's Weinkabinett	Germany	Wine

Moreover, Apple saves money by providing customer support through this medium. According to a recent Dataquest report, Americans will make an estimated 200 million calls to help-desks in 1996, up from 120 million four years ago, with the average length of a call now 13 minutes instead of 8. At an estimated cost of $1.50 a minute to the company, calls to help-desks cost the personal computer industry $3.9 billion annually.[10] International service per capita is higher due to the higher costs of mail and fax services. Because marginal costs to access via the Web are minimal, once the site is built to handle the volume, a company such as Apple can reap savings by providing such software support electronically around the globe. Finally, the availability of such Web site services can differentiate Apple and enhance its image among customers and developers.

Quadrant 2

The companies in Quadrant 2 have a similar domestic focus as those in Quadrant 1 but also offer transactions on-line (or immediately via phone or fax). Internationally, the potential of such transactions enables a company to reach consumers who may be inaccessible via other media, due to the company's small size or the limitations of local distribution systems. For example, CD Now is able to offer worldwide customers recordings that, even after shipping and handling costs, are priced lower than at foreign retail outlets. LIGHTNING Instrumentation SA, a Swiss networking equipment manufacturer, experienced a 20 percent increase in sales after establishing a Web site, almost all from outside its domestic market.[11]

A site like Mr. Upgrade, an Arizona computer parts distributor, will secure half its 1995 international sales through orders placed on its Web site, despite the site's simple design and the buyers' inability to conduct their transactions directly on-line for security reasons. (Customers must call an 800 number to place an order.) Of its twelve international accounts (with combined orders of $700,000), half came via the Internet.[12]

Quadrant 3

This quadrant includes those businesses whose primary motivation for the Web site is attracting an international audience. Moreover, international customers explicitly add value; i.e., the service is more valuable to all users because of the international scope of operations. For example, Sun Microsystems provides global product support, software updates, and hardware service to its worldwide network of internal and external hardware users and software developers. An owner of a Sun system with offices worldwide will benefit from Sun's "one stop" service center where Sun can design solutions for the customer's problems worldwide and distribute them directly via the Internet. Thus, even without transactions, the capability to provide service worldwide instantaneously makes this a valuable medium.

Federal Express's tracking service also adds value in this way by enabling customers to track packages and estimate delivery times anywhere in the world. In addition, this service alone will save Federal Express almost $2 million annually, as the Web site takes the place of more expensive human operators.[13] The Building Industry

Exchange is a new information resource that serves as a global directory for the fragmented construction industry. Consulting Inc.'s corporate site provides links to resources for expatriates, business travelers, and international publications. The site also contains a directory of more than 400 e-mail addresses for users to contact offices and industry groups around the world directly.

Quadrant 4

Quadrant 4 companies expand on the capabilities of those in Quadrant 3 by offering transactions to customers worldwide. However, as opposed to Quadrant 2, because these transactions tend to involve the matching of buyers and sellers, both reap direct benefits from the global scope of the site. For example, DYNABIT U.S.A.'s new TRADE'ex service creates an exchange for commercial buyers and resellers of computer equipment around the globe. CapEx is a German company that matches entrepreneurs and investors for a range of start-up investment opportunities. Both companies serve as "market makers" by enabling communication between small parties who would not have found each other without this medium. These companies make their profits by taking a commission on consummated transactions and charging registration fees to buyers or sellers.

Another example is Underground Music Archive (UMA), for which international sales represent 30 percent of its business. The added value of this music collection is its "inventory" of 800 artists from more than twenty countries who provide downloadable samples of their music unavailable through traditional channels.

Global value-added can occur whether companies are targeting existing customers and providing service (Sun) or are attracting new customers (TRADE'ex or UMA). The business models represented by Quadrants 3 and 4 are built on the advantages of network externalities, through which benefits multiply exponentially as the network expands. In the computer world, this is often referred to as "Metcalf's Law," which states, "The value of a network—defined as its utility to a population—is roughly proportional to the number of users squared."[14] The scope and depth of the markets served thus influence the value of the services provided.

The Impact on Markets: Effects on Efficiency

Standard Pricing

Advances in Web browsers and servers will facilitate rapid, frequent price changes and levels of price differentiation to a much finer degree than are currently achieved in alternative media like magazines and direct mail. Prices can be customized, not only by country market, but at the level of the individual user.[15] When a user accesses a Web site, the page she receives when she clicks on a link can be made dependent on her IP address, which is embedded in the commands sent from her browser to the server. This means instant customization of information and prices across borders (as in airline computer reservation systems), furthering the potential for more efficient markets.

While pricing may therefore become both less standardized and more volatile, users will quickly become aware of such price discrimination and may not tolerate it. MNCs with overseas distributors charging different prices in different country markets face especially difficult obstacles. Bob MacPherson, the webmaster for Laboratory Equipment Exchange, an information resource for the sale of used scientific equipment, explains:

> The companies that advertise through my service . . . have to recognize that there are international consequences to their promotions. For example, if a company were to offer a 20 percent discount on some products to my readers, readers all over the world would see this deal. But in some countries where you have distributors or don't need to discount to get business, the special offer is a problem. So my information network is not attracting MNCs but rather small and medium-size businesses. The big MNCs are really sitting on the Internet fence waiting to see what happens.[16]

In addition, smart agents, software programs that can search the Internet for products meeting prespecified criteria, may further combat attempts at price discrimination by uncovering different prices. Taken together, these factors suggest that the Internet will lead to increased standardization of prices across borders or, at least, narrower price spreads across country markets.

Changing Role of Intermediaries

The Internet can connect end users with producers directly and thereby reduce the importance of (and value extraction by) intermediaries. The ubiquitous availability of the Web enables buyers, particularly in emerging markets, to access a broader range of product choices, bypass local intermediaries, and purchase their goods on the world market at lower prices. A hospital in Saudi Arabia, for example, can put out a request for proposal for equipment over the Internet, secure bids, select a supplier without going through local brokers and distributors, and have the products delivered directly by DHL or Federal Express. Few buffer inventories will be needed in the worldwide distribution system and less working capital will therefore be tied up in inventory.

However, if intermediaries can perform a different mix of services, made necessary by the Internet, they will continue to play critical roles and extract value.[17] While the Internet makes direct contact between end users and producers more feasible, this may also be less efficient over the long term and across a broad range of products. The potential for "information overload" is enormous. An intermediary's value-added may no longer be principally in the physical distribution of goods, but in the collection, collation, interpretation, and dissemination of vast amounts of information. For example, the hospital in Saudi Arabia needs to purchase a broad range of products, probably in differing quantities and at different times. Although it can contact each supplier directly, it would be more efficient to use a single distributor to collect the pricing and product information required, acting much like the robotic software search agents we described above.

The critical resource for such a distributor would then be information, not inventory. In the international context, the value of such timely, accurate information may be even higher. A logistics company like DHL can handle the physical distribution of goods. When the intermediary roles can be separated, we may see a simultaneous growth and fragmentation at this level of the distribution chain. Since economies of scale for the marketer would then be reduced, smaller companies would be able to compete more effectively in international markets using the Internet.

Making Markets

There are new opportunities for businesses to serve primarily as market makers, assisting buyers and sellers in locating one another, in negotiating terms of trade, and in executing secure transactions. The two principal market-making vehicles are auctions and exchanges.

Electronic auctions are usually continuous, and the bidders are physically separated. At a site such as OnSale, which auctions off new, but discontinued or outdated, computer equipment, buyers place their bids electronically and are notified continually of their status. Japan's experience with electronic car auctions supports the auctions' potential for expansion to consumer goods on a wide scale. (The average selling price increased in national versus local auctions due to the increased number of bidders.)[18]

Exchanges prescreen buyers and sellers, introduce them to one another, and assist in the transaction process, but do not help them agree on a price. United Computer Exchange offers market-making services for consumers interested in buying and selling used computer equipment. Although the company was established as a phone service, it moved onto the Web to increase its market scope, since both buyers and sellers can participate without making costly, time-dependent phone calls during the bidding process. Exchanges are examples of businesses in which there is true value-added from the international scope of the operations. While most current Internet exchanges are in the computer field, possible product categories include all forms of specialized equipment and consumer durables on a global scale.

Efficient Capital Flows

The efficiency of international capital flows and foreign direct investment may also increase. American Venture Capital Exchange (AVCE) advertises investment opportunities on the Internet to prospective investors. AVCE accepts only investors who have submitted an application and passed a screening process. The company takes a fee on any deals that are finalized as a result of bringing investors and investment opportunities together. Recently, about 15 of their nearly 200 listings were companies based outside the United States—11 were in Russia. CapEx offers a similar matching service, in both German and English, for potential entrepreneurs and investors. Many start-up companies benefiting from this increased access to capital and investment opportunities are small and located in emerging markets. Improved access to capital will be another factor in leveling the playing field between large and small businesses competing internationally.

Internal Implications: The Intranet

While the early audiences for most Web sites have been external customers, the potential for serving internal customers may be equally as great. Creating internal networks to facilitate communications and transactions among employees, suppliers, independent contractors, and distributors may be the Internet's principal value for MNCs. A 1995 Forrester report defined an intranet as "Internal corporate TCP/IP [transmission control protocol/Internet protocol] networks that carry Internet-developed applications like the Web—and its future cousins." Based on interviews with fifty large corporations, Forrester reported that 22 percent had internal Web servers, and 40 percent were seriously investigating installation. A recent article on intranets revealed that sales of Intranet server software had surpassed sales of Internet servers by the end of 1995, as companies recognized broader uses from intranet applications.[19] Internal Web servers have a number of advantages over classic client-server solutions. They are cheaper, faster, and easier to set up than client-server network systems, given the existing use of TCP/IP for outside communications; vendors are quickly developing new products specifically for this market; the architecture is already established and built into PCs; and the platform offers room for growth and flexibility.[20] Web-based internal networks can also offer sufficient security based on encryption technologies and allow companies to adjust levels of access based on a user's status. For example, business partners (e.g., suppliers or developers) can be given more limited access to the internal system than employees, who may themselves be assigned differential access based on their department and position within the company.

We briefly examine the potential value of an intranet as an internal communications vehicle by reviewing the types of communication that it facilitates.[21] First, companies can use the traditional "one to many" or broadcast model to communicate corporate policies and product or market news to worldwide divisions. Similarly, companies can provide employees worldwide with immediate and up-to-date access to company databases, phone directories, and reports. Second, in the "many to one" model, MNCs can use the internal system to ask questions or collect information from divisions and individual employees. Third, in the "many to many" model, perhaps the model with the greatest potential impact, MNCs can use the network to enable real-time, synchronous discussion *among* operating units.

Several intranet applications of these communication models are in use, often aimed at expediting relatively simple but costly and time-consuming tasks like information distribution. Xerox plans to connect its 90,000 employees via its intranet and has begun testing the network with 15,000 employees in 120 offices, primarily to distribute customer support information to salespeople.[22] Digital Equipment's intranet, residing on 400 internal servers, currently connects the company's 61,000 employees and offers a biweekly corporate newsletter, a proprietary search engine, restricted information to corporate partners, and support for sales and service staff.[23]

More complicated two-way communications take fuller advantage of the new technologies. Companywide bulletin boards permit multiparty dialogue on specific problems. As expertise on intranet usage spreads from the MIS department to marketing to other functions, companies can bring together functional departments located at sites around the globe to learn, share, and solve problems. They can also use these real-time forums as training vehicles for selected employees worldwide. Sun Microsystems broadcasts its corporate executives' speeches to its employees and archives them for later access. At Lawrence Livermore National Laboratory in California, employees take safety orientation classes and exams using an internal Web server equipped with audio and video capabilities.[24] Eli Lilly & Co. is using its intranet to manage clinical trials and drug approval processes in more than 120 countries. The network enables employees worldwide to access databases detailing the complex requirements for drug testing and approval in each country, facilitating the process of moving drugs through trials.[25]

In addition, companies are testing intranets as tools for internal transactions. AT&T recently introduced digital transaction technology across divisions that buy and sell goods from one another, so it can test, in a safe and friendly environment, whether it can facilitate internal money transfers before expanding to external transactions.[26]

External Implications: Global Product Reach

The global expansion of the Internet will facilitate both finding markets for new products and developing products for new markets.

New Product Diffusion.   New product announcements on the Internet will spawn immediate demand. To respond and to avoid competitive preemption, manufacturers will have to be prepared to distribute and service new products overnight. Slow test-as-you-go rollouts of new products from one country market to another will be less common. At the same time, using sophisticated technologies, companies may find it easier to test multiple new product variations simultaneously if they can control the information flow between test markets. When able to discriminate by a visitor's Internet address, companies can target variations of new products at different groups and get instant feedback on the value of specific features and appeal of various prices. For example, Digital Equipment allows potential customers to obtain demonstrations of its hardware on line and can offer product variations on the Internet as beta tests for new products.

Local Adaptation and Customization.   Marketers are finding it easier to adapt their products inexpensively to local or national preferences, due to factory and marketing customization. The Internet's new communication capabilities may speed this trend. However, if the global community is able to communicate more openly, the global mass-market concept will thrive as consumers retain their desire to share in the latest trends around the world. For example, Asia's imitation of European and American fashion trends will be that much more rapid, due to the instant dissemination of fashion news and widespread availability of direct purchase from U.S. manufacturers via the Internet.

Online BookStore, a U.S.-based book publisher up-loads chapters of its forthcoming books in multiple languages for visitors worldwide to "sample." The samples often include feedback links to authors and links to other relevant materials on the Internet as the company aims to customize publishing. Its unique marketing strategy has spawned both new distribution channels and translation of materials into local languages as site visitors from around the world demand the books after sampling the content. This customization is unique because it is driven by end-consumer demand for titles, not by foreign distributor interest as is customary in this industry.[27]

Niche Products. Small companies offering specialized niche products should be able to find the critical mass of customers necessary to succeed through the worldwide reach of the Internet. The Internet's low-cost communications permits firms with limited capital to become global marketers at the early stages of their development.[28] Indeed, the risk that entrepreneurs in other parts of the world will preempt their unique ideas demands that they do so.

Manufacturers of specialized equipment, such as medical and scientific equipment, are beginning to find markets through exchanges such as the Laboratory Equipment Exchange. As Bob MacPherson, the webmaster, explains:

> People seeking limited production parts or very specialized hardware can try to locate what they are seeking through my service. An American might not find what he or she is looking for in the United States for two reasons: (1) it is an old piece of hardware and parts are hard to find; or (2) the OEM may have been an offshore company that once thrived in the United States, but has since closed its North American operations.

Overcoming Import Restrictions. Many Internet retailers (selling, for example, CDs, books, or clothing) are finding that they can offer products to consumers directly via their Web sites for a delivered cost significantly lower than most international consumers find in their local retail outlets. However, with the Internet stimulating cross-border product flows, government import regulations may become stiffer.

Information flows have come under similar scrutiny. For example, CompuServe recently bowed to the German government's disapproval of a number of Internet news groups' pornographic content. Due to limitations in its technology, CompuServe was forced to limit all subscriber access worldwide to more than 200 news groups. This, in turn, spawned customers' opposition in countries where such access is legal; they felt their freedoms had been violated. Although the issue was resolved when CompuServe acquired the technology to enable differential screening, defining the boundaries of international law and the carrier's level of responsibility for such information is still being debated among commercial service providers, content providers, and governments.

Understanding Global Consumers

The Internet promises to be an efficient new medium for conducting worldwide market research. Marketers can test both new product concepts and advertising copy over the Internet for instant feedback. They can also test varying levels of customer support to help managers define country market priorities and adapt the marketing mix. Marketers can also establish worldwide consumer panels to test proposed marketing programs across national, regional, or cross-cultural samples. Tracking individual customer behavior and preferences will become easier over time. Requesting customers' consent to monitor such data may prove superior to existing methods of gathering or buying customer information, since the site visitors who voluntarily provide information are likely to be high-potential customers. Moreover, the Internet permits new types of measurement tools that will expand the data available to marketers, including:

- On-line Surveys. Marketers can post surveys on sites and offer incentives for participation. Internet surveys are more powerful than mail surveys because of the medium's "branching" capabilities (asking different questions based on previous answers) and are cheaper than either mail or phone surveys.

- Bulletin Boards. On-line bulletin boards are much like the traditional cork board, except that the software enables "threading" messages, so readers can follow a conversation and easily check responses to each posting. Companies can monitor and participate in such group discussions in many countries simultaneously.

- Web Visitor Tracking. Servers automatically collect data on the paths that visitors travel while in the site, including time spent at each page. Marketers can assess the value of the information and correlate the observed traffic patterns with purchase behavior.

- Advertising Measurement. Since servers automatically record the link through which each Web visitor enters a site, marketers can accurately assess the traffic, as well as sales, generated by links placed on other Web sites.

- Customer Identification Systems. Both business-to-business and consumer marketers are installing registration procedures that enable them to identify individuals and track purchases over time, creating a "virtual panel."

- E-mail Marketing Lists. Many sites ask customers to sign up voluntarily on a mailing list for company news. The audience generated appears very different from that garnered through traditional direct marketing. Internationally, information can be disseminated quickly to the audiences on these lists at minimal cost.

Challenges for International Marketers

The growth of the Internet as a facilitator of international commerce presents different challenges and opportunities to small Internet start-up companies and to MNCs. Some of the obstacles are unique to each company, while others confront all marketers striving to succeed globally on the Internet.

MNCs usually already do business internationally but may have to revise their operations, strategies, and business models if they want to exploit the opportunities offered by the Internet. The start-up doing business primarily through the Internet must be prepared to operate globally from the outset, which can strain its resources. The company must have (1) twenty-four-hour order taking and customer service response capability, (2) regulatory and customs-handling expertise to ship internationally, and (3) in-depth understanding of foreign marketing environments to assess the relative advantages of its own products and services. Successful start-ups need sufficient staff with multilingual skills and access to information on local laws and trends.

Global Branding

A major challenge for MNCs is the management of global brands and corporate name or logo identification. Consumers may be confused if a company and its subsidiaries have several Web sites, each communicating a different format, image, message, and content. 3M, which has one site for its entire product line, has a focused corporate identity and firm control over the marketing actions of its divisions and subsidiaries. However, many MNCs with one brand name have allowed local entities to develop sites ad hoc and now have several sites around the globe that require tighter coordination. For example, Coopers & Lybrand offices around the world each have their own Web sites using different servers. The Saab USA home page differs greatly in both tone and content from the Saab home page in Sweden. In addition, both sites offer links to a number of individual dealers' Web sites and unofficial sites of Saab enthusiasts. Tupperware, Avon, and Mary Kay have no main company sites, but independent sales representatives from around the world offer their wares directly over the Internet in a range of formats.

On the other hand, developing one site for each brand—while costly and limiting to cross-selling—is preferable when the brands have distinct markets and images. Kraft has already applied for 134 domain names, and Proctor & Gamble has reserved 110, although they are currently using only a small number of them.[29] Guinness PLC has separate sites for its beer and single malt Scotch whiskeys.

New Internet users tend to explore the sites of familiar brands first. Trust is a critical factor in stimulating purchases over the Internet, especially at this early stage of commercial development; as a result, sites with known brand names enhance the credibility of the site sponsor, as well as the medium. Recognizing the importance of brand names, many MNCs are establishing single Web sites for each brand.

New Competition

The Web will reduce the competitive advantage of scale economies in many industries and make it easier for small marketers to compete worldwide. First, advertising as a barrier to entry will be reduced as the Web makes it possible to reach a global audience more cheaply. Paying to place links on pages with audiences that mirror or include a company's target customers is less expensive than traditional media. In addition, "free" advertising on other sites can often be exchanged for mutual links. Postings on Internet discussion groups on topics relevant for specific products or markets is another way for small marketers to attract visitors to their sites.

Second, increased advertising efficiency will be available to more marketers. While current Internet usage is skewed heavily toward young, relatively affluent, educated males, further growth will result in a user population that more closely mirrors the broad population. C/Net, a Web computer news service, will soon be able to alter the advertisements to its site visitors, depending on the registered user's reported purchase behavior. Large index and directory sites like Yahoo can selectively show advertisements, depending on visitor characteristics such as hardware platform, domain name, or search topics selected during the visit.

Third, as the role of intermediaries evolves, gaining visibility and distribution will become easier for small companies. In the new Web malls, like the German Electronic Mall Bodensee and the U.S. Internet Shopping Network, small entrepreneurs can reach vast audiences. The traditional networks of international distributors and subsidiaries that MNCs set up are less effective barriers to the entry of smaller competitors than they used to be—except perhaps in the case of products that require significant after-sales service. These existing networks may even impede MNCs' effective, timely response. MacPherson remarked:

> Some small companies will grow at the expense of big companies. And some of my small business sponsors are seeing their business opportunities quadruple . . . because of the exposure that my site is giving them. These opportunities are at the expense of the MNC.

However, providing on-site after-sales service will be difficult for manufacturers of products sold directly via the Internet. Local distributors currently fulfill this role but will be unlikely to take it on without profiting from the accompanying sale. MNCs must develop policies for providing such service without disrupting the existing channel arrangements.

Competitive Advantage

For companies marketing on the Internet, technology is a more important source of competitive advantage than size. For example, TRADE'ex has proprietary software that enables direct communication and simplified, secure transactions among its member businesses. The company is now considering licensing its software system to companies in other industries. Another example is Agents Inc., a music company that has patented preference-mapping software. Members, who register on entering the site, describe their music preferences to "teach" the system what music they like. As members continue to rate recommended music, the system becomes smarter in predicting preferences and suggesting new music. A small company like this can quickly become a big player internationally by leveraging technology in ways that respond to customer needs. Virtual Vineyards, an Internet-based wine merchant, has developed a proprietary wine-rating system. Visitors to the site can compare ratings of each wine on line and, in the future, to their personal taste profile stored by the system.

What does this mean for large MNCs? The advantages of size will erode. As a result, many will need to proactively invent new ways of using the Internet to address customer needs and also to connect their worldwide operations. The current defensive stance that many large MNCs have adopted, which involves merely establishing "banner" presences on the Internet and hoping that they do not develop into a transactional medium, may well prove unsustainable.

Organizational Challenges

The Internet presents especially serious organizational challenges for MNCs attempting to convert their global businesses to the new medium because its speed and worldwide presence make its audiences intolerant of inconsistencies and slow response. The services that an MNC offers on the Internet should be available to buyers in all countries to prevent confusion and dissatisfaction. For example, although Federal Express's home page currently offers the ability to track a package worldwide, information on delivery options, pricing, and schedules are available only in the United States. FedEx has long been planning worldwide expansion of its service but is hesitant to act too quickly. Robert Hamilton, FedEx's Internet/Online services manager, explained:

> One thing FedEx is facing is the fact that we have a global brand. A huge percentage of our hits are non-U.S. One of the challenges . . . is how to establish local relevance, yet at the same time put this out to serve a global medium . Once you get a new service, or set of services, you want to be able to speak to those [local] issues. For example certain [services] that are available to Canadian customers aren't relevant elsewhere.[30]

An MNC must set up a worldwide task force of executives to coordinate the presentation of its corporate identity on multiple, interconnected Web sites. It might appoint a particular office or operating unit that has been a leader in using the Internet as the center for home page development. It also must have a system for regular updating of Web site information, especially if prices change or inventories go out of stock. Managers of Internet task forces must keep informed about developments around the globe. In addition, an MNC must establish policies for allocating credit for sales orders placed via the home page to foreign subsidiaries, lest the performance measures of the subsidiaries be disrupted.

A specialized customer service staff may be needed to deal with Internet traffic. Internet users have high expectations for timely, efficient response, due to their knowledge of the company's expanded capabilities. For example, if the home page offers a visitor a way to give customer feedback or send questions to the company, customer service reps must answer quickly and monitor customers' e-mail for changes in content, tone, and origin. A company's Internet center should also analyze the server data that tracks customer site access and transactions.

Some sales may be consummated via the Internet, but the Web will probably not become the primary advertising and distribution vehicle for most products and services—except for financial and information services that can be completely delivered on the Web. Marketers will need to integrate their marketing communications and distribution for Internet customers with their existing strategies.

Disseminating Information

News of product quality problems and cross-border differences in quality, price, and availability will be hard to contain. Critical reviews of Intel's Pentium chip and Microsoft's Windows 95 software spread quickly across the Internet. News of bugs in Netscape's security system reached around the world in hours. There will inevitably be a need for a worldwide approach to crisis management; controversies, especially those surrounding global brands, will be impossible to contain at the national level.

There are other implications of the rapid information flow. Third-party "search agents" can collect pricing information through robots from various sources around the world, so consumers can compare prices and products. This is especially important in emerging markets where such sources of information (like *Consumer Reports*) are not widely available. For example, Andersen Consulting's "Smart Store" seeks the lowest prices on any certificate of deposit that a user requests.[31] In response, many sites are building software codes into their servers to block the robots so that they can continue to vary prices and product offerings by market.

Maintaining Web Sites

The creation of a Web site is not a one-time effort. A 1995 Forrester report shows that annual costs for site maintenance are two to four times the initial launch cost.[32] The current speed of technological innovation in Web site design and the increasing competitiveness of the medium require global marketers to continually assess their Internet sites' perceived value among target groups across countries. Sites must offer valuable, changing content that will not only attract new customers from many countries but also encourage them to return. Given that individuals around the world will have different product information needs, levels of brand familiarity, and bandwidth capacity, fulfilling such diverse needs on a single site will be challenging.

Currently, most company Web pages are merely online brochures, with added links to related information. Increased sophistication of server software will facilitate more complex content and more customized paths tailored to each visitor through a site. However, many Internet users outside the United States, at least in the short run, will have lower bandwidth and be paying higher prices for access, and therefore will not be able to access complicated graphics quickly and inexpensively. Site sponsors will need to recognize that the users' capabilities in hardware, software, and computer expertise will vary significantly across borders.

Most sites are organized as hierarchical layers of documents, with the rule of thumb that users should not have to delve more than three layers before they access valued information. However, new technologies will permit sophisticated matching of pages to user needs. For example, Software.net delivers Web pages dependent on the user's platform, identified by the server software. Macintosh users see Macintosh offers, while PC users see Windows software. Rockport plans to give its Web site visitors the option of classifying themselves as "rugged," "relaxed," or "refined." Based on each visitor's choice, he or she will see very different sites with specific navigation options. Federal Express recently announced plans to implement new software with different services, advertisements, and interfaces based on the user's country of origin, business type, and bandwidth.[33]

However, with new technologies and the proliferation of Web design and management companies, the temptation to customize content will have to be weighed against the value of maintaining a consistent worldwide image. In addition, companies will have to choose how to maintain, grow, and manage their sites. Should they outsource? Or should they strive to create proprietary content and software?

Language and Culture Barriers

The Web promises to reinforce the trend toward English as the lingua franca of commerce. There are significant obstacles in translating Chinese and Japanese to the computer, especially the large number of local dialects. In addition, the importance of vocal intonations in these spoken languages may further impede the transfer of business dialogue from voice to text.

Very few MNCs offer translations of their Web site content into local languages. Several translation services have opened on the Internet. In addition, exposure itself raises opportunities. For example, a Japanese company recently approached Catalog-Site, an Internet-based mall of catalogs to translate many of its catalogs into Japanese. One enterprising European on-line service based in Sardinia, Video On Line, is quickly expanding its user base by focusing on local content in local languages. The company overcomes the prohibitive costs of telephone use for Europeans by providing direct access through three high-speed dedicated lines between Sardinia, Stockholm, and the United States. Owner Nicola Grauso plans to expand from Sardinia and Italy to thirty countries in four continents, offering local language content in each, including more than a dozen African dialects.[34]

However, cultural barriers remain. When setting up a traditional business operation in a foreign country, managers usually have numerous conversations with local partners and visit the country several times. With a virtual business, the need for such contacts is minimized, and cultural differences may not be as apparent. To avoid cultural pitfalls, many small entrepreneurs without broad contacts use Internet discussion groups to become familiar with local customs, trends, and laws.

Government Influence and Involvement

Foreign government support and cooperation will be critical in determining how the international Internet business environment will evolve. Will foreign governments allow the free flow of trade and ideas? Will they be able to agree on issues such as data security, taxation on transactions, and pornography? Who will lead in developing the infrastructure, educating users, and providing access to the Internet for businesses and consumers?

Early initiatives by some governments, trade associations, and telecommunication companies bode well for future expansion. For example:

- More than 40 organizations in 10 eastern European nations provide Internet services to an estimated 350,000 local consumers and businesses, an increase from only 5,000 in 1992.[35]

- In Thailand, the National Electronics and Computer Technology Center, in cooperation with the state-owned telecommunications industry, is investing $10 million to develop the Internet infrastructure.

- In Russia, where only 500,000 computers were sold last year, the number of subscribers to on-line services is only 10 percent that in the United States, but increasing at 5 percent per month.[36]

- Israel has recently established a local search engine where inquirers can search for Israeli-based Internet resources.[37]

- Europe Online, the counterpart of America Online, attempts to bring together resources from around Europe, concentrating on entertainment, news, and travel.

- New Zealand focuses its national site, Gateway to New Zealand, on providing visitors with information on travel, commerce, education, weather, and recreation and on giving links to a range of local businesses that offer information and transactions on-line.

- In Latin America, there are more than 15,000 Internet connections, half established within the last year. Many Latin American sites are at universities or on servers in the United States.

- The National Telephone Company in Nicaragua has leased a satellite link to Florida to offer local Internet access to consumers and businesses.

- The Chilean National University Network gives commercial access to private businesses to fund its own growth and further Internet usage in the country.[38]

Some governments in Asia have aggressively led in development of the Internet infrastructure in their countries to further economic growth and to retain control over external access and internal usage. ChinaWeb actively promotes cross-border marketing by Chinese companies, highlighting how conducting business on the Internet can reduce costs and help companies reach specialized marker segments in diverse geographical locations. ChinaWeb also offers links to the Shanghai Stock Exchange, with daily updated stock quotes; the Pudong Investment Center, with information on Pudong's special economic zone; Air China, with online booking for its flights; a travel agency that offers additional travel arrangements within China; a career directory; and an e-mail database of exporters. The government of the People's Republic of China actively solicits corporate sponsorships by luring companies with the possibility of reaching Chinese people in the United States. However, ChinaWeb does not offer similar opportunities to foreign marketers seeking access to Chinese consumers.

The United Nations has established a "Global Trade Point Network" that assists small and medium-size companies eager to expand globally by linking interested entrepreneurs with information resources on trade regulations, trade associations, and local markets. Similarly, the Hong Kong Trade Development Council has established a computerized "Trade Enquiry Service" that matches overseas buyers with Hong Kong manufacturers and traders in a range of industries. The current database includes more than 320,000 importers, 140,000 Chinese businesses, and 70,000 Hong Kong manufacturers, classified by name, country, and product.[39]

Such government-sponsored "megasites" are more common in Europe and Asia than in the United States and reflect the countries' emphasis on government-led economic development. In Europe, small businesses are likely to establish an on-line presence through regional cooperatives and state organizations that promote local business. In the United States, individual small businesses have rapidly exploited the new opportunities on their own. While joint development efforts reduce costs and risks, they also limit an individual company's freedom to innovate and invest in aggressive marketing on the Web.[40]

Several countries have not yet signed the Bern Convention, which governs copyrights, or enforced the 1994 GATT policies on intellectual property. China and Thailand limit internal use of the Internet to research and academic projects. Quite recently, China has been reevaluating its internal access policies. The government is currently exploring the use of software that will enable it to screen the Internet information flows into, out of, and within the country, creating its own national Intranet.[41] In addition, many countries in central and eastern Europe resist the Internet because it threatens to open the culture and people to outside influences too broadly and rapidly.[42] The Internet Society Summit established an Internet Law Task Force in spring 1995 to explore solutions to problems such as privacy, warning labels, copyright and trademark protection, and taxation and to persuade reluctant governments to open Internet access.[43] Nonetheless, numerous issues remain to be resolved:

- Defining the scope of import tariffs and export controls.
- Delineating the boundaries of intellectual copyrights.
- Standardizing regulations on the use and sale of personal information.
- Defining the roles of national governments in limiting the inflow of ideas.
- Creating cross-national laws for regulated industries such as gambling, financial services, and liquor.

An equally daunting obstacle is the poor state of the current infrastructure and the regulation of the telecommunications industry abroad. For example, the Czech Republic's phone company cannot yet provide leased lines with adequate transmission speeds outside Prague. There are currently only 1.7 phones per 100 people in Africa, and little impetus and funds for state-owned monopoly telecommunication companies to invest.[44] In Mexico, consumers often have to wait more than a year for phone service installation. Similar situations prevail throughout developing countries in eastern Europe, Asia, Latin America, and Africa and highly regulated countries in western Europe. These countries need to invest in better telecommunications infrastructures and to promote internal competition before they can take full advantage of the opportunities the Internet offers for global commerce.

Conclusion

While the Internet offers many benefits to both existing MNCs and start-up companies—and, perhaps, to their customers—the challenges of an inadequate technological infrastructure, concerned public policymakers, and, especially for MNCs, existing distribution and organization structures all seem formidable. Any company eager to take advantage of the Internet on a global scale must select a business model for its Internet venture and define how information and transactions delivered through this new medium will influence its existing model. The company must also assess who its diverse Web audiences are, what specific customer needs the medium will satisfy, and how its Internet presence will respond to a changing customer base, evolving customer needs, competitor actions, and technological developments. For international marketers, achieving a balance between the new medium's ability to be customized and the desire to retain coherence, control, and consistency as they go to market worldwide will be a major challenge.

Notes

1. G.F. Colony, H.W. Deutsch, and T.B. Rhinelander, "Network Strategy Service: CIO Meets the Internet," *The Forrester Report*, volume 12 (Cambridge, Massachusetts: Forrester Consulting, May 1995).
2. As of July 1995, according to an Internet domain survey by Network Wizards, obtained from <http://www.nw.com>. Host computers are those connected directly to Internet gateways. A host computer can serve anywhere from one to hundreds of users, depending on the network set-up.
3. B. Bournellis, "Internet's Phenomenal Growth Is Mirrored in Startling Statistics," *Internet World*, volume 6, November 1995.
4. See <http://www.comnex.com>.
5. B. Giussani, "Why Europe Lags on the Web," *Inc.*, 15 November 1995, p. 23.
6. S. Gupta and J. Pitkow, "Consumer Survey of WWW Users: Preliminary Results from 4th Survey," December 1995, obtained from <http://www.umich.edu/~sgupta/hermes/>.
7. These figures, for the World Wide Web alone, were calculated from "Trends in the WorldWide Marketplace," Activmedia, at <http://www.activmedia.com>, 1996. Current estimates of transaction volume, especially predictions of future volume, vary widely based on the source of the data and the types of media included. For example, Forrester Research, in a May 1995 report, estimated 1996 transaction volume from all interactive retail (Internet, WWW, CD-ROMs, and commercial on-line services) at only $500 million.
8. Results reported from a Rochester Institute of Technology survey of 378 Internet shoppers conducted between February and May of 1995, obtained from <http://www.rit.edu>.
9. S. Butterbaugh, "More Than a Pretty Face: FedEx Gears up for a Brand-Intensive 1996," Interactive Monitor, Media Central, obtained from <http://mediacentral.com>, December 1995.
10. S. Lohr, "When Pointing and Clicking Fails to Click: More and More Questions, and Employees, at Computer Help Services, *New York Times*, 1 January 1996, p. 45.
11. T. Seiderman, "Making Net Export Profits," *International Business*, August 1995, pp. 47-50.
12. Giussani (1995).
13. A. Cortese, "Here Comes the Intranet," *Business Week*, 26 February 1996, p. 76.
14. C. Anderson, "The Accidental Superhighway," *The Economist*, 1 July 1995, pp. S1-S26.
15. Currently, there are some intricacies that may complicate this. Due to the international use of both domain (.edu, .com, .gov, .net) and country codes, it is sometimes difficult to identify the visitor's country if he or she is using a domain code. However, more comprehensive databases of hosts, more sophisticated server matching schemes, and user registration procedures can overcome this.
16. Quoted from personal interview with MacPherson via e-mail, January 1996.
17. See M.B. Sarkar, B. Butler, and C. Steinfeld, "Intermediaries and Cybermediaries: A Continuing Role for Mediating Players in the Electronic Marketplace," in R.R. Dholakia and D.R. Fortin, eds., *Proceedings from Conference on Telecommunications and Information Markets*, October 1995, pp. 82-92.
18. See A. Warbelow, J. Kokuryo, and B. Konsynski, "AUCNET" (Boston: Harvard Business School. Case #9-190-001, July 1989).
19. For examples of the range of Intranet applications in use, see. Cortese (1996), pp. 76-84.
20. P.D. Callahan, D. Goodtree, A.E. Trenkle, and D.F. Cho, "Network Strategy Service: The Intranet," *The Forrester Report*, volume 10 (Cambridge, Massachusetts: Forrester Consulting, December 1995).

21. For a review and application of these models to the new media, see:
D. Hoffman and T. Novak, "Marketing in Hypermedia Computer-Mediated Environments: Conceptual Foundations" (Nashville, Tennessee: Vanderbilt University, Owen Graduate School of Management, Working Paper No. 1, July 1995).

22. J.E. Frook, " 'Intranets' Grab Mind Share," *Communications Week*, 20 November 1995, p. 1.

23. J. Carl, "Digital's Intranet Comes Together," *Web Week*, volume 2, January 1996, p. 25.

24. K. Murphy, "Web Proves Useful as Training Platform," *Web Week*, volume 2, January 1996.

25. N. Gross, "Here Comes the Intranet," *Business Week*, 26 February 1996, p. 82.

26. E. Booker, "AT&T Using Internal Web to Test Digital Payments," *Web Week*, volume 1, December 1995.

27. See <http://www.obs-us.com/obs/>.

28. M.W. Rennie, "Global Competitiveness: Born Global," *McKinsey Quarterly*, 22 September 1993, pp. 45-52.

29. The policies of domain registration have created a frenzy to register brand names and trademarks since current trademark laws do not cover the registration of domain names. The company responsible for the allocation of the domain names, InterNIC, allocates names on a first-come, first-served basis with the agreement by domain holders that InterNIC will not be held liable for trademark infringements. For further information, see: "InterNIC Security," *Wired*, 4.01, January 1996, p. 74.

30. Butterbaugh (1995).

31. See <http://bf2.cstar.ac.com/smartstore/>.

32. J. Bernoff and A. Ott, "People and Technology: What Web Sites Cost," *The Forrester Report*, volume 2 (Cambridge, Massachusetts: Forrester Consulting, December 1995).

33. Butterbaugh (1995).

34. L. Marshall, "The Berlusconi of the Net," *Wired*, 4.01, January 1996, pp. 78-85.

35. D. Rocks, N. Ingelbrecht, R. Castillo, and D. Peachey, "Developing World Seeks Highway On-Ramp," *Communications Week*, 2 October 1995, p. 39.

36. J. Zander, "Russia Makes Net Progress," *TechWeb*, obtained from <http://techweb.cmp.com/ia/0108issue/0108issue.html>.

37. See <http://www.xpert.com/search/>.

38. Rocks et al. (1995).

39. See <http://www.tdc.org.hk/main/main.html>.

40. Guissani (1995).

41. J. Kahn, K. Chen, and M.W. Brauchli, "Chinese Firewall," *Wall Street Journal*, 31 January 1996, p. A1.

42. C. Grycz, "The International Aspects of Internetting" (Boston: Fall Internet World 1995 on CD-ROM, 1995).

43. C. Mendler, "Stop! Or I'll Yell Stop Again!," *Communications Week*, 2 October 1995, p. 28.

44. Rocks et al. (1995).

II

Implications of the Internet Age for Marketing

Peterson, Robert A, Sridhar Balasubramanian, and Bart J. Bronnenberg (1997), "Exploring the Implications of the Internet for Consumer Marketing," *Journal of the Academy of Marketing Science*, 25 (4), 329–346.

Burke, Raymond R. (1997), "Do You See What I See? The Future of Virtual Shopping," *Journal of the Academy of Marketing Science*, 25 (4), 352–360.

Peacock, Peter R. (1998), "Data Mining in Marketing: Part 1," *Marketing Management*, 6, (Winter), 8–18.

Peacock, Peter R. (1998), "Data Mining in Marketing: Part 2," *Marketing Management*, 7, (Spring), 15–25.

II

Implications of the Internet Age for Marketing

Part II contains papers that focus on implications for the existing "brick and mortar" marketing. For example, as the Internet enables consumers to gather information, interact, exchange and procure products and services at anytime and from anywhere; and as they become more co-producers with automation and integration of procurement and consumption, all product industries (agriculture and industrial) will become more and more services industries. In service industries, consumers are co-producers; there is simultaneity of procurement and consumption; and time and location boundaries are less far apart.

At the same time, the role of the intermediaries changes to one of an infomediary or an agent and the producer and the consumer more directly engage the market transactions. This is particularly relevant in international markets where an intermediary such as a distributor (wholesaler) and a dealer (retailer) are often more prevalent. The best examples of this international "disintermediation" are the direct global sales of personal computers by Dell and routers and servers by Cisco Systems. In most business-to-business marketing, this seems inevitable.

These and other broad implications of the Internet age for marketing are discussed by several reading in Part II. The Peterson and Balasubramanian's article, *Exploring the Implications of the Internet for Consumer Marketing* provides a framework for understanding possible impacts of the Internet on marketing to consumers. This is done by analyzing channel intermediary functions that can be performed on the Internet, suggesting classification schemes that clarify the potential impact of the Internet across different products and services, positioning the Internet against conventional retailing channels, and identifying similarities and differences that exist between them. The article concludes with a series of questions designed to stimulate the development of theory and strategy in the context of Internet-based marketing.

Burke's article (*Do You See What I See?*) suggests that marketers are most likely to use the Internet in cases where its unique characteristics make it a viable and attractive substitute for the functions of traditional channel intermediaries. Because of its ability to transform information quickly and inexpensively, the Internet will have the greatest impact on marketing communications, a moderate effect on sales transactions, and a minimal impact on logistics. The reasons why it has been so difficult to forecast the impact of new communication technologies on retailing are explored. The ways in which existing retailers might respond to this new technology are discussed.

Part II concludes with a two-part series. In the first one, *Data Mining in Marketing: Part 1*, Peacock examines several driving factors of the data mining revolution and applications to marketing problems. The article describes categories of data mining tasks and explains the principal weapons in the data mining arsenal, including query tools, descriptive statistics, visualization tools, regression-type models, association rules, decision trees, case-based reasoning, neural networks, and genetic algorithms.

Data Mining in Marketing: Part 2, posits that data mining is part of a much larger process known as *knowledge discovery in databases* (KDD). The knowledge discovery process includes 10 phases, from data funneling to recalibrating models. Senior marketing managers can put a KDD operation in place by following seven steps, but they also must be attuned to issues such as value measurement, consumer privacy concerns, and appropriate responses to the ongoing data explosion. While the first of the two article series is about the whys of data mining and KDD process, the second one addresses the issue of how to go about the KDD process.

6

Exploring the Implications of the Internet for Consumer Marketing

ROBERT A. PETERSON
SRIDHAR BALASUBRAMANIAN
BART J. BRONNENBERG
University of Texas at Austin

Past commentaries on the potential impact of the Internet on consumer marketing have typically failed to acknowledge that consumer markets are heterogeneous and complex and that the Internet is but one possible distribution, transaction, and communication channel in a world dominated by conventional retailing channels. This failure has led to excessively broad predictions regarding the effect of the Internet on the structure and performance of product and service markets. The objective of this article is to provide a framework for understanding possible impacts of the Internet on marketing to consumers. This is done by analyzing channel intermediary functions that can be performed on the Internet, suggesting classification schemes that clarify the potential impact of the Internet across different products and services, positioning the Internet against conventional retailing channels, and identifying similarities and differences that exist between them. The article concludes with a series of questions designed to stimulate the development of theory and strategy in the context of Internet-based marketing.

Robert A. Peterson holds the John T. Stuart III Centennial Chair in Business Administration and is the Charles E. Húrwitz fellow at the University of Texas at Austin. A former editor of the *Journal of the Academy of Marketing Science* and *Journal of Marketing Research*, he currently chairs the board of governors of the Academy of Marketing Science. **Sridhar Balasubramanian** (Ph.D., Yale University) is an assistant professor of marketing at the University of Texas at Austin. His research interests include the competitive and cooperative interface between electronic and traditional retail channels, customer equity modeling, and the application of options theory in marketing. **Bart J. Bronnenberg** is an assistant professor of marketing at the University of Texas at Austin. His research interests are psychological models of economic behavior, consumer choice and choice protocol and advertising. His work has been published in the *Journal of Marketing Research, Marketing Science, Journal of Retailing and Consumer Service*, and *R&D Management*.

Throughout the 20th century, pundits and prognosticators alike have proffered visions of consumers shopping electronically. For example, 30 years ago Doody and Davidson (1967) articulated a vision of electronic shopping that incorporated a flexible, yet comprehensive, shopping and distribution system for grocery products, drugs, and sundries. Consumers shopped by means of computer-type consoles linked electronically to a central distribution facility that employed, among other things, electronic funds transfer to control costs. Automated order filling of frequently purchased goods was routine, and next-day delivery was standard. In addition to presenting what turned out to be a remarkably prescient vision of electronic shopping (one similar to the current business models of such firms as Peapod, Streamline, and ShoppingLink), Doody and Davidson also noted several implications of their vision, including structural changes in marketing channels and changes in the roles of advertising and packaging.

Ten years later, Isaac Asimov (1977:53), a leading science fiction writer and noted futurist, expressed a similar vision:

> The year 2025 will see the "drive-in market," a kind of computerized convenience store. The customer will call the store by using his own computer, and make his grocery list. The order will automatically be picked off the shelves of a computerized warehouse, packed, and ready for pickup by car, or whatever mechanized vehicle we'll be driving in the next century. Only liquids will not be packaged this way.

The visions of Doody and Davidson and Asimov were extended by McNair and May (1978), Rosenberg and Hirschman (1980), and Schneiderman (1980), who shared the belief that electronic shopping would become the dominant mode of shopping. McNair and May (1978) wrote that "some authorities expect that by early in the twenty-first century, almost all food and other basic household needs will be acquired through the use of in-home television computer systems, and shopping choices will be made after viewing assortments, selections, prices, and brands on the television screen, together with programming of the household's customary wants, needs, customs, and habits" (p. 81). Rosenberg and Hirschman in particular believed that electronic shopping by consumers would irreversibly transform conventional retailing. Schneiderman (1980) went so far as to predict that by 1990, "American consumers will be buying fully one-half of all general merchandise without setting foot in a retail store" (p. 60).

In general, past visions of electronic shopping can be characterized as having enthusiastic presumptions regarding its pervasiveness and the influence it would have on marketing and consumer behavior. (Doody and Davidson believed that their vision would be operational in the 1970s.) Moreover, all of these visions implicitly assumed that shopping and purchasing would be accomplished through single-source electronic sales channels, computer-based systems that were closed (i.e., proprietary) and, by implication, incompatible with each other. Beginning in the late 1980s, however, several observers realized that single-source electronic sales channels were evolving into electronic markets wherein multiparty exchanges could take place (e.g., Bakos 1991; Malone, Yates, and Benjamin 1989). These electronic markets, as epitomized by the

SABRE and Apollo airline reservation systems, were envisioned as being operated by intermediaries, who could be buyers, sellers, independent third parties, or even multi-firm consortia (Bakos 1991). Like single-source electronic sales channels, electronic markets were assumed to be based on proprietary computer systems that had restricted access. Most discussions of electronic markets also focused on technical issues in the context of business-to-business marketing; consumer marketing received little attention.

Objective

Despite the ongoing interest in electronic shopping and electronic markets, until recently no one appears to have acknowledged the existence of the Internet or speculated on what, if any, role it might ultimately play in consumer marketing. For example, even such respected visionaries as Hyde, Steidtmann, and Sweeney (1990) failed to acknowledge the existence of the Internet and foresee its potential impact on marketing to consumers. Similarly, despite undertaking a major investigation of the implications of emerging technologies for marketing practice, Deloitte & Touche (1990) completely overlooked the existence of the Internet. These oversights may be attributed to the fact that the Internet was not widely accessible for commercial or public use until approximately 1992, although it had been operational a decade earlier. As recently as 1994, the number of commercial users was only in the hundreds.

Interest in the Internet is unprecedented, and its use in marketing is increasing exponentially. (For a good summary of marketing applications on the Internet, see the special section Selling in Cyberspace in the June 17, 1996, issue of the *Wall Street Journal*.) Even so, most of what is currently "known" about the potential impact of the Internet on consumer marketing is based on anecdotes, experiential evidence, and ad hoc descriptive studies (e.g., Bredenberg 1995; Taylor 1995). With few exceptions (e.g., Alba et al. 1997; Berthon, Pitt, and Watson 1996a; Quelch and Klein 1996), little systematic attention or serious thought has been given to the major long-term implications of the Internet for consumer marketing.

Examining the Internet in the context of consumer marketing and consumer behavior thus seems appropriate at this time. In particular, the present objective is to address a deceptively straightforward question: What are some of the major implications of the Internet for consumer marketing? Before attempting to answer this question, however, it is necessary to provide a brief history of the Internet to detail certain aspects that relate to consumer marketing. This history will serve as a frame of reference for the discussion to follow.

From virtually any perspective, the Internet can be considered a market discontinuity in the Mahajan and Wind (1989) sense because it represents a "shift in any of the market forces or their interrelationships that cannot be predicted by a continuation of historical trends and that, if it occurs, can dramatically affect the performance of a firm or an industry" (p. 187). Consequently, analogous to any market discontinuity, it is not possible to predict precisely the specific impacts of the Internet, especially given the velocity with which Internet-related changes are occurring and the increasingly assertive and unpredictable behavior of consumers (cf. Fox 1995; Molenaar 1996:102 ff).

Therefore, rather than attempt to "peer" into the future, an attempt will be made to provide a rudimentary foundation or framework for future analyses and predictions. In addition, two Internet-related issues currently attracting the attention of both academics and practitioners will be examined: market disintermediation and price competition. A major tenet of the article is that marketing implications of the Internet cannot be considered in isolation or limited to on-line commerce. All Internet-related marketing activities take place in the context of marketing activities in conventional marketing channels and must be considered in this context.

No attempt will be made to quantify the potential impact of the Internet or forecast the rate at which Internet access and usage will diffuse. Given the brief history and (epidemic-like) expansion of the Internet, any attempt at quantification would require unacceptable levels of speculation and would detract from the present objective. The article will conclude, in accordance with the editorial guidelines set forth by Cravens (1997), with a series of questions regarding the Internet's implications for marketing research, theory, and strategy.

Internet Background

Throughout this article, the term *Internet* will be used in a generic or conceptual sense to refer to a type of global information infrastructure consisting of computer hardware and software that is characterized as both general and open. The Internet is "general" in that it was not designed for a specific set of services. Indeed, many of the currently available services, such as direct, real-time interaction, had not even been conceived when the Internet was designed. The Internet is "open" in that all specifications required to use it are publicly available; anyone who observes certain protocols can access and traverse it. As such, the Internet is the antithesis of the centrally organized and managed electronic sales channels and electronic markets previously discussed.

Conceptually, the Internet represents an extremely efficient medium for accessing, organizing, and communicating information. As such, the Internet subsumes communications technologies ranging from the written and spoken word to visual images. Levy (1996) believed the Internet would ultimately become "the medium by which we keep in constant contact with our families, watch television, dash off a note to a friend, check the traffic, read the newspaper, prepare a report for work, make a phone call, buy a book" (p. 52).

Technically, the Internet is a highly decentralized network of computer networks that includes backbone networks, wide area networks (WANs), and local area networks (LANs). It originated in the 1960s when the Department of Defense, through its Advanced Research Projects Agency (ARPA), funded research on linking computer networks that were currently incompatible and automatically rerouting information around damaged or nonfunctioning components of a network. One result was the ARPANET backbone network. Subsequently, other networks not affiliated with ARPANET were created, such as BITNET and Usenet, and the National Science Foundation funded the creation of a much faster backbone network termed NSFNET. Although NSFNET eventually absorbed ARPANET and other networks, it was superseded in 1992 by ANSNET, a backbone network owned and operated by a consortium of firms. At this juncture, the Internet, which by then had become an amalgamation of many networks, became generally available for commercial ventures, with the consequences being well publicized (Comer 1995).

One of the consequences was the emergence of the World Wide Web (Web or WWW), an Internet service that organizes information using hypermedia and, at the moment, seems to possess the most potential for marketing (cf. Ainscough and Luckett 1996; Hoffman and Novak 1996). Berthon et al. (1996b) characterized the World Wide Web as the combination of an electronic trade show and a community flea market:

> As an electronic trade show, it resembles a giant international exhibition hall where potential buyers can enter at will and visit prospective sellers. They may do this passively by simply wandering around, enjoying the sights and sounds, pausing to pick up a pamphlet or brochure here, a sticker, key ring, or sample there. Some buyers might even become vigorously interactive in their search for information and want-satisfaction. They can talk to fellow attendees, actively seek the booths of particular exhibitors, carefully examine products and services, solicit richer information, and even engage in sales transactions with the exhibitor. . . . As a flea market, the Web possesses the fundamental characteristics of openness, informality, and interactivity— a combination of a community and a marketplace. (p. 25)

Numerous initiatives are under way to make the Internet more efficient and effective, including Internet2 and Next Generation Internet. Moreover, the federal government seems committed to creating what is commonly referred to as the information superhighway, or National Information Infrastructure (NII), of which the Internet is but the first part. These initiatives obviously have significant implications for society as a whole and for marketing in particular.

Because of the rapidity with which Internet initiatives and related technologies are unfolding and evolving, it is necessary to make four broad assumptions to facilitate the present analysis. Although these assumptions are not critical to the analysis or the conclusions, they simplify the analysis and eliminate potential distractions.

Facilitating Assumptions

The first assumption is that eventually there will be near-universal access to the Internet, at least in the United States. Although Internet usage may never become as ubiquitous as television viewing, a large and broad cross section of consumers will be able to access the Internet for both business and pleasure. This will result in part because of governmental concern that without broad access to the Internet, society will be bifurcated into those who are informationally impoverished and those who are not.

The second assumption is that use of the Internet for marketing purposes will not increase overall consumer spending. This assumption is not unique to this article (see, for example, Shi and Salesky 1994). There is no intuitive reason why the Internet, or any service based thereon, will in and of itself cause consumers to spend more. Rather, use of the Internet in marketing to consumers will more likely result in a redistribution of revenues among channels or among members within a channel (e.g., Hagel and Eisenmann 1994).

The third assumption relates to infrastructure technologies. As Economides (1996) so aptly noted, structurally the Internet consists of substitutes made of complements. Information transmission can be accomplished by dedicated landlines, television cables, standard telephone lines, wireless satellite links, and so forth. Access devices can be portable or fixed and range from television set-top boxes, workstations, personal computers, and network or Internet computers to information appliances (e.g., voice recognition and natural language processors) that are today unknown. Hence, one infrastructure technology issue relates to what combination of transmission modes and access devices, if any, will ultimately prevail (or, perhaps more appropriately, dominate) in the marketplace. Regardless of the outcome, the basic impact of the Internet on consumer marketing is likely to be unaffected.

An additional infrastructure technology issue relates to what some have forecast as the imminent collapse or demise of the Internet due to switching and transmission capabilities becoming congested and overwhelmed because of an unmanageable number of users. Although this possibility exists, it is assumed that the problem will be overcome through market forces and technical advances. For example, usage-based or priority pricing has been suggested as a mechanism for managing Internet activity (e.g., MacKie-Mason and Varian 1995). Likewise, technical advances on the order of ADSL (asymmetrical digital subscriber line) or even unforeseen market discontinuities are likely to materialize as solutions to transmission speed and congestion problems. In brief, both of the infrastructure technology issues (as well as related technology issues) will most likely be satisfactorily resolved and hence will not significantly influence the impact of the Internet on consumer marketing.

The fourth assumption relates to the issue of transaction security and privacy on the Internet. Transaction security (and authorization) is currently a high-profile issue. In many respects, however, this issue poses few long-term problems. It will probably be solved through a combination of E-cash or digital tokens, encryption/decryption technologies, and new forms of personal identification.

A more important issue involves network privacy and what information consumers will be willing to share with others. Information on Internet transactions can be easily captured, and it is possible to track a consumer's travels on the Internet in great detail. When a consumer's transactions and travel information are linked to other information residing in a myriad of massive databases, no secret is safe. Consumers may be willing to provide information about themselves, but at a cost to the requesting entity. Hagel and Rayport (1997) predicted that companies will emerge to represent consumers and manage their information (i.e., negotiate on their behalf and obtain remuneration for the use of information). Ultimately, as Leibrock (1997) noted, the issue of security and privacy on the Internet is a societal one and, as such, must be resolved at that level (see also Bloom, Milne, and Adler 1994 for related perspectives). Currently, the internet is like a frontier, there are few rules, and enforcement of the rules that do exist is frequently through vigilante-style justice (Spar and Bussgang 1996). Many technical, security, and privacy issues have yet to be resolved, and some will probably require government intervention. Still, the assumption is that such issues will be resolved and can therefore be ignored in the present analysis. To have generality and thus enduring value, any analysis of the Internet's long-term impact on consumer marketing must be relatively independent of issues that are likely to be resolved in the near term. Instead, it must incorporate general economic and behavioral factors relating to the Internet that are likely to influence the structure and performance of consumer markets in the long run.

Present Paradigms

As Miller (1996) astutely observed, "People tend to see the future of the Internet largely through the same color glasses they wear today" (p. 50). It is therefore not surprising that most firms currently seeking an Internet "presence" tend to be preoccupied with the Internet's communication and advertising potentials. Given the Internet's ability to foster real-time bilateral and multilateral communication and interaction, it is not surprising that "chat rooms" have become exceedingly popular. Indeed, their popularity could be easily predicted from the experience of France's Minitel service and even from the earliest precursor of the Internet, the Greek agorz (Fieischman 1993). The need to socialize seems to be a powerful, culture-free motivator for a variety of behaviors; Lanham (1993) argued that the Internet (electronic communication) will bring back an ancient emphasis on interaction, individuality, and open debate.

The most common advertising uses of the Internet appear to be home pages and interactive brochures. The media are rife with reports of the types of advertising most likely to be effective on the Internet, how to measure advertising effectiveness, and how to integrate Internet advertising with an overall communications strategy (cf. Ainscough and Luckett 1996; Berthon et al. 1996b). Rust and Varki (1996) went so far as to speculate that the Internet will functionally replace traditional mass media. Bank (1996) stated that the Internet is being transformed into a broadcast medium analogous to television, except that programming and advertising will be personalized for each user through "push" technology.

A second aspect of the Internet that has attracted attention is its potential in the marketing research arena. Scholars such as Burke (1996; Burke, Harian, Kahn, and Lodish 1992) and Urban (Urban, Hauser, Qualls, Weinberg, Bohlmann, and Chicos 1997; Urban, Weinberg, and Hauser 1996) have demonstrated the feasibility of using the Internet in various research situations, especially in the context of virtual stores and new product development. Numerous firms are attempting to take advantage of the capabilities it offers for communication and interaction by, for example, offering Internet-based focus groups and surveys (see, however, Hanson and Putler 1996 for a cautionary note on one on-line measure frequently used in Internet-related marketing research).

Other firms have attempted to harness the revenue generation potential offered by the Internet. Peterson (1997:11) opined that there are several approaches to generating revenue through the Internet. Many of these approaches—marketing products or services, charging fees for accessible content (e.g., on a Web site), charging fees for on-line transactions or links, providing technical services, and writing books and presenting lectures on using the Internet—are directed toward consumers. Peterson reported, somewhat facetiously, that of these approaches, writing books and presenting lectures seemed to be the only ones currently profitable, albeit at very low levels.

Eventually, most of the revenues generated through the Internet will probably be derived from marketing products and services to consumers (Shi and Salesky 1994). In theory, firms can use the Internet to generate revenues by selling more to existing customers and by attracting new customers. Both of these will occur because the Internet is not constrained by either location or time. A firm marketing its products or services through the Internet is, by definition, a global firm because consumers worldwide can access it (Quelch and Klein 1996). Similarly, marketing through the Internet has no time constraints; time zones have no meaning. Because of such characteristics, the Internet appears to be especially suitable for reaching thin markets—niche markets in which buyers and sellers are small and geographically dispersed, and the products or services are specialized or unique (e.g., rare collectibles). To date, however, revenues from marketing existing products and services to consumers are rather minuscule compared to total retail sales obtained through other channels. Firms that are successful in marketing through the Internet, such as Dell Computer Corporation, typically possess unique characteristics not easily generalized.

In brief, from the perspective of revenue generation, the Internet currently lacks such common appliances as the facsimile machine (i.e., broadcast fax) and the telephone (i.e., inbound and outbound telemarketing). The present value of the Internet for marketing to consumers probably resides more in its ability to reduce or eliminate costs (Phillips, Donoho, Keep, Mayberry, McCann, Shapiro, and Smith 1997) than in its ability to generate revenues. Its revenue-generating potential, however, will likely change as Internet access grows and firms gain more knowledge of its strategic, tactical, and operational implications for consumer marketing.

A Foundation for Analysis

As previously stated, the question motivating this article is deceptively straightforward: What are some of the major implications of the Internet for consumer marketing? Unfortunately, the answers to this question are not so straightforward. Although wide agreement seems to exist that the Internet will ultimately influence consumer marketing, there is little agreement as to exactly how the Internet will affect the structure and performance of consumer markets. This is partially because of the rigidity of the frameworks that have been used to analyze these markets. Extant literature on the structure and performance of conventional retail markets is both voluminous and sophisticated. Retailing activity has been studied from a variety of perspective, including spatial modeling (e.g., Hotelling 1929), franchising (e.g., Gallini and Lutz 1992), vertical integration strategy (e.g., McGuire and Staelin 1983), entry deterrence (e.g., Judd 1985), pricing strategies (e.g., Thisse and Vives 1988), and market coverage (e.g., Boyer and Moreaux 1993), and it may be possible to extend some of these perspectives to encompass the Internet. Many insights gained from investigating conventional retail markets can be applied to marketing analyses of the Internet. Because the Internet possesses certain unique characteristics that have no counterparts in conventional retailing, it might also be necessary to construct specialized theories that would explain the mechanics and consequences of marketing to consumers through the Internet. However, any analysis or theory that does not recognize both the substitutability and complementarity of the Internet and conventional retailing methods will likely yield an incomplete view of the Internet's competitive effects and overlook synergies derived from close coordination of it and conventional retailing.

It is tempting to undertake a comprehensive analysis that would address possible structural and performance changes in consumer markets due to the Internet. However, such an undertaking is overly ambitious and probably premature at this time, for reasons that have been amply discussed. Instead, it seems more fruitful to elucidate those factors that are likely to mediate or moderate the impact of the Internet on the structure and performance of consumer markets. Not only is this a more realistic and manageable undertaking, but it is also likely to be one that produces useful results. Therefore, as a starting point for a comprehensive analysis of the impact of the Internet on consumer marketing, it is first necessary to specify the characteristics of the Internet as a marketing channel and examine two broad categories of factors: channel intermediaries and product and service characteristics.

Internet Characteristics

As a marketing channel, the Internet has both unique characteristics and characteristics that are shared with other marketing channels. These characteristics include the following:

- The ability to inexpensively store vast amounts of information at different virtual locations

- The availability of powerful and inexpensive means of searching, organizing, and disseminating such information

- Interactivity and the ability to provide information on demand

- The ability to provide perceptual experiences that are far superior to a printed catalog, although not as rich as personal inspection

- The ability to serve as a transaction medium

- The ability to serve as a physical distribution medium for certain goods (e.g., software)

- Relatively low entry and establishment costs for sellers

No existing marketing channel possesses all of these characteristics. Even so, the present analysis may be relevant for future channels (as yet unknown) that may possess these characteristics.

Channel Intermediaries

Marketing activity occurs through three types of channels: distribution channels, transaction channels, and communication channels, each of which has a discrete function. The function of distribution channels is to facilitate the physical exchange of products and services. Transaction channels generate sales activities between buyers and sellers. Finally, communication channels enable the exchange of information between buyers and sellers. Although conceptually distinct, in the context of consumer marketing these channels frequently overlap, and channel members may be responsible for multiple functions.

The distribution function is typically more than facilitating physical exchanges. Frequently, it incorporates functions such as sorting, inventory holding, allocation, breaking bulk, and building up assortments (Alderson 1965). The existence of intermediaries in the distribution channel is supported primarily by the rationale of efficiency (Stern, El-Ansary, and Coughlan 1996). For example, assortment building of frequently purchased goods by supermarkets increases distribution efficiencies because the supermarkets carry out functions that are expensive or difficult to perform by producers and consumers.

The function of transaction channels is to facilitate economic exchanges between buyers and sellers. Although transaction channel intermediaries exist because of the efficiencies they provide, they differ from distribution channel intermediaries in that they assume some strategic control over marketing variables such as price and merchandising. Examples of transaction intermediaries include brokers, wholesalers, and retailers, some of which may never physically handle or take title to any product or service.

The primary function of communication channels is to inform buyers and prospective buyers about the availability and features of a seller's product or service offering; at times, they also allow buyers to communicate with sellers. Communication channel intermediaries generally create information for, and/or deliver information to, buyers and prospective buyers. They include advertising agencies and media, both broadcast and print, and are the consequence, analogous to intermediaries in other channels, of expertise and efficiencies offered.

Given that the Internet is a flexible, interactive, and efficient medium through which economic parties can communicate, the potential that it offers for efficiency improvements in channel functions will obviously vary across the three types of intermediaries. In particular, the specific impact of the Internet on the three types of channel intermediaries can be assessed by posing two questions. These questions implicitly assume that a firm wanting to replace a channel intermediary with its own Internet operation has the capability to do so efficiently. If so,

- Is an Internet operation a credible substitute for the function(s) of a traditional channel intermediary?

- Can the Internet operation significantly dominate the current performance of a traditional channel intermediary?

Figure 1 summarizes answers to these two questions for each of the three types of channel intermediaries.

Of the three types of channel intermediaries, the logistic functions of distribution intermediaries are probably the least dependent on the existence of a flexible, interactive, and efficient informational exchange between buyers and sellers. The added value created by a delivery service or a retailer providing a physical assortment to ultimate users seems quite robust in the presence of what might appear to be a near-perfect medium for producers. There is, however, a major exception—information goods that can be distributed through the Internet. Indeed, for goods consisting of digital assets (Rayport and Sviokla 1995), such as computer software, music, or

FIGURE 1	CHANNEL INTERMEDIARY FUNCTIONS AND THE INTERNET

Channel Type	Intermediary Function	Are Internet Operations a Substitute?	Does the Internet Dominate?
Distribution	Logistic operations Assorting Accumulating Sorting	No, unless the good is based on digital assets	No, unless the good is based on digital assets
Transaction	Sales, including control over the sales environment	Likely	Depends on the characteristics of the good
Communication	Creating information (e.g., role of ad agencies)	Possible	Possible
	Distributing information to buyers (e.g., role of broadcast media)	Very likely	Very likely

reports, the Internet may be the ideal distribution channel because the variable cost or distributing them is nearly zero.

Transaction channel intermediaries will probably be more affected by the existence of the Internet because it will be possible for sellers (producers or manufacturers in particular) to efficiently interact with individual buyers and potential buyers. Given the lack of distance and time constraints, sellers can internalize the transaction functions previously handled by local transaction channel intermediaries in geographically dispersed markets. Internalization of the transaction function will, however, be mediated by the characteristics of the products and services marketed (see the following section).

Communication channel intermediaries will probably be the most affected by the existence of the Internet. By definition, the Internet has been designed to deliver information efficiently and foster connectivity. It is more flexible than existing mass media channels, potentially superior in targeting individual buyers and prospective buyers, and it enables direct interaction. Moreover, the Internet can offer communication options that have virtually no variable costs.

Product and Service Characteristics

The suitability of the Internet for marketing to consumers depends to a large extent on the characteristics of the products and services being marketed. It is therefore necessary to explicitly consider product and service characteristics when evaluating the impact of the Internet. This can be done by formally incorporating a product and service classification into any analysis. For example, it is possible to classify products and services as being either search or experience goods. Features of a search good can be evaluated from externally provided information, whereas experience goods need to be personally inspected or tried. If a good is a search good and its features can be objectively assessed using readily available information, the Internet could serve significant transaction and communication functions and hence affect transaction channel and communication channel intermediaries involved with the good. If a good is an experience good, information about the good's features may not be sufficient for a consumer to engage in an Internet-based transaction. For a consumer wishing to experience the good prior to purchase, Internet-based marketing would seem to be a poor substitute for traditional transaction channels, where the good is available for inspection. However, a consumer might use a traditional transaction channel to experience the good and then revert to an Internet-based transaction channel when acquiring it. Additionally, as a communication channel, the Internet will be increasingly able to offer perceptual experiences that far transcend verbal descriptions of goods. Pictures of flower bouquets or fruits can be presented in great detail, and music from a CD can be sampled on-line. Finally, for routinely purchased experience goods in categories in which a consumer has considerable personal experience, the Internet may serve as an effective communication and transaction medium.

Although the search good-experience good dichotomy is useful, perhaps a better classification system is one in which products and services are categorized along three dimensions that are more relevant in the context of the Internet: cost and frequency of purchase, value proposition, and degree of differentiation. Goods vary along the first dimension from low-cost, frequently purchased goods (e.g., consumable products such as milk) to high-cost, infrequently purchased goods (e.g., durable products such as stereo systems). Even though this dimension is not strictly bipolar, it is still useful in that it illustrates differences in transaction and distribution costs depending on whether, and how, the Internet is used. In general, when purchase fulfillment requires physical delivery, the more frequent the purchase and the smaller the cost (e.g., milk), the less likely there is to be a good "fit" between a product or service and Internet-based marketing.

Goods vary along the second dimension according to their value proposition, whether they are tangible and physical or intangible and service related. As previously discussed, Internet-related marketing is particularly well suited to certain types of intangible, or service-related goods (i.e., those based on digital assets). To the extent that the value proposition is intangible, the greater the frequency of purchase or use of a good, the greater the advantage of the Internet as a transaction and distribution medium.

The third dimension reflects the degree to which a product or service is differentiable. In particular, it reflects the extent to which a seller is able to create a sustainable competitive advantage through product and service differentiation. Internet-related marketing can result in extreme price competition when products or services are incapable of significant differentiation. This can happen when they are perceived as commodities, partially because other factors that might moderate competition (e.g., store location) are absent and partially because of the relative efficiency of price searching engendered by the Internet. However, when products or services are capable of significant differentiation, the Internet can serve as an effective segmentation mechanism for guiding buyers to their ideal product or service. For example, consider a prospective buyer in the market for computer virus protection software. This product would be classified according to the present scheme as one that is relatively expensive, infrequently purchased, has an intangible value proposition, and is relatively high on differentiation. Searching on the Internet enables the prospective buyer to obtain information on various competing products, possibly sample the products for free,

| FIGURE 2 | PRODUCT AND SERVICE CLASSIFICATION GRID |

Dimension 1	*Dimension 2*	*Dimension 3*	*Examples of Products and Services*
Low outlay, frequently purchased goods	Value proposition **tangible** or **physical**	Differentiation potential **high**	Wines, soft drinks, cigarettes
		Differentiation potential **low**	Milk, eggs
	Value proposition **intangible** or **informational**	Differentiation potential **high**	On-line newspapers and magazines
		Differentiation potential **low**	Stock market quotes
High outlay, infrequently purchased goods	Value proposition **tangible** or **physical**	Differentiation potential **high**	Stereo systems, automobiles
		Differentiation potential **low**	Precious metal ingot of known weight and purity
	Value proposition **intangible** or **informational**	Differentiation potential **high**	Software packages
		Differentiation potential **low**	Automobile financing, insurance

and select the one that best meets his or her requirements. Consequently, sellers have an opportunity to charge a higher price, taking advantage of the good fit between buyer requirements and product characteristics. In a conventional retail setting, such detailed search and personal sampling is costly. Willingness to pay is tempered in this setting by uncertainty regarding how well the product meshes with the buyer's requirements. In such instances, Internet-related marketing may result in higher margins than conventional retailing.

Although the three dimensions are continuous, for expository ease they can be dichotomized, as has been done in Figure 2, which illustrates products or services for each of the resulting eight cells in the classification scheme or grid. When considered in conjunction with the conceptualized channel intermediary functions, the classification scheme or grid suggests several implications for marketing through the Internet.

The function conceptualization and classification schemes, although insightful, are only a useful starting point. They do not predict or explain either the structure or performance of consumer markets. To understand their implications for evaluating the impact of the Internet more fully, it is necessary to address consumers' information and brand acquisition strategies in the context of category or brand choice decisions and choice of seller platform (i.e., whether it is Internet-based.).

Consumer Decision Sequences

A rich melange of theoretical and strategic considerations emerges when the Internet and conventional retailing channels are treated as parallel, coexisting systems that are both complementary and competing. Each system offers communication, transaction, and distribution opportunities. In such a situation, the structure of a consumer market and its performance is mediated by (1) consumers' choice of communication, transaction, and distribution channel(s); (2) the product or service offering(s) being marketed; and (3) the specific sequence of decisions followed by consumers in carrying out their purchasing functions.

Specifically, consumers have the choice of (1) whether to focus on a product or service category or a brand at any stage of the information acquisition process, (2) whether to use the Internet or conventional retail channels for information acquisition, and (3) whether to use the Internet or a conventional retail channel for the final transaction and brand acquisition. Note that the competition between manufacturers ceases and shifts to the retail level once a consumer has focused on a brand. Figure 3 presents a framework containing various decision sequences that consumers might follow when acquiring a particular product or service. For simplicity, only two channels, Internet and conventional fixed-location retailing, and two activities, information search and brand acquisition, will be considered. The specific decision sequences used by consumers clearly influence the nature and intensity of competition among sellers—both horizontally (e.g., retailers vs. retailers, manufacturers vs. manufacturers) and vertically (e.g., retailers vs. manufacturers). Thus, it is important to incorporate consumers' alternative decision sequences into any analysis of consumer market structure and performance.

FIGURE 3   SOME POSSIBLE CONSUMER DECISION SEQUENCES

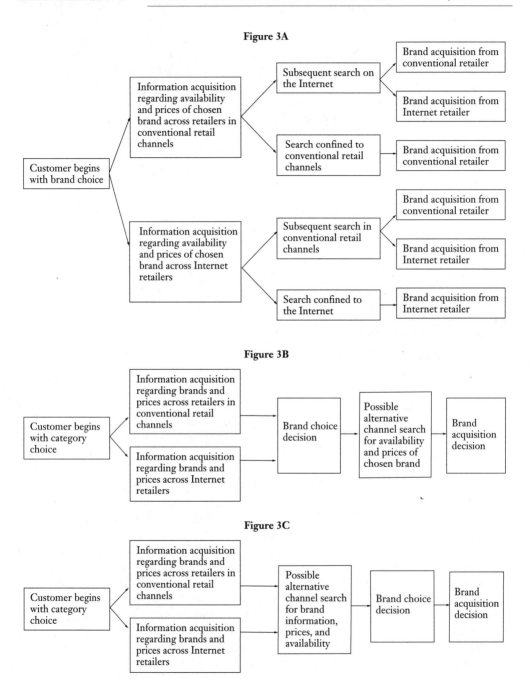

Figure 3A

Figure 3B

Figure 3C

Consider first the case of a consumer who begins the acquisition process with a brand already selected (Figure 3A). This situation may come about because the consumer has become aware of the brand through advertising, a personal recommendation, or prior experience. With the manufacturer predetermined, competition for this consumer is limited to retailers. Further, because the brand choice is clearly defined, the consumer will probably focus on price information and brand availability when conducting a search. The transaction could take place in either channel. Note that as long as the brand's manufacturer is not vertically integrated into retailing, substantial brand equity is probably required for strong performance in the context of the Internet as a transaction channel. (Empirical research by Jarvenpan and Todd 1997 suggested that, contrary to "common wisdom," all sellers are not equal on the Internet.) By indicating a brand choice at the beginning of the search process, the consumer forces retailers that stock the brand to compete on price by comparing their offerings across channels, thus promulgating intense price competition. Manufacturers are protected from this competition when the consumer selects a brand at the outset of the process.

What happens when brand choice is not clear at the outset and the consumer shops for a brand as well? In Figure 3B, brand choice is made after a consumer searches a single channel, whether Internet or conventional. For such a consumer, competition among manufacturers is limited to a single channel. If this consumer decides to shop for a low price, however, retailers will be forced to compete across channels. For example, a consumer in the market for a television set may decide on a particular brand after collecting information through the Internet but may then seek to consummate a transaction through either the Internet or a conventional retail channel.

Figure 3C presents the scenario of a consumer delaying a brand choice until completing a search of both the Internet and conventional retail channels. In this instance, the consumer possesses all relevant information on product attributes, including price, before making a purchase decision. For this consumer, manufacturers and retailers compete across both channels. Hence, competition is very broadly based.

Note that the existence of large numbers of consumers who are channel loyal— that is, who confine their information search and product acquisition activities to one channel—will moderate competition between the Internet and conventional retail channels. Channel loyalty can therefore effectively serve as a segmentation mechanism. At the same time, the existence of large segments of consumers who move from one channel to another during the decision process intensifies cross-channel competition.

Figure 4 links the product and service characteristics presented in Figure 2 to the decision sequences in Figure 3. Consider some of the implications of Figure 4. When products are low cost and frequently purchased, the conventional retail channel tends to dominate the Internet channel with respect to transaction and distribution functions, primarily because these functions do not offer economies of scale to the Internet marketer (unless there is a substantial delivery charge and/or several products are purchased and delivered together). As previously mentioned, however, if the value proposition is intangible or informational, the advantage shifts to the Internet marketer. Whether the potential for differentiation is high (e.g., on-line newspapers) or

FIGURE 4	PRODUCT AND SERVICE CHARACTERISTICS AND LIKELY CONSUMER DECISION SEQUENCES

Dimension 1	Dimension 2	Dimension 3	Likely decision sequences
Low outlay, frequently purchased goods	Value proposition **tangible** or **physical**	Differentiation potential **high**	(Example: Wines, soft drinks, cigarettes) • Brand choice likely after retail search. • Subsequent price search on the Internet is unlikely. • Final acquisition likely in retail store.
		Differentiation potential **low**	(Example: Milk, eggs) • Brand choice likely after retail search. • Subsequent price search on the Internet is unlikely. • Final acquisition likely in retail store.
	Value proposition **intangible** or **informational**	Differentiation potential **high**	(Example: On-line newspapers and magazines) • Brand choice likely after Internet search. • Subsequent price search in retail channels is unlikely. • Final acquisition likely on the Internet.
		Differentiation potential **low**	(Example: Stock market quotes) • Brand choice likely after Internet search. • Subsequent price search in retail channels is unlikely. • Final acquisition likely on the Internet.
High outlay, infrequently purchased goods	Value proposition **tangible** or **physical**	Differentiation potential **high**	(Example: Stereo systems, automobiles) • Brand choice likely after search of both channels. • Price search likely in both channels. • Final acquisition may occur in either channel. *(Comment: The need for personal product inspection may strongly influence the decision process in this case.)*
		Differentiation potential **low**	(Example: Precious metal ingot of known weight and purity) • Brand choice likely after search of both channels. • Price search likely in both channels. • Final acquisition may occur in either channel.
	Value proposition **intangible** or **informational**	Differentiation potential **high**	(Example: Software packages) • Brand choice likely after search of both channels. • Price search likely in both channels. • Final acquisition may occur in either channel. *(Comment: If prices are comparable, the Internet may be convenient for the final delivery of such products in the near future.)*
		Differentiation potential **low**	(Example: Automobile financing, insurance) • Brand choice likely after search of both channels. • Price search likely in both channels. • Final acquisition may occur in either channel.

low (e.g., stock market quotes), an intangible or informational value proposition favors the Internet marketer (due to the use of digital assets).

When products are expensive and infrequently purchased, the distribution constraint is reduced because delivery cost is a smaller proportion of the cost of the product. An Internet marketer therefore might be more likely to carry such a product. This likelihood, however, is counter-balanced by the probable need to personally inspect the product prior to purchase, and hence the traditional retailer is favored. Again, however, when the value proposition is intangible or informational, the Internet marketer is favored. Services such as automobile loans are easily arranged through the Internet, and software can be sampled, purchased, and distributed electronically. In general, it is expected that consumers will use traditional retail channels and the Internet jointly for high-value, infrequent transactions.

Collectively, the channel intermediary function conceptualization, product and service classification scheme, and consumer decision framework provide a foundation for analyzing the impact of the Internet on consumer marketing, especially in the situation when conventional retail channels are still a powerful presence. The channel intermediary function conceptualization focuses attention on where and how the Internet will likely substitute for and/or complement conventional channel intermediaries. The product and service classification scheme indicates that the impact of the Internet is sensitive to the nature of the products and services being marketed. The consumer decision framework emphasizes that consumers may use the Internet and traditional retail channels differentially to seek information, make brand choices, and take delivery of a product or service. All three influence the nature and degree of competition in a consumer market and, when applied in content, enable meaningful, precise predictions of the impact of the Internet in specific marketing situations.

Equilibrium Market Structures

Early visions of electronic marketing predicted the decline in importance of, and in some instances even the demise of, traditional channel intermediaries as consumers become able to directly access manufacturers. These predictions are still being made primarily on the basis of the Internet's offering flexible, low-cost information exchanges between consumers and manufacturers and the subsequent loss of location and time as bases of sustainable strategic advantage. Benjamin and Wigand (1995), for example, maintained that the Internet has the capacity to "eliminate retailers and wholesalers entirely" (p. 62).

These predictions are effectively conjectures on the equilibrium structures of consumer markets, and although they possess prima facie validity, they are probably too general. For example, the predictions do not seem to take into consideration that a market is a complex phenomenon consisting of a profusion of product and service categories with widely varying characteristics that are coupled with a mixture of consumers, retailers, wholesalers, manufacturers, and assorted other intermediaries bound together through a multitude of formal contractual and distribution agreements and informal arrangements. Nor do they appear to appreciate the fact that "equilibrium" is a sophisticated construct that imposes strong conditions on the stability of the strategies of all market participants.

It may well be that the Internet will eventually lead to structural changes in some consumer markets. As previously argued, under certain conditions the Internet will probably cause some degree of disintermediation or vertical integration compared with conventional retailing channels because of the distribution, transaction, and communication functions it can facilitate for some products and services. Even so, the Internet may also lead to more channel intermediaries than currently exist, such as rating services, automated ordering services, and order consolidation services (Sheth and Sisodia 1997).

A strategic reason for manufacturers to use transaction intermediaries is that doing so shields them from competing directly with each other. McGuire and Staelin (1983) showed analytically that if two competing products are highly substitutable, the respective manufacturers may be better off using independent retailers to protect themselves from possibly ruinous price competition, even though they lose control of retail prices. Similar results were advanced by Coughlan (1985), although Moorthy (1988) argued that McGuire and Staelin's conclusions held only in situations where prices are strategic complements, such that when one retailer raises the price it charges for a product, other retailers follow. Finally, Choi (1991, 1996) extended McGuire and Staelin's results to situations in which there are multibrand retailers and several manufacturers. Although some of the assumptions underlying these analyses need to be modified for the Internet, the underlying intuition, that manufacturers can protect themselves from competing directly with each other by a process of reintermediation, is especially appealing in the context of Internet-based marketing.

Despite its considerable advantages in efficiently providing information and facilitating transactions, the Internet will not lead to complete disintermediation in the foreseeable future for reasons that are economic, behavioral, and psychological. For instance, a single carton of milk will probably continue to be purchased at the nearest supermarket or convenience store because the distribution and transaction costs of such items are considerable as a proportion of the price paid. Of course, larger bundles of groceries may be amenable to Internet-based transactions.

A plethora of research (e.g., Berkowitz, Walton, and Walker 1979; Forman and Sriram 1991) shows that many consumers view the shopping experience as a source of enjoyment and an opportunity for social interaction. For these consumers, the process of shopping adds value to the products and services they purchase and variety to their lives, and consequently they may never use the Internet for shopping. Other consumers may decide not to use the Internet in their shopping and purchasing activities for reasons that include lack of access, technophobia, and inertia. Still other consumers, as discussed previously, will use Internet resources for certain aspects of purchasing while retaining conventional retailers for other aspects.

In sum, the structure of a consumer market depends on a variety of factors, but in general it evolves from the decision-making processes of market participants. For example, Balasubramanian (1997) showed empirically that the incidences of catalogs and fixed-location retail outlets vary widely across product and service categories. This variation depends in part on consumer perceptions of the categories as well as on their shopping experiences, the perceived need for future channel interactions, and the average dollar amount per purchase. Similarly, decisions of market participants and other moderating variables (e.g., products and services) influence the impact of the Internet on the structure of consumer markets. Figure 5 contains examples of such decisions and moderating variables. Although the Internet may influence both the structure and performance of certain consumer markets, the extent to which this

FIGURE 5	EXAMPLES OF DECISIONS OF INTERNET MARKET PARTICIPANTS THAT AFFECT CONSUMER MARKET STRUCTURE

Decisions of Internet Market Participants

Consumers
- Search strategies
- Joint use of Internet/conventional retail channels
- Aggregation of buying power

Retailers
- Decision on on-line transaction vs. on-line information provision
- Coordination of Internet with traditional retail channel
- Facilitation/obstruction of *consumer* coordination between the two channels.
- Stocking policies (exclusive/multiproduct)
- Pricing decisions and price-matching promises
- Depth and pattern of information presentation to consumers
- Nature of contractual relationship with manufacturer
- Nature of contractual relationship with (possible) information brokers

Manufacturers
- Degree of vertical and horizontal product or service differentiation
- Degree of vertical channel integration (sell directly to customer/use independent retailer)
- Nature of contracting relationship with retailer
- Pricing policy to retailers
- Coordination of information, product availability and pricing between Internet and conventional retail channels.
- Nature of contractual relationship with (possible) information brokers

Other intermediaries
- Information brokers: decision on charging consumers, retailers or manufacturers (or a combination of these participants) for information provided
- Decision on pricing structure for information: payment for purchases made or for information provided
- Decision on who operates information brokerages: consumer associations, retailers, or manufacturers

Internet characteristics → [diagram] → Equilibrium structure of products and service markets

occurs will be a function of numerous factors, both controllable and uncontrollable. Except for extreme cases, such as when digital assets are being employed in a service, the Internet will probably not eliminate or serve as a substitute for conventional retail channels.

The Internet and Price Competition

For homogeneous, commodity-type, or completely substitutable goods, it can be expected that the Internet will foster Bertrand-type competition. It is easy to point out conditions that lead to this expectation (see Tirole 1989, chap. 5, for conditions that generally facilitate Bertrand-type competition). In the context of an Internet-based market, there are large numbers of buyers and sellers (geography is not relevant) who possess near-perfect information on product and service attributes, including price. Market entry and exit are nearly costless, as are searches and transactions.

Under these conditions, the Bertrand model of competition predicts that firms will price at their marginal cost and that no firm can make positive profits because of intense price competition. This is paradoxical because it is not obvious why firms would enter or continue to compete in a market if it is not profitable to do so. Although theoretically appealing, the model's predictions may not hold for Internet-based marketing for several reasons.

The model assumes that firms interact only once and therefore anticipates that unilaterally undercutting competitors' prices will result in large demand effects and create more profit than charging the same price as competitors. Hence, a firm will undercut the price of its competitors, who in turn have the same incentive to undercut that firm's price, such that every competitor ends up pricing at marginal cost. However, it is unlikely that competitors who interact with each other over time and who realize their mutual dependencies will display such destructive pricing behavior. Specifically, in repeated interactions a firm not only should take into account the (mostly positive) present effects of undercutting competitors' prices, but it should also take into account the likelihood of invoking a long-term price war.

The model assumption that consumers have full knowledge of the availability and prices of competing products and services also may not hold, even though by definition the Internet provides virtually costless information. If consumers decide not to seek information on all available products and services, competition will reflect this fact. In a classic article, Stigler (1961) argued that consumers who value time will stop searching when the marginal benefits of search no longer outweigh the marginal costs; the implication of this argument is that, in general, full search across many alternatives will occur only when it is completely costless. Zettelmeyer (1996, 1997) proposed that firms use search cost as a control variable to reduce competition, even if it is costless to let consumers search their offerings. This logic seems to apply to the decisions of several marketers to not post prices on their Internet sites.

Finally, the model assumes that competing products and services are completely undifferentiated. This is a very strong assumption because it can be argued that firms will always be able to find a nonprice basis for differentiation (e.g., warranties, postsale service, image, and so on). Even minute differences in differentiation, such as how price is bundled with other offering attributes, may allow firms to price at higher than marginal cost.

In brief, the conclusion that the Internet is likely to promote intense price competition for products and services that are very substitutable may be overly general.

Not only are firms likely to be strategic about letting consumers use the Internet as a source of near-costless information, but they are also likely to create at least minimal differences, whether physical or perceptual, between their products and services and competing products and services and will recognize the interdependent nature of competition over time. Consequently, some consumers may be willing to pay higher prices for products and services marketed through the Internet because of its increased selection and convenience (cf. Rayport and Sviokla 1994). Even so, the advent of sophisticated and inexpensive search engines, shopping agents, and robotic software is likely to revolutionize the search processes of consumers and ultimately increase the level of competition for highly substitutable products and services. Finally, although most discussions of the impact of the Internet on competition emphasize the Internet's use as an electronic market, it was argued earlier in this article that whatever occurs on the Internet will also affect conventional retailers. The opportunity that the Internet offers consumers in terms of increasing choice sets by making a larger number and wider variety of competing firms available may of itself foster price reductions by conventional retailers.

.

Research Questions

Currently, one Internet conclusion is incontrovertible. No one can predict with certainty what the ultimate impact of the Internet will be on consumer marketing. There is virtually no information on how, or to what extent, consumers will use the Internet in the context of marketing or what new marketing paradigms will prove viable. It is already clear, however, that the Internet is changing the rules by which marketing is conducted and evaluated, and new consumer market structures will emerge in the next century as a consequence of the Internet or whatever succeeds it. Research conclusions and theories that have addressed such fundamental issues as imperfect information (e.g., Schlee 1996), information acquisition (e.g., Hauser, Urban, and Weinberg 1993), and retail location (e.g., Wolinsky 1983) will have to be carefully reconsidered in light of the Internet, and the consumer information systems envisioned by Beales, Mazis, Salop, and Staelin (1981) and Thorelli and Engledow (1980) must be visited anew. Moreover, from a regulatory and legal perspective, questions as to what constitutes a monopoly, unfair competition, or antitrust activities need to be addressed in light of a marketplace unfettered by geography or time.

The analysis reported in this article has spawned more questions than it has answered. Therefore, it seems appropriate to conclude the article with a series of questions that might motivate and guide the development of research on the Internet, as well as research on the Internet's implications for marketing theory and strategy. The questions are not meant to be either exhaustive or exclusive. Rather, they are illustrative of the types of questions that need to be answered before a comprehensive understanding of all the marketing implications of the Internet is possible. For expository case, the questions are organized around the themes of consumers, retailers, manufacturers, other channel intermediaries, and social planning.

Consumer-Oriented Questions

- How will the availability of automated search and information presentation mechanisms on the Internet affect the way consumers search for information and their subsequent decision making? In particular, how are optimizing and satisficing search processes affected?

- In what way are information and product or service acquisition strategies dependent on the specific characteristics of the product or service sought?

- What are the central reasons for selecting the Internet instead of a conventional retail channel for any component of the product or service acquisition process? What factors influence the implicit trade-off made when choosing one alternative over the other?

- How do consumers navigate the Internet and conventional retail channels during the search and acquisition process? How is the sequencing of decisions determined? How is the sequencing affected by the nature of the product or service sought?

- The Internet facilitates communication among consumers. Will this lead to an aggregation of buying power in the form of cooperative buying organizations?

- The Internet facilitates mass customization in some product and service categories. Mass customization can be interpreted as the availability of widely differentiated goods and services so that offerings can be tailored to suit individual demand. What are the implications of such a match between consumer needs and product characteristics on demand for products and services? What are the corresponding implications for product variety? Will mass customization lead to a lower emphasis on the advertising and promotional elements of the marketing mix?

Retailer-Oriented Questions

- The efficiency of the Internet may catalyze intense competition in some instances. The traditional spatial differentiation between retail stores, which strongly moderates competition, is nonexistent on the Internet. At the same time, the Internet offers fresh avenues for product and service design and distinct possibilities for consumer segmentation. What are the new avenues of sustainable differentiation possible on-line so that the value creation process is sustained and debilitating price competition is avoided?

- How can retailers coordinate their activities between the Internet and conventional retail channels? Should product offerings, price levels, and warranties differ across channels? If so, how?

- To what extent and in which directions should retailers facilitate consumers' attempts to coordinate their behavior across channels?

- What should be the nature and detail of product and service attribute information (including price) presented to consumers on-line?

- How can retailers segment and price discriminate between on-line shoppers?

- Should Internet retailers stock a single manufacturer's product in each category, or should they stock products from multiple manufacturers? How should the contracting agreement with manufacturers for on-line sales be designed?

- On-line sales could be supported by new promotion mechanisms. How should they be designed? What are the potential outlets of on-line advertising? Should (some) consumers be paid to visit on-line sites? How should new measures of store loyalty and brand loyalty be defined?

- Internet-based shopping malls offer one form of retail aggregation on-line. To what extent should retailers be aggregated? When is it profitable to be aggregated with similar retailers so that consumer demand is first drawn to the aggregation and then divided among retailers? How can competition be moderated between similar retailers in an Internet mall?

- The Internet facilitates the collection of information on consumer characteristics and search processes. How should such information be collected and used? What are the privacy issues involved?

Manufacturer-Oriented Questions

- To what extent should manufacturers be vertically integrated on the Internet? What are the advantages and disadvantages of selling directly to consumers? Under what conditions should independent retailers be used to buffer manufacturers from direct competition with each other?

- How should pricing and promotional policies to on-line retailers (or direct to consumers) be determined? How should contracts with retailers be designed? How should contracts with new intermediaries (e.g., information brokers, search engines) be designed?

- What degree of vertical (range of superior/more expensive and inferior/less expensive products and services) and horizontal (range of products and services of different types, not necessarily superior or inferior to each other) differentiation should be pursued? How should these offerings differ from those of the same manufacturer sold through other means? What are the new dimensions of differentiation possible that would create sustainable competitive advantage?

Other Channel-Intermediary-Oriented Questions

- The Internet is likely to generate information brokers and category-specific shopping search engines. How should such services be designed and priced?

- Should such information services be paid for by the manufacturer, retailer, or consumer? Should payment be contingent on use or on final successful transaction?

- If the information brokers search across manufacturers and retailers within a particular product category, how should searches be designed and executed to present unbiased and objective information to consumers?

- Who should own and operate information brokerages and search engines? Should they be independently owned or owned by manufacturers, retailers, or consumer associations?

Social-Planning-Oriented Questions

- How will the Internet affect the structure and performance of product and service markets? How will any consumer, retailer, or manufacturer surplus be redistributed? What will be the final impact of the Internet on social surplus?

- To what extent should efficiency be promoted to foster competition? Ruinous competition can lead to market exit by sellers, which then leads to concentrated, less competitive markets.

- How can the Internet's efficiency and information collection capabilities be balanced against genuine concerns about consumer privacy?

- How should the Internet be regulated to make it a safe and reliable transaction medium for consumers?

- Existing laws designed to keep product markets healthy and competitive are implicitly grounded in the spatially distributed nature of current markets. The rules of competition are substantially different on-line. How should existing regulations be adapted and new ones be designed to ensure the health and competitiveness of on-line markets?

Numerous questions must be asked and answered before the Internet can be effectively and efficiently applied in consumer marketing. It is hoped that this article will stimulate the questioning process.

Acknowledgment

The authors thank Susan M. Broniarczyk for her detailed and insightful comments on a previous version of this article.

Peterson, Robert A., Sridhar Balasubramanian, and Bart J. Bronnenberg.
Journal of the Academy of Marketing Science.
Volume 25, No. 4, pages 329–346.
Copyright © 1997 by Academy of Marketing Science.

References

Ainscough, Thomas L. and Michael G. Luckett. 1996. "The Internet for the Rest of Us: Marketing on the World Wide Web," *Journal of Consumer Marketing* 13 (September): 36–47.

Alba, Joseph, John Lynch, Barton Weltz, Chris Janiszewski, Richard Lutz, Alan Sawyer, and Stacy Wood. 1997. "Interactive Home Shopping: Consumer, Retailer, and Manufacturer Incentives to Participate in Electronic Marketplaces," *Journal of Marketing* 6 (July): 38–53.

Alderson, Wroe. 1965. *Dynamic Marketing Behavior: A Functionalist Theory of Marketing.* Homewood, IL: Irwin.

Asimov, Isaac. 1977. "The Supermarket 2077 A.D." *Progressive Grocer* 56 (June): 52–53.

Bakos, J. Yannis. 1991. "A Strategic Analysis of Electronic Marketplaces," *MIS Quarterly* 15 (September): 295–310.

Balasubramanian, Sridhar. 1997. "Two Essays in Direct Marketing." Ph.D. dissertation, Yale University, New Haven, CT.

Bank, David. 1996. "How Net is Becoming More Like Television to Draw Advertisers," *Wall Street Journal*, December 13, pp. A1, A8.

Beales, Howard, Michael B, Mazis, Steven C. Salop, and Richard Staelin. 1981. "Consumer Search and Public Policy," *Journal of Consumer Research* 8 (June): 11–22.

Benjamin, Robert and Rolf Wigand. 1995. "Electronic Markets and Virtual Value Chains on the Information Superhighway," *Sloan Management Review* 36 (Winter): 62–72.

Berkowitz, Eric N., John R. Walton, and Orville C. Walker Jr. 1979. "In-Home Shoppers: The Market for Innovative Distribution Systems," *Journal of Retailing* 55 (Summer): 15–33.

Berthon, Pierre, Leyland F. Pin, and Richard T. Watson. 1996a. "Marketing Communication and the World Wide Web." *Business Horizons* 39 (September–October): 24–32.

——, ——, and ——. 1996b. "The World Wide Web as an Advertising Medium: Toward an Understanding of Conversion Efficiency," *Journal of Advertising Research* 36 (January–February): 43–54.

Bloom, Paul N., Geroge R. Milne, and Robert Adler. 1994. "Avoiding Misuse of New Information Technologies: Legal and Societal Considerations." *Journal of Marketing* 58 (January): 98–110.

Boyer, Marcel and Michel Moreaux. 1993. "Strategic Market Coverage in Spatial Competition," *International Journal of Industrial Organization* 11 (Summer): 299–326.

Bredenberg, Al. 1995. "Seven Myths of Internet Marketing." *Target Marketing* 18 (September): 49–50.

Burks, Raymond R. 1996. "Virtual Shopping: Breakthrough in Marketing Research," *Harvard Business Review* 74 (March–April): 120–131.

——, Bari A. Harlam, Barbara E. Kahn, and Leonard M. Lodish. 1992. "Comparing Dynamic Consumer Choice in Real and Computer-Simulated Environments," *Journal of Consumer Research* 19 (June): 71–82.

Choi, S. Chan. 1991. "Price Competition in a Channel Structure With a Common Retailer," *Marketing Science* 10 (Fall): 271–296.

——. 1996. "Price Competition in a Duopoly Common Retailer Channel," *Journal of Retailing*, 72 (Summer): 117–134.

Comer, Douglas E. 1995. *The Internet Book.* Englewood Cliffs, NJ: Prentice Hall.

Coughlan, Anne T. 1985. "Competition and Coordination in Marketing Channel Choice: Theory and Application," *Marketing Science* 4 (Spring): 110–129.

Cavens, David W. 1997. "Looking Toward the Next 25 Years of *JAMS*," *Journal of the Academy of Marketing Science* 25 (Winter): 3.

Deloime & Touche, 1990. *A Special Report on the Impact of Technology on Direct Marketing in the 1990's.* New York: Direct Marketing Association.

Doody, Alron F. and William R. Davidson. 1967. "Next Revolution in Retailing," *Harvard Business Review* 45 (May–June): 4–16, 20, 188.

Economides, Nicholas. 1996. "The Economics of Networks." *International Journal of Industrial Organization* 14 (Fall): 673–699.

Fleischman, John, 1993. "In Classical Athens, a Market Trading in the Currency of Ideas." *Smithsonian*, July, pp. 38–42, 44, 46–47.

Forman, Andrew M. and Ven Sriram, 1991. "The Depersonalization of Retailing: Its Impact on the 'Lonely' Consumer." *Journal of Retailing* 67 (Summer): 226–243.

Fox, Bruce. 1995. "Retailing on the Internet: Seeking Truth Beyond the Hype," *Chain Store Age Executive* 71 (September): 33–72.

Gallini, Nancy T. and Nancy A. Lutz. 1992. "Dual Distribution and Royalty Fees in Franchising." *Journal of Law, Economics, and Organization* 8 (October): 471–501.

Hagel, John III and Thomas R. Eisenmann. 1994. "Navigating the Multimedia Landscape," *The McKinsey Quarterly* 30(3): 39–55.

Hagel, John III and Jeffrey F. Rayport. 1997. "The Coming Battle for Customer Information." *Harvard Business Review* 75 (January–February): 53–55, 58, 61, 64–65.

Hanson, Ward A. and Daniel S. Putler. 1996. "Hits and Misses: Herd Behavior and Online Product Popularity," *Marketing Letter* 7 (October): 297–305.

Hauser, John R., Glen L. Urban, and Bruce D. Weinberg. 1993. "How Consumers Allocate Their Time When Searching for Information," *Journal of Marketing Research* 30 (November): 452–466.

Hoffman, Donna L. and Thomas P. Novak. 1996. "Marketing in Hypermedia Computer-Mediated Environments: Conceptual Foundations," *Journal of Marketing* 60 (July): 50–68.

Hotelling, Harold T. 1929. "Stability in Competition," *Economic Journal* 95 (January): 41–57.

Hyde, Linda L., Carl E. Steidtmann, and Daniel J. Sweeney. 1990. *Retailing 2000*. Columbus. OH: Management Horizons.

Jarvenpaa, Sirkka L. and Peter A. Todd. 1997. "Is There a Future for Retailing on the Internet?" In *Electronic Marketing and the Consumer.* Ed. Robert A. Peterson. Thousand Oaks, CA: Sage, 139–154.

Judd, Kenneth L. 1985, "Credible Spatial Competition," *RAND Journal of Economics* 16 (Summer): 153–166.

Lanham, Richard A. 1993. *The Electronic Word: Democracy, Technology, and the Arts.* Chicago: University of Chicago Press.

Leibrock, Larry R. 1997. "Privacy, Surveillance, and Cookies." In *Electronic Marketing and the Consumer,* Ed. Robert A. Peterson. Thousand Oaks, CA: Sage, 155–162.

Levy, Steven. 1996. "Breathing Is Also Addictive," *Newsweek:*, December 30, pp. 52–53.

MacKie-Mason, Jeffrey K. and Hal R. Varian. 1995. "Some FAQs About Usage-Based Pricing." *Computer Networks and ISDN Systems* 28 (December): 257–265.

Mahajan, Vijay and Jerry Wind. 1989. "Market Discontinuities and Strategic Planning: A Research Agenda," *Technological Forecasting and Social Change* 36 (August): 185–199.

Malone, Thomas W., JoAnne Yates, and Robert I. Benjamin. 1989. "The Logic of Electronic Markets," *Harvard Business Review* 67 (May–June): 166–172.

McGuire, Timothy W. and Richard Staelin. 1983. "An Industry Equilibrium Analysis of Downstream Vertical Integration," *Marketing Science* 2 (Spring): 161–191.

McNair, Malcolm P. and Eleanor G. May. 1978. "The Next Revolution of the Retailing Wheel," *Harvard Business Review* 56 (September–October): 81–91.

Miller, Thomas E. 1996. "Segmenting the Internet." *American Demographics* 18 (July): 48–52.

Molenaar, Cor. 1996. *Interactive Marketing*. Aldershot, UK: Gower.

Moorthy, K. Sridhar. 1988. "Strategic Decentralization in Channels," *Marketing Science* 7 (Fall): 335–355.

Peterson, Robert A. 1997. "Electronic Marketing: Visions, Definitions, and Implications." In *Electronic Marketing and the Consumer.* Ed. Robert A. Peterson. Thousand Oaks, CA: Sage, 1–16.

Phillips, Fred, Andrew Donoho, William W. Keep, Walter Mayberry, John M. McCann, Karen Shapiro, and David Smith. 1997. "Electronically Connecting Retailers and Customers: Interim Summary of an Expert Roundtable." In *Electronic Marketing and the Consumer,* Ed. Robert A. Peterson. Thousand Oaks, CA: Sage, 101–122.

Quelch, John A. and Lisa R. Klein. 1996. "The Internet and International Marketing," *Sloan Management Review* 37 (Spring): 60–75.

Rayport, Jeffrey F. and John J. Sviokla. 1994. "Managing in the Marketspace," *Harvard Business Review* 72 (November–December): 141–150.

———— and ————. 1995. "Exploiting the Virtual Value Chain," *Harvard Business Review* 73 (November–December): 75–85.

Rosenberg, Larry J. and Elizabeth C. Hirschman. 1980. "Retailing Without Stores," *Harvard Business Review* 58 (July–August): 103–112.

Rust, Roland T. and Sajeev Varki. 1996. "Rising From the Ashes of Advertising," *Journal of Business Research* 37 (November): 173–181.

Schlee, Edward E. 1996. "The Value of Information About Product Quality," *RAND Journal of Economics* 27 (Winter): 803–815.

Schneiderman, Ron. 1980. "Non-Store Shopping Growing as Consumer Habits Change," *Merchandising* 5 (September): 60–61.

Sheth, Jagdish N. and Rajendra S. Sisodia. 1997. "Consumer Behavior in the Future." In *Electronic Marketing and the Consumer*, Ed. Robert A. Peterson. Thousand Oaks, CA: Sage, 17–38.

Shi, Christiana Smith and Andrew M. Salesky. 1994. "Building a Strategy for Electronic Home Shopping." *The McKinsey Quarterly* 4: 77–95.

Spar, Debra and Jeffrey J. Bussgang. 1996. "The Nat," *Harvard Business Review* 74 (May–June): 125–133.

Stern, Louis W., Adel I. El-Ansary, and Anne T. Coughlan. 1996. *Marketing Channels*, 5th ed. Upper Saddle River, NJ: Prentice Hall.

Stigler, George. 1961. "The Economics of Information," *Journal of Political Economy* 69 (January–February): 213–225.

Taylor, David. 1995. "Digital Dreaming, Part I: The Internet Marketing Primer," *Marketing Computers* 15 (March): 24–25.

Thisse, Jacques-Francois and Xavier Vives. 1988. "The Strategic Choice of Spatial Price Policy," *American Economic Review* 78 (March): 122–137.

Thorelli, Hans and Jack L. Engledow. 1980. "Information Seekers and Information Systems: A Policy Perspective." *Journal of Marketing* 44 (Spring): 9–27.

Tirole, Jean. 1989. *The Theory of Industrial Organization*. Cambridge, MA: MIT Press.

Urban, Glen L., John R. Hauser, William J. Qualls, Bruce D. Weinberg, Johnathan D. Bohlmann, and Roberta A. Chicos. 1997. "Information Acceleration: Validation and Lessons From the Field," *Journal of Marketing Research* 34 (February): 143–153.

————, Bruce D. Weinberg, and John R. Hauser. 1996. "Premarket Forecasting of Really New Products," *Journal of Marketing* 60 (January): 47–60.

Wolinsky, Asher. 1983. "Retail Trade Concentration Due to Consumers' Imperfect Information." *Bell Journal of Economics* 14 (Spring): 275–282.

Zettelmeyer, Florian. 1996. "The Strategic Use of Consumer Search Cost," Working Paper, William E. Simon Graduate School of Business Administration, University of Rochester, NY.

————. 1997. "Expanding to the Internet: Pricing and Communications. When Firms Compete on Multiple Channels." Working Paper, University of Rochester, NY.

7

Do You See What I See?
The Future of Virtual Shopping

RAYMOND R. BURKE
Indiana University

New technologies captivate our imaginations. We have seen a breathtaking stream of innovations—solar cells, nuclear fusion, biotechnology, genetic engineering, artificial intelligence, robotics, space travel, virtual reality, and many others—all promising to transform our lives. For better or worse, the actual impact of these innovations is often much less (and takes much longer) than what we expected. In some cases, unforeseen technical problems have stalled the development process, blocking an innovations's move from the laboratory into the marketplace. In others, consumers have resisted change, instead choosing to maintain the status quo. Existing technologies have also continued to evolve, making it unnecessary to switch to something new.

In recent years, the Internet has generated a tremendous level of excitement. Business magazines are filled with articles describing how life will be different in a digital age. High-technology stocks have soared on investors' expectations of the creation of new wealth and the transformation of existing businesses. Some of the most sensational predictions have been made with regard to electronic commerce. Maurice Saatchi, a prominent figure in the advertising industry, forecast that in 40 years, electronic retailing will eliminate the need for physical stores (Cope 1996:18). Andersen Consulting predicted that in the next decade, 20 percent of supermarket shopping will be conducted through nonstore electronic channels (McGrath 1994). Negroponte

Raymond R. Burke is the E. W. Kelley Professor of Business Administration at Indiana University and director of the Customer Interface Laboratory. His research focuses on understanding the influence of point-of-purchase factors (including new products, product packaging, pricing, promotions, assortments, and displays) on consumer behavior in conventional and virtual shopping environments. Prior to joining Indiana University, he was an associate professor of business administration at the Harvard Business School and an assistant professor of marketing at the University of Pennsylvania's Wharton School. His articles have appeared in various journals, including Harvard Business Review, Journal of Consumer Research, Journal of Marketing, International Journal of Research in Marketing, and Marketing Science. He is also coauthor of ADSTRAT: An Advertising Decision Support System.

(1995) argued that, as a consequence of electronic distribution, "videocassette-rental stores will go out of business in less than ten years" (p. 173). And Jupiter Communications, a New York market research firm, estimated that interactive home shopping would expand to $82.35 billion by the year 2003 (Conway 1994:26).

What is the future of virtual shopping on the Internet? Will it displace existing retail formats or serve as a natural complement to current marketing practices? Peterson, Balasubramanian, and Bronnenberg (1997) address this issue in their thoughtful and detailed analysis of the impact of the Internet on consumer marketing. They contend that many predictions regarding the future role of the Internet are overstated because they fail to consider the complexity and heterogeneity of consumer markets. The Internet is only one of many tools available to manufacturers and retailers for advertising, selling, and distributing their products to customers. Marketers are most likely to use the Internet in cases where its unique characteristics make it a viable and attractive substitute for the functions of traditional channel intermediaries. Because of its ability to transmit information quickly and inexpensively, the Internet will have the greatest impact on marketing communications, a moderate effect on sales transactions, and (with the exception of information goods) a minimal impact on logistics.

The goals of this article are to build on and extend the contributions of Peterson et al. (1997). In the following discussion, I will explore the reasons why it has been so difficult to forecast the impact of new communication technologies on retailing, discuss the ways in which existing retailers might respond to this new technology, consider how the Internet and electronic shopping will continue to evolve, and suggest how managers might plan for the future.

What's Wrong with Our Forecasting?

For the past 30 years, futurists have been predicting the advent of electronic shopping. They speculated that consumers would be able to shop for products from home and pay for the merchandise electronically, then have it delivered to their homes from a central distribution facility or pick it up at a drive-through depot. As Peterson et al. (1997) note, the researchers' predictions were surprisingly accurate, anticipating the launch of services like Peapod, Shoppers Advantage, Streamline, and Groceries-To-Go. However, they were overly optimistic about when this would happen—in some cases, missing the mark by 20 years. Even today, U.S. retail sales through electronic channels are unimpressive. In 1996, consumer sales over the Internet were just $520 million—less than 0.03 percent of the $2.2 trillion total (Burke 1998).

Why has it been so difficult to forecast the growth of electronic commerce? Peterson et al. (1997) contend that the new computer and communication technologies that will enable virtual shopping are market discontinuities, so it is impossible to use historical trends to forecast how they will affect the retailing industry. They note that "it is not possible to predict precisely the specific impacts of the Internet, especially given the velocity with which Internet-related changes are occurring and the increasingly assertive and unpredictable behavior of consumers" (p. 330). Yet, companies need some estimate of what the future holds to develop business plans and allocate resources productively. As Confucius once said, "If a man gives no thought about what is distant, he will find sorrow near at hand."

A major part of the forecasting problem is that multiple constituencies are involved—consumers, manufacturers, retailers, and technology firms—and each has a separate agenda. One needs to examine the motivations and constraints of each group when building forecasts.

Consumers

The changing demographic profile of the U.S. population, including the expanding number of dual-income and single-parent households and the increase in the average age of the household head, has created an opportunity for home shopping. A growing number of people are time constrained by obligations to work and family (Schor 1989). Individuals who are sick, disabled, or elderly may not have the ability to shop. And many people do not enjoy shopping, especially the routine chore of grocery shopping. "Some studies show that almost two thirds of people dislike the visit to the supermarket—roughly the same proportion as claim an aversion to the dentist" (Cope 1996:66). The concept of home shopping is appealing because of its potential to deliver greater convenience, more and better product information, and lower prices (Burke 1998).

Unfortunately, most existing services have failed to deliver these benefits. As Quelch and Takeuchi (1981) noted, consumers will be reluctant to shop in nonstore channels as long as the experience is inferior to the conventional store. Home shopping services typically do not provide the same levels of product information, personal service, entertainment, and social interaction as do physical stores. Consumers also find it difficult to comparison shop and are concerned about reliable product fulfillment and the loss of privacy. While Quelch and Takeuchi identified these problems in 1981, they remain a barrier today.

In a survey of 220 consumers who had shopped on the Internet, Jarvenpaa and Todd (1997) uncovered several other factors that may limit the growth of electronic commerce. They discovered that the main impediments to consumer acceptance of Internet shopping were not the frequently mentioned technical issues of network security and bandwidth. Instead, consumers complained that the Web was hard to navigate, that it was difficult to find specific items, and that the offerings of individual sites were too limited and not price competitive. Shoppers were generally disappointed by the customer service and expressed a preference for locally run stores and familiar merchants to the unknown retailers on the Internet.

Retailers

Existing retailers have also been reluctant to support electronic shopping. Building and maintaining a Web site requires a significant investment of time and money with an uncertain return on investment. If retailers post their prices on the Internet, customers and competitors have easy access to this information, increasing market efficiency and reducing margins. Electronic sales incur shipping and handling costs and have higher return rates, approaching 25 percent for television home shopping channels. As a consequence, many retailers have found that it is more expensive for them to sell to their customers electronically than through the conventional store.

Consider the case of Shopping Alternatives[1] (Koehn, Burke, and Verter 1996), a company based in Bethesda, Maryland, that provided home shopping services to a number of supermarket chains in the United States, including Cub Foods (Atlanta), Byerly's (Minnesota), Shaws (Massachusetts), as well as several Wal-Mart supercenters. When a customer placed an electronic order with Shopping Alternatives, the order was (1) transmitted to the closest retailer, (2) picked and packed by store employees, and (3) delivered by a courier service to the customer's home. Shopping Alternatives charged a $9 delivery fee to the customer and an $8 fee to the supermarket to provide this service. It cost the retailer approximately $5 to collect, scan, bag, and store the selected items. Therefore, the retailer incurred an additional $13 of expense to serve the home shopper.

On the positive side, delivery orders generated approximately 6 percent higher gross margins than in-store purchases, as customers were less likely to "cherry pick" sale items.[2] On an average order of $100, this provided an additional $6 of margin. The retailer's profits would also be higher if the electronic store attracted new customers rather than simply converting existing customers. This was more likely in smaller markets, where Shopping Alternatives was the only delivery service in town, than in major cities like Atlanta and Boston, where several retailers offered competing home shopping services (Cleland 1997).

Whereas electronic shopping may be threatening to existing retailers who have substantial investments in physical stores, it offers several benefits to a new breed of electronic merchant who designs his or her business from the ground up to maximize operational efficiency. By having one centralized warehouse instead of many individual stores, the merchant can carry less inventory, offer a greater variety of merchandise, and serve a larger geographic region. The warehouse can be located in an industrial area with low real estate costs. There is no need for wide aisles lined with expensive fixtures and multiple checkout counters. Because there is a time delay between when an order is placed and when it is delivered, the electronic retailer can handle slow-moving items more efficiently—in some cases, having them shipped directly from manufacturers. A study by Cap Gemini Consulting indicated that by eliminating the physical store and the associated operating costs, Internet retailers can triple profit margins (or cut prices by 12%) compared to the conventional retailer (see Cope 1996, fig. 1).

The Internet retailer is also in an excellent position to leverage customer information. Products, promotions, and advertising can be targeted much more efficiently than through conventional media. In the past, advertisers targeted customer segments by selecting media with matching demographic profiles. This resulted in two sources of error: (1) aggregate statistics on audience demographics hide considerable individual heterogeneity and (2) demographics are often a poor predictor of brand preference. Using the appropriate software, Internet-based retailers can communicate customized messages and promotions to individuals with the desired interests and shopping patterns (see, e.g., Williamson 1997). The Internet also provides retailers with instant control of marketing variables. Merchants can boost sales and profits by dynamically adjusting the mix of products, prices, and promotions in response to consumer demand (cf. Phillips, Donoho, Keep, Mayberry, McCann, Shapiro, and Smith 1997).

Manufacturers

Manufacturers are another important constituency in the development of Internet-based electronic commerce. In recent years, manufacturers have expressed concern that the balance of channel power may be shifting toward retailers, who have grown larger through consolidation and have become more sophisticated in their analysis of point-of-sale data. Manufacturers are often asked to create customized versions of products for specific chains and to pay substantial trade allowances to gain shelf space for new products and receive promotional and merchandising support for existing brands. At the same time, many retail "partners" have introduced private label products that compete directly with the national brands. This creates a powerful motivation for manufacturers to "go direct" to consumers.

One manufacturer offered the following scenario:

> Let's assume that a household buys three rolls of our paper towels each week. We could offer to sell that household 156 rolls, a year's supply, at a sizable discount. We would then deliver the product on a weekly basis and take back any unused merchandise. This simplifies life for the customer, who no longer needs to worry about buying paper towels. From our perspective, the household is taken "out of the market" for a year. There is no need to advertise or promote. And by having an accurate estimate of consumer demand, we can smooth out our production schedule.

As noted earlier, the Internet provides an inexpensive and targeted means for reaching consumers. By leveraging interactive technology, manufacturers can build one-to-one relationships with their customers, tailoring the marketing mix to individual preferences (Pine, Peppers, and Rogers 1995). And, as noted earlier, electronic marketing provides quick feedback on the effectiveness of marketing activities, enabling "performance-based marketing" (Peterson 1997). The quality of a manager's decisions concerning product assortment, pricing, advertising, and promotion can be directly measured in terms of revenues and profitability.

Despite the potential benefits, there are several reasons why manufacturers have hesitated to sell their products electronically. As Quelch and Takeuchi (1981) noted, manufacturers may not engage in direct marketing to avoid retaliation from the traditional retailers who account for most of their sales. Most manufacturers do not have sufficiently large product lines to satisfy consumers' needs for selection and variety, so they would need to cooperate with a channel intermediary in any case. And some products do not lend themselves to electronic purchase. These include heavy, bulky, and fragile items; low-margin items; products requiring in-store demonstration; and products that are needed urgently.

Both manufacturers and retailers have expressed concern that their merchandising options are limited on the Internet. Most existing shopping interfaces allow consumers to go directly to specific product categories and make their selections, avoiding the marketing distractions of the conventional store. As a consequence, shoppers may make fewer impulse purchases. The computer typically displays lists of brand names and model numbers with information on features, flavors, sizes, and prices. Consumers do not see the familiar product packages, so the brand equity communicated by the package shapes, colors, and logos is lost. Some shopping systems allow customers to sort products by price and ingredients, which draws their attention away from the brand names and tends to commoditize the purchase.

Technology Firms

Due to the diligent efforts of the computer industry over the past 15 years, many of the technical barriers to electronic retailing identified by Quelch and Takeuchi (1981) have been overcome. American homes now hold more than 40 million PCs. Computers are less expensive and easier to use. They can display multimedia information and three-dimensional graphics. Search engines are readily available to help find desired information. While existing shopping interfaces do not (and may never be able to) provide the familiar and engaging shopping experiences of the conventional store, computer and communications technologies will continue to improve.

Some of the most promising forecasts of the future growth of the Internet and electronic commerce have come from high-technology firms. These companies often have a good grasp of how the technology will evolve and understand the engineering hurdles that must be overcome. However, managers must be cautious not to confuse technology forecasts of what is scientifically possible with market forecasts of consumer demand and product adoption. Technology is just a platform for change. How firms use the technology to create value for customers is what will determine the size and growth rate of the market.

Managers should also question the motivations behind many of these forecasts. Brody (1991) noted, "Rosy predictions often originate with people who have a financial stake in a new technology" (p. 40). Entrepreneurs in search of capital are inclined to overstate the future opportunity and underestimate the technical problems to gain support. In fact, many high-tech companies have "evangelists" on staff to promote their new projects. Market analysts and the media, always on the lookout for a hot story to boost their own businesses, are quick to pick up and repeat these overblown forecasts.

Environment

Finally, one must consider the regulatory environment. While the U.S. government has been generally supportive of electronic commerce, there are still many issues that need to be resolved, including issues concerning on-line privacy, marketing to children, unsolicited e-mail, and taxation. For example, several states in the United States have proposed that local Internet service providers should be considered "agents" of electronic retailers; therefore, all commerce over the Internet should be treated as "local" with regard to taxation. This would raise the price of on-line merchandise by 5 to 10 percent in most states, slowing the growth of electronic sales.

This review suggests that in the short run, many factors will inhibit the growth of Internet-based electronic commerce. Consumers are frustrated by poorly implemented shopping interfaces, limited selections of on-line merchandise, and high prices. Retailers are constrained by the high overhead costs of existing facilities, high delivery charges and return rates, and the fear of lost impulse sales. Manufacturers feel that their hands are tied given their current dependence on conventional retailers. However, in the long run, there are tremendous opportunities for electronic commerce. Consumers are demanding greater convenience and economy and are acquiring the skills and technology necessary to shop electronically. Retailers and manufacturers are searching for new ways to expand their markets and build customer loyalty, and some have developed profitable business models for on-line commerce. This suggests that, as with many revolutionary technologies (e.g., color television, the refrigerator, and the VCR), we will see a long introduction period followed by rapid growth and eventually high levels of penetration (cf. Bayus 1993). Of course, this depends on the evolution of existing retail channels and communications technologies. These issues are explored in the next section.

How Will Conventional Retailing Evolve?

The factors that drive total retail sales differ markedly from those that determine the share of any particular shopping medium (such as the Internet, television shopping channels, kiosks, catalogs, toll-free telephone numbers, and conventional retail stores; cf. Barnett 1988). Total retail sales are a function of the number of consumers, consumers' needs and habits, economic conditions, and the rate of product consumption and replacement. Demand for Internet-based shopping depends, instead, on how well this new format compares on price and performance to other, substitute retail formats. As Peterson et al. (1997) note, "There is no intuitive reason why the Internet, or any service based thereon, will in and of itself cause consumers to spend more. Rather, use of the Internet in marketing to consumers will more likely result in a redistribution of revenues among channels or among members within a channel" (p. 331).

To predict the percentage of total retail sales that will be captured by the Internet, it is necessary to identify the relative advantages of Internet-based marketing over conventional retailing both now and in the future. Several unique characteristics of the Internet were highlighted here and in Peterson et al. (1997). These include inexpensive, instantaneous, and global communication with customers; the ability to know about, interact with, and market to customers as individuals; and, for information-based products and services, instantaneous distribution. These attributes translate into a number of possible benefits for consumers, including greater shopping convenience, more current and complete product information, custom-tailored products and services, and potentially lower prices.

To the extent that existing retailers can duplicate these advantages or leverage their own unique characteristics, this could slow or even reverse the growth of electronic commerce. Brody (1991) noted, "Technological forecasts tend to go astray partly because they underestimate the possibilities for advances in existing technology" (p. 41). He quotes Robert Lucky, executive director for communications science research at Bell Labs: "People forget that there are always an army of people working on improving an old technology and only a handful of people working on a new technology" (Brody 1991:42). In the following discussion, I review several ways in which conventional retailers can enhance their future prospects by building on their strengths and overcoming potential weaknesses relative to Internet-based shopping.

Convenience

In a survey of 220 consumers from Austin, Texas, Jarvenpaa and Todd (1997) found that convenience was the single most salient benefit of Internet shopping. Similarly, Burke (1998), who conducted six focus groups in the eastern, midwestern, and western regions of the United States, discovered that convenience was the most frequently cited reason for wanting to shop electronically. Summarizing the comments of participants, Burke reported:

> Shoppers appreciated the ability to visit the virtual store at any hour, and to perform other activities, like exercise, cooking, and child care, while shopping. They could shop even when transportation was unavailable, and avoid crowded parking lots or bad weather. The [home shopping system] eliminated drive time and checkout time, and allowed shoppers access to distant stores. The weight and bulk of packages no longer constrained the size of their orders.

Conventional retailers can address their potential vulnerability on this dimension by making shopping more convenient for their increasingly time-pressed customers. Some stores are staying open 24 hours a day. Others are providing free and plentiful parking, expanding their selections of merchandise to allow one-stop shopping, organizing products according to customers' needs and lifestyles, and locating frequently purchased items in the front of the store. Progressive food retailers are using "shopping basket analysis" to identify which items are purchased together and are grouping complementary items into "meal solutions" at the point of purchase. Ukrops, a chain in Richmond, Virginia, reports that its What's for Dinner Tonight program has achieved sales increases of 50 to 600 percent (Higgins 1997). Many retailers offer to load heavy and bulky purchases into customers' vehicles, and a few provide drive-through windows so customers can shop from their cars.

Consumers often complain about having to wait in long checkout lines. Some retailers accept this as a fact of life. They assume that an employee must be at the checkout counter to total up the merchandise, handle payment and coupons, and bag the merchandise. They see long lines as an opportunity to sell high-profit impulse purchase items like magazines and candy. Other merchants are looking for ways to speed up the process by expanding the number of checkout lanes, opening special lanes for small orders, and using UPC laser scanners to quickly total items. Several new technologies may eliminate lines altogether. ICL Retail Systems has developed a "supertag" system that can instantly scan tagged items in a shopping basket (Cope 1996). UPC radio tags send signals to the register, which allows items to be totaled as the consumer walks through the checkout lane. Companies are also experimenting with systems where consumers self-scan their purchases.

Many retailers have offered, and will continue to offer, the convenience of home shopping through media other than the Internet. These include toll-free telephone numbers, touchpad- or voice-based ordering systems, catalogs, television shopping channels, electronic kiosks, automated teller machines (ATMs), video conferencing, and fax machines. Each approach has unique advantages and disadvantages (Phillips et al. 1997). For the moment, the telephone, television, catalog, and, to a lesser extent, the fax machine dominate computer shopping in terms of low acquisition cost, high household penetration, and superior ease of use. Electronic kiosks and ATMs provide customers with state-of-the-art technology in public locations and can dispense cash and printed receipts. From the customer's perspective, the most convenient technology is the one that best matches his or her shopping and media habits. In a project with a Boston-area bank, Burke (1998) found that about one-third of the bank's patrons preferred to use ATMs for most of their transactions, one-third used bank tellers for some services and ATMs for others, and one-third were "branch wed," refusing to use electronic media. To accommodate personal preferences, the bank allowed customers to conduct transactions by accessing its customer and product databases through either a human teller (using face-to-face interaction or a video-conferencing kiosk) or the computer (using an ATM, the Internet, or touch-tone telephone).

Product Information

In recent years, mass merchandisers like Wal-Mart and Target, supercenters like Meijer, and "category killers" like Home Depot, Barnes & Noble Booksellers, and Toys 'R Us have changed the landscape of retailing. By building large stores in inexpensive locations and using sophisticated information systems, bulk purchasing, centralized inventory, and continuous replenishment to cut costs, these chains can offer shoppers extensive selections of products at low prices. Yet, these are the same advantages that are driving the expansion of Internet-based retailers like amazon.com, now with 2.5 million book titles, and CUC International's netMarket, an on-line shopping club. In head-to-head battles with conventional retailers, the Internet merchants would seem to have the advantage. They are unencumbered by the overhead of physical stores, have larger trading areas, and can offer an almost unlimited selection of merchandise.

Conventional retailers can still gain the upper hand by providing more complete and relevant product information. Most existing Internet-based shopping systems are designed to replace expensive human labor with computerized assistants. These software agents can provide copious amounts of product information through hierarchical lists of product categories, brands, and models; product photographs and feature descriptions; filtering mechanisms; and search engines. However, even with this flexibility, it is difficult to create one shopping interface that addresses everyone's needs, especially when consumers have widely varying levels of prior knowledge and must select among several complex products, as is the case for products like insurance, financial services, and travel (Burke 1998). Internet shopping systems typically do not have a human agent to clarify or interpret product information, respond to specific questions (except as anticipated by a "frequently asked questions" list), or discuss how to solve customers' problems. "Chat windows" and e-mail provide only limited opportunities for interaction. To gain an advantage on this dimension, conventional retailers will need to do a better job of merchandising their stores and training their salespeople, transforming them from clerks who just ring up orders into sales professionals and product specialists who can talk intelligently about the stores' products and services.

Customized Products and Services

Most retailers design their stores, product offerings, promotions, and services for the masses. They treat all shoppers alike, despite the fact that customers differ in terms of their needs and wants and the volume and profitability of their purchases. Retailers' actions are driven by several assumptions: (1) there are too many different customers or customer segments to tailor a store's offerings; (2) managers do not have the time, knowledge, or technology to analyze individual-level data; and (3) there is insufficient return on investment (or an uncertain return on investment) for customizing marketing programs for individuals. As noted earlier, this puts retailers at a distinct disadvantage relative to those electronic retailers who can adjust their marketing programs in real time to match the needs of individual shoppers.

Advances in database marketing are helping to overcome these problems. By setting up frequent shopper programs and linking customer profiles to UPC scanner data, retailers can track the shopping patterns, sales volume, and profitability of their patrons. They can mail out customer-specific fliers and promotions. When shoppers enter the store and swipe their frequent shopper cards through a reader, a computer can print out customized shopping lists complete with recipes, coupons, and suggestions for replenishment purchases. In-store kiosks and electronic displays can highlight products that meet customers' requirements. Service personnel can access customer profiles at point-of-sale terminals and make suggestions based on a knowledge of past purchases, household characteristics, and preferences.

Several forward-thinking companies are already leveraging information technology to build closer relationships with their customers. Mitchell's Clothing in Westport, Connecticut, tracks the clothing preferences, work environments, and budgets of its customers. Salespeople can use this information to alert customers when new merchandise arrives in the appropriate sizes, styles, and price ranges and to match new clothing items with prior purchases. British Airways uses System ESS to track the preferences of its frequent flyers. This allows flight attendants to great passengers with their favorite magazines, beverages, and meals and reduces the costs of inventory. Merv Griffin's Resorts, a casino in Atlantic City, New Jersey, targets events and promotions to individual customers based on their spending patterns and game preferences (Sviokla and Langbert 1992). And GTE Telesystems developed a terminal for customer service people that provides instant feedback on customer characteristics. It displays calendar pages to indicate customer longevity, sticks of dynamite to show past service problems, and moneybags to indicate sales volume.

Enhancing the Shopping Experience

Many people have suggested that the best way for retailers to respond to the threat of Internet-based shopping is to improve the in-store shopping experience. Cope (1996) argued, "[Traditional retailers] will need to compete on added value and quality by utilizing the advantages the virtual retailers cannot match. This will mean higher levels of service, more highly trained staff and improved stores that are entertaining, fun and a pleasure to visit" (p. 19). Retailers have tried several approaches to adding entertainment, ambience, and social interaction to the shopping experience. Ogden Corporation created American Wilderness, a nature preserve located in a shopping mall, with 160 wild animals, a restaurant, and a shopping boutique (Bird 1997). Land Rover dealerships built off-road test tracks so customers can experience the thrill of driving sport utility vehicles (Fournier 1996). Athletic shoe stores have installed basketball courts and rock-climbing walls. Some grocery stores have scheduled "singles nights," with contemporary music, name tags, food samples, and flattering lighting to emphasize the social aspects of shopping (Saulny 1997).

These are only a few of the ways in which conventional retailers might sustain and grow their businesses in the face of increased competition from Internet-based shopping. As a starting point, retailers can improve shopping convenience, emphasize knowledgeable and personalized service, and enhance the entertainment value and ambience of their stores. Creative retailers will go far beyond this list of suggestions, developing both high-tech and high-touch selling approaches. They can use database systems to track major life events (e.g., births, deaths, marriage, graduations, moves) to market products to customers at the precise times when customers' needs are most salient. They can employ infrared and video-tracking systems to monitor shoppers' traffic patterns and reset store layouts and displays to maximize impact. They can install electronic shelf tags and dynamically alter the prices of merchandise to manage demand. Retailers can satisfy the heterogeneous needs of customers by carrying just a few basic products, which they customize at the point of purchase (e.g., by adding components to computers, ingredients to food, colors and patterns to clothing items). They can work with members of the local community (hospitals, government, civic groups) to create products and services that are tailored to regional needs and interests. The opportunities for enhancing conventional retailing are limited only by one's imagination. Of course, the same is true for virtual shopping.

How Will Internet-Based Marketing Evolve?

Is the Internet a "phenomenal marketing opportunity," as Hoffman and Novak (1996) suggested, or "just another communication improvement, following language, the printing press, newspapers, mail, telegraph, telephone, TV, and fax, and to some extent the automobile," as Lehmann (1997:131) contended? Both statements are correct. The Internet provides merchants with several potential advantages over conventional media, as discussed earlier. However, most existing Web sites have not capitalized on these advantages, instead taking a very traditional approach to retailing (Jarvenpaa and Todd 1997). James Utterback, a professor of engineering at MIT, noted, "New things are viewed in the clothing of the old." The problem with this, he argued, is that "old things are optimized for what they do already" (Brody 1991:43).

As companies move forward with electronic commerce, we are likely to see the greatest success stories in cases where firms are able to leverage the unique characteristics of the medium to sell their products and services and where the profiles of their target customers match those of Internet users (see Hoffman, Kalsbeek, and Novak 1996 for detailed demographic information). Peterson et al. (1997) hypothesize that consumers are more likely to search for product information, make a brand selection, and acquire the product or service on the Internet when the value proposition is intangible or informational (see, e.g., a discussion of the music industry in Reilly 1997). For physical products, consumers are most likely to search for product information and make purchases using the Internet when the products are expensive, infrequently purchased, and can be easily evaluated using on-line information. For these products, the potential economic savings from shopping on the Internet more than offset the time required to electronically search for the best product and price.

Dell Computer Company and Gateway 2000, Inc., two of the largest direct marketers of personal computers, are both excellent examples of how to capitalize on the unique benefits of Internet shopping, and both have seen recent, dramatic growth in on-line sales. These firms use the Internet to communicate detailed, up-to-date information on their fast-changing line of products to a computer-literate audience of customers. Shoppers can custom design a computer by selecting options from an on-screen form and see the immediate impact on price. When the shopper is satisfied with the configuration and places an order, the company records delivery and billing information, builds the computer to specification, and ships the computer to the customer's home. This ensures that the customer will receive the latest technology and protects the manufacturer from being saddled with obsolete inventory.

For Internet-based shopping to extend beyond these applications and achieve mass market penetration, it must be made substantially easier to use. At a minimum, customers must be able to connect to the Internet in a simple and reliable way. In a field trial of residential Internet service, Kraut, Scherlis, Mukhopadhyay, Manning, and Kiesler (1996) reported, "Even with help and our simplified procedure, HomeNet participants had trouble connecting to the Internet for a variety of reasons, including bad telephone lines and busy signals, passwords forgotten, misunderstood user interfaces, depressed shift-lock keys on keyboards, erased login scripts, and buggy software" (p. 57). Franzke and McClard (1996) reported similar frustrations in their study of 50 Internet households from Winona, Minnesota.

In addition, the customer interface must be dramatically improved. The original World Wide Web interface, the NCSA Mosaic browser, was introduced in 1992 and was relatively easy to use. It displayed primarily textual HTML documents on the user's screen. By clicking on highlighted words (called hypertext links), the user could navigate through a (typically hierarchical) set of documents. The Internet of today is much more complex. Browsers can display text, graphics, animation, and video. Users navigate with buttons, frames, pull-down menus, image maps, search engines, Java applets, ActiveX controls, and so on. As software companies battle for technological and market dominance of the Internet, even more features and complexity are added. Every electronic commerce site has a different appearance, a different set of product categories, a different way to search for product and price information, and a different procedure for placing an order. Needless to say, this is confusing and frustrating for the average consumer.

We can learn from the success of the fax machine, whose growth eclipsed e-mail in the 1980s. Negroponte (1995) noted that fax was inferior to e-mail, lacking the computer readability that allows electronic storage, retrieval, and manipulation. However, fax machines were standardized and very easy to use, thus making them accessible to a broad segment of the population. In the same way that the Apple Macintosh and Microsoft Windows user interface made personal computers useful by providing a consistent and familiar means to interact with the computer, consumers need a consistent and familiar means to shop electronically. Indiana University's Customer Interface Lab is currently studying how consumers learn and interact with a variety of new electronic shopping interfaces, including text-based interfaces, two- and three-dimensional graphical displays, stereo imaging, touch-screen kiosks, video conferencing, and voice recognition.

Manufacturers and retailers must also search for ways to reduce the perceived risk of on-line purchasing. Quelch and Takeuchi (1981) noted that direct marketers have been able to broaden the range of products that consumers are willing to purchase by offering free trials, money-back guarantees, and toll-free complaint hotlines. Electronic merchants have several other options available, including using trained and licensed raters to personally inspect and evaluate products; word-of-mouth endorsements from other, similar customers; three-dimensional product simulations so shoppers can virtually experience new products; and specially designated "trial stores" where people can see and try the latest goods and services.

Forecasting Revisited: From Prediction to Management

Niels Bohr, the Nobel Prize-winning physicist, once said, "Forecasting is always difficult, and it's especially difficult when trying to forecast the future." This is certainly true of electronic commerce. Computer and communication technologies continue to evolve. Consumers, retailers, and manufacturers each have unique motivations and constraints with respect to electronic shopping. Yet, their plans and actions are interdependent. The success of Internet-based shopping programs depends on how well the programs are executed and promoted and the quantity and quality of competitive response. Even after a careful analysis of current conditions and trends, it is hard to predict the future growth of virtual shopping without making many questionable assumptions.

This leaves managers with two options. The first is to plan contingently. Firms can pursue their current marketing practices while learning about and monitoring the growth of Internet-based commerce. When the technology reaches a critical level of acceptance, stability, and productivity, they can jump onto the Internet bandwagon. This is the approach that most manufacturers and retailers have taken up until now and is a primary reason for the slow growth of electronic commerce. Gloomy predictions have become self-fulfilling prophecies.

The alternative approach is for managers to take an active role in defining and managing the future. They can work to establish standards for commerce over the Internet, partner with high-tech firms to create technology that is usable and useful, and develop distribution and payment systems that complement Internet-based marketing. They can treat each of the limitations of electronic shopping discussed earlier in this article as an obstacle that needs to be overcome to gain acceptance. By challenging the assumptions of established players, these firms open the door to creating new industries.

Which assumptions should be challenged? There is a long list of candidates: "The catalog is the best metaphor for electronic shopping," "Internet retailers should compete on variety and price," "Customers will not buy perishable products electronically," "Virtual shopping is less entertaining than physical shopping," "Customers must search for information and make decisions before buying," "People will not make impulse purchases on-line," and so on. Through experimentation, manufacturers and retailers can learn which of these assumptions are most tenuous and which new technologies are most promising. Rather than embracing new approaches on blind faith (with potentially ruinous consequences) or conducting large-scale tests that may turn into public embarrassments, firms can maximize their learning by testing several different approaches in small-scale experiments. By evaluating revolutionary ideas through an iterative process of prototyping, testing, and refinement, companies can successfully manage the risk of pioneering the future.

Journal of the Academy of Marketing Science.
Volume 25, No. 4, pages 352–360.
Copyright © 1997 by Academy of Marketing Science.

Notes

1. In 1997, Shopping Alternatives was acquired by Streamline, a home shopping service based in Westwood, Massachusetts. Unlike most existing grocery shopping services (such as Shopping Alternatives, Shoppers Express, and Peapod), which handled fulfillment from a conventional retail store, Streamline delivered orders from a centralized warehouse. While the construction of a dedicated fulfillment center significantly increased the up-front capital investment, it reduced the long-term costs of operation. The interested reader should consult Cope (1996) and Burke (1998) for more detailed discussions of the electronic grocery shopping industry.
2. Shopping Alternatives did not provide prices in its electronic catalogs. One could argue that when prices are included (perhaps as a result of competitive pressure), gross margins will fall, both because consumers are able to comparison shop on price and because the service may attract more price-sensitive shoppers. In fact, people who shop with a text-based shopping interface may become more price sensitive than those who shop in the conventional store due to the increased visual prominence of the price information (Burke, Harlam, Kahn, and Lodish 1992).

References

Barnett, F. William. 1988. "Four Steps to Forecast Total Market Demand." *Harvard Business Review* 66 (4): 28–33.

Bayus, Barry L. 1993. "High-Definition Television: Assessing Demand Forecasts for a Next Generation Consumer Durable." *Management Science* 39 (11): 1319–1333.

Bird, Laura. 1997. "Move Over Mall Rats, Wild Beasts Are Taking Your Turf." *Wall Street Journal*, July 8, pp. B1, B7.

Brody, Herb. 1991. "Great Expectations: Why Technology Predictions Go Awry." *Technology Review*, July, pp. 39–44.

Burke, Raymond R. Forthcoming. "Real Shopping in a Virtual Store." In *Sense and Respond: Capturing the Value in the Network Era*. Eds. Stephen P. Bradley and Richard L. Nolan. Boston: Harvard Business School.

Burke, Raymond R., Bari Harlam, Barbara Kahn, and Leonard Lodish. 1992. "Comparing Dynamic Consumer Choice in Real and Computer-Simulated Environments." *Journal of Consumer Research* 19 (1): 71–82.

Cleland, Kim. 1997. "Peapod, Shoppers Express Vie for Online Grocery Business." *Advertising Age*, June 9, p. 40.

Conway, Claire. 1994. *The 1994 Home Shopping Report*. New York: Jupiter Communications.

Cope, Nigel. 1996. *Retail in the Digital Age*. London: Bowerdean.

Fournier, Susan. 1996. "Land Rover North America, Inc." Case No. 9-596-036, Harvard Business School, Boston.

Franzke, Marita and Anne McClard. 1996. "Winona Gets Wired: Technical Difficulties in the Home." *Communications of the ACM* 39 (12): 64–66.

Higgins, Kieran. 1997. "Focus: Selling Solutions." *CIES Food Business News* 5 (May): 1–2.

Hoffman, Donna L., William D. Kalsbeek, and Thomas P. Novak. 1996. "Internet and Web Use in the U.S." *Communications of the ACM* 39 (12): 36–46.

Hoffman, Donna L. and Thomas P. Novak. 1996. "Marketing in Hypermedia Computer-Mediated Environments: Conceptual Foundations." *Journal of Marketing* 60 (July): 50–68.

Jarvenpaa, Sirkka L. and Peter A. Todd. 1997. "Is There a Future for Retailing on the Internet?" In *Electronic Marketing and the Consumer*. Ed. Robert A. Peterson. Thousand Oaks, CA: Sage, 139–154.

Koehn, Nancy F., Raymond R. Burke, and Geoffrey Verter. 1996. "Shopping Alternatives, Inc: Home Shopping in the Information Revolution." Case No. 9-796-132, Harvard Business School, Boston.

Kraut, Robert, William Scherlis, Tridas Mukhopadhyay, Jane Manning, and Sara Kiesler. 1996. "The Home Net Field Trial of Residential Internet Services." *Communications of the ACM* 39 (12): 55–63.

Lehmann, Donald R. 1997. "Some Thoughts on the Futures of Marketing." In *Reflections on the Futures of Marketing*. Eds. Donald R. Lehmann and Katherine E. Jocz. Cambridge, MA: Marketing Science Institute, 121–135.

McGrath, Betsy Grover. 1994. "Food Shopping for Couch Potatoes." *Catalog Age*, July.

Negroponte, Nicholas. 1995. *Being Digital*. New York: Knopf.

Peterson, Robert A. 1997. "Electronic Marketing: Visions, Definitions, and Implications." In *Electronic Marketing and the Consumer*. Ed. Robert A. Peterson. Thousand Oaks, CA: Sage, 1–16.

Peterson, Robert A., Sridhar Balasubramanian, and Bart J. Bronnenberg. 1997. "Exploring the Implications of the Internet for Consumer Marketing." *Journal of the Academy of Marketing Science* 25 (Fall): 329–346.

Phillips, Fred, Andrew Donoho, William W. Keep, Walter Mayberry, John M. McCann, Karen Shapiro, and David Smith. 1997. "Electronically Connecting Retailers and Customers: Interim Summary of an Expert Roundtable." In *Electronic Marketing and the Consumer*. Ed. Robert A. Peterson. Thousand Oaks, CA: Sage, 101–122.

Pine, B. Joseph II, Don Peppers, and Martha Rogers. 1995. "Do You Want to Keep Your Customers Forever?" *Harvard Business Review* 73 (2): 692–703.

Quelch, John A. and Hirotaka Takeuchi. 1981. "Nonstore Marketing: Fast Track or Slow?" *Harvard Business Review* 59 (4): 75–84.

Reilly, Patrick M. 1997. "Honey, They're Downloading Our Song." *Wall Street Journal*, July 17, p. B1.

Saulny, Susan. 1997. "Grocery Store Turns Into Shop for Available Singles." *Marketing News*, July 21, p. 38.

Schor, Juliet. 1989. *The Overworked American: The Unexpected Decline of Leisure*. New York: Basic Books.

Sviokla, John J. and Jon A. Langbert. 1992. "Merv Griffin's Resorts." Case No. 9-192-105, Harvard Business School, Boston.

Williamson, Debra Aho. 1997. "Wanted: Info on You and Your Interests." *Advertising Age*, May 19, pp. 60, 64.

8

Data Mining in Marketing: Part 1

The Revolution Is Upon Us,
So Choose Your Weapons Carefully.

PETER R. PEACOCK

The data flood unleashed by advances in information technology has only just begun, but it already threatens to wash away those marketing managers who fail to recognize and deal with its consequences. Data mining and the closely related concept known as "knowledge discovery in databases" are potential bulwarks against this surge. This first article in a two-part series examines several driving factors of the data mining revolution and applications to marketing problems. The article also describes categories of data mining tasks and explains the principal weapons in the data mining arsenal.

During the last three years, Marriott's Vacation Club International has cut the volume of direct mail needed to produce target levels of response to its offers. How? By taking information from its own database, augmenting it with "enhancement" information provided by a data compiler, and then applying a predictive model to the augmented data set.

Prudential Insurance Co. recently combined demographic data on 10 million households provided by the same data compiler with its own life, securities, real estate, and credit card operational systems. Why? So the entire annuity product prospect pool could be distilled to exclude prospects with little interest in annuity products. The payoff: A pilot test conducted in the Northeast generated twice the response that randomly selecting prospects from the entire pool would have produced.

Peter R. Peacock is Associate Professor of Marketing and Information Systems at the Babcock Graduate School of Management at Wake Forest University. He has been a consultant in marketing, marketing research, and information technology to R.J. Reynolds Tobacco Co., Novartis, Hanes Dye and Finishing Co., Bob Timberlake Inc., and Sara Lee. A member of the Babcock faculty for many years, Peter has taught courses in marketing research, database marketing, and information systems. His varied research interests have resulted in articles published in the *Journal of Business,* the *Journal of Consumer Research*, the *Journal of Marketing Research*, the *Journal of Office Systems Research*, *Business Horizons*, and *Marketing Management*. Currently, Peter is doing research in the areas of data mining, data transformations, and direct marketing strategy and database structures. He received his PhD from the University of Chicago.

American Express is using a neural network to examine the hundreds of millions of entries in its database that tell how and where individual card-holders transact business. The result is a set of "purchase propensity scores," for each cardholder. Based on these scores, AmEx matches offers from affiliated merchants to the purchase histories of individual cardholders and encloses these offers with their monthly statements. The benefits are reduced expenses for AmEx and information of higher value for its cardholders.

Defining Data Mining

These are just a few examples of how data mining is being used to improve marketing efficiency by many of America's largest companies. The trade press brims with countless additional examples. But, despite this attention, there is much confusion about the meaning of the term, "data mining." Data mining is defined within a narrow scope by some experts, within a broad scope by others, and within a very broad scope by still others.

Narrow Scope

Narrowly defined, data mining is the automated discovery of "interesting," nonobvious patterns hidden in a database that have a high potential for contributing to the bottom line. As it is used here, the word "interesting" has special meaning to the data mining community: "Interesting" relationships are those that could have an impact on strategy or tactics and ultimately on an organization's objectives. The narrow scope of data mining encompasses computer-based methods—generally called "machine-learning" methods—that extract patterns or information from data while requiring only limited human involvement. Most of these methods are of relatively recent origin and have their roots in artificial intelligence (AI). Examples of machine-learning methods are neural networks, association rules, decision trees, and genetic algorithms.

Note the emphasis here on the process of discovery. Discovery means that we're looking for relationships we didn't know about beforehand, and, in that sense, discovery is akin to surfing—that is, searching for interesting patterns and following the data trail wherever it leads. The discovery process often involves sifting through massive quantities of data; electronic point-of-sale transactions, inventory records, and online customer orders matched with demographics can easily use up hundreds of gigabytes of data storage.

Although the volumes of data with which marketing decision makers must work are already very large and will get much larger still, tools are available to help with the heavy lifting. For example, the judicious use of probability sampling, predictive modeling, and machine-learning methods can yield valid results while reducing the data management task significantly.

Broad Scope

Within the broad-scope definition, data mining also encompasses "confirmation" or the testing of relationships revealed through the discovery process. Here, we employ classical and Bayesian statistical methods and formally assess hypotheses turned up at the discovery stage, or we search for and confirm relationships that support the theories, models, and hypotheses formulated within the narrow data mining scope or with the aid of other kinds of evidence whose structures are weak and not well-understood.

Prior to confirmation, our beliefs are more akin to hunches than they are to consistent, propositional connections between phenomena or events. Also, within the broad scope, the data mining umbrella opens up to encompass simple queries and traditional investigative procedures, most of which have their roots in statistics. Examples of these procedures are exploratory data analysis, ordinary least squares regression, logistic regression, and discriminant analysis.

These more traditional techniques are typified by greater emphasis on human learning and less emphasis on machine learning. These activities are best described as computer-assisted and are semiautomatic in the sense that analysts use statistical and AI tools to confirm patterns in data rather than to identify them. Within the broad scope definition, there is also more involvement of the manager and analyst in structuring the investigation, identifying important variables prior to analysis, and attempting to ensure that the variables are in a form suitable for analysis.

Very Broad Scope

In its broadest scope, data mining is referred to as "knowledge discovery in databases" (KDD), and it incorporates the following activities:

- Acquiring data from internal and external sources.

- Translating, cleaning, and formatting the data.

- Analyzing, validating, and attaching meaning to data (this includes narrow scope data mining).

- Scoring databases.

- Building and implementing decision support tools and systems to make data mining results available to decision makers and lower level staff.

- Recalibrating models and maintaining delivery systems.

The individual steps included in the KDD process have been taken ever since the first business enterprise was formed thousands of years ago. In those ancient times, and even up to very recently, however, individual activities were performed in an ad hoc, catch-as-catch-can support role. For many firms today, however, the KDD process and narrow scope data mining are taking on a central, business-driving role. The process is being formally managed, is being placed in continuous operation, and is moving to the core of business operations.

Driving Factors

Two questions marketers often ask are: (1) "What's driving the data mining revolution we hear about so often?" and (2) "What can data mining do for me that my regular marketing research organization doesn't already do?

Data mining is obviously important. For example, the *Wall Street Journal* reported recently that: "The Palo Alto Management Group, an industry research firm, estimates companies will spend $73 billion on hardware, software, and services related to sorting out customer data in 2001, up from $10 billion today. The payoff will be a much faster return on investment when more of the right customers are hit."

But despite all the hoopla and media attention, data mining is not really revolutionary. Its roots reach back to the methodology of John Tukey of Princeton and Bell Labs, a statistician whose ideas were first introduced in the mid-'70s. Tukey called his methodology, "exploratory data analysis" (EDA), and it's still referred to by that name; moreover, EDA continues to be used on a daily basis by researchers and analysts working in a broad range of disciplines.

What's different today is that data volumes have proliferated to the extent that analysts are unable to extract meaningful information using traditional EDA approaches, even those that incorporate statistical sampling methodologies to tackle the problem of data management. Because data volumes have become so large, data mining professionals are turning increasingly to information technology as a way to float above the data flood.

The principal differences between EDA of the '70s, EDA as it continues to be practiced widely today by statisticians and analysts, and data mining in the narrow scope is that data mining substitutes machine learning for human learning and it is frequently applied to entire data sets (often very large data sets) rather than to samples drawn from them.

Several closely related developments have motivated the growth of the data mining industry. Grouping them into a "supply-side" factor set and "demand-side" factor set aids in understanding their effects.

Supply-Side Factors

On the supply side are the effects of information technology advances. For example, advances in data storage and data processing technology such as parallel-processing computers have led to deep reductions in the cost of collecting and storing the operational data flowing from retail point-of-sale terminals, direct marketing order-entry systems, and the interrelated systems of financial services firms.

A second factor is the declining cost of electronic communication. Not so many years ago, only the analysts working directly with mainframes could gain access to data easily. With today's widespread networks, however, almost anyone with a PC can connect to a corporate network, intranet, extranet, or the World Wide Web and work directly with large data files.

A third factor is the emergence of new analysis techniques that have enabled analysts to turn much of the work of discovery over to computers. Examples are neural networks, genetic algorithms, decision trees, and induction rules.

A fourth factor is the computer architecture revolution IS types refer to as "client/server" and friendlier user interfaces such as Microsoft Windows.

And a final supply-side factor is the development of the data warehouse and the data mart. Lumped together, these technological advances are causing the amount of information in the world to grow exponentially (see Data Warehouses and Marts box on page 168).

Demand-Side Factors

One demand-side factor is the growing need for ever-faster analytical results in an increasingly competitive business environment as the relevant market for most industries becomes worldwide in scope.

A second factor is the squashing of the organizational hierarchy. Just a few years ago, marketing managers turned to staff support analysts for the answers they needed. But, today, most of the support analysts are gone, and the marketing manager must either become a part-time analyst or sail by dead reckoning. Another alternative for the marketing manager is to develop ongoing partnerships with a few marketing research firms that provide close analytical support for a variety of needs. In more and more firms, the partnering research firm has employees at the client site providing support with data mining and other analysis tasks on almost a permanent basis.

A final and unexpected demand-side factor is the boomlet in books and articles focusing attention on building and maintaining customer relationships. Perhaps the best known example of this genre is *The One To One Future* by Don Peppers and Martha Rogers, but there have been many such publications in recent years. This literature has increased the sensitivity of marketing managers to the value of information in their companies' databases and stimulated demand for ways to get at it.

Data Mining and Marketing

Data mining has many potential uses in marketing. Four of these—customer acquisition, customer retention, customer abandonment, and market basket analysis—have wide application:

- *Customer acquisition.* In the first stage of a two-stage process, direct marketers apply data mining methods to discover attributes that predict customer responses to offers and communications programs such as catalogs. Then, in the second stage, the attributes of customers that the model says are most likely to respond are matched to corresponding attributes appended to rented lists of noncustomers to select only the noncustomer households most likely to respond to a new offer or communication.

- *Customer retention.* In a typical marketing application, data mining identifies those customers who contribute to the company's bottom line but who are likely to leave and go to a competitor. With this information, the company can target the vulnerable customers for special offers and other inducements not available to nonvulnerables.

- *Customer abandonment.* Some customers cost more than they contribute and should be encouraged to take their business elsewhere. This situation often exists in retail banking when young customers keep rock-bottom balances but require high levels of bank support services. Unprofitable customers also populate the files of traditional direct marketers, placing lots of small orders or habitually ordering merchandise and then returning it. When data mining is

---

DATA WAREHOUSES AND MARTS

Data mining is possible without a data warehouse, but having one up and running greatly eases the data mining task. A data warehouse is an enterprise-level data repository that draws its contents from all critical operational systems and selected external data sources. It is built according to an enterprise "data model" that must be drawn up ahead of time in an often time- and resource-consuming cross-functional effort. Data warehouses can cost in excess of $10 million to build and take anywhere from one to three years to complete.

A data mart, in contrast, is a functional, subject-area, or departmental data repository that draws its contents from systems that are critical to the unit owning the data mart and from selected external sources. Data marts can be constructed as individual components within the scope of a comprehensive data warehouse plan (called "top-down" design) and, if time and cost requirements aren't constraining, that's recognized as the best approach. In most cases, however, data marts are cobbled together independently of data warehouse initiatives (called "bottom-up" design) because cost and time almost always are constraints.

Data marts usually cost between $10,000 and $1 million to build and can be brought on line in less than six months. The major drawback of the bottom-up approach is that the architecture of the data mart (specified in a set of formalized rules called "meta data") often turns out to be inconsistent with the architecture of other data marts and the data warehouse (when it does get built).

---

applied to the purchase histories of such customers, their negative impact on the bottom line often becomes evident.

- *Market basket analysis.* By identifying the associations between product purchases in point-of-sale transactions, retailers and direct marketers can spot product affinities and develop focused promotion strategies that work more effectively than traditional "one-size-fits-all" approaches. The American Express selective envelope-stuffing strategy cited earlier is an example of how market basket analysis can be employed to increase marketing efficiency.

Data Mining Tasks and Tools

Although data mining can be applied to lists of individuals, objects, ideas, text fragments, or any other construct that can be represented as an electronic list, most marketing applications model individuals or households. Five foundation-level analysis tasks are the "reasons why" of data mining: summarization, predictive modeling, clustering/segmentation, classification, and link analysis.

Summarization. Summarization refers to methods that collapse large amounts of data into the summary measures that provide general descriptions of variables and their relationships. Examples of summarization methods are simple structured query language (SQL) "selects" that produce counts, averages, and totals; descriptive statistics that include measures of central tendency such as the mean and median; measures of dispersion such as the standard deviation; and measures that describe distributions of variables such as the range, skewness, and kurtosis indicators. Simple cross-tabs and visualization techniques such as pie charts and histograms also fall into the summarization category. Although summary measures provide useful overviews and "big-picture" insights, they miss the details and idiosyncrasies that typify individual observations and contribute significantly to our understanding of consumer behavior.

Predictive Modeling.   Predictive modeling includes methods employed to predict outcomes using one or more independent variables to specify the value of a criterion or dependent variable. The outcomes can be binary—for example, respond to an offer or not, remain an active customer or not—and, in these cases, models are used to predict the probability of an outcome. Outcomes also can be continuous—for example, average yearly purchase volume or average monthly credit balance. Traditional tools used for predictive modeling are ordinary least squares regression, logistic regression, and discriminant analysis. Newer techniques are association rules, decision trees, neural networks, and genetic algorithms.

Clustering.   Clustering, or segmentation, refers to the process of forming groups of individuals or households based on information contained in the sets of variables that describe them. Its purpose is to assist in the development of customized marketing programs that can be targeted to cluster members in hopes that they will buy more or become more loyal.

For example, demographic characteristics, lifestyle descriptors, and actual product purchases might be used to segment mail-order cycling product customers into mountain bike, road bike, triathlete, touring, and "gift-giving" segments. Assuming segmentation is successful, marketing programs can be customized to appeal differentially to the individual segments, producing a more efficient design than the "one-size-fits-all" approach.

Clustering can be performed with traditional statistical cluster analysis techniques, with decision-tree-based methods such as CHAID (chi-square automatic interaction detector), with neural networks, and with genetic algorithms.

Classification.   Classification methods assign prospects to existing groups using the information contained in sets of predictor variables. Classification can be performed with older techniques such as discriminant analysis and logistic regression or with newer tools such as association rules, case-based reasoning, and neural networks. Returning to the cycling example, demographic and lifestyle data purchased from a data compiler could be used to assign brand new cycling product customers to existing segments.

Link Analysis.   Link analysis refers to a family of methods that is employed to correlate purchase patterns cross-sectionally or over time. Market basket analysis, a link analysis method, uses the information implicit in the products customers have already purchased to predict which products they're likely to buy if they're given special offers or even if they're just made aware of them. For example, an individual who buys aero bars and deep-rim wheels (bicycle components with special appeal to triathletes) is much more likely to buy a wet suit on special than would a customer buying mostly mountain bike components.

Sequential pattern modeling is analogous to market basket, analysis except that products purchased or other behavior patterns captured at one point in time are used to predict the likelihood of purchasing product or service categories in the future.

The Data Miner's Tool Kit

Many analytical techniques can be classified as data mining tools, but, for now at least, agreement on exactly which techniques should and should not be included in the tool set is not widespread. Nonetheless, books and articles in this area do suggest that the data miner's tool kit would probably include nine tools or tool sets:

- Query tools.
- Descriptive statistics.
- Visualization tools.
- Regression-type models.
- Association rules.
- Decision trees.
- Case-based reasoning.
- Neural networks.
- Genetic algorithms.

Decision trees, association rules, case-based learning tools, neural networks, and genetic algorithms are categorized as "machine-learning" methods, whereas the others can be classified as "machine-assisted" aids to support human learning.

Query Tools. The user who already knows what to look for employs query tools to produce lists of individuals or households having specified characteristics and simple summary measures such as counts, totals, and averages. Query tools are typified by structured query language (SQL), the standard query language of almost all relational database management systems.

For the analyst or manager who is comfortable with SQL, who knows the structure of the database, and who has a good understanding of what to look for, running SQL queries against a database can produce quick and informative results. But even for the less sophisticated analyst, there are excellent query tools available because IT advances have produced graphical point-and-click interfaces that greatly simplify the creation of queries. Microsoft Access is one widely available application that provides easy-to-use query tools; another good tool is Q & A.

Descriptive Statistics. Near the front end of the KDD process, simple descriptive statistics such as averages and measures of variation, counts and percentages, and cross-tabs and simple correlations are useful for understanding the structure of the data and for identifying potential problems with and misconceptions about data.

At the back end of the data mining stage of the KDD process, descriptive statistics provide additional support to user-analysts attempting to interpret patterns discovered by data mining engines. Simple statistical tools are familiar to most managers and can be quite useful. However, they often suffer in comparison with visual data displays because they don't provide "the look and feel" of the data to which users of desktop application visualization tools have become accustomed.

Visualization. Data visualization is primarily a discovery technique. Visualization is particularly effective for interpreting large amounts of data because it takes advantage of our natural ability to recognize and distinguish between patterns of observable characteristics.

Visualization techniques are effective for condensing large amounts of messy data down to a concise, economic, and comprehensible picture. Visualization techniques used in data mining range from low-level univariate and bivariate analysis tools such as simple histograms, box plots, and scatter diagrams to more advanced tools such as rotating 3D surface plots that reveal the subtleties in distributions and relationships involving three variables.

Regression-Type Models. These models are used mainly for confirmation. The complete regression tool set includes several related families of models, but the techniques employed most often are: (1) ordinary least squares (OLS) regression, (2) logistic regression, and (3) discriminant analysis. OLS regression and discriminant analysis have been in the statistician's tool bag for more than 60 years; logistic regression is a more recently acquired tool.

OLS regression is best suited for modeling or predicting naturally continuous quantities such as average monthly purchases when the distributions of the quantities don't differ markedly from the normal distribution, when the relationships between independent variables and the dependent variable are linear, and when the independent variables do not interact. (Interactions occur when the values of an independent variable affect the relationship between the dependent variable and a second independent variable.) OLS regression is also favored when understanding the nature of the relationship between the dependent variable and the predictor is important because regression results are more informative than the output from other data mining tools such as neural networks.

Logistic regression is best suited to predicting categorical outcomes such as responses to direct marketing offers or customer attrition (attrition either does or does not happen; there's no middle ground). A plus for logistic regression relative to OLS regression is that the assumptions underpinning the procedure are less restrictive than the assumptions underpinning linear regression. An advantage of logistic regression relative to other non-regression-type methods is that it produces assessment statistics that are analogous to the assessment statistics of linear regression packages, making it easier to understand the impact of the predictors on the criterion variable.

Discriminant analysis is a regression-type tool used to assign new individuals or households into one of two or more existing groups or clusters. On the plus side, discriminant analysis software packages produce assessment statistics that are comparable to those produced by regression packages. On the minus side, the technique is subject to fairly restrictive assumptions—all predictor variables are assumed to be normal and the variance structures of all groups are assumed to be the same—causing analysts to have some reluctance to use the tool.

Association Rules.   Association rules are statements about relationships between the attributes of a known group of individuals and one or more aspects of their behavior that enable predictions to be made about the behavior of other individuals who are not in the group but who possess the same attributes. Association rules are always stated in dichotomous terms—for example, "make a purchase or not"—and usually assign probability-like numbers to actions.

To see how association rules work, consider the following example. Assume we're interested in promoting a cycling jersey to phone-in customers who have just finished ordering several other items. Promoting the jersey to customers who aren't interested will waste our phone representatives' time and may even antagonize some callers. Therefore, we'd like to restrict the offers to just those callers who have a high probability of buying the jersey. That's where association rules come in. They use the information in customer purchase histories to formulate probabilistic rules pertaining to subsequent purchases.

Returning to our example, analysis of purchase records with association rule methods may tell us that callers who purchased helmets and biking shorts on one call were far more likely to buy jerseys on a subsequent call than, say, callers who ordered Power Bars, tires, or tools. Therefore, when the association rules are incorporated in our order entry system and the system sees that the customer on the phone recently ordered shorts and a helmet, it can trigger the phone representative to make the offer on jerseys. On the other hand, if the system finds that the caller bought tires and Power Bars on the last call, the built-in decision rules incorporate a low probability of jersey purchase and the phone rep is not prompted to make the jersey offer.

Decision Trees.   Tree-based methods are the most common implementation of what are usually referred to as "induction" techniques. They construct decision trees from data automatically, yielding a sequence of stepwise rules, such as "If the household has purchased at least twice in the last six months, assign it to this node of the tree." Tree-based methods are good at identifying important variables, nonlinear relationships, and interactions between predictor variables, and they work well when predictors are numerous and many are irrelevant. They also lend themselves well to visualization and, compared with other data mining tools, are relatively easy for users to understand and interpret. Finally, decision tree algorithms are robust to outliers and erroneous data in the predictors or response variable, and they usually run quickly on all but the largest data sets. Leading examples of decision tree algorithms are CHAID, CART, and C4.5.

On the negative side, trees use up data very rapidly in the training process, so they should never be used with small data sets (see Training vs. Estimation box on page 174). They are also highly sensitive to noise in the data and they try to fit the data exactly. Another way to express this last notion is to say that trees tend to overfit data. What overfitting means is that the specification of a model is in large part an artifact of the idiosyncrasies of the data set used to build it. When a model suffers from overfitting, it is unlikely to have external validity (it won't hold up when applied to a new data set). Therefore, cross-validation of decision tree results is critical. Cross-validation involves the application of a model constructed using one data sample (often called a "calibration" sample) to a second, independently drawn sample (often called, not surprisingly, a "validation" sample) to see if the performance of the model is reproducible.

Case-Based Reasoning.   In case-based reasoning (CBR) systems, sets of attributes of new problem situations are compared with corresponding attribute sets in a collection of previously encountered "cases" to find one or more template-like examples that provide generally good outcomes or solutions.

Consider this example of a case-based reasoning system that defines the specifications—square footage, number of checkouts, whether the store has a bakery or deli section, and so forth—for potential grocery store sites. In the application, the essential attributes of a site—population density, traffic flow, average household income, and average age of household heads—might be compared to the rows in a database containing corresponding attributes for all of the company's existing stores, together with their design specifications, and perhaps performance indexes as well.

With the information provided, the CBR system would quickly identify the existing locations that most closely resemble the proposed locations and suggest what design specifications they should incorporate—the "template" notion. Of course, it would be most unusual for all the attributes of any proposed site to duplicate exactly all attributes of any one or a small group of existing sites, and so some modifications of the potential site's design specification would usually be required to accommodate its unique characteristics. In that respect, the most similar case identified by the system is analogous to a spreadsheet template; it's a good model, but it's likely to require modification to meet needs that are not inherent in even the most comparable case in the database.

Case-based reasoning systems are effective because they convert abstract concepts into real images, forcing users to focus directly on the similarities and differences between different situations in a structured way using the attributes that define the cases. In addition, CBRs are intuitive and easy for managers to understand. They accommodate qualitative data and discontinuous, lumpy relationships between attributes very well, and computation is fast.

The primary drawback of CBRs is that the solutions included in the case database may not be optimal in any sense because they represent what has actually been done in the past, not necessarily what should have been done under similar circumstances. Therefore, using them may simply perpetuate earlier mistakes. Other limitations of CBRs are the time required to establish and maintain the database and the expertise needed, first, to identify attributes that are related to specific outcomes and, then, to assign weights so that new situations can be matched to the most appropriate outcomes. A final limitation is that CBRs don't work well when there are significant interactions between attributes.

Neural networks.   Neural networks are computer applications mimicking the processes of the human brain that are capable of learning from examples to find patterns in data. They are good at combining information from many predictors, and

TRAINING VS. ESTIMATION

A regression model is said to be "estimated" by applying a regression package to a data set. But a neural network model is said to be "trained." Conceptually, however, estimation and training are analogous. Estimation involves reading sample data and then calculating predictor-variable weights by using optimization techniques based on calculus. Training involves reading sample data and iteratively adjusting network weights to produce a best prediction. In either case, once weights are determined, new data can be applied to the model to generate predictions quickly.

they work well when many of the independent variables are correlated and when non-linearities and missing data cause problems for traditional linear models such as OLS regression and discriminant analysis. Neural networks have a significant advantage over regression-type models because they are able to detect nonlinear relationships automatically.

A purported advantage of neural networks relative to procedures whose solutions are easier for users to understand—such as logistic regression—is the time required for adjusting models to compensate for changes in the relationships they are supposed to capture. Generally, rebuilding regression models so that they accurately represent changes in the relationships they are thought to model is time-consuming. As a result, neural networks are considered to be especially appropriate in dynamic, fast-changing situations when the relationship between behavior—for example, customer attrition—and a set of predictors is subject to frequent change.

On the negative side, building the initial neural network model can be especially time-intensive because input processing almost always means that raw data must be transformed, and variable screening and selection requires large amounts of analyst time and skill. Also, for the user without a technical background, figuring out how neural networks operate underneath the hood is far from obvious. An even more serious limitation is that neural nets provide little to explain the outcomes they produce; they are said to be opaque.

Another limitation of neural networks is that they require large training sets, that is, many data points. This requirement is usually not difficult to fulfill in data mining situations, however. Finally, a confusingly large array of neural network procedures exists, so for anyone other than the neural network expert, the multitude of analysis tools available can be bewildering.

Genetic Algorithms. Genetic algorithms (GAs) operate through procedures modeled upon the evolutionary biological processes of selection, reproduction, mutation, and survival of the fittest to search for very good solutions to prediction and classification problems. GAs are used to solve prediction and classification problems or to develop sets of decision rules similar to the rules that can be inferred from the output of decision-tree models.

GAs are especially effective for solving poorly understood, poorly structured problems because they attempt to find many solutions simultaneously, whereas a regression model, for example, attempts to find a single best solution. Another strength of GAs is that they can explicitly model any decision criterion in the "fitness function," an objective system used to assess a GA's performance. For example, a GA can explicitly model maximizing the percentage of responses in the top two deciles of a direct marketing lift analysis, something logistic regression cannot do.

Another benefit of GAs relative to other procedures that can be applied to the same problem—such as logistic regression to a prediction problem—is that they can produce novel solutions. For example, they might discover combinations of predictor variables that no one would have expected to be predictive beforehand. A final benefit of GAs is that they can be applied fruitfully in cases where the user doesn't know enough about analytical procedures to select the most appropriate tool for the job. They tend to be forgiving of a user's lack of technical expertise.

Although GA software operates very efficiently on relatively small problems with relatively small numbers of variables and can be run effectively on a PC, GAs tend to operate slowly when large numbers of variables are included. This happens because of the process of evaluation of the fitness function. Therefore, they are not appropriate for automatic searching through very large numbers of candidate variables to find a subset of variables with relatively high predictive power—a task to which decision trees are especially well suited.

In addition, the hands-on work associated with constructing GAs is often quite time-consuming and many runs may be required in the fitting process. Finally, in contrast to regression models, for example. GA solutions are difficult to explain. They do not provide interpretive statistical measures that enable the user to understand why the procedure arrived at a particular solution.

Quicksand

Ponder for just a moment about the billions of marketing transactions that occur every day, year after year in the retail sector, in business-to-business marketing, and in the direct channel. An absolute flood of data that has disappeared into the sand. Think for another moment about all the useful information contained in those transactions that was simply thrown away because it was just not economic to collect, store, extract, and interpret it.

Now, realize that precipitous and continuing reductions in data storage costs, development of ever-faster processors, discovery and commercialization of sophisticated analysis techniques, and a growing army of bright, well-trained data miners will enable the conversion of this waste by-product into a great new resource for providing added value to customers. Are you getting ready to incorporate this new resource into your marketing production process? Do you know how to seize the opportunity?

I will discuss the important activities that make up the KDD process in Part 2 of this article, which will appear in the next issue of *Marketing Management.* That article also will focus on how a senior marketing manager can put together a KDD operation and address important related issues of value measurement, addressing consumer concerns, and preparing to respond to the continuing data explosion.

Reprinted with permission from the Winter 1998 issue of Marketing Management, *published by the American Marketing Association, Peter R. Peacock, Winter 1998/Vol. 6. pp 8–18.*

9

Data Mining in Marketing: Part 2

Dig Deep to Unearth Knowledge Inherent in Databases

Data mining is part of a much larger process known as "knowledge discovery in databases." The knowledge discovery process includes 10 phases, from data funneling to recalibrating models. Senior marketing managers can put a KDD operation in place by following seven steps, but they also must be attuned to issues such as value measurement, consumer privacy concerns, and appropriate responses to the ongoing data explosion.

As chief operating officer of Paceline Inc., a supplier of bicycles and accessories to hard-core cyclists and triathletes as well as more casual riders, Gary Bright long has wondered how to increase the effectiveness of the catalog mailings from the mail-order side of his business. He's also wondered how Paceline's customer support representatives can best cross-sell additional merchandise when customers place phone orders. And, Bright has pondered how he can move more retail customers to mail order and more mail-order customers to retail. Inspired by a seminar presentation on data mining and some additional reading, he decided the large databases supporting Paceline's mail-order and retail operations just might yield some answers to those questions.

Most managers ask the same types of questions, and because of the attention paid to data mining in the information technology community in recent years, many of them are attempting to apply this process to their own businesses.

In the last issue of *Marketing Management*, we defined data mining narrowly, as the data miners themselves define it, and more broadly, as most of the rest of the business world defines it. We also discussed some of the driving forces behind the explosive adoption of data mining, considered some specific data mining tools, and sketched out the workings of the most popular techniques in this tool set. This issue, we broaden our scope and examine the larger framework in which data mining is but a component: knowledge discovery in databases, or KDD.

The Process

To become productively engaged in knowledge discovery activities, marketing managers should possess a firm grasp of what these activities entail. Figure 1 outlines the knowledge discovery process. Although the exhibit omits feedback loops between

FIGURE 1	THE KNOWLEDGE DISCOVERY PROCESS

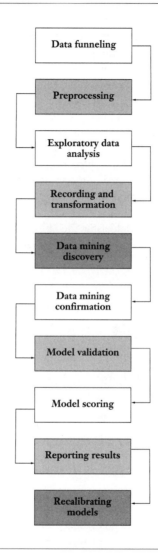

elements of the diagram, it should be understood that the KDD process is "iterative" and that there is a substantial flow of information back to prior steps in the process.

Data Funneling

This element represents the procedures through which data are gathered to ensure suitability for analysis. This is important because when data are badly flawed, even the most sophisticated data mining tools perform badly. Data mining tools assume high data quality levels; it is not their purpose to identify, correct, or remove data garbage.

Data funneling operations include the identification of internal operational data and external enhancement data appropriate to the data mining objective.[1] They also involve the movement of internally generated and enhancement data to a central collection point, or data repository. Finally, they include procedures for evaluating data quality and rejection of data that do not meet quality standards.

Procedures for assessing data quality include scanning the results by running simple queries, applying basic visualization techniques, and running automated procedures that ensure that incoming data types match expected data types and that individual data items fall within acceptable ranges. Almost all data sets have minor flaws, but it isn't the purpose of the screening process to catch minor flaws. The objective is to identify catastrophic problems such as data elements that are in the wrong columns, numeric elements that have been truncated from seven places to three, or variables that have not been converted from alphabetic representation to numeric. Data funneling also includes selecting the subset of variables to be analyzed from the larger set of all characteristics available in the data repository.

Preprocessing

Data preprocessing includes five operations that ensure that raw material conforms to input standards:

- Reformatting. Data from different sources are converted to a common format.

- Standardizing. It is usually necessary to standardize data attributes—especially text-based—to conform to common external or corporate standard specifications.

- Removing sparse records. When individual records lack data on many important attributes, it makes little sense to retain them in a data mining repository. Specifying criteria for removing sparse records and then deleting them from the repository (or making them inaccessible to analysis routines) is important.

- De-duping. Duplicate instances of the same individual or household resulting from address changes, input keying errors, and fraud are common in databases that are not cleaned regularly. Identifying and removing duplicates is obviously an important preprocessing activity.

- Householding. The natural target unit for many marketing programs is the household rather than the individual. In such cases, individuals must be assigned to households by software that looks for sets of common attributes such as last names, address components, and phone numbers.

Exploratory Data Analysis

After the preprocessing is complete, the next step is to conduct exploratory data analysis, the investigation of preprocessed data by an analyst using computer-assisted methods. A major purpose of EDA is identifying the anomalies and outliers remaining in a data set after it has passed quality checks and been reformatted and standardized.

Another purpose of EDA is giving the analyst a feel for the preprocessed data. The analyst looks for largest and smallest values, central tendency (if any), dispersion, the shapes of the distributions of individual variables, and the structure of the relationships among variables. He or she is on the alert for nonlinear relationships and empirical distributions that depart significantly from the classic normal shape.

A third purpose of EDA is the discovery of data patterns and relationships among variables suggesting hypotheses of cause and effect which did not exist beforehand. When these occur, they should be formally recorded in an intelligent database so the findings can be sorted and aggregated by subject, issue, or topic area. Tools that support EDA are query engines such as SQL, descriptive statistics, and visualization techniques.

Recoding and Transformation

In the recoding and transformation phase, some or all preprocessed variables are transformed into new values. This can be done by taking their logarithms or square roots, or by performing other mathematical operations on their preprocessed values. Preprocessed data also might be recoded into other values using simple decision rules.

Variable transformations are employed to improve the performance of predictive and classification modeling techniques or to construct a new predictor or criterion variable whose empirical distribution conforms more closely than does the preprocessed variable to an assumed distribution, such as the normal. Recoding converts continuous data into a categorical form for use with tools such as neural nets and decision trees, or it converts nominal text label data into numeric values. For example, a state designator such as "CA" might be assigned a value of 4.

Data Mining/Discovery

This step involves the techniques and algorithms referred to as "narrow-scope" data mining, essentially machine learning from patterns in data performed by the major discovery tools such as association rules and decision trees.

Data Mining/Confirmation

The techniques and algorithms referred to as "broad-scope" data mining are the procedures that test hypotheses discovered via EDA or narrow-scope data mining. This is the construction phase of any data mining project whose purpose is model building. Techniques used include classical statistical procedures such as logistic regression as well as artificial intelligence-based techniques such as neural nets, employed for confirmation of hypotheses rather than pattern discovery.

Model Validation

This is the step where model quality is assessed. Validation is especially critical because a model almost always predicts more accurately when it is applied to the data set used for estimation or training than when data from an independent sample are used. This situation occurs when a model captures subtleties in the data that arise only in the sample used to build the model, and it's called overfitting.

The standard approach to model validation is to draw two random samples from the preprocessed data. A calibration sample is used to build the model. A validation, or holdout, sample is used to evaluate the model produced using the calibration sample. Generally, a well-constructed model produces good results when applied to a validation sample, but some reduction in performance can be expected. When the model performs very poorly—no better than chance, for example—the analyst must once again begin the model-building process from scratch.

Model Scoring

In the scoring phase, the validated predictive model, or a set of classification rules, is applied to the entire database. A model such as $y = b_0 + b_1x_1 + b_2x_2$ developed from a sample of the data is applied to the entire population of records. Scoring is accomplished by substituting corresponding population data for the variables—x_1, x_2, x_3, and so forth—that were in the sample. The calculated scores, the y's, are placed in a new column in the database.

The predicted values are the scores, and the process of applying the equation to the preprocessed variables is called scoring. Scoring also refers to the process of coding cluster membership of individual observations when clustering is performed. Scoring is obviously a crucial step in the KDD process and must be precise.

Quality assurance is an important four-step supplemental process. First, a set of sample records is selected randomly from the entire database and scored using the newly developed model. Second, these sample records are checked carefully to ensure that the scoring algorithm worked correctly. Third, in a completely separate operation performed under production conditions, the entire database (including the records selected in step 1) is scored with the new model. Finally, the records matching the sample drawn earlier are again pulled from the database and their scores are compared to the scores assigned on their first appearance. The two sets of scores must match exactly or the scoring process is defective.

Reporting Results

This step includes interpreting results and providing support information to decision makers. Decision support information can be produced in the EDA phase or in the discovery or confirmation phases of data mining, and the results can be in the form of standard paper reports or in an electronic form made available over the corporate network or intranet.

Recalibrating the Model

Individual behavior changes, households reconstitute themselves, and the marketing environment of every company evolves. Even the best-constructed model is unlikely to be best for long. Some models are productive for two or three years, others are useless after only a few months, but all deteriorate over time. Recalibration that is done regularly and according to a schedule established before the very first model is built is critical.

Recalibrating involves repeating the model-building process with a recently constructed data set. Because business dynamics will cause the data used for recalibration to differ from the data used to build the existing model, the parameters of the recalibrated model will differ from those of the existing model. The recalibrated model may even have a totally different structure—it might include new parameters, or its mathematical formulation may differ.

Required Infrastructure

Three infrastructure components are requisites to knowledge discovery. The most important is a repository containing data on customers and other entities—identifiers such as customer name and address, demographic and lifestyle variables, purchase history, and response to previous marketing efforts. The data repository can be a full-scale "data warehouse" serving the entire organization or a more modest "data mart" supporting the analytical requirements of an individual department. It also could be a "virtual warehouse" in software and communications links between a customer information file and the company's operational systems.

KDD also requires one or more high-performance computers for processing the many variables needed to predict customer behavior, identify market segments, or classify new customers into existing groups. Once models have been built, large-scale computing power is useful for quickly "scoring the database": inserting numerical values in customer records that are used as keys to select sets of records for use in marketing programs. The scored database is often a large multiple of the sample used to build the model. At present, symmetric multiprocessor and massively parallel computers are the machines of choice for delivering the performance needed for these activities.

An alternative to those processors is dedicated departmental computers—usually reduced instruction set computers (RISC) with lots of disk space. After the necessary data is extracted from the main customer information file, the RISC machine does the scoring and other processing. Scored or modified fields are shipped back to the main file.

The third infrastructure component is the entire set of procedures, operations, and supporting software that make results available to decision makers in the output phase. This can involve paper reports or electronic text and graphics accessible via software tools on the desktop client machines of marketing managers and their support staffs.

Organizing for KDD

Be prepared to commit significant time, money, and intellectual resources to the organizing effort. Hidden costs almost always crop up when trying to solve ill-structured business problems. For most companies, assembling the individual pieces of the KDD process to support data mining is a large-scale innovation undertaken to solve not one but many problems.

Figure 2 shows the tasks involved in building a data mining operation. Tasks are listed stepwise in the order of their accomplishment. The most important step is to

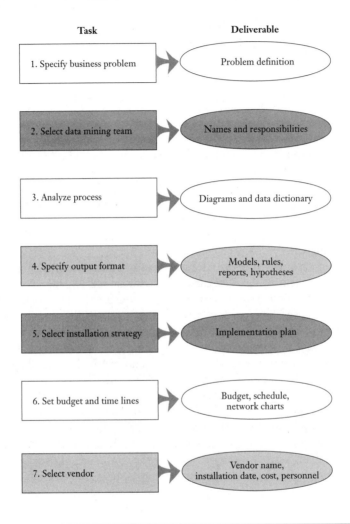

FIGURE 2 ORGANIZING FOR KNOWLEDGE DISCOVERY

Task	Deliverable
1. Specify business problem	Problem definition
2. Select data mining team	Names and responsibilities
3. Analyze process	Diagrams and data dictionary
4. Specify output format	Models, rules, reports, hypotheses
5. Select installation strategy	Implementation plan
6. Set budget and time lines	Budget, schedule, network charts
7. Select vendor	Vendor name, installation date, cost, personnel

define the problem and focus all efforts on solving it. The scope should be defined narrowly in the sense that it should affect no more than a small number of corporate units and should be quickly resolvable, certainly in no more than a year. A sin committed all too often by managers new to data mining is being overly ambitious. At the outset, they want to gather all the data required to solve any conceivable business problem emerging within the next quarter century.

Excess ambition is understandable, but it usually results in the creation of a data repository that's too large, too costly, too dirty, and years behind schedule. Defining the business problem narrowly and then creating a data repository specific to it is best at the commencement of a program. The written statement of the business problem to be solved by the data mining effort should include the effort's objective, a general time frame, and a list of affected business units.

At the start, concepts will be ill-defined, objectives will be vague, and policies will be conflicting and contradictory. Therefore, the data mining team should be a small task force whose primary role is problem investigation and feasibility analysis. The data mining team should include the marketing manager, the database administrator, and the analyst.

- The marketing manager is the team leader and "domain expert." He or she is closest to the business problem and best understands the business environment, knows what questions to ask, and knows how to translate answers into action. The marketing manager is also closest to top-level support for the data mining effort and is the effort's natural "champion." This individual must be zealously dedicated to the project and have the persistence and force of will to see it through to completion. Identifying champions isn't easy, but ignoring this key dimension puts the entire project at risk.

- The database administrator is responsible for the back end of the process. He or she has the technical knowledge to extract data from the database most efficiently as well as an awareness of the kinds of information actually residing on the database.

- The analyst is responsible for the front end. He or she defines and executes the necessary analyses and is responsible for the day-to-day activities of the team. This usually is the only key player who would work full time on the project.

In the early stages, providing data mining consulting support to the team makes sense. Administrative support staff and junior analysts would be added to the team as needed. And technical experts in telecommunications and database design could be assigned to the team on a temporary basis. A list of the names and assigned responsibilities of all members of the data mining team should indicate each team member's "home" department or business unit and the number of hours allocated to the data mining effort.

After the problem identification and team selection, all members of the team should become familiar with operational data germane to the marketing problem and help identify sources of enhancement data and other important external data. They also should understand where operational data originate, how they are processed, and what is done with them after processing. Knowing where the data are achieved and the procedures for cleaning and quality assessment are also important.

When data are examined before loading into a data warehouse, they often are found to be less than accurate, less than complete, or both. Incompleteness and inaccuracy usually come about because many data elements have more of an operational than an analytical purpose. Only when data are being readied for analysis are their deficiencies discovered. As part of the overall process analysis, the data mining team should grasp five realities:

- The importance of high-quality data.

- The concomitant need to assess data quality.

- The need to develop methods and procedures to ensure data completeness and accuracy.

- The unanticipated time and expense that data cleaning can add to a project.

- The need to work with upstream operations to fix "dirty data" problems so future remedial action can be avoided.

Data flow diagrams and entity-relationship diagrams are tools commonly used by IT professionals involved in systems design. They are easy to learn and can be instructive to all data mining team members. The data dictionary, a comprehensive catalog of a data repository, is another tool from the IT tool box.

Output Format

The team should specify what the output categories of the KDD process should be, to what individual or business unit they are to be delivered, and the schedule. Examples of output categories are models, decision rules, reports, and hypotheses about interesting relationships that might be discovered in the data sets.

Model formats might include the language to be used for coding scoring algorithms, documentation describing the algorithms and how they are to be run, and the names of online computer directories where they are to be stored. Formats for decision rules would include the language or software system within which the rules are coded, descriptive and instructional documentation, the names of libraries or directories where they can be found, and access restriction specifications.

Formal reports can be delivered in electronic or paper formats, in straight text or multimedia, or through a variety of other communications media—regular or intraorganizational mail, e-mail, or Web-based delivery. Hypotheses about relationships would normally be presented in descriptive text in a working paper or brief ad hoc report. Format specifications for short reports on hypotheses would correspond to the specifications for formal reports.

Installation Strategy

Three installation strategies can be taken in data mining: a tools approach, an application approach, or an outsourcing approach. A combination of these strategies might also be selected. A company adopting the tools approach acquires the data mining software tools together with hardware and software components of the KDD infrastructure, including the data server, application package, data preparation software, and the support staff.

A company adopting the application approach identifies a specific data mining application such as fraud detection and then selects software from a vendor specializing in that area. If another application is identified later—reducing customer attrition, for example—the company would have to acquire additional specialty software.

Although the infrastructure required to support the application approach will be less extensive than the infrastructure required to support the tools approach, the company adopting an application approach must provide some components of the support infrastructure.

In the outsourcing approach, most of the aspects of data mining are turned over to a specialist, with the company retaining only those aspects having to do with policy, objective setting, and implementation of the marketing strategy and tactics that grow out of the data mining results.

If a company is relatively unsophisticated and wishes to take a low-risk (but potentially more expensive) approach, outsourcing is probably the most appropriate solution. If the problem to be solved is narrow and well defined and expectations are limited, then an application strategy probably makes the most sense. When the company possesses depth in analysis and IT support, sees clear benefits from data mining, or is committed to a large-scale KDD effort, then the tools strategy holds the greatest promise. But the tools strategy also carries the greatest risk.

Budget and Time Lines

Once the team has established an installation strategy, it should establish a detailed budget and specify when all of the project milestones are to be reached. Some items that should appear in the budget are:

- Full-time and partial personnel equivalents

- Computer hardware and software costs

- Communication costs

- System maintenance and training costs

- Facilities expenses

- Supply expenses

- Utilities expenses

- Consulting fees

Budget projections for several years are essential, and they should make explicit costs that can easily be hidden because no one thinks of them until they show up later in large unanticipated budget overruns. Time spent in informal training sessions, talking to analysts, and figuring out how to solve system-related problems are typical overlooked costs. Included in the project budget and schedule package would be Gantl charts, PERT charts, and similar output from a project management software package.

Vendor Selection

Many data mining vendors are available, and new companies seem to enter the field on a daily basis. Here are some traditional rules of thumb for selecting a vendor:

- Select a vendor with some longevity in the business.

- Look for an enthusiastic customer base.

- Confirm the vendor's financial stability.

- Choose a vendor with a strong support program, both when the system is being implemented and when it's up and running.

- Ensure that a prospective vendor's solution provides adequate computing power to mine the largest database your company might build. Alternatively, ensure that the vendor's software is scaleable and will operate comfortably on computers with ever-greater horsepower.

- Be alert to marketing hype and over promising. Because data mining is a new industry and a highly technical one, many sales reps will promise phantom capabilities because they simply don't know enough about the inner workings of their products to do otherwise.

Figure 3 lists some of the major data mining vendors offering products and services, and additional listings can be found at www.sentrytech.com. These vendors' computing platforms, approximate price ranges, and product descriptions are readily available by linking to their web sites. Many vendors also provide downloadable, limited-use demo copies of their software applications.

Measuring Value

After creating a framework, a work plan, and a time schedule, the data mining team's major responsibility is to perform a cost-benefit analysis of the proposed data mining effort. In doing this, the team should judge the project in terms of whether it will make enough money to offset its costs of implementation and operation, a judgment that can be difficult to accomplish.

Estimating the cost of hardware, software, facilities, personnel, and consulting support is reasonably straightforward, provided the project is not open-ended. The organization's IT department should be able to provide useful guidance in this area, and tapping that particular source of assistance should be on the database administrator's agenda. Costs such as training time and materials, lost productivity, software maintenance, and time spent in meetings are more elusive, but they should still be factored into the equation. Other subtle costs of a data mining initiative include disruption to normal business processes and the higher wages of staff experts who can support sophisticated technology.

Over time, the costs to be included will vary according to the project, but life-cycle costs may include upgrades: support, staffing, telecommunications, and facilities charges. If consultants will be retained or part of the project outsourced, those hard dollar expenses must be included in the estimates. As a general rule, hardware usually accounts for only one-fifth to one-third of information technology costs.

Data mining benefits tend to be difficult to estimate. Uncertainty surrounds how much additional revenue an improvement in operations will return though the

FIGURE 3 **DATA MINING VENDORS**

Vendor	Products	Product types	Web site
Angoss International	Knowledge Seeker Knowledge Studio	Data mining tool	www.angoss.com
Business Objects	BusinessMiner	Decision tree-based mining tool	www.businessobjects.com
Cognos	Scenario 4Thought	Analysis and segmentation tools	www.cognos.com
Data Mind	DataMind DataCruncher	Data mining tools connecting directly to data sources	www.datamincorp.com
Exchange Applications	Valex Marketing Management System	Direct marketing campaign automation	www.exapps.com
Group 1 Software	Model 1	Four-module, multi-model data mining tool for marketing applications	www.g1.com
IBM	Intelligent Miner	Data mining applications suite	www.ibm.com/bi
Information Discovery	IDIS	Pattern discovery within relational DBMS's	www.datamining.com
Knowledge Discovery One (KD1)	Retail Discovery Suite	Retail customer purchase prediction	www.kd1.com
NCR	Knowledge Discovery Workbench Management Discovery Tool	End user visual data mining tool Rule-based tool that searches for changes and trends	www.ncr.com
NeoVista Software	Decision Series	Analysis, data cleaning, and developer tools	www.neovista.com
Neural Ware	Predict Plus	Neural net development tool	www.neuralware.com
Pilot Software	Pilot Discovery Server	Sales and market segmentation tool	www.pilotsw.com
SAS Institute	Enterprise Miner	Data mining toolset	www.sas.com
SPL Infoware	Customer Profiling System	Customer switching prediction tool	www.spl-infoware.com
SPSS	SPSS base AnswerTree	Statistical data mining package	www.spss.com
Sybase	Sybase MPP	Parallel architecture RDBMS	www.sybase.com
Thinking Machines	Darwin	Multi-algorithm data mining tool	www.think.com
Torrent Systems	Orchestrate	Data mining application development tools	www.torrent.com

marketing manager may provide a reasonably accurate estimate of this unknown. Supplemental estimates from internal sources or from one or more experienced consultants may be appropriate

Uncertainty also surrounds the predictive power of the model or models that will emerge from the data mining effort. Unfortunately, a model's predictive ability simply cannot be ascertained ahead of time with any assurance. One data set produces a highly predictive "killer" model; another yields up a model that turns out to be a bust. Unfortunately, no one can tell ahead of time which will be which. Benefits must be estimated on the basis of results obtained by similar companies in similar situations.

At prespecified milestone points, the team should determine if anticipated data mining benefits actually have been achieved and at what cost. Performing a formal post-project assessment is expensive and will be painful for some in the organization, but it helps avoid future mistakes. On a more positive note, if the project is a success, formal recognition of the accomplishment following the post-project audit promotes the next project and makes it easier to obtain project approval.

Privacy Concerns

In the electronic age, individual privacy is a hot-button issue. New laws restricting access to data and how they may be used almost seem inevitable. Companies with existing data mining operations as well as those contemplating them must be aware of the legislative arena and how the changes there will restrict operations and add cost.

To consumers, the term data mining itself often connotes a process with sinister purpose. Many interpret the term to mean the discovery and exploitation of their behavior patterns in order to manipulate them subtly and secretly. An earlier parallel was the furor created by so-called subliminal advertising, the principle underpinning of which was the assumption that an advertiser can plant a small number of frames in a commercial that are imperceptible to the viewer of the commercial at the conscious level. At the same time, however, those few and supposedly innocuous frames unconsciously induce viewers to take some action benefiting the commercial's sponsor.

Dismissed now as the product of junk science and journalistic excess, subliminal advertising was a salient marketing issue in its time. Should data mining be covered by a particularly clever and malevolent journalist, the resulting public reaction will be at least on the order of the subliminal advertising affair. In recognition of this, marketers should take a proactive stance and work to diffuse the issue before it becomes a major problem.

The Future

With the emergence of interactive TV, the continued expansion of the World Wide Web, and increasing capabilities of ATMs and other point-of-sale technologies, customer contact points will become increasingly more common and produce ever-larger transaction streams. For many companies, formerly independent operations and analysis activities will become strongly interdependent. Even today, most data mining applications are static, with historical data patterns used to build models that support batch-type marketing programs such as direct mail offers, catalog drops, and customer reactivation efforts.

Increasingly, however, we will encounter applications of embedded data mining, where data mining capabilities are incorporated directly into dynamic, real-time operations. Companies that integrate their operational systems and data mining infrastructures will be far better prepared than their competitors to implement the increasingly important share-of-customer market development strategy.

Data mining is still in its infancy and evolving in unexpected ways. Nevertheless, several important trends can be identified even at this point of the revolution. First, both the number of operational data sets and their volumes will continue to grow exponentially well into the next millennium as the costs of information technology decline steadily.

Second, the quality and consistency of data produced by operational systems will improve significantly because managers are coming to comprehend the residual value in high-quality transactions data. Operational data add value to the efficiency of the transactions process; operational data also can add value to organizational effectiveness via results analysis and prediction of future marketing programs outcomes.

Data mining tools will continue to grow in power, analytical sophistication, and ease of use. Tool suites rather than individual tools will become the standard offering from major vendors. Data mining tools will also become easier to use. As knowledge about these techniques spreads, marketing managers will assume more and more data mining responsibilities. But this evolution will take several years to complete.

Meanwhile, executives like Paceline's Gary Bright are taking the kinds of incremental steps that will make data mining a marketing mainstay in the near future. In Bright's case, data mining seemed like a reasonable remedy to as many as five or six of the problems that were bugging him. He selected just one problem, the one that looked easiest to solve and, coincidentally had the highest payoff. Gary knew that getting started with a single, straightforward problem with a high payoff made sense because he also realized that a new data mining operation would need plenty of teeth-cutting before it worked smoothly.

After creating the data mining team, Bright announced its composition to the rest of the Pace-line organization and emphasized to everyone that the data mining initiative had A-level priority and his complete support. Gary's next step was to specify that the group's initial responsibility was to construct a data mart stocked with a very clean set of historical data from the company's retail and direct marketing order entry systems and overlay it with demographic and psychographic data from a major data compiler.

The team members spent considerable time evaluating various data mining tool suites before settling on one that included visualization, decision tree, and neural net capabilities as well as a set of standard statistical routines and a query engine. Now they are ready to plunge into KDD.

Reprinted with permission from the Spring 1998 issue of Marketing Management, published by the American Marketing Association, Peacock, Peter R., Spring 1998/Vol. 7, pp. 15–25.

Note

1. Enhancement data, also called overlay data, are additional attributes such as customer age or income that can be purchased from data compilers and added to the customer database. Some of the leading source of such information are Acxiom. Donnelley Marketing, and R.L. Polk. Some enhancement data elements, such as income, are inferred from aggregates such as the average income for the block on which a household lives. Other data, such as automobile model year, are specific to the household. Inferred income and some other household attributes are available for just about all households. For other attributes, enhancement data are sparse.

III

Improving Marketing Productivity in the Internet Age

Sheth, Jagdish N. and Rajendra S. Sisodia (1995), "Feeling the Heat—Part 1," *Marketing Management*, 4, Fall, 8–23.

Sheth, Jagdish N. and Rajendra S. Sisodia (1995), "Feeling the Heat—Part 2,"*Marketing Management*, 4, Winter, 19–32.

III A: Product Innovation in the Internet Age

Iansiti, Marco and Alan MacCormack (1997), "Developing Products on Internet Time," *Harvard Business Review*, 75 (September/October), 108–117.

III B: Reintermediation and Disintermediation in the Internet Age

Sarkar, Mitrabarun, Brian Butler, and Charles Steinfield (1998), "Cyber-mediaries in Electronic Marketspace: Toward Theory Building," *Journal of Business Research*, 41 (March), 215–222.

Hagel, John III and Jeffrey F. Rayport (1997), "The New Infomediaries," *The McKinsey Quarterly*, Number 4, 54–70.

III C: Pricing in the Internet Age

Docters, Robert G. (1997), "Price Strategy: Time to Choose Your Weapons," *The Journal of Business Strategy*, 18 (September/October), pp. 11–15.

Cortese, Amy E. and Marcia Stepanek (1998), "E-Commerce: Good-Bye to Fixed Pricing? How electronic commerce could create the most efficient market of them all," *Business Week,*
May 4, p 70.

III D: Advertising in the Internet Age

Cartellieri, Caroline, Andrew J. Parsons, Varsha Rao, and Micheal P. Zeisser (1997), "The Real Impact of Internet Advertising," *The McKinsey Quarterly,* Number 3, 45–62.

Briggs, Rex and Nigel Hollis (1997), "Advertising on the Web: Is There Response Before Click-Through?" *Journal of Advertising Research,* 37 (March/April), 33–45.

III E: Sales and Customer Service in the Internet Age

Cravens, David (1995), "The Changing Role of the Sales Force," *Marketing Management,* 4 (Fall), 48–57.

Freedman, Jennifer, and Ruby Sudoyo (1999), "Technology's Effect on Customer Service: Building Meaningful Relationships Through Dialogue," *Integrated Marketing Communications Research Journal,* 5, Spring, 3–8.

III

Improving Marketing Productivity in the Internet Age

The Internet age has moved the issue of the productivity of marketing resources (the 4 Ps of Marketing) to the forefront. Improving customer loyalty through better targeting, feedback, personalization and customization are critical success factors in the Internet age. In other words, marketing has begun a shift from product centric mass marketing to customer centric segment marketing. It is ironic that the impact of the Internet age may be greater on the marketing function than on the production function because marketing has so much potential to improve both in customer satisfaction and in resource efficiency. It is similar to the dramatic improvement in management organization and support functions such as information services, procurement, legal, finance and human resource functions.

The readings assembled in Part III are intended to offer valuable perspectives on how information technology can be utilized to improve productivity in marketing resources. We begin with two readings by Sheth and Sisodia who provide the context for the remaining articles, which focus on each of the Four Ps of Marketing plus sales and customer service functions.

In *Feeling the Heat—Part 1*, Sheth and Sisodia remind us that marketing does not produce anything making marketing productivity very difficult to measure. They argue that marketing productivity should be defined as the amount of desirable output per unit of input; in other words, output should be measured in terms of quality as well as quantity. Stated simply, the ultimate output of marketing is acquiring and retaining customers profitably. A good measure of marketing productivity, therefore, must include the economics of both customer acquisition and retention. Sheth and Sisodia conclude the article by discussing ways to improve marketing productivity.

The central theme of *Feeling the Heat—Part 2* by Sheth and Sisodia is that the goal of acquiring and retaining customer profitably can be achieved by the pursuit of the ideal of effective efficiency—doing the right things and doing things right. Information technology can improve and eventually alter marketing practice in several ways, including lowering the cost of providing a particular service to customers and reducing the demand for personnel-based customer service. The authors further propose ways to enhance marketing productivity.

A. Product Innovation in the Internet Age

The focus of this section is on product innovation in the Internet age. Iansiti and Mac-Cormack in *Developing Products on Internet Time* describe how innovative companies have replaced the traditional product-development process with a flexible process in the Internet age. Such a process allows designers to continue to define and shape products even after implementation has begun. This innovation enables Internet companies to incorporate rapidly evolving customer requirements and changing technologies into their designs until the last possible moment before a product is introduced to the market.

B. Reintermediation and Disintermediation in the Internet Age

What role will the intermediaries play in the Internet Age? Will they be disintermediated, or will the "brick and mortar" retailing converge with "point and click" to create an integrated hybrid called "click and mortar." In general, the consensus seems to emerge that the sales and service (fulfillment and maintenance) functions will be divorced; and intermediaries will become less sales intermediaries and more service intermediaries. At the same time, there will be emergence of infomediaries who will be paid either by users or by providers or by advertisers to gather, organize and update information on a continuous basis (very similar to stock market ticker tape or Nielsen television ratings).

These issues are discussed in more detail in the two reading in this section. In the first one, *Cybermediaries in Electronic Marketspace: Toward Theory Building* Mitrabarun and Butler argue that the advent of ubiquitous information infrastructures is not likely to lead to the demise of intermediaries in electronic markets. On the contrary, not only is it likely that widely available information infrastructures will reinforce the position of traditional intermediaries, but that networks will also promote the growth of a new generation of intermediaries. These new players, which they term "Cybermediaries," are organizations that perform the mediating tasks in the world of electronic commerce. They illustrate that the case for the elimination of intermediaries in the move to create direct producer-consumer links is based on questionable assumptions. Then the functions of intermediaries that are not easily absorbed by producers are examined noting the new needs that electronic commerce imposes on producers and consumers, thus noting the role of the new cybermediary.

The second reading in this section, *The New Infomediaries* by Hagel and Rayport, suggests that in the past information about customers was taken for granted; in the future, it will have to be purchased. As consumers become more keenly aware of the value of information about their behavior and preferences, companies will have to negotiate with them to gain access to it. A new kind of player, the infomediary, will emerge to handle this bargaining process and add value in the treatment of customer information. It will act as an agent by helping them obtain maximum value from their information profiles, serve as a proxy by representing their interests in negotiations with vendors, and perform a filter function by screening commercial messages for relevance.

C. Pricing in the Internet Age

Similarly, price as the third P of marketing is likely to be impacted significantly. Price is, after all, a piece of information also. Market inefficiencies exist because price information is not available at the same time and the same place to all customers and consumers. Also, there is enormous price variation across sellers and service providers. The Internet will make price information more standardized and on real time across global markets reducing price discrimination. This will result in most products and services becoming commodities and, therefore, suppliers will have to do true product innovation or value added services that differentiate them from competition to command higher prices.

At the same time, price as a unit of exchange will be impacted by reverse auctions as eBay and Priceline become more prevalent. It is interesting to note that Priceline has announced it will provide reverse auction for gasoline purchases where consumers can specify online what they are willing to pay for a gallon of gasoline and solicit bids for their business!

The first article in this section, titled *Price Strategy: Time to Choose Your Weapons* by Docters, examines how corporate strategists can utilize the requisite management skills, knowledge base, and information technology to achieve the kind of pricing sophistication exhibited by such veteran competitors as airlines and commodity chemical manufacturers, a company must.

The second reading, *E-Commerce: Good-Bye to Fixed Pricing? How Electronic Commerce Could Create the Most Efficient Market of Them All* by Cortese, maintains that there is a revolution brewing in pricing that promises to profoundly alter the way goods are marketed and sold. In the future, marketers will offer special deals—tailored specifically for the consumer, just for the moment—on everything from theater tickets to bank loans to camcorders. The Internet, corporate networks, and wireless setups are linking people, machines, and companies around the globe. This is enabling buyers to quickly and easily compare products and prices, putting them in a better bargaining position. At the same time, the technology allows sellers to collect detailed data about customers' buying habits so they can tailor their products and prices. As buyers and sellers do battle in the electronic world, the struggle should result in prices that more closely reflect their true market value.

D. Advertising in the Internet Age

The impact of the Internet age on advertising and promotion is as significant and swift as price and distribution. Indeed, it may be more significant and swifter! After all, advertising and promotion are information and communication, and they always have been affected by the media. As Marshall McCluhan has said, "Medium becomes the message." The Internet as a medium of communication, information and transaction is, therefore, already having massive impact on the advertising function and advertising agencies.

First, the Internet has democratized the media access better than any other medium. Today, it is possible for a small business and even self-employed individuals to create and maintain Web sites. It is cheaper than local radio advertising, local yellow pages as well as local newspaper ads. Furthermore, it can be dynamically changed and updated on a continuous basis. The cost of change in production is minimal as compared to other media. Finally, the versatility of web advertising is enormous. It can provide voice, video, and written texts, and in a more integrated and creative way than any other medium. Indeed, the dream of integrated marketing communication (IMC) is more becoming a reality because of the Internet and the Internet age.

Perhaps the single biggest advantage of the Internet advertising is the direct correlation between the advertisement and the response at an individual level. One can do both cross-sectional as well as longitudinal panel type measurement of the impact of advertising expenditures on market behavior. It is direct, instantaneous, and a more controlled measure of advertising effectiveness and efficiency. This is both good news and bad news. The good news is that it will encourage companies to support advertising and promotion dollars because they deliver revenue growth and profitability to the company. It is bad news because the all-speculative and "trust me" culture of creativity and non-accountability of advertising and promotion campaigns will be bought less and less by company's marketing managers.

The articles in this section provide additional insights on some of the issues discussed above. The first reading by Cartellieri, et al.—*The Real Impact of Internet Advertising*—suggests that a growing proportion of overall advertising expenditure will be devoted to the Internet, and that practices first developed or deployed there will spill over into traditional marketing activities. In particular, marketers with experience of Internet advertising are likely to be inspired to adopt new creative approaches elsewhere; to reevaluate their investments in traditional media; to acquire a better understanding of customers' needs, preferences, and product usage; and to develop higher expectations of the effectiveness and measurability of other media.

In the second reading (*Advertising on the Web: Is There Response Before Click-Through?*), Briggs and Hollis report the results of an empirical study of Web banner advertising that measured attitudes and behavior. The authors found important attitudinal shifts even without click-through. By using Millward Brown's BrandDynamics system, along with other copy testing measures, increases in advertising awareness and brand perceptions to Web banner ads for apparel as well as technology goods have been documented.

E. Sales and Customer Service in the Internet Age

Two other areas of marketing that are likely to be impacted are sales force and customer service. In both cases, automation and integration with the use of the Internet and information is radically improving efficiency of otherwise people-intensive functions, and ironically, improving customer satisfaction. For example, automated customer services, such as telephone calls without the operators or ATM machines without the tellers are becoming increasingly popular for all business support functions especially in business-to-business marketing. Today, more call centers are becoming Web centers with e-mail as a predominant method of communication and interaction. Also, using the existing technologies, customers are directly accessing the supplier company's databases for information and even transactions for such routine activities as checking flight information, marketing airline restrictions, or buying electronic tickets. The Amazon.com phenomenon is as real as the Domino Pizza phenomenon was a generation ago when we offered home delivery as a value-added Customer Service. Today, it is everywhere whether for office supplies, books, or any home sourcing services.

Customer service and sales force will, therefore, experience extreme and contradictory repositioning. Most routine transactions will be automated and integrated and customers will become do it yourself (DIY), especially in business-to-business marketing. At the same time, more non-routine, complex first time transactions will require a team approach involving a cross functional team similar to project management.

Two articles in this section further elaborate on the impact of the Internet age on sales and customer service. In the sales area, Cravens' article, *The Changing Role of the Sales Force*, argues that as companies restructure to lower costs and leverage their capabilities to build customer satisfaction, reinventing the sales organization is becoming a critical item on their agendas. The reforming process requires redesigning the traditional sales organization, leveraging information technology to lower costs and provide quick response, designing the sales strategy to meet different customer needs and building long-term relationships with customers and business partners. The contribution of the sales force to the sales, profit, and customer satisfaction performance of many companies highlights the urgency of designing selling strategies to match the demands and uncertainties of the rapidly changing marketplace. Examining the role of the sales force starts with a candid look at how the sales strategy measures up to what is being done in other organizations in several important areas.

The focus of the second reading is on customer service. In *Technology's Effect on Customer Service: Building Meaningful Relationships Through Dialogue*, Freedman and Sudoyo emphasize the importance of "dialogue" in building customer relationships. The authors contend that technology has to be used judiciously in providing customer service. It is quite likely that, if used indiscriminately, technology may actually come in the way of customer service by attenuating the dialogue component of the relationship. Based on the results of a study the authors provide some pointers on conducting a customer service audit for both—telephone customer service system and the Internet customer service system.

10

Feeling the Heat—Part 1

*More than ever before, marketing is under fire
to account for what it spends.*

JAGDISH N. SHETH

RAJENDRA S. SISODIA

Concluding that marketing has overspent and underdelivered, top management now expects other business functions to perform more marketing tasks. CEOs are demanding that marketers prove their worth or be gradually starved of resources. These pressures, coupled with a strong tendency toward "business as usual," spell a productivity crisis in marketing that cannot be ignored. In this first of a two-part series, the authors define marketing productivity and outline a concrete plan for improvement that focuses on horizontal and vertical collaboration and ways to rationalize different elements of the marketing mix.

As a corporate function and a societal institution, marketing is increasingly being regarded as a "necessary evil" rather than a value-creating activity, focusing renewed attention on its productivity. That customers today have a great variety of high-quality products and services available at reasonable prices is attributable, in part, to marketing's ascendancy in the modern corporation. Yet in many companies, the marketing function appears to consume a disproportionately high share of resources, inviting intense scrutiny from corporate cost-cutters. (See "The Productivity Crisis in Marketing".)

Furthermore, at a macro level, the correlation between the level of marketing spending and overall financial performance or competitive position is low. Many firms are even getting negative returns on incremental marketing spending.

Because marketing must contend with the uncertainties associated with managing external forces: such as customers and competitors, it has some inherent characteristics that confound measurement. If it's true that "you cannot improve what you cannot measure," then we may never see the dramatic improvements experienced in manufacturing. But it's still possible for marketing productivity to soar beyond historical levels.

In the past, marketing productivity was viewed purely in terms of efficiency. Early attempts at improvement focused predominantly on minimizing costs. This was driven, in part, by the recognition that it was difficult to measure the output of marketing

THE PRODUCTIVITY CRISIS IN MARKETING

Every business comprises three broadly defined areas: marketing, management, and manufacturing or production—colloquially speaking, the "finders, minders, and grinders." In the quest for greater efficiency and higher quality, the latter two functional areas have undergone fundamental, frequently wrenching changes in the past few decades:

- Manufacturing/production has become substantially more efficient (through automation, the use of just-in-time approaches, product redesign for assembly and manufacture, flexible manufacturing systems, service process blueprinting, and so on) and quality-focused. As a very rough estimate, manufacturing now accounts for about 30% of total corporate costs, down from approximately 50% after World War II.

- "Management" (defined here to include finance, accounting, human resources, and support functions such as legal departments and R&D) has raised its efficiency through "downsizing," "right-sizing," outsourcing, and business process re-engineering. As a result, the approximate share of corporate costs attributable to management has fallen from 30% to 20%.

- That leaves about 50% for marketing (up from 20%), including the costs of product development, outbound logistics, order fulfillment, selling, distribution, advertising, sales promotion, public relations, customer service, and so on.

Marketing costs more today, but it also carries more of the competitive burden. The marketing function's importance—along with the size of its budget—is increasing as companies face higher levels of competition in increasingly global markets. Its exalted status as the generator of corporate revenues, profitability, and visibility often shielded marketing from the deep cuts other departments have endured in the past decade. Indeed, though marketing is the biggest discretionary spending area in most companies, many wish they could devote even more resources to it.

But marketing's heyday may soon be over. In fact, there are already clear signs that CEOs are demanding major cost savings and a higher level of accountability from marketing than ever before. Numerous companies are downsizing the sales force and closing regional sales offices; others are downsizing the headquarters marketing function and transferring marketing personnel and functions to the sales force. In many companies, other functional areas have adopted more outward-looking customer orientations with the expectation that they will do so more effectively and economically. For example, marketing's two major traditional areas of focus—competition and customers—are now the primary concerns of strategic planning and business operations, respectively.

Improving marketing productivity has become a major concern, for several additional reasons:

- As market orientation increases, the cost of marketing goes up. More companies in more industries are becoming more market-driven (because of deregulation, privatization, greater competition, and technological change), adding huge cost centers. For example, marketing costs in the telecommunications, banking, electric utility, and health care industries have been rising rapidly as these industries move toward unfettered competition.

(Continues)

- A major driver of new thinking in marketing has been a dramatic surge in the sales of private label products. The growing success of such products in Europe and the United States suggests that the value-added by intensive (and expensive) marketing programs is often not sufficient to justify a price premium. This has spurred a heightened interest in what has been called "lean marketing."

- Marketing is not done just in the marketing department anymore but dispersed across all the functions. The question of who is responsible for marketing and how to account for it has become an increasingly important issue.

- There is an enormous degree of cross-subsidization across accounts in marketing; a few highly profitable accounts often hide the inefficiency in serving the rest. Such a marketing system is highly vulnerable to bypass or cherry-picking.

- Many marketing phenomena are still not accurately measurable. Without reliable measurement, meaningful improvements in efficiency levels are extremely difficult to achieve. Marketing is beginning to resemble manufacturing in the "pre-quality" days. Whereas the TQM philosophy resolved many of manufacturing's problems, a similar change still awaits marketing. Although a few writers have discussed the concept of "total quality marketing," the idea is still largely unexplored.

adequately. But it was also driven by an implicit belief that marketing did not create value in any tangible sense and, hence, was an activity on which the minimum necessary amount of resources should be expended.

Today we have ample evidence that judiciously expended marketing resources can be tremendously productive. For example, the return on $1 of advertising for AT&T's early "Reach out and touch someone" campaign (when the company still had a dominant market share in the long-distance telecommunications market) was estimated to be over $4, most of it profit. John Little's advocacy in the late 1970s of "response reporting" was mainly done in this spirit; by determining the elasticity of sales and profits to various marketing stimuli, marketing resources could be expended in a highly productive manner.

As Robert Buzzell pointed out in his seminal dissertation on marketing productivity, marketing does not produce anything: it performs functions around goods and services, making productivity very difficult to measure. Furthermore, many functions performed by marketing become sufficiently routine over time that they are absorbed into other functional areas. For example, many food products used to be sold in bulk to retailers, who would then sell to customers in smaller packages. When manufacturers began shipping their products in multiple sizes, a marketing function became a manufacturing function. In the long term, this type of shift can create the illusion that marketing productivity is diminishing. (See "How We Got Here".)

Because marketing initiates most manufacturing changes, this "problem" could become even more acute in the future. As companies adopt mass customization approaches, many more of marketing's value-added contributions likely will be performed by manufacturing.

Marketing efficiency was relatively high when the consumer market was homogenous and mass media dominated. Many basic needs had not yet been met, and the intensity of competition (certainly from global competitors) was much lower. All of these conditions are now the exception rather than the rule.

From Doing Less With More . . .

Marketing's response to the tremendously heightened competitive intensity of the past few decades has been two-fold. Its first response was to increase expenditures on virtually every aspect of marketing, from greater and more frequent discounting to more pervasive advertising to intensified selling efforts. The second was to proliferate greater variety in products, prices, distribution channels, and so on. Each of these actions, while perhaps justifiable in isolation and on short-run considerations, contributed to making the marketing function increasingly unwieldy and expensive.

In 1980, Fred Webster of Dartmouth College interviewed the CEOs of 30 major corporations to determine their views of the marketing function. Two of the four key areas of concern were the diminishing productivity of marketing expenditures and a poor understanding of the financial implications of marketing actions. A third concern—a lack of innovation and entrepreneurial thinking—also relates to marketing's failure to address the productivity issue in new ways.

Unfortunately, in the ensuing decade and a half, not much has improved. The high-flying '80s left us with even greater marketing bloat. Rapidly expanding markets in many industries obscured underlying problems of waste and inefficiency. Now that growth has slowed, these problems are coming into sharp focus.

. . . To Doing More With Less

In most industries the new competitive realities are stark: Companies must deliver more performance with fewer resources in every area. Global competition and ever-savvier customers have seen to that. For example, a recent cover story in *Business Week* described the dilemma of companies that are unable to raise their prices. What was once true only for industries such as computing and consumer electronics is now hitting many industries: Customers expect real prices to fall over time while product quality continues to improve. In an era of intensified global competition, there have been plenty of suppliers ready to do just that.

"The auto industry says real costs have to come down by 2%–3% a year, or you won't be a supplier," said Corning Inc. CEO Jamie Houghton in the Jan. 17 issue of *Financial Times*. "Optical fiber has to keep coming down by 5% a year. I operate under the assumption that over time, our costs must go down 3%–5% a year in real terms." Since the 1980s, Corning has worked through eight generations of manufacturing technology for optical fiber. According to Houghton. "It wasn't long ago that we were selling fiber at $1 a meter. Now it's five cents and our margins have been good throughout."

Measuring Productivity

These challenges notwithstanding, there is so much to be gained from improvements in marketing productivity that even imperfect measurements can be of great value. However, we must measure the right things: otherwise, our attempts at improvement will, by definition, be misdirected.

Traditionally, productivity has been measured in terms of the *quantity* of output for a given amount of input. However, such measures are unsatisfactory in that they fail to adjust for changes in the *desirability* of the output. In an often-cited example, the output of a steel mill is measured in "tons of steel," disregarding the fact that the quality and value-added of such steel may increase substantially over time.

The Intangibles Factor

This problem is especially acute for marketing measurements because marketing deals with so many intangibles. To address it, we suggest that marketing productivity be defined as the amount of desirable output per unit of input; in other words, output should be measured in terms of quality as well as quantity.

The productivity of a salesperson, for example, is more than the number of sales calls made or even the number of transactions that result. It also includes the effectiveness of those sales calls (that is, their long-run impact on the relationship with those customers), the profitability of the resulting transactions, and the impact of today's business mix on the future. Likewise, a productive advertisement could be defined as one that maximizes the quality-adjusted amount of positive exposure for a given budget.

Ultimately, the desired output of marketing can be stated in simple terms: acquiring and retaining customers profitably. A good measure of marketing productivity, therefore, must include the economics of both customer acquisition and retention.

Acquiring Customers. This measure consists of the revenues attributable to marketing actions that bring in new customers, divided by the costs of those actions, adjusted by a customer satisfaction index (CSI). This formula reflects the idea that highly satisfying exchanges, rather than "hard sell" techniques or deceptive advertising, form the basis of new customer acquisitions. Overpromising and then underdelivering on heightened expectations usually leads to customer dissatisfaction.

Retaining Customers. Because retaining a customer requires more than maintaining high satisfaction, we suggest adjusting the measure of revenues/costs for existing customers by what we call a customer loyalty index (CLI). Even ostensibly satisfied customers can be induced to switch to a rival unless they have been strongly bonded to a firm's offering. The CLI addresses customer "churn," which is a significant problem in a number of industries today. See Figure 1.

Effective Efficiency

Using this method, the overall marketing productivity for a firm would be a weighted combination of the productivity of customer acquisition and customer retention. The weights should reflect the relative importance of acquisition and retention according to the company's objectives. For example, a startup firm in a growing market would place greater relative emphasis on acquisition, whereas an established firm in a slow-growing market might be primarily concerned with retaining its best customers.

In this broader sense, marketing productivity includes both the dimensions of efficiency (doing things right) and effectiveness (doing the right things), as depicted in

| FIGURE 1 | MARKETING EFFICIENCY AND EFFECTIVENESS |

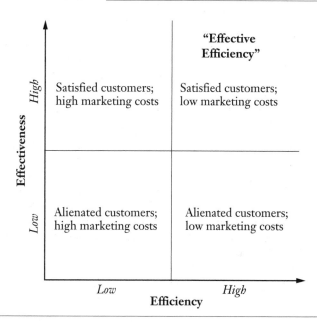

Exhibit 1. Ideally, the marketing function should generate satisfied customers at low cost. Too often, however, companies either create satisfied customers at unacceptably high cost, or alienate customers (as well as employees) in their search for marketing efficiencies.[1] In far too many cases, the marketing function accomplishes neither. (See "Symptoms of Marketing Malaise.")

To make the necessary improvements, we first must adopt a broader view of productivity. Marketing must pursue the ideal of "effective efficiency" in all of its programs and processes; neither objective is adequate by itself.

Achieving Balance

To a certain extent, marketing's productivity problem is simply due to poor marketing; in other words, companies often fail to apply marketing concepts in a balanced manner. Too many, for example, emphasize capturing market share over growing the market—a crucial distinction that leads to an escalating spiral of misapplied marketing dollars and heavy competitive retaliation.

Likewise, many companies demonstrate a poor understanding of how the elements of the marketing mix interrelate and deploy excessive resources on some aspects to the detriment of others. For example, if a company misses the fact that its "weak link" is inadequate market coverage, it might lower prices or end up squandering excessive resources on advertising.

SYMPTOMS OF MARKETING MALAISE

Several recent reports from prominent consulting firms have contributed to a growing sense of urgency within the marketing function. In 1993, Coopers & Lybrand surveyed 100 of Great Britain's leading companies and found that marketing departments were "ill-focused and over-indulged." They tended to overstate their contribution to the corporation, but could not specify what the nature of the contribution was. The measures frequently used—such as sales growth and market share—are affected by other functional areas as well as marketing.

"The marketing department is critically ill. Marketing . . . has been outflanked by other disciplines, in finance and manufacturing," concluded Coopers & Lybrand in the study report. "Companies certainly need a marketing philosophy. But many marketing departments aren't making it live within the organization."

Likewise, management consultant Booz Allen & Hamilton issued a report in early 1994 warning that "brand managers were failing to get to grips with commercial realities." In 1993, McKinsey released a report attacking the failures of marketers: "Doubts are surfacing about the very basis of contemporary marketing." Marketing departments have shown themselves to be "unimaginative," generating "few new ideas," and have simply stopped "picking up the right signals. Fairly or unfairly, many consumer-goods CEOs are beginning to think that marketing is no longer delivering."

- Many companies today practice "just-in-time" manufacturing but "just-in-case" marketing. The data on this are clear: Between 1982 and 1993, manufacturers reduced their inventory levels dramatically, from 2 times monthly sales to around 1.4 times monthly sales. In contrast, retail and wholesale inventories actually rose during the same time period. Companies are failing to leverage their efficient demand-driven production systems by coupling them with similar marketing systems; they continue to practice forecast-driven marketing. Once these forecasts are enshrined in formal targets and budgets, companies deploy their marketing arsenals to achieve those (almost always top-line) goals—too often at the expense of profitability and the long-run health of the business.

- Companies misallocate marketing resources. For example, advertising is most effective when there is a strong product to sell; however, a recent McKinsey study found that advertising spending is highest where product differentiation is lowest. For most products, differentiation based purely on image cannot be long sustained. As a result, customers are becoming ever more willing to purchase private label products.

- Many companies rely too heavily on expensive internal sales channels and fail to leverage more efficient third-party distribution channels. For example, Compaq has cut its sales force in half while doubling sales, and AT&T is one of many companies closing unproductive regional sales offices and requiring laptop-computer-equipped salespersons to work out of their homes and cars.

- Companies engage in wasteful and even harmful sales promotion activity. *Forbes* reported that packaged-goods manufacturers spent $6.1 billion on more than 300 billion coupons in 1993. Of these, only 1.8% were redeemed, and of those, 80% were redeemed by shoppers who would have bought the brand anyway. Of the other 20%, many are redeemed by pure deal shoppers, who are unlikely ever to purchase the brand without a large incentive.

(Continues)

- The vast majority of trade promotions are ineffective and almost all actually lose money. Excessive trade promotions add an estimated $20 billion a year to the grocery bills of U.S. consumers, much of it due to the practice of "forward buying." As a result, it takes almost three months for a product to get from the manufacturer to the consumer.

- Management focuses too much of the marketing arsenal on getting new customers; in most companies, keeping the customer is somebody else's (or nobody's) job. In many industries such as long-distance telecommunications, customer "churn" has become a major drain on marketing resources and company profitability.

A good business strategy makes marketing much easier and productivity much more achievable. By the same token, even the most productive and enlightened marketing efforts cannot compensate for a flawed strategy in the long run. Marketing can thus be an uphill battle or downhill glide, depending on how sound the business strategy is.

For example, Southwest Airlines has spent far less on marketing over the years than its rivals have, yet it has outperformed them on every measure. That is because Southwest recognized that it didn't have to spend heavily to push a message that is intrinsically attractive to a large and growing part of the market. The airline also has been highly consistent in its marketing efforts over the years and advertises on local, rather than national television to avoid reaching markets where it has no presence. In the markets that it does serve, Southwest's market share now tops 60%.

In contrast, US Air has struggled mightily to compete as a full-line national player, fighting the "Big Three" on one front while staving off regional players such as Southwest and ValueJet on another. US Air's marketing resources are spread thinly, and the company has lost huge amounts of money.

Beyond correcting such fundamental marketing mistakes, we have identified 20 ways to improve marketing productivity and classified them into four broad categories: collaborating, rationalizing, "informationalizing", and managing.

Collaborating

Several collaborative marketing approaches help improve productivity. In particular, three of these approaches—partnering, relationship marketing, and marketing alliances—allow for greater resource efficiency as well as improved customer satisfaction.

Partnering

When buyers and sellers agree to work together, they can achieve dramatic gains in distribution and marketing efficiencies. "Partnering" between members of a value chain, such as retailers and manufacturers, represents a major departure from their traditionally antagonistic relationship; both become part of a single process—distributing products to customers—which technology can greatly streamline and simplify. For example, Black & Decker describes its new distribution philosophy as "Sell one, ship one, build one." Inventory is pulled through the system rather than pushed down, resulting in much lower average levels of inventory, coupled with higher levels of product availability for customers.

Maintaining such availability is key; when a customer does not find a desired product on the shelf, the manufacturer not only loses the margin on that sale, but also presents a rival with a free customer trial.

Through partnering, buyers and sellers reap the advantages of vertical integration without the attendant drawbacks—sometimes referred to as "virtual integration." With its roots in the apparel industry's "quick response" (QR) movement, partnering is known as "efficient consumer response" (ECR) in the grocery business. A Food Marketing Institute report on ECR says that it has the potential to reduce inventory by 41% and save $30 billion a year. The ECR system is based on timely, accurate, and paperless information flow between suppliers, distributors, retail stores, and consumer households. Its objective is to provide a "smooth, continual product flow matched to consumption," focusing on the efficiency of the total supply system, rather than any of its components.

According to the report, four ECR strategies contribute to performance improvements: efficient store assortments, replenishment, promotion, and product introductions (see Figure 2). In addition to cost savings, ECR also provides important intangible benefits to the consumer (increased choice and shopping convenience,

---

FIGURE 2	EFFICIENT CONSUMER RESPONSE STRATEGIES

Strategy	*Objective*	*Major impact areas*
Efficient store assortments	Optimize the productivity of inventories and store space at the consumer interface	Increased sales and gross margin per retail square foot, increased inventory turns
Efficient replenishment	Optimize time and cost in the replenishment system	Automated retail and warehouse ordering, flow-through logistics, reduced damages, reduced supplier and distributor wholesale inventories
Efficient promotion	Maximize the total system efficiency of trade and consumer promotion	Warehousing, transportation, administration, and manufacturing efficiencies; reduced forward buy supplier inventories and warehousing expense
Efficient product introductions	Maximize the effectiveness of new product development and introduction activities	Fewer unsuccessful introductions, better value products

Source: *Efficient Consumer Response: Enhancing Consumer Value in the Grocery Industry*, Kurt Salmon Associates, Inc. 1993.

reduced out-of-stock items, fresher products), the distributor (increased consumer loyalty, better consumer knowledge, improved supplier relationships), and the supplier (reduced stockouts, enhanced brand integrity, improved distributor relationships).

The impact of ECR on the grocery business is expected to be dramatic, similar to the impact the QR movement has had in the general merchandising industry.

Central to such partnering arrangements are the enabling technologies of bar-coded product identification and electronic data interchange (EDI), along with the re-engineering of business processes both within as well as across firms in the value chain. The systems improve efficiencies and customer service, primarily by replacing physical assets with information. They reduce the retailer's inventory while providing a supply of merchandise that is closely coordinated with the actual buying patterns of consumers.

These systems also allow retailers to make purchase commitments closer to the time of sale and deploy resources previously tied up in inventory to increased advertising, new product lines, or the bottom line. The result is a win-win-win: Consumers consistently find the merchandise they want in stock (often at lower prices); suppliers increase sales, lower costs, and cement ties with retailers; and retailers gain increased sales and inventory turns and more satisfied customers.

Relationship Marketing

Related to partnering, but one step short, is relationship marketing—long-term, mutually beneficial arrangements in which both the buyer and seller focus on value enhancement through the creation of more satisfying exchanges. At the same time, both buyers and sellers are able to reduce their costs; buyers do it by reducing their search and transaction costs while sellers are able to lower advertising and selling expenses.

Maintaining strong relationships with customers involves fulfilling orders faster and more accurately in the short run and managing orders better in the long run. It also requires companies to be responsive to special customer needs, provide personalized service, and continuously increase value to customers over time.

Be Selective. Implied in the concept of relationship marketing is the idea of customer selectivity. It is neither feasible nor worthwhile to establish such relationships with all customers. By channeling resources into customers who can be served profitably, companies can increase marketing productivity.

The profitability of serving different customers can be analyzed using "customer retention economics." For example, data from the banking industry indicate that a customer who has been with a bank for five years is several times more profitable than one who has been with the bank for one year. Likewise, it has been estimated that automobile insurance policies have to be held five years before they turn profitable.

Reward Loyalty. Companies in a variety of industries now recognize the value of customer longevity by offering "frequent buyer" rewards. While these programs are generally inexpensive, effectiveness depends on their uniqueness and the value they provide to customers. Customer retention and overall service quality are closely linked. As evidence, three winners of the Malcolm Baldrige National Quality Award—FedEx, AT&T Universal Card and Ritz-Carlton—also are leaders in customer retention.

Most companies do not measure and monitor loyalty in any formal way; as a result, customer retention often receives inadequate budgetary support. However, this appears to be changing. Recently, consulting firm Marketing Metrics conducted a study of 165 companies and found that 53% of their marketing budgets were allocated (implicitly rather than explicitly) to customer retention vs. 47% for customer acquisition, reversing the figures from 1991.

"Ultimately, this will mean a shift of funds out of advertising into customer service programs," said Marketing Metrics president, Terry Vavra in the Nov. 1, 1994, issue of *Investor's Business Daily*. "The goal has shifted from gaining share of market to increasing share of the customer, intensifying his loyalty."

If marketing expenditures for a given customer don't decline over time, they are being misdirected. However, we should be careful to allocate an appropriate amount to customer retention because these customers will drive profitability. Furthermore, the nature of spending has to change over time: Dollars should be shifted away from advertising and sales promotion to consultative selling, customer business development, and logistical enhancements. Such resources could visibly accumulate in a "Customer Business Development" fund, and customers should influence how those resources are spent.

Marketing Alliances

By combining forces with another company interested in reaching a similar target market with a distinctive or complementary offering, companies can almost double the productivity of some of their marketing resources. Marketing alliances are most readily formed for advertising, selling, or distribution purposes, but they could also extend into product development or creative product bundling arrangements.

An increasingly popular type of alliance is co-branding: Kellogg's Pop Tarts made with Smucker's jam; Nabisco's Cranberry Newtons filled with Ocean Spray cranberries; Cracker Jacks packaged with Blue Diamond almonds. Benefits include greater differentiation and thus a greater ability to woo customers away from generics and private labels, the ability of two brands to attract each other's core loyal customers, and lowered costs. Co-branding can also be a way to tap into the equity in a particularly strong brand, in which case the "host" brand might pay a royalty to link itself with a strong "guest" brand.

"Affinity-group" marketing is another form of marketing alliance. Under such arrangements, companies can market to a group of customers who are members of an affinity group (such as alumni of a university or members of an association), typically by developing offerings customized for the needs of that group. Marketing efforts often piggyback on the communication efforts of the affinity group.

A third type of marketing alliance is a "cross-selling" agreement. Typically, such alliances are formed between units or divisions of the same company whose separate offerings have appeal to each other's customers. For example, the credit card division of American Express works with the travel and publishing divisions of that company to cross-sell their offerings. Different divisions of a bank might sell diverse services to the same customer. Such capabilities are enhanced through shared customer information files used in database marketing.

Cross-marketing agreements also can occur across different companies. For example, companies marketing complementary products on the Internet to similar groups of customers engage in "cross-linking": providing direct connections to each other's sites. In this way, companies can raise their customer throughput with little added expense.

Marketing alliances clearly improve marketing efficiency because they achieve synergy in resource utilization. They also improve marketing effectiveness because customers are offered convenient "one-stop-shop" access to more products.

Rationalizing

There are two major ways in which marketing can be rationalized.[2] The first is by better defining where marketing tasks should be performed, up the value chain (outsourcing to suppliers) and down the value chain (getting customers to take over some tasks). Another possibility is to move marketing tasks into other parts of the company, which can achieve the same results more efficiently or effectively (or both). For example, certain tasks performed by customer service could be designed into the product, thus reducing the need for customer service.

The second dimension of rationalizing relates to the problem of poor resource allocation among the elements of the marketing mix. Productivity can sometimes be improved simply by pulling back in some areas and deploying all or some part of those resources elsewhere. For example, Procter & Gamble has improved its marketing (and corporate) performance by drastically cutting its spending on sales promotions in favor of advertising and R&D.

Competitive pressures have led marketing to add more and more variations in elements of the marketing mix. If these variations are unrelated to actual differences in customer preferences, though, they can add complexity and cost without adding offsetting value. For example, the airline and long-distance telephone service industries have proliferated pricing schemes to such a degree that customers are confused and often resentful.

For companies serving a wide range of product-markets, marketing activities can become highly scattered and thus very expensive if undertaken in an uncoordinated, excessively decentralized manner. However, such companies also have the opportunity to be very productive in their marketing, provided they can reduce redundancies, increase economies of scale in marketing efforts, develop mechanisms for cross-marketing, and so on.

For example, 3M sells an astounding variety of products—approximately 60,000 in all. All of those products carry the 3M brand name, giving the company so much visibility that very little corporate advertising is needed. In its quest for marketing efficiencies, 3M also has developed sophisticated information systems that allow salespersons from any part of the company to sell all 3M products to a particular customer.

Companies can spend marketing dollars at several different levels: brand, divisional, corporate, and even the industry level. Productivity improvements can sometimes be realized simply by shifting resources from one level to the next (usually, though not always, to a higher level).

For example, a company can try to use advertising to grow the overall market for a product by pointing out new uses or highlighting its advantages over substitute products. Unless a company has the lion's share of the market, it would probably be more productive to undertake such an effort in cooperation with its rivals in the industry. In the 1970s, Pioneer Electronics tried to develop the hi-fi market using its own advertising dollars, despite having a relatively small share of the market. Even though this did result in a substantially larger hi-fi market over time (benefiting Pioneer as well as its competitors), it is probable that the same effect could have been achieved at less cost to Pioneer if it had led an industrywide effort in this direction.

In a similar vein, reallocating marketing dollars between the areas of advertising, sales promotion, public relations, and the nurturing/managing of word-of-mouth communications among customers can have a significant impact on marketing productivity. PR and word-of-mouth have received inadequate attention from most companies, but the latter type of communication will likely take on greater import with the increased use of online networks for marketing purposes. We discuss these developments in detail in the next issue of *Marketing Management*.

Make Vs. Buy

Every marketing activity should be evaluated in terms of a "make vs. buy" decision, but this is especially important for advertising, sales, and distribution. In the Spring 1986 issue of *Sloan Management Review*, Erin Anderson and Barton Weitz suggested that a transaction cost analysis framework is useful for determining the most efficient way to perform these functions.

Specifically, they maintained that efficiency is a function of scale economies, company-specific capabilities, the ability to monitor performance, the extent of free-riding potential, and environmental uncertainty.

The framework suggests outsourcing when there is a high degree of specialization in performing a marketing activity. Over time, more marketing activities are becoming specialized, making them good candidates for outsourcing.

The trend to outsource marketing activities is picking up momentum: By one estimate, PepsiCo now outsources approximately 80% of its marketing activities; RJReynolds outsources many things, including package design; and P&G outsources 90% of its custom market research projects.[3] With noncore marketing activities being outsourced and core activities being spread among other functional areas, it becomes evident that the marketing department faces a squeeze from two sides.

Some activities, such as advertising, have traditionally been outsourced, and others, such as market research, are heading in the same direction. Many companies do too many activities in-house while others outsource activities they should retain control over. For example, firms can profitably outsource the *creation* of relationships (via third-party distribution channels and so on) but not relationship *management;* maintaining a relationship with the customer is too important to be left exclusively to an intermediary. This is why marketers themselves should make informed evaluations of which tasks should be outsourced and which should be done in-house.

Some marketing activities that are candidates for outsourcing include sales, sales management (just as many companies are already outsourcing the human resource function), sales promotion, logistics, marketing information systems, customer service, and so on.

Outsourcing can contribute tremendously to marketing productivity if it involves taking a secondary or "back-burner" activity and handing it over to a specialist for whom it is a "front-burner" activity. The specialist enjoys economies of scale and scope in performing the activity and provides leading-edge capabilities through investments in emerging technologies. Direct marketer Laura Ashley, for example, successfully outsourced its inbound and outbound logistics functions to Federal Express' Business Logistics Division. The result was a 10% reduction in costs, coupled with a dramatic improvement in product availability and the launch of a new worldwide, 48-hour direct delivery service.

Bringing Customers Into the Value Chain

One of the ironies of marketing is that customers are often more satisfied when they perform some tasks that marketers normally would perform. Companies could simultaneously lower their costs and increase customer satisfaction by identifying such areas. For example, the leading telecommunications companies have accomplished this by providing billing information to their business customers on floppy disk, CD-ROM, or computer tape. Rather than the telecommunications company providing detailed reports, customers use software (also provided by the telecommunications company) to analyze the data themselves.

Numerous activities—from ATM banking to pumping gas to direct dialing long-distance calls—today are routinely and preferentially performed by customers. Direct dialing is an interesting case. Until 1970, almost half of all long distance calls were being placed by operators. In 1971, AT&T launched a marketing campaign to get customers to dial direct, with the advertising theme, "We have two reasons for urging you to dial direct. You save and we save too." By the end of 1973, 75% of calls were direct dialed, and AT&T estimated productivity savings of $37 million a year. In recent years, the use of direct dialing for calling cards reduced costs for phone companies and made customers happier.

Companies can increase customer satisfaction and lower personnel costs by allowing customers direct access to company databases. For example, FedEx, UPS, most major airlines, and a number of banks are currently using this technology. FedEx and UPS have had great success by providing customers with terminals and software to access their information systems for queries regarding package pickup, tracking, and delivery. Likewise, telecommunications companies provide customers the ability to "self-provision" certain services instantaneously, instead of waiting for hours or days for the company to do it for them. For example, Cellular One now allows customers to set up their own voice mail service immediately.

The win-win aspect of all such changes is critical. Lacking a "win" for the customer, productivity enhancing measures are viewed as self-serving and lead to customer defections. In some instances, the "win" is not immediately evident, and may require extensive customer education or the continued provision of traditional service for some segments. The "high-tech" aspects of such service changes must be balanced by adequate attention to "high-touch" issues.

In the early 1980s, Citibank attempted to speed the use of ATMs in New York by requiring customers with total account balances below a set amount to use only ATMs for a specified list of transactions. This policy led to protests by customers, much adverse publicity, and many account closings. Customers like multiple options and usually will not stand for ultimatums.

As Benjamin Schneider and David Bowen note in their new book, *Winning the Service Game*, "Customers may . . . be delighted if their participation leads to productivity increases in which they get to share through lower prices. But this is not the most important point. The important point is that customers who are offered an opportunity to participate are more likely to be satisfied *regardless of whether they actually participate*—because customers like *choices.*"

Conversely, there are many tasks customers now perform that could be performed more productively by specialists. The intensifying time shortage facing many consumers today has led to burgeoning demand for a whole variety of convenience-oriented services. Consumers are "outsourcing" more and more tasks such as house cleaning, lawn care, food preparation, and so on.

Many of these functions are more accurately classified as operational rather than marketing. But the boundaries between the two functions need to be redrawn; all customer-involving operations should be treated, at least indirectly, as marketing concerns. Beyond that, there are opportunities to get the customer to perform more purely marketing tasks, such as self-qualifying, order placement, order follow-up, and so on.

Companies can also leverage their own satisfied customers as salespeople, either directly, as MCI has done with its highly successful Friends & Family program, or indirectly, through word-of-mouth marketing.

The following checklist can help determine if customers should be asked to perform tasks ordinarily performed by marketing or customer service.

- Does the change save the customer time?

- How much additional effort does it entail?

- Does it protect the customer's privacy?

- Can the customer automate the process to any extent? Can we provide tools to accomplish this?

- Can the customer customize it to a greater degree?

- Does the change maintain or increase the accuracy with which the task is performed?

- Is personal (human) help available immediately if the customer needs it?

Reducing Product and Attribute Proliferation

The adoption of flexible manufacturing systems and various software-driven manufacturing processes now enables many firms to increase the assortment of products they can produce without substantially increasing unit costs. Ironically, this capability frequently contributes to declining marketing productivity because the ability to produce products efficiently does not mean that they can be marketed efficiently.

In many cases, firms have expanded the range of their product offerings beyond what the market needs. This has fragmented as well as increased the need for advertising and sales forces. It has also increased the difficulty of forecasting sales, resulting in more unsold inventory. As a result, the marketing costs for the product line increase substantially, lowering or eliminating profits for the line.

For example, when it sold its housewares business to Black & Decker in 1984, General Electric produced 150 products in 14 product categories, including 14 models of steam irons. To obtain distribution support for its entire line, the company had to administer a whole range of incentive programs for retailers, including early-buy allowances, full-line forcing programs, and so on. Black & Decker is gradually backing off of this approach, offering a rationalized product line and relying on a replenishment logistics approach instead to move toward its goal of "sell one, ship one, build one."

A similar argument can be made about product attributes. Many add much more value than they do cost, leading to higher margins. But, more often, numerous incidental attributes add more cost than value, creating a drain on profitability. Some attributes may cost little, but mean even less to customers, such as the ability to program VCRs a full year in advance.

Southwest Airlines has eliminated many frills to concentrate on providing a better core service; on-time arrivals, no lost baggage, no complaints. Some "frills" may be relatively inexpensive in dollar terms—such as baggage transfers between airlines—but have the potential to hurt the quality of the core offering by delaying some flights or causing luggage to be misrouted.

Umbrella Branding

Product proliferation typically leads to brand proliferation, which lowers the economies of scale associated with advertising. Because each new brand requires a high threshold of advertising spending just to be noticed, the breakeven market share becomes very high.

While "brand equity" is a powerful force in consumer decision making, it can be very expensive to create and sustain. The typical "national" brand name can cost $50 million–$100 million a year to support. Companies are finding that, by capitalizing on existing brand names whenever feasible, they can achieve the benefits of a powerful brand without investing the resources to create a new one.

Of course, this can only be done if the same image is appropriate for both products. The problem with extending a brand is that many brands have been defined (mostly through past advertising) in too narrow a fashion; as a result, they have become very product-specific and difficult to extend.

Conversely, some firms have been slow to recognize the value of the brand equity in some of their products and have underutilized those assets. For example, P&G discovered some years ago that Ivory was really an umbrella brand that didn't just stand for soap. It has since leveraged Ivory's considerable brand equity into leadership positions in dishwashing liquid, shampoo, conditioner, and laundry detergent.

Japanese companies, such as Matsushita (Panasonic), Mitsubishi, and Yamaha, have been very successful at using their brand names across an extremely wide variety of products as has GE in the United States.

Rethinking Advertising

By making information sources such as newspapers, magazines, TV, and radio virtually free to most end-users, advertising has played a tremendous role in creating huge and profitable markets for these media. However, advertising is so rife with productivity problems that its role as a marketing tool is under increasingly harsh scrutiny.

An estimated $159 billion will be spent on advertising in the United States this year. This amount will buy an average of 1,500 person-exposures every day! Of these messages, perhaps one-tenth are actually noticed at all, a fraction of that are remembered, and fewer than that are remembered in a positive way. Little surprise, then, that some industry experts estimate that advertisers waste as much as $40 billion a year in the United States alone on ineffective campaigns in pursuit of largely intangible results.

Given these dismal numbers, it is not surprising that the advertising industry is being transformed—even reinvented—through the evolution of information technology. For example, Ed Artzt, the influential former chairman of Procter & Gamble (one of the largest advertisers in the country) has called for the advertising profession to reinvent itself for the coming information age, suggesting that "business as usual" will simply not work. The key problem is the poor targetability of current advertising and its highly intrusive nature.

The overall thrust of future changes in advertising will be to make it more "yield-based," with the costs of advertising directly linked to its effectiveness. Early forms of yield-based advertising can already be seen in TV ads for which advertisers are charged only for the calls generated from their 800-number, rather than on some estimate of viewership.

Advertising does create value for customers, and many seek out advertiser-generated information on their own. Unfortunately, much advertising today still is developed for broadcast to mass markets, many of which long ago fragmented into smaller markets. To be successful in the future, advertising will have to move from its broadcast mode to more narrowcasting and eventually "monocasting" or "pointcasting" to segments of one. Meanwhile, managers can improve advertising productivity by managing expectations, budgeting carefully, adjusting compensation methods, and recycling campaigns.

Manage Expectations.   In most companies, advertising sets customer expectations, and the rest of the marketing function—along with operations, customer service, and so forth—must deliver on them. Unfortunately, most companies exercise inadequate control over the setting of expectations, allowing advertising agencies too much discretion in the matter. These agencies typically set such unrealistic expectations that even a high level of actual performance may still leave the customer dissatisfied. Managers at client firms and ad agencies must take responsibility for better managing customer expectations, by underpromising and overdelivering rather than the reverse.

Budget Better.   Advertising must be very carefully budgeted, since the effect of advertising spending on profitability is extremely high. Additions to the advertising budget reduce immediate profits by a like amount and reductions enhance it. In many cases, a reduction in R&D spending also accompanies advertising spending increases. John Philip Jones of Syracuse University has shown that sales of large brands can be maintained with a relatively low (and sometimes declining) level of advertising spending. Similarly, brands with very small market shares (usually newer entrants) typically must spend at a level exceeding that suggested by their market share.

Adjust Compensation. The traditional practice of compensating ad agencies with a negotiated percentage of media billings creates a perverse incentive. Research has shown that an outstanding commercial is many times more effective than an average one. For example, Campbell Soup Co. found that the quality elasticity of advertising was 18 times greater than the quantity elasticity. Outstanding ads need to be run much less frequently than mediocre ones to achieve a given exposure level. However, under the traditional practice, this would result in lower total compensation for the agency.

Clearly, agencies should be compensated for the effectiveness of their advertising and given incentives to achieve effective results with the lowest possible expenditure on media. One solution is to unbundle the creation of advertising from media scheduling and purchasing, as the Coca-Cola Co. and others have recently done.

Recycle. When struggling with the issue of advertising wearout, marketers make two kinds of mistakes: sticking with poor campaigns long after it becomes evident that they are failing and prematurely terminating very successful campaigns. Several companies have successfully "recycled" old ad campaigns, often (but not always) tied in to a nostalgia theme.

Marketers should ask their ad agencies to create advertising that is not time-sensitive to avoid material that rapidly becomes dated. Also, agencies can recycle their own creative work by converting approaches that have worked well in one context into another, noncompeting context. Technology can be a great help here. P&G is developing an expert-system database of commercial advertising copy aggregating over 3,500 commercials. P&G personnel in any part of the world will be able to access tried and proven advertising copy sorted by the "sizzle" being sold. If copy conveying "shine" is needed, for instance, whether for shampoo or floor wax, the database will provide it.

Focusing Promotions

Sales promotion activity has gotten out of hand, especially in the packaged-goods industry. While advertising can be viewed as an investment, sales promotion is a purely short-term fix, typically intended to buttress the top line or market share.

Consider the sales promotion activity of couponing. Traditional coupons are of four broad types, and each has been found to be inefficient as well as ineffective:

- Magazine and newspaper coupons reach people who might throw away free-standing inserts (FSIs) or direct mail coupons without looking at them; however, they have high media costs and low redemption rates (1.6% in 1991).

- In- or on-product coupons always reach the users of a product and so are appropriate for encouraging the purchase of product line extensions and increasing brand loyalty. However, they are not effective for gaining trial among non-users.

- Direct mail coupons are sent directly to consumers' homes. When they are mass mailed, redemption rates are very low. If the coupons are matched to a desired customer profile (often based on Zip-code analysis), the redemption rate rises (4.3% in 1991).

- Free-standing inserts make up the bulk of traditional coupons, representing 88% of the 323 billion coupons distributed annually and $1.8 billion of the $2.1-billion coupon industry in 1992. However, their shotgun approach yields a national redemption rate of only 1.8%–2.3%. FSIs have a tremendously high "cost per coupon redeemed by the user of a competitive product." The cost of running an FSI, including processing and redemption, is approximately $19.75 per 1,000 coupons distributed. Of these 1,000, only three on average are redeemed by users of competing brands, making the cost per competitive trial $6.58. This type of couponing can be effective for companies with very low market share because most redeemers are likely to be users of competing brands.

In addition to these failings, traditional coupons have a long redemption process, meaning that information on the coupon promotion is not available to brand managers until three to six months after the expiration date on the coupon. Furthermore, the amount of information available is very limited; the brand manager can only find out the total number redeemed, the total dollar value, and how quickly they were redeemed.

One company, Catalina Marketing Corp. of St. Petersburg, Fla., is making consumer promotions much more productive. Catalina has created a unique niche for itself based on its ability to address the tremendous inefficiency of traditional coupon promotions in the packaged-goods industry.

Catalina's Checkout Coupon system works by printing out coupons based on products "just purchased." With a redemption rate of between 6.5%–10%, the cost per competitive user trial is $2.22–$2.42. It is interesting to note that the average cost per coupon redeemed is in fact substantially higher for Catalina compared to FSIs ($2.30 vs. 90¢); the main advantage is in virtually eliminating windfall redemptions by customers who would have bought the product anyway.

Besides the lower cost, Catalina's automated system enables brand managers to obtain information on the results of promotions in a much more timely manner. Catalina can provide several types of coupons: competitive, continuity, tie-in, cross-category and own-user coupons, as well as ones with specific advertising messages on them. Coupons can also be created for retailers, for example, offering X dollars off the next visit to entice heavy shoppers to return to the store (the amount can be related to the average amount spent by that shopper per visit).

While Catalina and its competitors offer a substantially better way to do coupon-based sales promotions, manufacturers such as P&G prefer to gain trial through advertising. Advertising is considered the highest value way of gaining trial because customers are buying the product "for the right reasons." In other words, they have been convinced that the product is superior, whereas with a coupon-induced trial, they might be buying it simply because it is less expensive.

Also, P&G believes that people who use coupons are very likely to switch again, which further lessens the value of trial. The implication is that the lifetime value of customers gained through advertising is greater than that of a customer gained through couponing. Unfortunately, there is no reliable way to track advertising-driven trial, though that too will change when interactive advertising becomes more widespread.

Dynamic Pricing

Many companies continue to use some variation of cost-plus pricing. By so doing, they tend to sacrifice significant profit opportunities in the long run as well as shield many operating and marketing inefficiencies. By moving to more market-driven pricing—and, consequently, price-based costing—they force many of their costs down because no artificial umbrella exists to shield high costs. For example, a company might use cost-plus pricing to sell cellular phones for several hundred dollars apiece and then charge a high per-minute rate based on an average cost formula (dividing the cost of building and running the network by the minutes used and adding a markup).

With these high prices, a company can have high margins on paper that allow it to spend heavily to acquire new customers. However, if it were to move to a price-based costing approach (as most in the industry have done), the company would determine that the profit-maximizing strategy is to subsidize the phones to get them in people's hands and then price calls low to drive up usage. Even though total spending on marketing would rise in the process, so would marketing productivity because costs on a per-customer basis would have to fall.

Southwest Airlines has created a very low cost-structure that allows it to turn a profit on a $50 ticket. Clearly, it cannot afford to spend $25 of marketing effort on getting that customer! The use of price-based costing leads to a price that "hits the sweet spot" in the market, making marketing's task that much easier.

Another major way pricing can improve marketing productivity is through the use of modified yield management (YM), systems, such as those used in the airline and hotel industries to maximize revenues and profits.

YM systems can streamline pricing and capacity management processes, especially for service businesses. However, as Rashi Glazer of the University of California at Berkeley points out, they also have important implications for companies using flexible manufacturing systems. Because such systems produce customized products on demand, they represent expensive fixed assets with varying levels of capacity utilization over time; the systems become idle when demand does not materialize, and YM helps smooth out demand.

Dynamic pricing systems will increase in importance as flexible pricing permeates education, health care, and other domains. Flexible pricing also could be used in retail to give shoppers lower prices at off-peak shopping times.

Unbundling and Rebundling Services

Customer service is rightly viewed as an essential component of good marketing but many firms have become trapped in an escalating spiral of increasing service costs. When service is bundled with the core product, it can rapidly raise the costs of marketing and erode profitability. It also leads to the cross-subsidization of heavy users of service by light users, which contributes to marketing inefficiency and provides opportunities for competitors to steal the profitable low-service customers by offering them lower prices.

The answer is not to reduce or eliminate service but to package it in different ways. Firms can provide a base level of service to all customers and then offer different levels of service to different customer groups for a fee. Alternatively, they can choose to continue offering the service free to their most frequent and profitable customers.

Such an approach increases marketing productivity by increasing revenues (through the sale of value-added services to high-end customers) and lowering costs (by reducing the incidence of unprofitable service provision to other customers). The personal computer software industry has been particularly successful in making this transition, offering varying levels of support under different fee structures for different segments of consumers and businesses.

Service costs also can be reduced and service quality enhanced through the redesign of products for greater serviceability. "Smart" products can diagnose themselves (using sensors and expert systems) and alert the service provider (through wired or wireless telecommunications) of impending problems. Such features are becoming commonplace in high-end copiers and medical diagnostic equipment, where the costs associated with downtime are very high. They allow companies to price service contracts very attractively and still make a large profit margin on them.

Computer software and hardware companies are increasingly designing their systems for remote trouble shooting; technicians can take control of a user's computer from afar and find and fix problems. The enabling technologies are becoming so affordable that the day of the smart toaster may not be too far off.

In the next issue, we expand on the role of information technology in boosting marketing productivity and discuss how the marketing function can be better managed for effective efficiency.

Reprinted with permission from the Fall 1995 issue of Marketing Management, *published by the American Marketing Association, Sheth, Jagdish N. and Rajendra S. Sisodia, Fall 1995/Vol 4, pp. 8–23.*

Notes

1. The classic example of this is telemarketing; with $40 billion-$60 billion a year in estimated telecommunications fraud in the United States alone, this is fast becoming the most efficient way ever devised to alienate customers.
2. The term "rationalizing" in this connection has been used by Fred Wiersema of the CSC/Index Consulting Group. See CSC Index Alliance presentations on *Lean Marketing: The Immediate Imperative* by Fred Wiersema ("More Bang for the Buck") and Michael Treacy ("The Strategic Context for Lean Marketing") at the 1993 Executive Forum in Tucson.
3. P&G has even outsourced its central switchboard, with receptionists provided by an outside vendor.

Additional Reading

Anderson, Erin and Barton A. Weitz (1986), "Make-or-Buy Decisions: Vertical Integration and Marketing Productivity," *Sloan Management Review,* 27 (Spring), 3–19.

Berry, John M. (1994), "For Many Firms, Benefit of Cutting Inventories is Worth the Risk," *The Washington Post*, (Oct. 6), D1.

Buckingham, Lisa (1993), "20/20: Over-Marketing Mystery," *The Guardian*, (Dec. 18), 36.

Jacob, Rahul (1994), "Why Some Customers Are More Equal Than Others," *Fortune*, (September), 215.

Lovelock, Christopher H. and Robert F. Young (1979), "Look to Consumers to Increase Productivity," *Harvard Business Review*, (May–June), 168–78.

Mitchell, Alan (1994), "Dark Night of Marketing or a New Dawn? Changes in the Marketing Function," *Marketing*, (Feb. 17), 22.

Reichheld, Frederick (1994), "Loyalty and the Renaissance of Marketing," *Marketing Management*, 2 (4), 10–21.

——— (1993), "Loyalty-Based Management," *Harvard Business Review*, (March–April), 64.

Schneider, Benjamin and David Bowen (1995), Winning the Service Game. Cambridge, MA: *Harvard Business School Press*.

Walsh, Matt (1994), "Point of Sale Persuaders," *Forbes*, Oct. 24, 232–34.

11

Feeling the Heat—Part 2

*Information technology, creative management
boost marketing productivity.*

JAGDISH N. SHETH

RAJENDRA S. SISODIA

*When marketing becomes more productive, everyone wins, especially customers. Part 1
of this article described collaborative marketing strategies that improve marketing productivity as well as various ways to rationalize expenditures. Part 2 emphasizes the huge
role information technology plays in the quest for "effective efficiency" and offers some
innovative management strategies. With all of this focus on refining the science of marketing, though, we must take care never to lose sight of marketing as an art.*

In the last issue, we talked about the growing productivity crisis in marketing and
how difficult it is to measure the true output of an activity that involves so many
intangibles. Even so, with cost cutters demanding accountability, even imperfect
measures help make the case for marketers if they measure the right things.

The desired output of marketing is to acquire and maintain customers profitably.
To accomplish this, marketing must pursue the ideal of "effective efficiency"—doing
things right and doing the right things. We have identified 20 ways to improve marketing productivity and classified them into four broad categories: collaborating,
rationalizing, "informationalizing," and managing. (For an overview, see "Improving
Marketing Productivity.")

In Part 1, we focused on the first two categories, collaborating and rationalizing.
Now, we discuss how to boost marketing productivity by using information technology and better managing the function for effective efficiency.

'Informationalizing'

Many of the productivity improvements in aspects of business other than marketing
have occurred through the deployment of information technology (IT). Particularly
in the last decade (since PCs infiltrated the workplace), IT spending has been imper-
vious to economic recessions or industry downturns because of its anticipated impact
on productivity. In the last few years, the impact of that spending has indeed become

IMPROVING MARKETING PRODUCTIVITY

Collaborating

- Partnering: Treat suppliers and customers as partners in lowering system-wide costs and adding value.
- Relationship marketing: Be selective about customers, and take a long-term win-win perspective.
- Marketing alliances: Share resources and opportunities with other companies serving the same customers.

Rationalizing

- Make vs. buy: Focus on your marketing core competences, and let outside experts handle the rest.
- Bringing customers into the value chain: Lower costs and increase customer satisfaction by adding customers to the value chain.
- Reducing product and attribute proliferation: Variety does not always equate to value; reduce customer confusion and marketing costs by matching product lines with distinct market segments, and by adding product attributes that matter.
- Umbrella branding: Increase "Return on Branding" by developing brand names with broad applicability to multiple products and markets.
- Rethinking advertising: Better manage the setting of customer expectations, budget for advertising based on objectives, remote conflicts-of-interest and perverse incentives in agency compensation methods, unbundle advertising creation and placement, and understand advertising wearout.
- Focusing promotions: Stop creating "deal junkies," end windfalls to existing customers and surgically target promotional incentives to achieve greater trial.
- Dynamic pricing: Use market-based pricing to increase profits and decrease marketing waste, and consider the use of dynamic pricing approaches such as yield management systems.

- Unbundling and rebundling services: Uncover the hidden costs of free service, and create new revenue sources.

'Informationalizing'

- Market response modeling: Use well-established marketing models when high quality data is available.
- Database marketing: Target marketing efforts more precisely, but ensure that you are creating additional value for the customer and are acutely sensitive to privacy concerns.
- Front-line information systems: Deploy information tools where they have the greatest impact on customer service and satisfaction—at the front-line.
- Net-based marketing: Prepare now for a radically different, more integrated mode of marketing in the future, predicated on "total customer convenience;" Position yourselves for a future of one-to-one interactive marketing.
- Re-engineering marketing processes: Develop radically different and information technology-enabled ways of conducting key marketing processes.

Managing

- Activity-based costing: Understand where resources are being spent, where customer value is being created, and where money is being made or lost.
- Zero-based budgeting: Overcome inertia in marketing budgets and improve accountability by linking marketing spending with specific objectives.
- Adjusting compensation of marketing personnel: Compensation drivers must be linked with the need for effective efficiency in all marketing activities.
- Continuous assessment of marketing practices: Beware of creeping marketing incrementalism; take a periodic "zero-based" view of marketing practices.

apparent, and the so-called "Productivity Paradox"—a perceived lack of correlation between IT spending and overall productivity—has been laid to rest.

Several of the productivity enhancers discussed in Part 1 are based on the use of the new capabilities of today's computing and communications technologies. Technology can improve and eventually alter marketing practice, in several ways.

IT is not an automatic solution to marketing productivity problems; simply "automating" aspects of an otherwise unchanged marketing process leads to the classic result that students of business process re-engineering know very well: marginal improvements at best, and many new and hidden costs. Clearly, the fundamental processes of marketing must be addressed first, with the redesign recognizing and appreciating the power of new technologies. Even then, IT can prove to be a productivity hindrance in the short run as the organizational culture adapts to accept and integrate the new technology into various marketing processes.

For sustained competitive advantage, companies need an IT "platform" that uniquely blends core marketing competencies with seamless technology. Over time, IT becomes less of a driving force and more of a requisite infrastructure. And this leads to the development of technology-based core competencies that are not readily duplicated by others because they cannot be purchased "off-the-shelf."

Companies such Frito-Lay, FedEx, Citibank, and American Airlines, for example, are outstanding at technology assessment, integration, and absorption. They have developed close partnering relationships with technology vendors and work with them on state-of-the-art solutions to problems others have not even experienced yet.

IT can improve marketing productivity in a number of ways. It can lower the cost of providing a particular service to customers as well as make it more convenient. It also can reduce the demand for personnel-based customer service. At FedEx, for example, customers with access to the World Wide Web can track the status of their package in seconds, without ever dealing with a live representative.

At 3M, customers used to select and order products from a five-inch thick catalog listing the company's 60,000 products. Known among sales representatives and customers as the "bible," this catalog was a burden to thumb through, expensive to produce and distribute, and subject to rapid obsolescence. To replace it, 3M has developed a CD-ROM version that can be produced for $1.50. In addition to eliminating the paper barrage of brochures, mailers, and product binders the company sent to clients to keep them updated, the technology has also decreased the demand for customer service. In the past, many customers called a customer service rep because it was faster and easier than using the catalog.

Marketers have only begun to feel the impact of IT. In the past decade, scanner systems allowed packaged-goods marketers to make better informed and more timely decisions, but without appreciably changing what they did. However, the availability, affordability, and capability of IT are fast approaching a level where wholesale changes will be made—changes that offer the promise of raising marketing productivity to a new level.

The primary technological drivers are:

- Greater computing power in more portable form at increasingly affordable prices. Computing power that used to cost a million dollars can be had today for less than a dollar.

- Greater communication band width, along with more availability of wireless data transmission capabilities.

- Increasingly sophisticated and user-friendly software, including the popularization of embedded and stand-alone expert systems, as well as a variety of "performance support systems."

- Real-time capture and distribution of pertinent marketing data, including transaction data as well as various stimulus variables such as advertising.

- Rapid progress in the area of voice recognition technology.

The impact of these enormously powerful technologies on marketing will be profound. To attain their full benefit, many marketing processes will have to be *re-engineered*, or redesigned "from the ground up" to take advantage of available information tools.

The relationship between IT and marketing productivity will manifest itself in five areas: analytical marketing models, database marketing, front-line information systems, net-based marketing, (the likely impact of the so-called information highway), and the re-engineering of key marketing processes.

Market Response Modeling

Market response models help companies develop strategies that lead to increased marketing effectiveness as well as significant cost savings. Most companies could benefit from a more analytical approach to marketing decision making than they have had in the past. Used in the appropriate contexts and with the right data, models can be very effective. For example:

- In over a thousand applications, the new product pretesting model "Assessor" is highly accurate in predicting a new brand's eventual market share. Studies have shown that actual market shares are within 10% of predicted market shares 90% of the time. Furthermore, companies can use Assessor and similar models to "fine-tune" the marketing mix before launching their product.

- The sales planning system "Call Plan" is very effective in improving decisions pertaining to optimal sales force size and deployment, as well as call planning at the salesperson level.

- Media planning systems such as "MEDIAC" are indispensable tools for making effective decisions on media selection, scheduling, and budgeting.

- The use of analytical approaches to evaluating advertising has allowed companies such as Anheuser-Busch and Campbell Soup to reduce advertising spending while increasing its overall impact.

The usefulness of models and the quality of their performance depends greatly on the availability of good data. For many aspects of marketing today, there is no dearth of highly accurate, timely, and affordable data. For example, supermarket scanners have created a virtual avalanche of clean, timely data. The ability to leverage these data into actionable insights is greater today than ever before. The potential value of models is thus higher.

Two relatively recent developments augur well for the increased use of market response models in the future. First, many such models now incorporate expert system approaches, providing managerial judgment as well as analytic insight. They are able to respond to "What if?" queries with a richer set of responses as well as make proactive suggestions for managers to consider.

The second development pertains to the interface. Models are increasingly shielding the user from their inner complexity through the use of graphical interfaces as well as through more natural language capabilities. For example, an expert system called Cover Story provides managers of consumer products with a one-page memo in English summarizing the key insights gleaned from enormous quantities of scanner data.

Clearly, such tools lead to more effective and efficient marketing decisions, and it will be increasingly necessary for firms to adopt them in order to compete. Widespread availability and affordability will no doubt reduce their value as a source of competitive advantage, though some proprietary advantages might accrue to firms with sophisticated internal "knowledge bases."

Database Marketing

Just as all politics is local, once upon a time all marketing was local—and personal. Marketers had long-standing one-to-one relationships with their customers. However, the rise of mass markets, mass advertising, and mass merchants led to the onset of impersonal mass marketing. Customers are now quite remote from marketers, buffered by time, place, and multiple intermediaries. Database marketing (DBM) is once again starting to close the gap between marketers and customers.

This should not be surprising; more and better information about customers is at the heart of marketing. Marketers are recognizing that past behavior, as recorded in transaction records, is the best indicator of future behavior. DBM is now rightly moving into the marketing mainstream, and increasingly must be used by almost all marketers.

The use of DBM is spreading fast:

- Donnelley Marketing Inc. found that, in 1994, 56% of manufacturers and retailers were building a database, an additional 10% planned to do so, and 85% believed they would need database marketing to be competitive beyond the year 2000.

- GM now has a database of 12 million GM credit card holders, giving the company access to a great deal of data on their buying habits. GM also surveys these customers to get information on driving habits and needs.

- Blockbuster has a database of 36 million households and 2 million daily transactions. It uses the technology to suggest additional movie choices and cross-promote its affiliates such as Discovery Zone for children.

- Philip Morris' database of 26 million smokers is used to market cigarettes as well as solicit support in lobbying efforts.

- Claridge Hotel and Casino now distributes a "frequent-gambler" card, known as CompCard Gold, to 350,000 "members."

Direct marketing and database marketing are not synonymous, although direct marketers have long led the way in using databases. With better targeting of prospects for products and promotions, greater ability to customize marketing messages and programs, and so on, DBM clearly contributes to greater marketing efficiency. When practiced properly, it yields double-digit response rates, compared to 2%–4% for "junk mail."

For example, Hilton Hotels offers targeted promotions to senior citizens through its Senior Honors program, prompting almost half of the members to take previously unplanned trips that included stays at Hilton.

While DBM is not inexpensive and must be cost-justified like any other initiative, it can "piggy-back" on existing costs. American Express, for example, has initiated what it calls "relationship billing," or customized monthly bills that include offers triggered by specific purchases, such as flights and special store sales. Relationship billing has been rolled out in Europe, Canada, and Mexico, and AMEX claims an increase of 15%–20% in year-over-year cardmember spending in Europe.

Relationship billing allows AMEX to move closer to "mass customization," the tailoring of communications/offers to individual customers. For example, rather than using broad demographics, AMEX might now define a market segment as "female business travelers who bought jewelry abroad on their last trip." Some of the company's offers have gone out to as few as 20 people, but received very high response rates.

DBM provides tremendous opportunities for cross-selling related products. For example, Canon Computer Systems maintains a database of its 1.3 million customers. The company obtained a 50% response rate in a direct mail solicitation asking printer owners if they wanted information on a new color scanner; buyers of scanners received four free ink cartridges for their printers.

We see several issues affecting database marketing in the future:

- Privacy issues will increasingly come to the fore. Unless the marketing profession (not just the Direct Marketing Association) develops an approach to deal with privacy concerns, it could lead to very restrictive government-imposed rules on the use of customer information, such as those already in force in Europe.

- DBM must focus on greater value creation for the customer in addition to marketing efficiency enhancement; in other words, the customer's "profit" in the relationship must increase.

- As technological capabilities expand, companies will have access to virtually unlimited data and broadband interactive multimedia communication channels with their customers. The winners will be companies that are best able to use these efficiency-increasing capabilities to satisfy customers.

- The analytical processes used in DBM have been quite basic—in many cases, limited to sorting and weighting. With the increasing accessibility of fuzzy logic and massively parallel technology, more can and will be done to extract real value from customer and prospect databases.

- In particular, the use of better models in conjunction with database marketing can identify customers with a high propensity to buy and a low likelihood of attrition.

Front-Line Information Systems

In the traditional hierarchical corporation, customer contact personnel occupy the lowest tier in terms of status, responsibility, and compensation levels (see Figure 1). However, their impact on customer satisfaction is arguably greater than that of any other group. Typically, in such corporations, the most sophisticated IT is deployed at the top tier of management for "executive information systems" (EIS). The next priority tends to be "management information systems" (MIS) for middle managers. Employees below that level have traditionally been provided with low-level transaction-support technologies.

This represents a misplaced sense of priorities, however, because the most powerful impact of this technology is felt when it is harnessed at the front lines. Companies that invest in and deploy cutting-edge "front-line information systems" (FIS) achieve breakthrough improvements in service quality and reliability, and thus very high levels of customer satisfaction. By adopting sophisticated FIS, firms will achieve quantum improvements in the effective efficiency of their marketing activities.

Many of today's FIS models were designed primarily to process customers efficiently and were not conceived as marketing tools. This has started to change, however. Dollar Rent-A-Car, for example, is rebuilding its counter systems to include a graphical

---

FIGURE 1　　**FRONT-LINE INFORMATION SYSTEMS (FIS)**

Traditional top-down approach　　**The bottom-up approach**

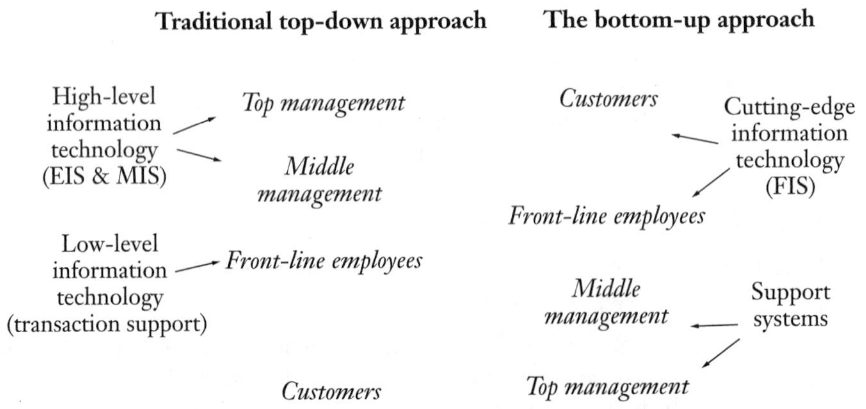

interface that gives the sales agent access to a customer's complete itinerary. Dollar's system will be integrated with those of travel agents and airlines to take advantage of distributed processing capabilities. As car reservations are made, they will be combined with other information and downloaded to the counter database.

Classic Hawaii, a travel agent, uses ANI (automatic number identification) to identify customers, call up their travel itinerary, and greet them by name. The system also automatically routes customers to the agent who made the original booking, providing a high level of familiarity and comfort.

Other examples of companies using high-end FIS include FedEx, Frito-Lay, and Hertz, each of which equips front-line personnel with technologies that enable them to do their work faster and better. Not incidentally, such companies also tend to have high levels of front-line employee satisfaction. Furthermore, because they are using sophisticated tools to perform the work, they're gathering all the data needed for managerial control purposes; such data then "trickle up" to the MIS and EIS levels.

Well-conceived investments in FIS (such as those used by salespeople and customer service representatives) provide very substantial returns, far more so than those intended to automate back-office operations or improve management information systems. FIS investments tend to promote efficiency (through faster and more accurate processing) as well as effectiveness (by improving the quality of service received by the customer).

For example, many companies that provided their sales forces with sophisticated laptop computers and wireless communications have improved their performance and productivity in the areas of account management, lead management, literature fulfillment, reporting (using templates), proposal generation, customer inquiry response, quote status, inventory checking, and so on. Salespeople spend less time on sales administration and paperwork; there is no need for a salesperson to contact marketing for literature or manufacturing for inventory availability. And, because salespeople are not available 24 hours a day, IT can be used to answer customer questions and fulfill their needs around the clock.

For example, by providing an FIS capability to its sales organization at a cost of $30 million, Campbell Soup Co. expects to save $18 million a year through shorter order cycle time, more accurate invoicing, and better control of product promotion funds.

Anderson Consulting now equips its consultants with a CD-ROM called the "Global Best Practices Knowledge Base," which contains best practice information on about 170 business processes. By deploying FIS capabilities for their sales forces, AT&T and Compaq have largely freed salespeople from the constraints of reporting to an office. They now employ the concept of "hoteling," whereby permanent office space for salespeople is replaced by temporary space on an as-needed basis. This lowers costs as well as encourages salespeople to spend as much time as possible in contact with customers.

Net-Based Marketing

The long-awaited "information highway" will be the most significant driver of dramatic change in marketing processes in coming years. Widely available, interactive broadband communication will allow companies to integrate advertising, sales promotion, personal selling, and even distribution to a far greater extent than is now possible, possibly spelling the end of time and place constraints on customers.

Predicted to become widespread in the United States by the year 2005, this technology will dramatically transform the marketing functions of advertising, personal selling, and physical distribution. It will reconfigure industries such as retailing, health care, and education while significantly affecting nearly all others.

Marketing in this new environment will be predicated upon "monocasting" or "pointcasting" of communications, mass customization of all marketing mix elements, a high degree of customer involvement and control, and greater integration between marketing and operations. Companies that successfully make the transition to this new way of marketing will be characterized by fewer wasted marketing resources and minimal customer alienation resulting from misapplied marketing stimuli. All companies will experience enormous pressures to deliver greater value, more global competition, and intense jostling for the loyalties of "desirable" customers.

An early version of the information highway is already here. Some are calling the World Wide Web (WWW) the most important new marketing tool since the television commercial.

The WWW is a part of the global Internet system of linked computers. Those with access to the Internet (now numbering over 35 million in the United States alone and growing rapidly) can be connected to a company's "Home Page" in an instant. From there, they can receive information, order product literature or purchase products, submit queries, check the status of orders or shipments, interact with other customers, "link" to any other related site worldwide—and anything else an imaginative designer can concoct. All of this incorporates multimedia capabilities as appropriate, including audio and video clips and full-color photographs and illustrations.

While the WWW represents a true breakthrough with major implications for marketing, it really represents only a glimpse of more dramatic changes to come, as processing power continues to improve, two-way communication bandwidths explode, and imaging moves toward high definition.

Marketing has a great deal riding on the information highway (which some are calling the marketing highway); it is here that much of the waste that seems inescapable with traditional marketing can be removed. It is also here that new forms of customer-company and customer-customer communication can take place, giving rise to many new opportunities for value creation.

The Internet, as it has evolved in the last two years, gives us an early glimpse of the possibilities for marketing on the information highway. Though constrained by its availability to a small subset of the population and its very narrow communications bandwidth, the power of the medium is already apparent to many and is leading to an explosion of activity in establishing new "sites."

Some industry observers are calling the kind of marketing that will prevail in this new medium "Intelligent Marketing." We refer to it as "Net-Based Marketing" (NBM). In any event, it will be a mode of marketing that is cost-effective, accountable, individualized, interactive, and relationship-based—the very essence of "effective efficiency."

Several characteristics of this new medium make it a significant development.

Few Barriers. Although only 7% of the U.S. population currently subscribes to any kind of online network, growth rates are increasing exponentially and eliminating barriers to use. The absence of encryption and other means of providing for the security of network transactions has also hindered the spread of commercial transactions thus far. However, such standardization and security issues are expected to be resolved by the end of 1996.

Customer Interaction.   Customer relationships and satisfaction will become even more important. NBM will greatly raise the stakes for the delivery and management of customer satisfaction. To a far greater extent than ever before, a company's customers will have the ability to interact among themselves, rather than simply with the seller. This can be a tremendous source of value-enhancement because loyal and satisfied customers can be creatively used as resources to support the needs of newer customers.

The potential clearly exists to foster unprecedented levels of customer loyalty. As Nick Gassman, a participant in the Internet-based INET discussion group, said, "The Internet creates personal relationships. They choose to visit you on the Web, they talk about you with others in the newsgroups, and you join in. And you talk to them privately by e-mail. If you do it right, you make good friends with your customers."

However, the nurturing of such "customer communities" (akin to organizations such as the Acura Buyers Club, where communication among customers is enabled through more cumbersome traditional means) can also backfire. By drastically increasing the "connectivity of opinion," net-based marketing can create a snowball effect in which one customer's complaint can rapidly escalate into a customer relations nightmare (as with Intel's Pentium debacle). Companies must develop realistic contingency plans for such scenarios.

By the same token, however, companies providing superior products and services will probably prosper even more than before at the expense of those for whom reality falls short of promises. In all likelihood, the Internet promises to be an inhospitable habitat for marginal performing companies of any kind.

Customer Retention.   As we mentioned in Part 1, too much of marketing's attention is devoted to customer acquisition and too little to customer retention and growth. It appears that NBM has the greatest potential for the latter, primarily because of its greatly enhanced ability to provide superior customer service through the WWW.

For example, FedEx's site allows customers to key in their package tracking code and immediately receive details on every stop made by a package on its journey. To the extent that NBM can facilitate longitudinal data capture and store a customer's transactions and preferences, value delivery can increase over time.

Egalitarianism.   In many ways, the Internet promises to become a "great equalizer" for businesses:

- "Store-fronts" on the WWW are as readily created by individuals or small businesses as by large corporations.

- The entry cost is low. It has been estimated that a sophisticated site could be created for $200,000—less than half the cost of a single 30-second spot on a top network TV program.

- Advertising and other marketing materials can be created for less, can be modified more easily, and can be reused as appropriate.

- Establishing a brand name becomes a potentially less capital-intensive proposition.

Co-op Marketing. A major key to success with NBM is the ability to attract traffic to a site. Some of the more popular sites (such as the one maintained by *Wired* magazine) already charge upwards of $30,000 a month to provide an advertising link into a sponsor's site. For small companies, more affordable alternatives exist. For example, they could "co-market" their site with others targeting the same customers by providing mutual cross-linkages. The power of such networking will increase the prevalence of cooperative marketing. In either case, the marketing skill set differs considerably. Content and value will drive browsers (prospects) and buyers (customers) to a site.

Micromarketing. The Internet is an ideal tool for targeting market fragments—market segments far smaller than any considered before. Interactions with fragments are usually characterized by very high levels of customer involvement. Such niche markets can be reached at a fraction of the cost of direct mail and other forms of advertising.

Integrated Functions. NBM integrates marketing sub-functions and marketing with other functions. It will redefine sub-functional boundaries within marketing as well as across business functions. For example, marketing, sales, and order processing are integrated functions with NBM.

The need for such integration has been keenly felt; according to a Chilton Publishing report, sales tends to ignore 85% of leads generated by marketing through trade shows and advertising. In Web-based marketing, however, "A person visits the site, gathers information, qualifies himself, asks questions, provides answers to questions, builds an interactive relationship, and offers or responds to an offer to do business," said Ken Sethney of the Sethney Group in INET discussions.

NBM also promotes integration beyond the marketing function. The same resource can be used also to perform customer service and order-processing functions as well as address suppliers, business partners, shareholders, and employees. And all of this communication occurs faster, more accurately, interactively, and at lower cost through NBM than is possible with any other alternative.

Value-Added. As a result of this ability to integrate functions and services, and because customers will gain the ability to obtain the lowest price instantaneously on a given stand-alone item, the locus of competition will shift to providing bundles of benefits—combinations of products and services enhanced through customization, database capabilities, updates, and so on. Marketers will slowly shift from treating buyers as customers to regarding them as clients.

Redefined Advertising. Given a higher level of customer involvement, marketing communication in the new medium will move from providing simple (and, companies hope, memorable) messages to delivering real information (based on the customer's requirements) and eliciting a response.

"Think content, not hype," said Jill Ellsworth, author of *Marketing on the Internet* and another INET discussant. Highly creative, hype-dominated advertising serves the needs of the advertiser far more effectively than those of the client. While visual style and panache are every bit as important in NBM, they must be accompanied by real substance.

Devastate "Traditional" Marketers.   The strategy for many new NBM entrants might be based primarily on technology. This is already true for a host of online businesses. Many new entrants will be powerful companies looking to expand geographically, primarily in a virtual sense. Others may be telecommunications or credit card companies leveraging their information assets and detailed customer databases to provide a wider array of products and services to customers.

Such competitors will come in without any organizational inertia or sunk investment in existing ways of doing business. If the new entrants are successful (as some inevitably will be), traditional marketers will end up with huge "stranded assets": networks of warehouses around the country, distributed customer service operations, expensive retail real estate, and so on.

Just as cellular companies have historically been valued on "potential customers in licensed region" rather than on physical assets, NBM companies may be valued on the basis of analogous measures, such as "potential customers served." Over time, of course, potential customers must become actual customers for this type of company to sustain its value.

Empower Customers.   Though it has become almost a cliché to talk about increasing customer power, it is indeed the case that future customers will call the shots to a far greater extent than ever before. Marketing must move quickly to make customers their allies rather than uneasy adversaries. Customers will no longer be innocent bystanders or passive targets of marketing; they will seek to control it to their advantage.

Indeed, with IT, the very nature of the relationship between buyers and sellers could be altered, with buyers becoming marketers and sellers becoming prospects. In this environment, marketing management becomes demand management. Databases containing information on product image, prices, inventory availability, and so forth will be used by customers as well as by marketers. Purchase decisions in the future may be influenced by database search and display programs, instead of salespeople.

Re-engineering Marketing Processes

Rather than upgrading with piecemeal IT additions, companies will achieve far better results by re-engineering their marketing processes (based on the principles of effective efficiency) and incorporating technology as an inherent element of the redesign.

In the last few years, the re-engineering wave has swept through corporations worldwide. However, relative to other business functions, marketing has been slow to adopt a re-engineering mindset.

As Thomas Davenport pointed out in *Process Innovation:* ". . . Nothing is more critical to a firm's competitive success than its ability to develop new products and services and deliver them to customers. . . . Product/service development and delivery are [thus] likely candidates for innovation in virtually any company. *Yet few companies have adopted a process view of these activities, applied innovative thinking to the processes, and employed IT or human resources to enable radical change*" (italics added).

Davenport suggests that the reason for this has to do with the very nature of marketing activities: "The open-ended nature of marketing makes it difficult to know when and whether a particular set of activities results in a transaction or relationship. The primary output of a marketing process is thus highly uncertain, and this accounts for many companies' unwillingness to consider marketing in process terms."

Although we won't be able to address re-engineering marketing processes in detail, Figure 2 illustrates how re-engineering might affect three key marketing processes: new product development, order management, and customer retention/relationship management.

Ultimately, to be successful, companies will need to have competency in both marketing and technology. Neither alone will suffice.

Managing

Tasks such as planning, analysis, control, compensation systems, and the like all require better marketing management—in the traditional sense of that word. One of the key reasons for poor marketing productivity is that most companies—approximately 70%, according to a 1989 survey by the Institute of Management Accountants—treat marketing activities as revenue centers rather than profit centers. As a result, most marketing managers are under little pressure to deliver high contribution margins.

FIGURE 2 RE-ENGINEERING'S EFFECT ON KEY MARKETING PROCESSES

Process	Problem	Nature of rethinking	IT enablers
New product development	Slow, costly, too much iteration, results in products lacking "integrity"	Involve marketing, manufacturing, design, and so on in a platform team from day one; facilitate communication among them through technology	CAD/CAM, photorealistic visualization, groupware, holography, video-conferencing
Order management	Expensive, slow, frequent errors	JIT marketing, automatic replenishment, vendor managed inventory, virtual inventory, partnership, cross docking	EDI, POS terminals linked to vendor, bar-coding, expert systems, locational systems
Customer retention/ relationship management	High churn, deal-prone customers, focus on last transaction, no learning	Lifetime revenues, win-win relationships, process and goal convergence	Linked information systems, database marketing, mass customization

Many companies that do treat marketing as a profit center rely too much on transfer pricing based on actual costs, rather than standard costs. By using standard costs, it becomes possible to separate manufacturing cost performance from marketing performance; the former is typically outside the control of the marketing manager.

Marketing productivity would be greatly enhanced by (1) adopting activity-based costing, (2) budgeting better, (3) linking compensation with effective efficiency, and (4) conducting an ongoing auditing of marketing activities.

Activity-Based Costing

As Philip Kotler points out in the latest edition of his classic *Marketing Management* text, companies such as General Foods, Du Pont, and Johnson & Johnson have established a "marketing controller" position to help improve efficiency. However, this practice is still limited to a few companies and focuses heavily on efficiency of expenditures and profitability; it does not address the effectiveness dimension. To develop a comprehensive marketing accounting discipline, marketing must work with the accounting function.

Developments in this field are occurring rapidly, from the concept of "Economic Value Added" (linking corporate spending to shareholder value creation) to more recent attempts at measuring intellectual capital. These efforts grapple with the measurement of the largely intangible elements that constitute much of the assets and added value in today's businesses. As such, they are potentially very valuable tools for measuring (and thus improving) marketing productivity.

One accounting tool that is clearly of great importance for marketing is activity-based costing. According to Robert Kaplan, one of the pioneers in the ABC field, "Failure to [completely] understand cost drivers leads to SKU proliferation; pricing divorced from actual operating costs; poor understanding of product, brand, and customer profitability; ineffective vendor relationships; and hidden costs from inefficient processes."

The fundamental question posed through the use of ABC is: "Would the customer pay for this activity if they knew you were doing it?" For many marketing activities, the answer is "No."

Traditional accounting methods allocate over-head as a percentage of direct labor. ABC is based on some fairly simple principles. The first is, because most business activities support the production and delivery of goods and services, they should be regarded as direct product costs. ABC thus abandons the traditional accounting practice of treating large blocks of corporate and overhead expenditures as "fixed costs" allocated evenly across all products. Rather, it defines a much wider section of corporate activities and costs as "variable," allocating them as directly as possible to specific goods and services.

Activity-based costing becomes especially critical when a company achieves the "preferred supplier" status. In such situations, the customer/partner typically requires that the supplier open its company books, detailing costs for materials, assembly, labor, sales, marketing, and so on. Customers can then bypass entire categories of cost; for example, they may see no need to pay for sales and marketing because the partnership arrangement makes most of those activities unnecessary.

Understandably, activity-based costing is an element that frightens many suppliers and makes them wary of customer partnerships. Indeed, it can expose suppliers to strong-arm abuse; a customer might insist that a supplier sell at 10% over its cost of manufacturing, with no allowance for research and development, technical support, or other activities considered essential to the businesses.

In successful partnerships, however, customers appreciate the supplier's need to make a good profit. By lowering total system costs, both partners are able to benefit without an adverse impact on profitability. A striking illustration of this comes from Chrysler, a company that works very closely with its suppliers. Chrysler currently has the lowest cost structure of the Big Three carmakers, makes the highest profit per vehicle, and has the most profitable suppliers.

In the grocery business, the use of direct product profitability (DPP) has led to substantial improvements in overall productivity. Marketing productivity can be measured at the account level in a similar way, using a combination of activity-based and account-based costing for marketing activities. ABC enables companies to eliminate the unintended (i.e., hidden) cross-subsidies between accounts that often invite "cream-skimming" competitors to take away highly profitable customers.

The use of ABC in marketing raises effective efficiency through possible reduction in, and more balanced application of marketing resources.

Zero-Based Budgeting

Marketing budgets should be set to achieve specific objectives, rather than fund self-perpetuating commitments. This requires a greater degree of resource flexibility than is traditionally present in most companies.

Marketing dollars also should be reallocated across brands. Well-known, mature brands, for example, should be able to prosper with greatly reduced marketing expenditures. Consider P&G's Ivory brand, which has extraordinarily high levels of consumer awareness and trial. Allocating a large advertising budget to Ivory would be far less productive than using those resources to support a less well-established brand.

Some companies also are experimenting with budgets based on customer acquisition, customer relationship management, customer relationship enhancement, and so forth. This is a sound approach because it forces the integration of marketing elements to achieve a particular objective.

Adjusting Compensation

"The customer pays the bills, but not the wages," said Robert Heller in a January 1994 *Management Today* article. ". . . [D]ecisions on promotions, powers, positions, perks, punishments are made internally. The practice of internal politics, in most companies, heavily outweighs the theory of putting customers first and foremost."

To improve effective efficiency, companies must create transparent incentive schemes to focus all marketing personnel on the essentials: increasing the profitability of what they do and increasing customer satisfaction. Companies such as IBM have adopted precisely those two criteria in determining sales force compensation, and such approaches could be spread into all areas of marketing.

One area that companies need to look at more carefully is the use of commissions. Many companies, such as Best Buy, Home Depot, and Charles Schwab, have come to the conclusion that commission-based selling is inherently antithetical to achieving a high level of customer satisfaction. While we would not go that far, we do recommend designing sales incentive mechanisms with utmost care so salespeople are rewarded for effective efficiency.

Continuous Assessment

As in any other human or business endeavor, marketing practices suffer from substantial inertia; new practices are added on slowly and old ones are discarded even more slowly. As with creeping product proliferation, marketing programs have a way of accumulating by perpetuating themselves even after they have outlived their usefulness.

Michael Treacy of CSC/Index Consulting Group has suggested that innovative marketing programs start to lose their effectiveness after three or four companies adopt them. It's important to distinguish here between marketing innovations that are short-lived and those which represent a lasting improvement; the latter may cease to be sources of competitive advantage after others adopt them, but are certainly not candidates for termination. We believe that the relationship marketing paradigm falls under this category.

Marketing could achieve "addition through subtraction" by periodically reviewing and rationalizing the whole gamut of marketing activities, programs, and offerings—a "marketing productivity audit." As always, the criterion to use should be whether or not the elements in question contribute to the achievement of effective efficiency.

In Figure 3, we have classified the 20 approaches to improving marketing productivity on the basis of their primary impact. Each approach has both efficiency and effectiveness enhancing potential, though the primary impact may be only in one area. For a number of approaches, the impacts are strong and nicely balanced between efficiency and effectiveness; most of these have to do with collaborative strategies and the informed use of information technologies.

Science *and* Art

Conducting business in today's globalized, highly competitive marketplace is risky and unpredictable. Customers worldwide are becoming accustomed to outstanding levels of quality at affordable prices. They are no longer willing to subsidize unproductive expenditures by companies, be they on convoluted product development processes, ruinously expensive attempts to push inventory down the distribution pipeline, inefficient purchasing strategies, inefficient provision of support services, or a host of other areas.

Marketing is ultimately about pleasing (even delighting) the customer to such an extent that he or she is willing, even anxious, to engage in a continuous relationship with the seller (see "Productivity Lessons From Most-Admired Companies.") Incessant pressures to increase marketing efficiency without regard for marketing effectiveness can easily lead to customer alienation, rebellion, and ultimately defection.

| FIGURE 3 | CLASSIFYING APPROACHES TO IMPROVE MARKETING PRODUCTIVITY |

Effectiveness impact

Dynamic pricing
Activity-based costing
Zero-based budgeting
Adjusting compensation
of marketing personnel
Continuous assessment
of marketing practices

Partnering
Relationship marketing
Insourcing vs. outsourcing
Customers in the value chain
Market response modeling
Data-base marketing
Front-line information systems
Net-based marketing
Re-engineering marketing

Marketing alliances
Reducing product and
attribute proliferation
Umbrella branding
Rethinking advertising
Focusing promotions
Unbundling and rebundling services

Efficiency impact

Companies must excel at both the art and science of marketing but, unfortunately, most attempts to improve marketing practice focus on the latter. Even though we agree that marketing needs to become more scientific (in so doing, it's bound to become more productive in the traditional sense), this must not occur at the expense of devaluing the art of marketing.

The goals for improving marketing productivity are not all quantifiable. For example, at 3M, marketing goals include increasing earnings by 10% a year as well as achieving the "preferred supplier" status with top customers. The marketing department is assessed in terms of its overall effectiveness to the company—specifically, the amount of sales brought in by a particular product line, customer satisfaction ratings, and budget/cost analyses.

Ideally, the science of marketing must incorporate within it those human elements normally associated with the art of marketing. Continued, intense pressure for efficiency improvements alone can only lead to an increasingly dehumanizing experience for employees as well as for customers. Such a downward spiral benefits no one except competitors.

Over time, the market will become more efficient through the increased availability of information and knowledge. Companies that improve marketing productivity by today's standards will still be vulnerable. Marketing productivity must be considered relative to other companies. As the overall market becomes more efficient, the companies that make more than marginal profits will be those best able to tailor their offerings for

PRODUCTIVITY LESSONS FROM MOST-ADMIRED COMPANIES

The most-admired company in the United States for two years in a row, according to *Fortune* magazine, has been Rubbermaid. In 1994, Rubbermaid experienced its 43rd consecutive year of sales growth, its 57th consecutive year of profitable performance, and its 40th consecutive year of increased dividends paid per share. The company uses a number of internal programs to assess and improve its marketing productivity.

Its Value Improvement Process (VIP) program focuses on continuous value improvement in three areas: productivity, supplier rationalization, and administrative and technology standardization. For example, as part of its product development process, Rubbermaid has sped up mold and color changes. It has also reduced the number of hues from 426 to 109 (it went from 18 shades of black to only 2). And the number of SKUs has been reduced, for a 35% improvement in inventory turns.

With regard to supplier rationalization, the company has a plan to reduce its supplier base by 80% over three years, leading to closer partnerships and greater economies of scale. Rubbermaid uses electronic data interchange (EDI) and vendor-managed replenishment to standardize links with customers and suppliers. These technologies allow Rubbermaid to improve its market forecasting, inventory management, and customer service. Other computer systems (CAD/CAE/CAM) are used to design, engineer, and manufacture new products more efficiently, reducing the average product development cycle by up to 11 weeks.

Rubbermaid gains a further advantage in the marketplace by forgoing test marketing of its new products, relying instead on focus groups and other evaluation methods. As a result, the company brings out products faster and thwarts copycat competitors. Despite the speed of entry, Rubbermaid's efforts are highly successful, with more than 90% of its new products turning a profit.

Another approach to improving marketing productivity begins with analyzing the top 100 Rubbermaid accounts with respect to percent of purchases, how many products they sell, what colors they stock, and so on. This information is fed into the company's "Best Practices" program, which helps retailers stock and display Rubbermaid products in the most effective manner. The company even has a "Best Practices" room where retailers can view sample displays of various product mixes and other ways to increase sales.

Finally, Rubbermaid's customer service function is handled by a group called "Invincible Customer Service," which is a part of operations. "Invincible" refers to a commitment to provide customer service on a real-time basis. ICS has complete autonomy and needs no authorization from other areas to fulfill its responsibilities to customers.

Another widely admired company, Home Depot, has one simple rule: Spend only on what directly benefits customers. Its stores are cement-floored, warehouse-style outlets with little ambiance. The company does very little advertising and rarely entices shoppers with promotional sales. It employs EDI to reduce the expenses associated with ordering, shipping, receiving, and paying for merchandise. Because all of its suppliers must make shipments directly to individual stores, the company has eliminated all costs associated with product storage and distribution.

Marketing at Home Depot is based on great value and outstanding customer service. The company hires only 2% of job applicants, searching for the right mix of attitude and ability to learn. The bottom line for the company is satisfied customers who keep coming back for more.

market fragments and discriminate by price across customer groups. In a highly efficient market, effectiveness becomes all the more crucial.

The push for productivity in marketing spending is in no way contradictory to creating and maintaining a market orientation. Being customer-oriented, however, does not automatically mean spending more on marketing. The fact is that too many companies use marketing dollars as a blunt weapon, believing that if they spend enough, they will become customer-oriented. Instead, they subject existing customers to a barrage of redundant advertising and sales promotions. Focused and tailored marketing spending not only is more efficient, but also reduces the amount of marketing noise and improves customer contentment.

Marketing reform must come from within, rather than being imposed from above. That is the only way to ensure that the changes increase the efficiency as well as the effectiveness of marketing actions.

In the future, marketing will be called upon to make even greater contributions to the corporation than it has in the past. More and more, corporate "top line" success (revenues and market share) will depend on the quality of marketing efforts; at the same time, corporate "bottom line" success (profitability) will depend on how cost-effectively marketing is able to perform its tasks.

Reprinted with permission from the Winter 1995 issue of Marketing Management, *published by the American Marketing Association, Sheth, Jagdish N. and Rajendra S. Sisodia, Winter 1995/Vol. 4, pp. 19–32.*

Additional Reading

Berry, Jonathan, (1994), "Database Marketing: A Potent New Tool for Selling," *Business Week*, (Sept. 5), 56.

Buzzell, Robert D. and Rajendra S. Sisodia (1995), "Information Technology and Marketing," in *Companion Encyclopedia of Marketing*, Michael J. Baker, ed. London: Routledge.

Cooper, Robin and Robert S. Kaplan (1988), "Measure Costs Right: Make the Right Decisions," *Harvard Business Review*, (September–October).

Davenport, Thomas (1993), Process Innovation, Cambridge, MA: *Harvard Business School Press*.

Heller, Robert (1994), "Customer Focus Means Commitment to Constant Change," *Management Today*, (January), 19.

Jacob, Rahul (1994), "Why Some Customers Are More Equal Than Others," *Fortune*, (Sept. 19), 215.

Loewe, Pierre M. and Dominique M. Hanssens (1994), "Taking the Mystery Out of Marketing," *Management Review*, 80 (August), 32.

Sheth, Jagdish N. and Rajendra S. Sisodia (1993), "The Information Mall," *Telecommunications Policy*, (July), 376.

Sisodia, Rajendra S. (1992) "Expert Marketing With Expert Systems," *Marketing Management*, 1 (2), 32.

Stewart, Thomas A. (1994), "Your Company's Most Valuable Asset: Intellectual Capital," *Fortune*, (Oct. 3), 68–74.

12

Developing Products on Internet Time

MARCO IANSITI
ALAN MACCORMACK

In today's turbulent business environments, more and more companies need a development process that embraces change—not one that resists it.

The rise of the World Wide Web has provided one of the most challenging environments for product development in recent history. The market needs that a product is meant to satisfy and the technologies required to satisfy them can change radically—even as the product is under development. In response to such factors, companies have had to modify the traditional product-development process in which design implementation begins only once a product's concept has been determined in its entirety. Instead, they have pioneered a *flexible* product-development process that allows designers to continue to define and shape products even after implementation has begun. This innovation enables Internet companies to incorporate rapidly changing customer requirements and evolving technologies into their designs until the last possible moment before a product is introduced to the market.

Flexible product development has been most fully realized in the Internet environment because of the turbulence found there, but the foundations for it exist in a wide range of industries where the need for responsiveness is paramount. Product developers in industries from computer workstations to banking increasingly face dynamic and unpredictable environments characterized by rapidly evolving technologies, changing customer tastes, and sweeping regulatory changes. In these industries, companies that have begun to adopt more flexible product-development approaches are setting new competitive standards.

Marco Iansiti is an associate professor at the Harvard Business School in Boston, Massachusetts, where his research focuses on the factors that influence R&D performance. He is the author of *Technology Integration: Making Critical Choices in a Dynamic World,* which will be published by the Harvard Business School Press in the fall of 1997. His last article for HBR was "Technology Integration: Turning Great Research into Great Products" (May–June 1997). **Alan MacCormack** is a doctoral candidate in the Technology and Operations Management group at the Harvard Business School. His research explores how companies manage product development in rapidly changing business environments.

What's involved in increasing the flexibility of the product development process? Many of the companies we studied have adopted a coherent set of mechanisms that allow product developers to generate and respond to new information about what customers want and about how technology has evolved over the course of a project. These mechanisms not only enable a continuous flow of information about customer needs and new technologies but also reduce both the cost and the time it takes to integrate that information into the evolving product design. They allow designers continually *to sense* customer needs, *to test* alternative technical solutions, and *to integrate* the acquired knowledge into a coherent product design. This flexible process continues iteratively throughout the development process.

The traditional development processes that many companies use are highly structured. A future product is designed, developed, transferred to production, and rolled out to the market in clearly articulated, sequential phases. Such processes usually begin with the identification of users' needs and an assessment of the various technological possibilities. Then a detailed set of product specifications is created and, once approved by senior management, is set in stone. At that point, attention shifts to implementation as a functionally integrated team translates the concept into reality. If the up-front work has been done correctly, inherently expensive changes to the product's specifications are kept to a minimum. Indeed, the number of engineering changes is often used as a measure of a project's effectiveness: many changes signify an inferior effort.

In contrast, flexible product development delays until as late as possible any commitment to a final design configuration. The concept development phase and the implementation phase thus overlap instead of following each other sequentially. By accepting the need for and reducing the cost of changes, companies are able to respond to new information that arises during the course of a product's development. Systemic changes in a project's definition and basic direction are managed proactively; designers begin this process with no precise idea of how it will end. (See Figure 1.)

When technology, product features, and competitive conditions are predictable or evolve slowly, a traditional development process works well. But in turbulent business environments, a sequential approach to product development is more than inefficient; it risks creating an obsolete product—one that fails to address customer needs and to make use of the latest technologies. When new competitors and technologies are likely to appear overnight, when standards and regulations are in flux, and when a company's entire customer base can easily switch to other suppliers, businesses don't need a development process that resists change—they need one that embraces it.

A Flexible Process at Work

Not every company interested in developing a flexible product-development process would have to go to the extremes that Netscape did. But by looking at Netscape's experiences, we can see how a highly flexible process works. Founded in 1994, the company pioneered the easy-to-use Web browser: a software interface that provides access to the World Wide Web. The Web browser has transformed the Internet from

FIGURE 1	TWO APPROACHES TO PRODUCT DEVELOPMENT

The Traditional Approach

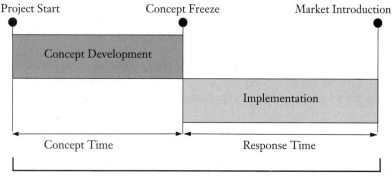

The Flexible Approach

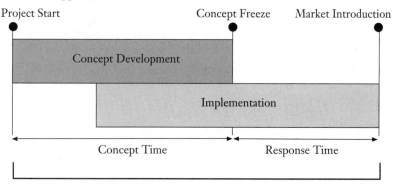

Speed is a subtle concept in this model. *Total lead time*—the time taken to fulfill the initial objectives of the project—is clearly important; but *concept time* and *response time* are critical measures themselves. Concept time is the window of opportunity for including new information and for optimizing the match between the technology and its application context. Response time is the period during which the window is closed, the product's architecture is frozen, and the project is unable to react to new information. Although the total lead time is the same for both processes above, the flexible process has a shorter response time and is therefore preferable in rapidly changing environments.

a communications channel for scientists and technicians into a network connecting millions of ordinary users across time and space—and thus into an industry in its own right.

But Netscape faced no easy task in developing its Web browser, Navigator. In the rapidly evolving Internet industry, many alternative technologies and applications compete for attention, and product development is a project manager's nightmare. The major challenge in the development of a Web browser is the level of technical complexity involved: a typical program rivals a traditional word processing or spreadsheet application in size, and it must work seamlessly with myriad different hardware and software platforms. The level of uncertainty is so high that even the most basic decisions about a product must be continually revised as new information arises. And the fact that industry giant Microsoft, which had already developed its own flexible product-development process, was readying a product to compete with Navigator only added to the complexity and urgency of Netscape's development effort.

Netscape introduced Navigator 2.0 to the market in January of 1996 and immediately thereafter began to develop the next version of the Web browser, Navigator 3.0, which was to be released in August of the same year. (See Figure 2.) The Netscape development group—which included staff from engineering, marketing, and customer support—produced the first prototype quickly. By February 14, just six weeks into the project, it had put a Beta 0 version of the program up on the company's internal project Web site for testing by the development staff. Although many of the intended functions were not yet available, the prototype captured enough of the essence of the new product to generate meaningful feedback from members of the development group. On February 22, less than two weeks later, the team posted an updated version, Beta 1, again for internal development staff only. In early March, with major bugs in the product worked out, the first public release, Beta 2, appeared on Netscape's Internet Web site. Additional public releases followed thereafter every few weeks until the official release date in August, with gradual refinements appearing in each beta iteration.

The sequence of beta versions was extremely useful to Netscape because it enabled the development team to react both to feedback from users and to changes in

FIGURE 2   THE DEVELOPMENT OF NAVIGATOR 3.0: A TIMELINE

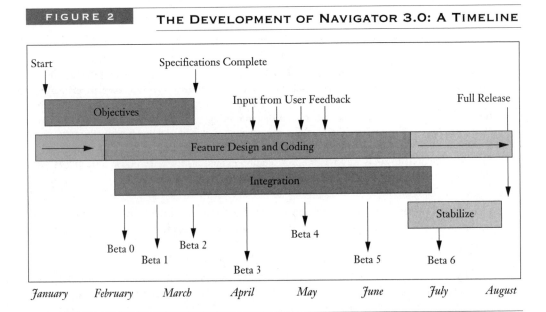

the marketplace while the team was still working on the Web browser's design. Beta users by and large are more sophisticated than Netscape's broader customer base and therefore are a valuable source of information. Most useful among them are developers from other Internet software companies, who tend to be extremely vocal customers. Because many of these customers use the Navigator browser as part of the environment in which their own products operate, they are often the first to find the more complicated bugs—bugs that are revealed only when the product is stretched to the limits of its performance in complex applications.

Getting input from users was one way in which the Navigator team generated new information during the course of the project. During the seven-month development cycle, however, the team also paid careful attention to competing products. As the largest and most powerful software developer in the industry, Microsoft was considered a very serious threat to Netscape's then-dominant position in the browser market. The software giant had just undertaken a dramatic—and very public—switch in strategy, refocusing its formidable talents squarely on the Internet. As a result, Netscape continually monitored the latest beta versions of Microsoft's competing product, Explorer, to compare features and formats. Based on the information that it gathered, the Netscape team would often add format or feature changes to the current beta version of its own product.

In order to respond to the constant stream of new information being brought into the development process, the team carried out extensive experimentation and testing. Subgroups working on individual features went through numerous design-build-test cycles, gradually adding functionality to the product. As features were completed, the team integrated them into the evolving product, then conducted tests to ensure that the new feature did not produce unwanted interactions with other parts of the system. These so-called system builds occurred with increasing frequency as the project progressed; they were performed at least daily in the run-up to the official release.

To facilitate the integration of the vast amounts of information generated during the project, Netscape set up a project Web site on its intranet. The site contained the product's development schedule and specifications, each of which was updated as target dates changed or new features were added. In addition, it contained bulletin boards through which team members could monitor the evolution of various parts of the design, noting the completion of specific features and logging problems in the existing version. Once the Navigator moved to public beta testing, these intranet features became especially valuable because an increasing amount of information then had to be received, classified, and processed.

Netscape built into its product-development process considerable flexibility to respond to changes in market demands and technology. And what is already true of companies in the Internet industry is becoming true of companies elsewhere. Our research on the computer-workstation-and-server industry has shown that there, too, a more flexible process is associated with greater performance. In this environment, companies with a faster response time, as measured from the construction of the first physical prototype to commercial shipping, clearly outperform those with slower response times. The use of sophisticated simulation tools allows teams to work with a virtual prototype for much of the project—in effect, creating a significant overlap between the concept and the design implementation phases.

According to Allen Ward and his colleagues in "The Second Toyota Paradox: How Delaying Decisions Can Make Better Cars Faster" (*Sloan Management Review*, Spring 1995), there also is evidence that a more flexible model has emerged in the automotive industry. Toyota's development process allows it to delay many design decisions until later in the development cycle. The development team creates seve;ral sets of design options and, finally, through a process of elimination, selects only one for implementation. As a result, Toyota can respond to changing market conditions at a later stage than many of its competitors.

The Foundations of a Flexible Process

How should companies create a flexible development process? The experiences of leading companies suggest that senior managers first must understand what gives the process its flexibility. Product development flexibility is rooted in the ability to manage jointly the evolution of a product and its application context. The goal is to capture a rich understanding of customer needs and alternative technical solutions as a project progresses, then to integrate that knowledge into the evolving product design. The faster a project can integrate that information, the faster that project can respond to changes in the product's environment.

The value of flexible product development, however, is only as good as the quality of the process it uses to generate information about the interaction between technical choices and market requirements. Unlike traditional development projects, which rely on periodic bursts of input on users' needs, projects in turbulent business environments require continual feedback. To acquire and use this information, the development process must be able to sense customer needs, to test alternative technical solutions, and to integrate the knowledge gained of both markets and technologies into a coherent product. (See Figure 3.)

As we describe how leading companies have achieved a more flexible development process, many of the examples we cite come from our work with several software companies that have recently launched Internet products or services. But bear in mind that this is not the only industry in which these lessons apply. We also describe specific practices from other, more traditional industries to illustrate that the approaches used are not unique to the Internet. In fact, they represent cutting-edge practice across a range of environments where change is—or is becoming—the norm.

Sensing the Market. The first element of a flexible process is sensing the needs of customers and the market. Flexible projects establish mechanisms for getting continual feedback from the market on how the evolving design meets customers' requirements. They do so by creating intensive links with the customer base—links that range from broad experimentation with many customers to selective experiences with a few lead users. Furthermore, these customers do not have to be external to the company: leading companies make extensive use of internal staff and resources to provide a test bed for evolving new products.

Gaining continual feedback from customers was particularly critical at Netscape because of its dramatic head-to-head race with Microsoft. Netscape's broad-based

| FIGURE 3 | THE STRUCTURE OF A FLEXIBLE PRODUCT-DEVELOPMENT PROCESS |

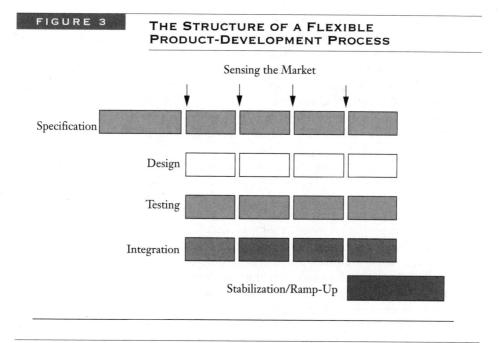

release of multiple beta versions to its entire customer base allowed users to play a significant role in the evolving product design. At the same time, it allowed Netscape to test an extremely complex technical product. Although not all Netscape's customers actually experimented with beta versions, the Web browser's most advanced users had to because they themselves were creating products that needed to work seamlessly with the Navigator release. And their feedback clearly had an impact: a significant portion of the new code, features, and technology that were integrated into the new release was developed only after the first beta version went public.

Microsoft, Netscape's chief rival, was slow to recognize the opportunities offered by the World Wide Web. Not until the end of 1995 did the company begin to focus on developing Internet products. Yet when Bill Gates and the rest of the senior management team finally acknowledged the need for a strategic shift, Microsoft's development expertise was unleashed with astonishing speed. In the six months from the end of 1995 to the middle of 1996, the company went from having no presence in the critical browser market to offering a product that several industry experts claimed was comparable to or better than Netscape's Navigator.

Microsoft was able to react quickly because its existing product-development process had been founded on the rapid iteration of prototypes, early beta releases, and a flexible approach to product architecture and specification. (For a detailed account of Microsoft's development process, see Michael A. Cusumano and Richard W. Selby, *Microsoft Secrets* [Free Press, 1995].) The process that Microsoft followed in developing its Internet Explorer was similar to Netscape's but was more internally oriented.

With more than 18,000 employees to Netscape's 1,000 at the time, Microsoft could test successive Explorer beta versions extensively just by putting them up on its own intranet. "Everyone around Microsoft is encouraged to play with it," explained a Microsoft program manager. "Internal testing means that we release it to thousands of people who really hammer away at it. We use the product much more heavily than the average Web user." Microsoft combined broad internal testing by employees with carefully staged external beta releases, using only two or three in contrast to Netscape's six or seven. The company thus limited the risk that imperfections in early releases might damage its reputation.

A similar flexible philosophy can be used in the development of services. Consider Yahoo!. Founded in 1995, the company offers search, directory, and programming services for navigating the World Wide Web. As a service provider, the company believes that before a new offering is released to the outside world, it needs to be more robust than the typical Internet software beta. The market risk of broad, public testing is too high: users who try a new service once and have an unsatisfactory experience with it either are unlikely to return or, worse, may defect to competitors. Furthermore, Yahoo! assumes that competing companies will copy the innovative features of a new service once it has been released. These factors suggest delaying external testing to late in the development cycle.

For these reasons, Yahoo! puts early versions of new services on-line for internal use only. Given its development team's technical skills and breadth of experience, these trials expose any major technical flaws in the service and provide additional suggestions for improving functionality. Only then does Yahoo! begin a "soft release" of the offering: the service is put up on Yahoo!'s Web site but without any links to highly frequented parts of the site. As a result, only the more technically aggressive users are likely to find and use the service at this stage. Yahoo! also asks some of the 30,000 users, who have volunteered to be beta testers, to try the new service—thus exposing the service to rigorous external testing without revealing it to unsophisticated users who might be frustrated by a slow, incomplete, or error-ridden version.

The Netscape, Yahoo!, and Microsoft examples illustrate several approaches to sensing customer and market needs: broad consumer testing, broad internal testing, and testing by lead users. Companies adopting a flexible development approach should consider the merits of each, as well as the potential for using a balanced combination of all. It is important to emphasize, however, that these techniques are not unique to the Internet. Advances in information technology now allow companies to sense customer needs in ways not possible a few years ago. Leading companies in many industries have begun to use these new capabilities.

Fiat, for example, used a broad, external testing approach, not unlike Netscape's, to evaluate several automobile concepts. A link on the company's Web site directed customers to a page aimed at evaluating users' needs for the next generation of the Fiat Punto, its highest-volume car, which sells about 600,000 units per year. Customers were asked to fill out a survey indicating their preferences in automobile design. They could prioritize the following five considerations: style, comfort, performance, price, and safety. Then they were asked to describe what they hated most in a car and to suggest ideas for new features. Next the software allowed customers to design a car themselves. They could select from a variety of body styles, wheel designs, and styles for the front and rear of the automobile. They also could examine different types of headlights, details, and features. In this way, users could experiment with different designs and see the results immediately on the screen. The software captured the final results; in addition, it traced the sequence that customers went through in evaluating and selecting options. This information told designers much about the logic customers used to evaluate features, styles, and characteristics in order to arrive at a given design solution.

Fiat received more than 3,000 surveys in a three-month period, each comprising about ten pages of detailed information. The ideas suggested ranged from clever (an umbrella holder inside the car) to significant (a single bench front seat). Fiat used the information to inform a variety of styling and concept decisions for the next-generation Punto. And the total cost of the exercise was only $35,000, about the cost of running a few focus groups. Moreover, Fiat executives claimed that the surveys provided them with precisely the data they needed. The profile of the survey's participants—trend-setting individuals with high incomes, who are 31 to 40 years old and frequent car buyers—was the target segment most useful to Fiat.

General Motors' Electro-Motive division has adopted a similar philosophy in its new virtual-product-development process. That process allows engineers to give customers digital tours of next-generation locomotives even as their development proceeds. Although the GM system is still evolving, the aim is to move to an all-digital environment in which the product moves electronically through concept design, analysis, prototyping, and manufacture, and along the way makes several stops on the customer's desktop for feedback.

Testing Technical Solutions. Sensing customer and market needs as a project progresses is one element of a flexible development process. If companies are going to allow a product's design to evolve well into the design implementation phase, however, they also must adopt mechanisms that lower the cost of changes, speed their implementation, and test their impact on the overall system. Such mechanisms allow companies to evaluate and test alternative technical solutions at a rapid rate: the second element of a flexible development process.

Early prototypes and tests of alternative technologies are critical to establishing the direction of a project. Consider NetDynamics, a company that develops sophisticated tools for linking Web servers to large databases. The single most important technical decision confronting NetDynamics during the development of its second product release was the early choice of language in its product. Either the company could develop a proprietary language, or it could use Java. At that time, in early 1996, the Java programming language had received a lot of publicity, but it was still highly unstable, relatively immature, and little understood. "We knew Java was going to be big," recalled chief engineer Yarden Malka, "but it was still only available as a Beta 1 version. This meant that the development tools that went along with it were either terribly buggy or nonexistent. If we chose it, we knew we also had to develop many of our own tools."

NetDynamics' commitment to an open platform tended to favor Java. If there was a standard—either existing or emerging—it should be used, and Java appeared to be that standard. To make the decision, however, NetDynamics' engineers spent considerable time experimenting with various options, trying to become as comfortable as possible with the benefits and risks of each language. They began by developing simple prototypes and gradually migrated to more complex programs, attempting to gauge the advantages each would give the user. This "user-centric" approach to prototyping and experimentation was critical to the final choice and stands in stark contrast to the approach often adopted by high-tech companies in which technologies often are evaluated purely on the basis of the advantages they give the design team.

As a project progresses, the design team must have the capacity to evaluate and test alternative design solutions quickly and cheaply. Yahoo! can easily do just that because of the way it has elected to provide its Internet service. The company meets its processing needs with many inexpensive computers instead of a few large (and expensive) servers. The small investment required for each machine allows Yahoo! to scale up its capacity smoothly to meet new demand. It also means that Yahoo! can easily run experiments to test different design options. According to Farzad Nazem, the vice president of engineering, "Our Web site setup works just like a spigot valve. If we want to test out a new product or feature on several thousand users, we promote it on the home page of only a few machines. As users access the service and we reach the required volume, we can turn off the promotion on each machine. We can also conduct comparative experiments by running multiple versions of the same service on different computers in the network, then track the results to see which version attracts more customers."

To reduce the cost of testing alternative design choices, companies outside the software industry increasingly have invested in new technologies for virtual design. By designing and testing product designs through simulation, for example, companies achieve the flexibility to respond to new information and to resolve uncertainties by quickly exploring alternatives. Computer-aided design software also has dramatically reduced the cost of design changes, while at the same time speeding up experimentation. At Boeing, for example, the all-digital development of the 777 aircraft made use of a computer-generated "human" who would climb inside the three-dimensional design on-screen to show how difficult maintenance access would be for a live mechanic. Such computer modeling allowed engineers to spot design errors—say, a navigation light that would have been difficult to service—that otherwise would have remained undiscovered until a person negotiated a physical prototype. By avoiding the time and cost associated with building physical prototypes at several stages, Boeing's development process has acquired the flexibility to evaluate a wider range of design options than was previously possible.

Integrating Customer Needs with Technical Solutions. It's no good knowing what customers want in a product under development if the development team can't integrate that information with the available technical solutions. As a result, all the organizations we discuss have established dynamic integration mechanisms. Some of them are based on well-understood concepts, such as using dedicated teams—an approach adopted by Netscape, NetDynamics, and Microsoft. Others are less traditional. All three companies, for example, use their intranets to integrate tasks, synchronize design changes, and capture customer information as projects evolve. Thus project teams are able to keep track of the evolving relationships among tasks, schedules, and design changes in a dynamic way. Such integrating mechanisms are essential for managing a flexible process, given the many rounds of experimentation and the wide range of information generated. Without a way of capturing and integrating knowledge, the development process can quickly dissolve into chaos, with ad hoc design changes creating masses of rework because of unanticipated interactions with other components in the system.

In the Internet world, integrating mechanisms are dictated by the nature of the product—software. Each of the projects we describe adopted sophisticated design-integration tools to hold the master version of the emerging product. As team members went to work on individual components, they checked out the code for that part of the system. Once finished, they had to run a series of tests to ensure that the component did not create problematic interactions with the rest of the system. Only then could they check in the new component. At the end of each day, when all the new components had been checked in, engineers ran the program. Any problems that occurred had to be corrected before new code could be permanently integrated.

Similar approaches are found in projects outside the Internet world where new information systems allow companies to share knowledge more effectively. At Silicon Graphics, a leading manufacturer of workstations and servers, a new product-introduction process makes extensive use of the company's intranet to coordinate development activities. Managers and engineers throughout the world, who respond daily to the problems of current customers, provide input during the concept-generation stage. In addition, lead users in target application segments (referred to as "lighthouse" customers) are linked directly to the development teams, allowing the teams to get fast and effective guidance on critical decisions as the project evolves. The intranet also is used to integrate design tasks on a daily basis. Project engineers work from a shared body of software that simulates the hardware design. As with the Internet projects, when team members want to make a change, they check out the relevant code, make the desired design improvements, test it for errors and unanticipated interactions, then check it back in.

Such approaches are not limited to high-technology products. Booz Allen & Hamilton, a management consulting firm, approaches the problem of integrating a diverse and geographically dispersed knowledge base by using its intranet. The intranet allows consulting staff quickly to locate and contact industry experts with specific skills and to identify previous studies that are relevant to current projects. In this way, the collective experience of the organization is available to all employees on-line. The intranet also allows the company to develop its intellectual capital. In management consulting, new-product development consists of developing new frameworks, industry best practices, performance benchmarks, and other information that can be applied across projects. By having these products on-line during development and thereafter, Booz Allen can integrate new information and experiences into its knowledge base.

Integrating within the company, however, is not always sufficient. In some cases, the ability to integrate knowledge across networks of organizations may also be important. For Internet software companies, given the novelty and complexity inherent in their products and the rapidity of their development cycles, no single organization can research, make, and market products alone. Instead, they take advantage of technical possibilities that are beyond the boundaries of any individual company; those technologies can then be integrated into their own core products. (Internet users will be familiar with Java applets and Web browser plug-ins.) Doing so, however, means that just as the technologies must be seamlessly integrated into a product, so must the organization accommodate a changing cast of players. The companies we describe have built alliances with third-party developers, engaged in joint development projects, and worked hard to foster open product architectures and modular designs. And such arrangements are not peculiar to software. Workstation manufacturers such as Sun, Hewlett-Packard, and Silicon Graphics frequently engage in joint development efforts with other hardware companies (such as Siemens, Intel, Fujitsu, Toshiba, and NEC) to leverage the performance of their systems.

Putting Flexibility to the Test

In combination, the foundations of a flexible product-development process allow a company to respond to changes in markets and technologies *during* the development cycle. We found a striking example of how that is done in a setting that is about as far from the typical high-tech world as one can get: the America's Cup. In 1995, a small team from New Zealand dominated the races from start to finish. Team New Zealand's effort shows how the mechanisms we have described can be combined to dramatic effect in a flexible process.

Team New Zealand recruited Doug Peterson, who had been on the winning America's Cup team in 1992, as its lead designer. It also recruited an experienced simulation team to make use of advanced design software. Although Peterson's extensive experience drove the initial concept design, once the team's yachts were constructed the emphasis shifted to evaluating design changes through thousands of computer-simulated design iterations. The simulations were run on a small network of workstations located a few feet from the dock. To ensure rapid feedback on the performance of design changes, the team built two boats. Each day, one of them was fitted with a design change for evaluation; then the two boats raced each other to gauge the impact of the change.

Team New Zealand's flexible process sensed "market needs" through the two-boat testing program, which generated feedback each day on how the evolving design fit the racing environment. It tested alternative designs through a simulation program that was directed by one of the world's most experienced yacht designers. And it integrated knowledge by making the resulting information available locally. The crew, design team, and management were therefore able to make suggestions for the design, to see the impact of potential changes, and to know what to expect when those changes were tested on the water.

The U.S. boat that Team New Zealand faced in the final race had been designed on the latest supercomputers with the support of large, well-heeled corporations. Although the U.S. team could test a massive number of experimental designs, the computers were located hundreds of miles from the dock. As a result, there were significant delays between detailing a design and getting feedback on results. Furthermore, the team had only one boat on which to test design changes; given the varying sea and wind conditions, it took far longer than its rival to verify the impact of a change.

Team New Zealand's approach had better mechanisms than its U.S. rival for sensing, testing, and integrating what it had learned. Its flexible process produced a yacht of superior design, which many observers believed to be a full generation ahead of its competitors' boats. As Paul Cayard, skipper of Team New Zealand's opponent in the final race, remarked, "I've been in some uphill battles in my life. But I've never been in a race where I felt I had so little control over the outcome. It's the largest discrepancy in boat speed I've ever seen."

We have seen a similar pattern throughout many environments we have studied. Organizations that have adopted a flexible product-development process have begun to transform the very industries that forced them to adopt it. They have implemented strategies that companies clinging to traditional approaches cannot follow. Competitors without flexible development processes will almost certainly find their industries growing more and more turbulent in appearance. And in such an environment, their products and services will always seem to be one step behind those of their more flexible rivals.

13

Cybermediaries in Electronic Marketspace: Toward Theory Building

MITRABARUN SARKAR
Michigan State University

BRIAN BUTLER
Carnegie Mellon University

CHARLES STEINFIELD
Michigan State University

The increasing importance of electronic commerce makes it essential to develop a theory of virtual value chains. This article considers the intermediation process between producers and consumers within electronic markets. We argue that, contrary to existing wisdom, intermediaries will play a key role in electronic markets. Drawing on channel evolution literature and transaction cost economics, we present a set of propositions regarding the emergence of cybermediaries and the development of virtual channel systems.

The increasing popularity of the World Wide Web (WWW) and explosive growth of the Internet has generated significant interest in the development of electronic commerce. Electronic data interchange and other interorganizational systems, which have existed for decades, use telecommunications technology to support business-to-business transactions. The Internet adds the capability of directly linking firms with individual consumers. As a result, the potential for transformation of individual value systems (Porter, 1985; Porter and Millar, 1985) is increased. Many firms, drawn by potential access to millions of consumers, have already invested heavily in establishing a marketing presence on the WWW (for examples see *Business Week*, 1994; Hoffman, Novak, and Chatterjee, 1995). Moreover, telecommunications and information technology firms have shown significant interest in the Internet as the basis for expansion into electronic commerce.

As a result, the Internet has the potential to evolve into an interconnected electronic marketplace bringing buyers and sellers together to facilitate commercial exchanges. Electronic markets may support many activities, ranging from the provision of product information to the execution of complete transactions. For information goods, such as software and graphic images, the Internet can also provide product distribution facilities. The development of electronic marketplaces is expected to redefine industry value systems by supporting a radical restructuring of the processes and organizations that connect manufacturers and consumers.

One common vision of the electronic marketplace is of an ideal electronic market in which consumers interact directly with producers. Software tools including intelligent agents and distributed databases, would enable consumers to efficiently search for and purchase a wide variety of goods directly from producers. Thus, it is argued by some that developing electronic marketplaces will threaten intermediaries as direct producer-consumer interactions become the dominant structure in electronic commerce (Benjamin and Wigand, 1995; Hoffman and Novak, 1996; Office of Technology Assessment, 1994).

However, further analysis demonstrates that a more likely, outcome is the emergence of a class of commercial service providers which we term cybermediaries. Cybermediaries are organizations that operate in electronic markets to facilitate exchanges between producers and consumers by meeting the needs of both producers and consumers (Sarkar, Butler, and Steinfield, 1995; Butler, 1996). Cybermediaries also increase the efficiency of electronic markets, in a role similar to intermediaries, by aggregating transactions to create economies of scale and scope (Alderson, 1954; Coyle and Andraski, 1990; Sarkar, Butler, and Steinfield, 1995). According to this view, multi-organization structures will play an important role in emerging electronic markets.

How will electronic marketplaces be structured? To what extent will producers and consumers take advantage of the new technology to form direct ties? What role, if any, will cybermediaries play in these new markets? This article examines the nature of intermediation in electronic markets and its implications for the structure of electronic commerce. First, we consider the view that intermediaries are fundamentally threatened by electronic marketplaces. Then we present our analysis and arguments for the emergence of cybermediaries, followed by propositions regarding the evolution of cybermediary organizations and the structure of electronic marketplaces. We conclude with a discussion of the implications of this work for future electronic commerce research.

Transaction Costs and the Threatened Intermediaries Hypothesis

Williamson's (1975, 1985) work on transaction costs provides a theoretical framework for analyzing the structure of commercial activity. Transaction cost models focus on a firm's choice between internalizing an activity and relying on external market agents. In these models, organizations choose from structures ranging from hierarchical relationships to open-market transactions (Anderson and Coughlan, 1987; Klein, 1989). Although traditional studies deal with the two extremes of markets and hierarchies, i.e., full reliance on market forces or total vertical integration, the model has been extended to include quasi-hierarchical and quasi-market structures (Gulati, 1995).

However, the basic concept remains the same: firms choose structures that minimize transaction governance and execution costs.

Prior empirical research has validated the transaction cost models in the context of traditional marketing channels (see Rangan, Menezes, and Maier, 1992). Transaction cost theory also serves as the basis, either implicitly or explicitly, for much of the research on the structure of electronic marketplaces. In this literature it has been noted that intermediaries add significant costs to the value chain, which are then reflected in higher final prices to consumers. For example, to motivate their discussion of electronic markets, Benjamin and Wigand (1995) describe how the retail price in the high quality shirt market would be reduced by almost 62% if wholesalers and retailers were eliminated. Similarly, an Office of Technology Assessment (1994) report states that the widespread availability of data communications networks and technologies will facilitate direct exchange between producers and consumers, thereby reducing the costs of commercial activity. Electronic networks, it is argued, support the coordination of exchanges and reduce the transaction costs that producers and consumers would normally incur (Malone, Yates, and Benjamin, 1987). By this reasoning, manufacturing firms and consumers have both the means and the incentive to use telecommunications to bypass intermediaries in traditional value systems (Benjamin and Wigand, 1995). This implies that emerging electronic marketplaces pose a direct threat to traditional intermediaries.

Transaction Costs Revisited: The Case for Cybermediaries

However, reconsideration of the transaction cost model reveals that the threatened intermediaries hypothesis relies on several key assumptions (Sarkar et al., 1995). Specifically, by focusing on the connection between producers and consumers, prior work overlooks the impact of new communication technologies on the other relationships within the electronic marketplace. When a full system transaction cost analysis of channel services is considered, very different structures emerge.

Transaction cost models characterize the problem facing firms in terms of two types of costs: production and governance costs. Production costs are defined as the cost of completing the desired activity. Governance costs are the costs incurred by a firm as a result of its efforts to coordinate and control the entity performing the activity. Firms choose the transaction structure which minimizes the sum of these costs. Transaction cost analyses of industrial structures consider both the production cost of channel services (T2 vs. T2') and the governance costs associated with coordinating and controlling the organization or unit which provides those services (T1 vs. T1') (Sharma and Dominguez, 1992) (Fig. 1). Because of economies of scope and scale, channel functions often can be provided at a lower cost by specialized intermediaries (T2' < T2) (Williamson, 1981; Anderson and Coughlan, 1987). As a result, coordination costs play a key role in firms' choice of channel structure. Because external production costs are typically lower, firms will prefer to internalize channel activities and deal directly with consumers only if the costs of coordinating intermediaries (T1') is substantially higher than the cost associated with governing an internal unit (T1). Furthermore, if the development of a widespread data communications infrastructure

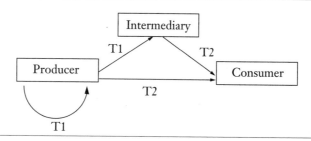

FIGURE 1   **TRANSACTION COST MODEL OF DIRECT VS. INTERMEDIATED CHANNELS**

reduces coordination costs between producers and consumers (T2) it is also likely that the costs of coordinating producer-intermediary (T1′) and intermediary-consumer interactions will be reduced as well (T2′) (Sarkar et al., 1995). Rather than threatening intermediaries, it is likely that the development of an extensive public telecommunications infrastructure will provide new opportunities for external firms to provide channel services. This argument leads to the following general alternative to the threatened intermediary hypothesis: it is likely that intermediary organizations will play an important role in developing electronic marketplaces.

Nature of Cybermediaries

As noted in Sarkar et al. (1995), conceptualizing electronic commerce only in terms of coordination can be deceiving. In any commercial exchange, both producers and consumers have a variety of needs that must be met (Butler, 1996). Traditional intermediaries provide a range of services, including product information, customization, quality assurance, lot size adjustments, one-stop shopping convenience through maintaining assortment, proximal and temporal availability, after-sales service, and logistics (Rangan et al., 1992). Understanding commercial structures and the nature of cybermediaries in emerging electronic markets requires that the composite nature of channel services be recognized.

Although the *need* for the channel functions described above remains strong, the *form* of organizations providing the services may change. For example, a ubiquitous data infrastructure is likely to lead to "unbundling" of channel functions. Just as lower coordination costs are likely induce producers to seek the services of cybermediaries, it is also likely that cheaper coordination will lead to the existence of focused firms, which ultimately provide a virtual bundle of channel services. Lower external transaction costs should result in greater horizontal de-integration of channel functions with increased specialization. Thus we propose that:

P1: In an electronic market, the number of organizations involved in a complete producer-consumer exchange will be greater than in a comparable exchange in a traditional market.

The composite nature of channel services and the potential for unbundling presented by the developing information infrastructure also have implications for the types of cybermediaries that are likely to exist. Williamson (1981) has argued that manufacturers are more likely to diversify into the production of other products where their expertise lie, than to integrate forward and handle a wider variety of goods as an intermediary. This is also supported by a resource-based view of the firm, which states that firms have limited managerial and other resources that are invested only where they can appropriate the highest rent. Since a producer firm is likely to have developed competencies in *producing*, it is more likely to pursue diversification in its core area of competence rather than move into *distribution*, which requires a very different skill set.

In electronic marketplaces, the need for special skill sets is even more pronounced. For example, Hoffman and Novak (1996) have argued that the WWW has certain unique characteristics that distinguish it from conventional media and markets. They refer to the issues of telepresence, experiential behavior, and the perceived challenges of the interaction process as unique characteristics that define the WWW. The telecommunications technologies and commerce-related software systems that serve as the basis for electronic markets are also rapidly developing technologies that require specialized expertise to develop, maintain, and operate. Thus, in electronic marketplaces unique features of environment, the nature of the underlying technology, and other traditional economies of scope and scale combine to make it unlikely that the average production firm will be able to perform channel functions as efficiently as specialized cybermediaries. Services that rely on new technologies or specialized skills, such as transaction security, product presentation, and on-line store management, are more likely to be acquired from external cybermediaries. In contrast, functions such as paper-based billing and telephone order-processing, which do not require use of complex, changing technology or electronic marketplace specific skills, are less likely to be performed by new cybermediaries.

P2a: Channel functions that rely on electronic market specific skill sets or technologies will be more likely to be provided by cybermediaries.

P2b: Channel functions that do not require electronic market specific skill sets or technologies will be more likely to be performed by producers.

Another important feature of any marketplace is the ability to attract a large number of potential consumers. In physical marketplaces, secondary services such as food and entertainment are often provided with the goal of drawing consumers to a particular location. Similarly, in electronic markets it is necessary to develop an audience of individuals who are interested in a firm's goods or services. Many types of user services, such as general search facilities or specialized content that attracts audiences, can be developed on the Internet. However, specialized resources and knowledge are needed to develop the consumer base in electronic markets. As a result, audience creation and maintenance is one area in which cybermediaries are likely to play an important role.

P3: In electronic markets, channel functions related to attracting a community of potential consumers will more likely be performed by cybermediaries.

The current state of Internet-based electronic commerce provides general support for these propositions regarding the nature of cybermediaries. Researchers have noted the proliferation of commercial exchange facilitators on the Internet (see Hoffman et al., 1995), providing an indication that cybermediary services are an efficient mechanism for supporting electronic exchanges. Examples of Internet-based exchange facilitators include gateways, directories, search services, on-line malls, electronic publishers, and virtual resellers (Sarkar et al., 1995). The emergence of on-line content and search service providers, which develop audiences to generate advertising revenue, provides another example of the role of specialized cybermediaries. Though still in the early stages of development. Internet-based electronic markets provide anecdotal evidence regarding the nature of emerging cybermediaries.

Structure of Electronic Marketplaces

Researchers have noted that study of channel structures is a fundamental research task (Anderson, 1985; Klein, Frazier, and Roth, 1990; Stern and Reve, 1980). The following sections consider the implications of the cybermediary argument for the structure and evolution of electronic markets. We also discuss how organization and cultural factors, such as power and consumer perceptions, are likely to encourage or hinder the development of complex structures within electronic marketplaces.

Channel length is defined as the number of organizations through which products move as they go from producers to end consumers (Stern, El-Ansary, and Coughlan, 1996). Channel length, which is often equated with the number of intermediaries involved in the exchange, is seen as an important characteristic of market structures (Sharma and Dominguez, 1992). The relationship between the number of intermediaries and the length of a channel is an important issue to both business strategists (Anderson and Coughlan, 1987) and public policy analysts (Sharma and Dominguez, 1992).

However, in electronic markets the straightforward relationship between the length of the physical channel and the number of intermediaries may not apply. As Rayport and Sviokla (1995) have argued, electronic marketplaces consist of both physical and information, or virtual, channels. It is also claimed that whereas the physical value chain is composed of a linear sequence of activities, the virtual value chain is nonlinear. Furthermore, the unbundling of channel functions resulting from lower coordination costs is likely to contribute to the separation of physical distribution from other cybermediary functions. This can simplify and shorten physical distribution (e.g., Federal Express as the distribution system) while producing complex and longer networks of informational intermediaries (e.g., some firms may locate products, others provide evaluations of related products, others provide training, others provide settlement services, etc.). In contrast to the traditional notion that shorter channels imply a greater degree of vertical integration by producers (Bucklin, 1970; Anderson and Coughlan, 1987), electronic marketplaces may support shorter physical channels and less overall vertical integration. This implies that:

> **P4:** In electronic markets, due to the unbundling of channel functions, the length of the physical channel will be lower than for comparable exchanges in traditional markets.

P5a: As a result of the network structure of virtual channels, consumers in electronic marketplaces will interact with a greater number of intermediary firms than similar consumers in traditional markets.

P5b: As a result of the network structure of virtual value chains, the number of information channels from the producer to the consumer will be greater in an electronic market than in comparable traditional markets.

Unlike the linear flows that characterize traditional channels (Stern, El-Ansary, and Coughlan, 1996), electronic markets are likely to be characterized by a shorter linear physical channel supplemented by nonlinear processes provided by a network of cybermediary organizations.

Evolution of Electronic Market Structures

Up to this point, our analysis has implicitly relied on static models. Whereas this type of analysis may adequately capture the general impact of electronic markets, it provides little insight into how the structure of these markets is likely to develop. Mallen (1975) notes that early in the development of new markets, firms are more likely to utilize intermediaries rather than performing channel functions internally. The small entrepreneurial producers who typically develop new markets often find it advantageous to outsource channel functions to specialized intermediaries that possess the specialized skills needed to quickly achieve economies of scale and scope. This is consistent with our earlier prediction (P1) that a large number of cybermediaries will emerge in the early stages of the electronic market.

However, research has shown that it is common for longer traditional channels to be reduced as the market develops (for a review, see Sharma and Dominguez, 1992). The evolutionary model suggests that as markets develop, competition intensifies, and producers who control channel functions gain competitive advantages (Guiltinan, 1974). From a transaction cost perspective, increasing volume enables some producers to achieve economies of scale in-house and as a result the difference between internal and external channel service production costs is reduced (T2 and T2′ in Figure 1). Furthermore, because the cost of coordinating with a large number of traditional intermediaries is high, using many traditional intermediaries can hinder a firm's ability to maneuver. (Sharma and Dominguez, 1992). Therefore, as markets develop and mature, firms will tend to shorten and simplify their traditional channels by internalizing intermediary functions.

Similar changes in the cost of internally providing channel services (T2 in Figure 1) are also likely to occur in electronic markets. However, in electronic markets the trend toward simpler channel structures and fewer intermediaries will be inhibited (Figure 2). In traditional markets, a decrease in the cost of providing a channel service internally (T2) results in more firms performing that service in-house as the total cost of in-house production (T1 + T2) falls below the cost of using an intermediary (T1′ + T2′). However, in electronic markets the cost of coordinating a cybermediary (T1′)

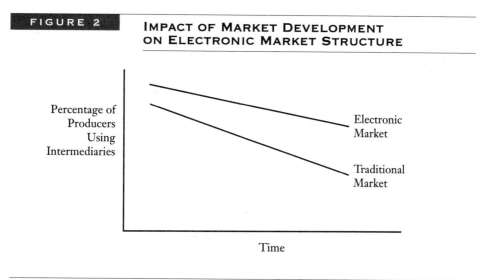

FIGURE 2   IMPACT OF MARKET DEVELOPMENT ON ELECTRONIC MARKET STRUCTURE

is lower and the difference between internal and external coordination costs (T1 vs. T1') is not as large. As a result, a greater reduction in the cost of performing the channel service internally is required to shift organizations from the use of external intermediaries. Consequently, although it is likely that some firms will choose to internalize cybermediary functions, in electronic markets the trend towards simplified market structures will be reduced.

> **P6:** The number of producers using cybermediaries to perform a particular channel service in an electronic market will decline at a slower rate than the number of producers in a comparable traditional market.

Power and Socio-Cultural Influences

Prior studies of channel management have considered how both producers and distributors use their power base to achieve their objectives (Frazer and Rody, 1991; Beier and Stern, 1969; Gaski, 1984). Conflict and cooperation are central themes in this line of research (Anderson and Narus, 1990). Firms obviously cannot always completely control the behavior of other firms to effect desired outcomes, and bargaining and negotiating often play an important role in determining channel structures (Gomes-Casseres, 1990). Thus, it is likely that the evolution of electronic market structures will be affected by the distribution of power in the existing channel systems. The presence of a dominant producer in an existing market may encourage other producers to move into electronic markets as an alternate channel for reaching customers. This in turn would create a producer-side demand for cybermediary services. On the other hand, powerful intermediaries in existing markets may hinder the development of electronic markets. If the new structure conflicts with the interests of powerful players in existing markets, firms may be unable to develop electronic markets. The power of intermediaries, often stemming from their relationships with customers, may force producers to abandon efforts to bypass traditional intermediaries in fear of retaliation.

One example of this is the experience of Air France on the French Minitel system, Minitel, which is available throughout France in most businesses and 40% of households (Streeter et al., 1993), is used by Air France to permit on-line seat reservations. They considered distributing ticket printers, allowing large corporate customers to completely bypass travel agencies and avoid the commissions associated with airline ticketing. However, fear of retaliation from travel agents led Air France to reject this plan, especially because the number of people actually using Minitel to reserve seats paled in comparison to the number who use travel agencies. Instead, a system was developed in which reservations could be made electronically, but traditional intermediaries continued to provide the actual ticketing service (Steinfield, Caby, and Vialle, 1992). Until the electronic means of reaching customers offers better access than traditional means, producer firms will be reluctant to attempt complete bypass of the traditional intermediary. Consideration of power distribution in channel structures leads to the following propositions.

P7: In product markets characterized by an imbalance of power in favor of particular producers, competing producers will be motivated to offer their products within electronic markets. As a result, cybermediaries will be more common in these product-markets.

P8: In product markets characterized by an imbalance of power in favor of one or more traditional intermediaries, producers will be reluctant to offer their products through channels in electronic markets until the electronic market channels offer greater access to customers than traditional channels. As a result, cybermediaries will be less common in these markets.

The intermediary's ability to personalize efforts and add customer services, such as liberal return and credit policies, can act as powerful deterrents to forward integration by producers (Heide and John, 1988). However, whereas cybermediaries are capable of providing specialized services for consumers, it is unclear whether they can provide the social atmosphere and support that consumers expect from many traditional intermediaries. Research on channel evolution has also shown that cultural values significantly affect the adoption of new distributive institutions and practices (Sharma and Dominguez, 1992). Sociologists and anthropologists have long recognized that economic activity is embedded in a social structure, and that existing social relations influence patterns of economic exchange (Granovetter, 1985). Finally, culturally bound shopping behavior is known to affect retail institutions and channel structure (Shimagushi and Lazer, 1979). Therefore we propose:

P9: In product markets where social interaction is crucial for supporting consumer purchasing behavior, cybermediaries will be less common.

Conclusions

This article addresses the nature of intermediation in electronic marketplaces. We have argued against the idea that intermediaries are likely to disappear. In fact, it is our contention that within electronic markets, cybermediary firms are likely to be more common and diverse than intermediaries in traditional markets. The transaction cost analysis presented above suggests that increased outsourcing of channel functions is likely to result in a prominent role for cybermediaries in the electronic environment. Electronic markets will require a more complex set of producer-consumer mediating needs, which in many cases will be best provided by cybermediary firms.

Our analyses highlight a number of areas for future conceptual and empirical work. One avenue for future work involves the formalization of the transaction cost models underlying this and previous electronic commerce research. Other research should operationalize and empirically test these propositions and models in specific electronic marketplaces with both cross-sectional and longitudinal data. Studies of the evolution of electronic marketplaces provide a valuable opportunity for developing our understanding of commercial structures and processes. The changes brought about by the developing information infrastructure will enable researchers to challenge and improve the models underlying our understanding of organizations, consumers, and commercial-activities.

Reprinted from Journal of Business Research, *Vol. 41, 1998, with permission from Elsevier Science.*

References

Alderson, Wroe: Factors Governing the Development of Marketing Channels, in *Marketing Channels for Manufactured Products*, R. M. Clewett, ed., Richard D. Irwin, Homewood, IL. 1954.

Anderson, Erin: The Salesperson as Outside Agent or Employee: A Transaction Cost Analysis. *Marketing Science* 4 (Summer 1985): 234–254.

Anderson, Erin, and Coughlan, Anne T.: International Market Entry and Expansion Via Independent or Integrated Channels of Distribution. *Journal of Marketing* 51 (January 1987): 71–82.

Anderson, Erin, and Narus, James A.: A Model of Distributor Firm and Manufacturer Firm Working Partnerships. *Journal of Marketing* 54 (January 1990): 42–58.

Beier, F., and Stern, Louis: Power in the Channels of Distribution, in *Distribution Channels: Behavioral Dimensions*, Louis Stern, ed., Houghton Mifflin, Boston, MA. 1969, pp. 92–116.

Benjamin, R., and Wigand, R.: Electronic Markets and Virtual Value Chains on the Information Superhighway. *Sloan Management Review* 36 (2) (1995): 62–72.

Bucklin, Louis P.: Macro Models of Vertical Marketing Systems, in *Vertical Marketing Systems*, Louis P. Bucklin, ed., Scott, Foreman and Company, Glenview, IL. 1970, pp. 116–134.

Business Week: The Internet: How It Will Change the Way You Do Business. *Business Week,* November 14, 1994, pp. 80–88.

Butler, Brian: Product, Information, and Risk: An Exchange System Model of Electronic Retailing. Working Paper. Carnegie-Mellon University, Pittsburgh, PA. 1996.

Coyle, J., and Andraski, J.: Managing Channel Relationships, *Annual Conference Proceedings of the Council of Logistics Management*, 1990, pp. 245–258.

Frazer, G. L., and Rody, R. C.: The Use of Influence Strategies in Interfirm Relationships in Industrial Product Channels. *Journal of Marketing* 55 (January 1991): 52–69.

Gaski, J. F.: The Theory of Power and Conflict in Channels of Distribution. *Journal of Marketing* 48 (Summer 1984): 9–29.

Gomes-Casseres, Benjamin: Firm Ownership Preferences and Host Government Restrictions: An Integrated Approach. *Journal of International Business* 20 (1) (1990): 1–22.

Granovetter, M.: Economic Action and Social Structure: The Problem of Embeddedness. *American Journal of Sociology* 91 (3) (1985): 481–510.

Guiltinan, J. P.: Planned and Evolutionary Changes in Distribution Channels. *Journal of Retailing* 2 (Summer 1974): 79–91.

Gulati, Ranjay: Does Familiarity Breed Trust? The Implications of Repeated Ties for Contractual Choice in Alliances. *Academy of Management Journal* 38 (1) (1995): 85–112.

Heide, Jon B., and John, G.: The Role of Dependence Balancing in Safeguarding Transaction-Specific Assets in Conventional Channels. *Journal of Marketing* 52 (January 1988): 20–35.

Hoffman, Donna L., Novak, Thomas P., and Chatterjee, Patrali: Commercial Scenarios for the Web: Opportunities and Challenges. *Journal of Computer Mediated Communication*, Special Issue on Electronic Commerce, 1 (3) (1995). [http://shum.huji.ac.il/jcmc/vol1/issue3/vol1no3.html]

Hoffman, Donna L., and Novak, Thomas P.: A New Marketing Paradigm for Electronic Commerce. Project 2000 Working Paper, Owen Graduate School of Management, Vanderbilt University, Nashville, TN. 1996. [http://www2000.ogsm.vanderbilt.edu/novak/new.marketing.paradigm.html]

Klein, S.: A Transaction Cost Explanation of Vertical Integration in International Markets. *Journal of the Academy of Marketing Science* 17 (May 1989): 196–208.

Klein, S., Frazier, G., and Roth, V. J.: A Transaction Cost Model of Channel Integration in International Markets. *Journal of Marketing* 17 (May 1990): 196–208.

Mallen B.: Marketing Channels and Economic Development: A Literature Review. *International Journal of Physical Distribution and Materials Management* 5 (5) (1975): 230–237.

Malone, Thomas, Yates, J., and Benjamin, R.: Electronic Markets and Electronic Hierarchies: Effects of Information Technology on Market Structure and Corporate Strategies. *Communications of the ACM* 30 (6) (1987): 484–497.

Office of Technology Assessment: *Electronic Enterprises: Looking to the Future*, U.S. Government Printing Office, Washington, DC. 1994.

Porter, Michael: *Competitive Advantage*, The Free Press, New York, 1985.

Porter, Michael, and Millar, Victor: How Information Gives You Competitive Advantage. *Harvard Business Review* (July-August 1985): 149–160.

Rangan, Kasturi, Menezes, M., and Maier, E.: Channel Selection for New Industrial Products: A Framework, Method, and Application. *Journal of Marketing* 56 (1992): 69–82.

Rayport, J. F., and Sviokla, J. J.: Exploiting the Virtual Value Chain. *Harvard Business Review* 73 (6) (1995): 75–85.

Sarkar, Mitrbarun, Butler, Brian, and Steinfield, Charles: Intermediaries and Cybermediaries: The Continuing Role for Mediating Players in the Electronic Marketplace. *Journal of Computer-mediated Communications*, Special Issue on Electronic Commerce. 1 (3) (1995). [http://shum.huji.ac.il/jcmc/vol1/issue3/vol1no3.html].

Sharma, Arun, and Dominguez, Luiz V.: Channel Evolution: A Framework for Analysis. *Journal of the Academy of Marketing Science* 20 (1) (1992): 1–15.

Shimagushi, M., and Lazer, W.: Japanese Distribution Channels: Invisible Barriers to Entry. *MSU Business Topics* 27 (Winter 1979): 49–62.

Sternfield, Charles, Caby, Lawrence, and Vialle, P. Exploring the Role of Videotex in the International Strategy of the Firm. Paper presented to the *Telecommunications Policy Research Conference*, Solomons Island, MD, September 1992.

Stern, Louis W., and Reeve, T.: Distribution Channels as Political Economies. *Journal of Marketing* 44 (Summer 1980): 52–64.

Stern, Louis, El-Ansary, A., and Coughlan, Anne T.: *Marketing Channels*, 5th edition, Prentice Hall, Englewood Cliffs, NJ. 1996.

Streeter, Lynn A., Kraut, Robert E., Lucas, H. C., and Caby, Lawrence: The Impact of National Data Networks on Firm Performance and Market Structure. Unpublished Bellcore manuscript, 1993.

Williamson, Oliver E.: *Markets and Hierarchies: Analysis and Antitrust Implications*, The Free Press, New York. 1975.

Williamson, Oliver E.: The Economies of Organizations: The Transaction Cost Approach. *American Journal of Sociology* 87 (3) (1981): 548–577.

Williamson, Oliver E.: *The Economic Institutions of Capitalism*, The Free Press, New York. 1985.

14

The New Infomediaries

JOHN HAGEL III
JEFFREY F. RAYPORT

Will they dominate the networked economy?

Agents, proxies, and filters whose first allegiance will be to customers and to the information they guard

Their challenge? Managing the interplay between trust and value received

Received wisdom has it that there are two fundamental truths about the networked economy. First, that every networked business is ideally positioned to capture information about its customers—information that represents the main source of value in this economy. Second, that any players specializing in customer information that may emerge will naturally serve vendors, not customers. We take issue with both of these assertions.

Our view is that firms established to capture customer information will serve customers rather than vendors. They will enjoy low capital costs and high ROI—the hallmarks of an emerging category of business that we call infomediaries. As its activities start to generate increasing returns, we predict this category will become more and more concentrated, with rising entry barriers excluding mature and new players alike. While infomediaries will emerge first in networked sectors of the economy, we anticipate that they will eventually expand into physical business transactions too, thereby transforming the competitive landscape for traditional as well as networked players.

The scale of this transformation could be formidable. A concentration of large infomediaries in the United States could account for as much as $10 billion in revenue a decade from now, representing market capitalization of at least $40 billion.

Players in this new game will find that success depends on their ability to build strong bonds of trust with their customers. While trust has always been important in business, it will become even more so in the online world, with its expanding choices

John Hagel is a principal in McKinsey's Silicon Valley office; **Jeffrey Rayport** is an associate professor in the Service Management Interest Group at Harvard Business School.

and declining switching barriers. In the past, information about customers has been taken for granted; in the future, it will have to be purchased. Indeed, if firms fail to establish trust-based relationships with customers, it may not be available at any price.

Few companies appreciate the scale of the challenge. Many still seem to take trust much too lightly. Witness America Online's announcement in summer 1997 that it would sell its members' telephone numbers to telemarketers—a decision that was rapidly rescinded after members protested. As consumers become more keenly aware of the value of information about their own tastes and actions, traditional players will have more difficulty gaining access to it. This will enable new entrants—infomediaries—to become customer information specialists in a new information-intensive economy. We define *infomediary* as follows:

> [**infomediary**] *a business whose sole or main source of revenue derives from capturing consumer information and developing detailed profiles of individual customers for use by selected third-party vendors.*

The emergence of infomediaries will be driven by two key developments. In a networked economy, customers' ability to capture information about their own behavior and preferences implies that they can also choose to withhold this information from vendors that seek it. At the same time, the sheer accessibility of such information has raised a host of concerns about privacy. These two shifts in the nature of economic activity will lead, we believe, to a state of affairs in which companies will negotiate with customers to gain access to information about them.[1] This bargaining process will create a need for infomediaries that can handle negotiations and payments and add value by the way they process customer information.

The Business Model

The infomediaries we see today fall into the vendor-oriented category. In other words, they use customer information to aid vendors in targeting products, services, and promotions to consumers in competitive markets.

Vendor-Oriented Infomediaries

Two basic types of vendor-oriented intermediary have already appeared on line:

Audience brokers capture information about users across multiple Web sites to help advertisers reach the most appropriate audiences. A leading example is DoubleClick. Audience brokers also exist in the physical world: for example, print brokers in newspapers and magazines, and rep firms in radio and television, use their knowledge of audience composition to help place advertising packages. While they may position themselves as media buyers, their primary value lies in their ability to find the best audiences for advertisers.

Lead generators aggregate potential customers according to their profiles, preferences, and other criteria, translate this data into specific product and service needs, and then direct customers to vendors whose offerings meet those needs. Prime examples on the Web are Auto-By-Tel, which provides a national network of 2,200 car dealers with consumer requests in exclusive sales territories in return for a fee per lead, and 1-800-PCFlowers, which distributes orders to independent florists throughout the United States. Similar services also exist in the physical world: FTD uses a phone and fax network to distribute orders for flowers, while mortgage brokers amass customer profiling data to place mortgages with appropriate lenders.

Customer-Oriented Infomediaries

We anticipate, however, that a new breed of infomediary will emerge that is distinguished by its overt allegiance to customers rather than vendors. It will:

- Help customers get maximum value from their information profiles by using choices they have made in the past to deduce which product or service would best match their current needs, and then finding the vendor that can deliver the preferred product or service at the cheapest price (**agent** function);

- Represent customers' interests in negotiations with vendors that seek access to information about them (**proxy** function); and

- Screen commercial messages from vendors so that they are relevant to the customer (**filter** function).

These five informediary types—audience brokers, lead generators, agents, proxies, and filters—will operate according to a variety of economic models.

Vendor-oriented infomediaries will be paid a commission to help vendors target and reach relevant customers. **Audience brokers** and **lead generators** will in effect charge for eyeballs, impressions, click-throughs, and leads on a CPM or segment-of-one basis. Take the audience broker DoubleClick. In return for placing an ad on various Web sites in its network and reporting back on the ad's performance, DoubleClick receives a payment from the advertiser based on the total number of impressions generated. Rates start at $40 per thousand impressions. Meanwhile, the lead generator Auto-By-Tel receives sign-up fees of $2,500 to $6,500 and fees totalling $10,000 to $25,000 per year from participating auto dealers in exchange for qualified leads of prospective car buyers generated through its Web site.

Customer-oriented infomediaries are likely to operate under a radically different economic model reflecting the value that they generate for their clients. Revenues are likely to consist of either payments made directly by clients for services rendered, or commission on revenues accruing to clients from vendors as a result of services provided by infomediaries.

Filters are likely to base their services on a flat fee per client. This fee will probably be modest, given consumers' limited willingness to pay third parties to screen vendors on their behalf. CUC International, a successful purchasing service that preselects vendors offering a wide range of consumer goods and services, levies a membership fee of only $59 per year, for instance.

Agents will probably evolve toward a commission structure. Customers will save time and money by using agents that can perform quick and efficient searches for the goods they need and negotiate prices with vendors on their behalf. In return, they will pay agents a proportion of the savings they make. However, agents may seek, especially in the early stages, to implement flat-fee pricing in an effort to maximize incentives for consumers to purchase through infomediaries.

Proxies are the most likely to be commission based. They represent the interests of customers to vendors (either blindly like Firefly Network, where the vendor is not able to identify individual customers, or transparently like CyberGold, where customers are rewarded for revealing their identities), and aim to extract maximum value for their customers' information. They will take a commission on the revenues they generate for their customers by selling information to vendors.

An Industry Is Born

As infomediaries spring up to take advantage of the opportunity to help consumers profit from the value of their own information, a new industry will be created. This industry will eventually be dominated by customer-rather than vendor-oriented players. Its participants will proliferate rapidly—and perhaps become concentrated just as rapidly. It will generate substantial revenues and create significant value, but only after an initial period of slow growth. And it will change the nature of business in the physical world too.

Customer-Oriented Players Win

While vendor-oriented infomediaries are likely to abound on networks in the near term, customer-oriented infomediaries should eventually prevail as new technologies are deployed and customers become more aware of opportunities to capture for themselves the value of information about their own activities and preferences.

Vendor-oriented infomediaries will predominate initially because of vendors' interest in exploiting the opportunities to capture information offered by networks such as the Internet. As Web sites proliferate and generate an oversupply of advertising venues, the need will arise for someone to help aggregate customer information across fragmented sites—an important intermediary function for audience brokers. Lead generators will play an equally valuable role by helping vendors exploit scale advantages in marketing and by aggregating profiles of sales prospects that can be parceled out to the most suitable vendors.

In time, however, the early success of vendor-oriented infomediaries is likely to be undermined by the advent of technologies giving customers more control over personal information. At present, customers leave a trail of information about themselves as they move from one Web site to another. This information is available to the site operators as a "free good" simply because they are able to attract customers in the first place. Customers are often unaware of the information they are leaving behind—or, in some cases, storing in their own computers through "cookie" software that allows Web site owners to access it each time the customers return to their sites.

Technologies are now becoming available that will turn the tables on vendors; they include new forms of electronic cash, "anonymizer" software, and modifications to cookie software. Their main impact will be to allow customers to visit Web sites and conduct transactions in total anonymity. This then creates a bargaining opportunity for customers to reveal information selectively to specific vendors in return for value. Hence, information that was once a free good automatically captured by vendors during interactions with customers now becomes an economic good that must be "purchased" by vendors in exchange for cash or tangible value.

Technology is merely the enabler in this transformation, which is really driven by operational efficiencies. A customer's computer is a far more efficient place to capture an integrated profile of his or her activities and preferences than a fragmented set of vendors could ever be.

Needless to say, the transformation implies a major shift in customers' beliefs and behavior, and will take some time to play out. But customer-oriented infomediaries are likely to speed up the process by providing the necessary technology tools, a portfolio of services to maximize the value of the information captured, and aggressive marketing to make customers aware of the value of the information they are currently giving away. When this happens, vendor-oriented infomediaries will find it harder to survive, since customer-oriented infomediaries will preemptively capture the customer information on which they rely, and deliver—more efficiently—the services they used to provide.

Proliferation Followed by Concentration

As value creation shifts from vendor- to customer-oriented infomediaries, rapid infomediary proliferation is likely to be followed by a ruthless industry shakeout culminating in concentration and rising barriers to entry.

When the right technology tools become available, there will be a rush to set up customer-oriented infomediary businesses. In the early days, specialized niche players are likely to target specific agent, filter, and proxy service opportunities. Eventually, however, these niche players may find themselves at a disadvantage to full-service infomediaries. The agent, filter, and proxy services they offer all depend on the capture and analysis of the same customer profiles. A situation where multiple specialized providers independently capture and manage the same information is far less efficient than one where the full range of services is delivered from a single database—a fact that is likely to drive the first wave of consolidation.

Full-service customer-oriented infomediaries will themselves begin to consolidate, prompted by economies of scope and increasing returns dynamics. Two main economies of scope will arise.

First, infomediaries with large, diverse customer bases will enjoy an advantage over those with narrower customer bases thanks to new collaborative agent/filtering technology. This identifies clusters of customers who display similar needs and interests. When certain customers within a cluster buy a particular product or service, the collaborative agent/filter suggests to the other customers within that cluster that they might also like the product or service. The broader the sample set of customers, the more accurate the clusters are likely to be, and the more valid the recommendations made by the collaborative agent/filter.

Firefly Network has used this technology to register its members' tastes in music. By developing clusters of preferences among like-minded members on its site, now owned by 2Way Media, it has been able to recommend CDs that individual members might not know about, but would be likely to enjoy. The second economy of scope driving consolidation will be the insight derived from building a customer profile that encompasses many product categories. Early customer-oriented infomediaries are most likely to emerge within particular product categories, but they will soon find they are able to deliver more value by expanding their reach across product categories. A book buyer who purchases travel guides to Bali is probably intending to spend a holiday there, for instance, while a couple that starts asking for information about baby food may soon be ready to trade in their sports car for a roomier family model. In this way, product-focused infomediaries should give way to broad-based infomediaries serving the full range of their customers' product and service needs.

In addition to these economies of scope, powerful increasing returns dynamics will drive industry concentration over time. These increasing returns result from the powerful interplay between trust and value delivered to the client. Trust is the infomediary's lifeblood. How else could it persuade clients to divulge their most sensitive information? Trust is difficult to build at the outset, but deepens over time and as the client base broadens.

Trust is also reinforced by the increasing value a consumer receives from an infomediary that understands not just that particular individual, but also others with similar tastes and habits. The more interaction an infomediary has with consumers, the more insight it gains into their needs, and the more proactive and precise it can be in delivering agent and filter services. The information profiles it offers to vendors in turn become more compelling and thus generate larger revenues. As consumers see the value of the infomediary's understanding, their trust grows deeper.

The interplay between trust and value also serves to build barriers to entry. As with most cases of increasing returns, a business that at the outset is relatively easy to enter becomes more difficult and costly to enter over time. Imagine trying to compete as a new entrant with a well-established and trusted infomediary. No matter how compelling your service offering may be, you will find it difficult to persuade clients to switch from their established relationship. Trust locks customers in to a particular infomediary. The costs of client acquisition rise prohibitively for latecomers.

The Value at Stake

The customer-oriented infomediary business is likely to generate substantial revenues for the winners in the consolidation game. It could generate $10 billion a year in the US consumer market alone within the next decade.

To see how, let us assume that 10 percent of US households (roughly 10 million households) subscribe to an infomediary service by 2007. Since customer-oriented infomediary services are likely to be linked initially to purchases made on line, and will thus attract the more affluent households first, our model assumes that this 10 percent of households represents 20 percent of US retail sales. It also assumes that only 20 percent of these households' retail purchases are made on line. Thus, the online purchases of infomediary clients ten years from now represent 4 percent of total US retail sales.

To put this estimate in context, the total thus arrived at, $99 billion, is less than the current sales volume derived from mail order and other forms of direct marketing, which stands at $113 billion. To be conservative, we have assumed no growth in overall retail sales volume or advertising expenditure over the next ten years.

Each household subscribing to a full-service infomediary will pay, according to our model, a basic fee of $55 (roughly equivalent to an annual credit card fee). The remaining infomediary revenue of roughly $950 per average client represents a proportion of the value received by the client and is derived from commissions. This value has three components: (1) cash revenue averaging $730 per household for the sale of customer information (calculated on the basis of that household's likely purchasing activity and the amount that vendors currently spend on advertising and promotion to reach similar households); (2) net savings averaging $1,250 per household (or 15 percent less a 2 1/2 percent agency fee) made on online retail purchases as a result of agent services; and (3) substantial savings in the time households spend in searching for products, capturing and managing purchasing information, and similar activities.

If customer-oriented infomediaries achieve the high level of concentration characteristic of other increasing returns businesses, it is likely that the leading player, representing 40 percent of the market, could achieve annual revenue of $4 billion within 10 years. Two other leading players, each representing approximately 20 percent of the market, could account for $2 billion in revenue apiece.

Slow Early Growth, Then Acceleration

Because this is an increasing returns business, it will take time for revenue and profitability to build. Once the business gains momentum, however, volumes will rise with remarkable rapidity.

Increasing returns businesses typically grow slowly at the outset, when the network effects that eventually drive increasing returns are being formed. In the case of customer-oriented infomediaries, the challenge will be to build trust among a critical mass of clients. An infomediary with no clients will have a hard time convincing the first client to entrust it with information. Accumulating information profiles that are deep and broad enough to create substantial value for clients is also a slow process. As more clients join and more value is generated by the infomediary on their behalf, it becomes progressively easier to convince the next client to join.

Eventually, an inflection point is reached when the accumulation of a critical mass of clients and information profiles crosses a threshold in terms of perceived value to current and potential clients. Revenue and profitability take off as the value of the service becomes compelling to a larger and larger market. The economic challenge for an aspiring infomediary is to reach this inflection point as quickly as possible, while at the same time ensuring that investors have realistic expectations of the level of funding required and the interval before an acceptable return on investment can be realized.

In this case, there are likely to be several such inflection points as different economic thresholds are reached. One threshold will involve acquiring a critical mass of clients, a second will involve accumulating sufficiently rich profiles of these clients to generate higher revenues, and a third will involve building a robust network of appropriate vendors to maximize the value of the profiles. All of these will take time to achieve.

High ROI Eventually

Given the economics of increasing returns businesses—namely, increases in the value generated per incremental unit of investment and strong tendencies toward concentration—it is likely that customer-oriented infomediaries will enjoy substantial returns over time. Operating via networks gives them the added advantage of being able to achieve national and even global reach without having to make expensive investments in bricks-and-mortar sales outlets.

Initially, however, it will be necessary to invest in acquiring clients and building database management capabilities well in advance of the inflection point, so that cash will be consumed and profitability depressed. If the business is highly fragmented, as we might expect in the early stages, the aspiring infomediary faces the prospect of spending heavily on marketing to differentiate itself from the pack while it is suffering intense pressure on prices and margins as other players seek to acquire share preemptively.

Once inflection points are reached and the expected shakeout occurs, the value of these businesses should soar as investors begin to see rapid growth and rising barriers to entry. The combination of improving margins and accelerating growth should generate substantial shareholder value. The leading infomediary ten years from now, with $4 billion in annual revenue, strong profitability, and high growth potential (since we assumed only 10 percent of households would be penetrated in the first wave), might conceivably represent shareholder value of $20 billion. The two other large contenders with revenues of $2 billion could each represent shareholder value of $5 to $10 billion.

The Impact on Physical Markets

The rise of infomediaries will change the nature of business in the physical world too. Traditional businesses may well find themselves under pressure to profit by gathering customer information or exploiting it in their own operations. As consumers become accustomed to personalized service on line, for instance, they will come to expect it in hotels, restaurants, airlines, and stores. These businesses will also find themselves in demand as collectors of data from their everyday interactions with customers. They too will call upon infomediary services.

As smart card and other low-cost information capture technologies spread, infomediaries will rapidly extend the scope of their services to transactions in physical space. It would not be difficult, for example, for an infomediary to modify emerging smart card technology to perform information capture as well as value transfer functions. If it equipped its clients with modified smart cards for making purchases from traditional retail establishments, the resulting transaction records could be regularly downloaded from the smart cards via PCs to broaden its customer profiles. Such an approach would mean the infomediary would no longer be confined by the boundary between network and physical space.

Although smart card technology could help infomediaries record transactions in physical space, they would still find it difficult to log related details such as advertisements viewed and retail establishments browsed in. But even these may begin to be accessible; for example, infomediaries might equip their clients with electronic monitors to record TV viewing patterns, much as Nielsen does today for small sample audiences (the so-called "Nielsen households"). Households might also be asked to make all media purchases (especially newspapers and magazines) with smart cards to build a profile of reading habits.

The point is that as clients perceive the value of the infomediary on the network, they will begin to want the same services in physical space. Aided by advances in technology and market pressures on traditional retailers, infomediaries are likely to exploit their strong positions on line to expand their services beyond the network.

Who Can Play?

Existing players should ask themselves whether they possess the assets they would need to become infomediaries, namely:

- **Brand breadth.** Do we have a sufficiently broad or flexible brand positioning among our target customers to allow us to market a diverse range of products and services?

- **Emotional bond.** Are our linkages to our target customers sufficiently deep and emotionally based to engender high levels of trust?

- **Transaction intensity.** Do we process, or have access to, a sufficient volume of transactions across a variety of products and services to extract detailed profiles of customer preferences and purchases?

Emotional bond and transaction intensity ensure **access to information,** the first as a result of trust (without which consumers will be unwilling to reveal much about themselves) and the second as a result of the data richness that comes from intensive economic activity (without which consumer profiles will generate insufficient data to support powerful insights).

Brand breadth, on the other hand, ensures **quality of information.** Only brands that enjoy broad, cross-category relationships with customers will furnish a context in which horizontal (as opposed to vertical or single-category) patterns of consumer behavior can be observed and interpreted effectively. Narrow brands cannot compete because the relationships they engender are too tightly focused to support the kinds of insight that come from seeing how consumers behave across a range of product and service sectors.

Among existing players, we can identify five separate businesses that may have the potential to play an infomediary role: fiduciaries, retailers, purchasing brokers, database players, and media players.

Fiduciaries

These are companies with large, loyal populations of affluent customers who have grown accustomed to sharing personal information with them. They can be found in financial, entertainment, community-oriented, and lifestyle services.

In financial services, American Express and USAA are prime candidates. Amex has managed its customers' access to purchasing power for decades, first in the form of traveler's checks and later via charge cards and credit cards. Its customer base numbers tens of millions throughout the world. Through its travel and leisure services, Amex markets everything from package holidays to consumer products. More recently, it has extended into financial advice, small business services, and investment vehicles.

The company still performs its familiar role in the lives of travelers overseas. In cities around the globe, Amex offices provide instant credit, replacement checks and cards, and a postal address for tourists and expatriates. It is thus well placed to harness the emotional bond, brand breadth, and transaction intensity to act as an infomediary in building, maintaining, and marketing detailed cross-category customer profiles.

USAA is ideally positioned to pursue a similar strategy among its core community: individuals with past or present affiliations to the US military. Like Amex, USAA has emotional resonance for its customers as a reliable, responsive supplier of financial services. It was the first US property and casualty insurer to offer solutions rather than settlements, purchasing replacements for lost or stolen household items itself instead of haggling over claims and sending checks. As a result, it is one of the nation's leading merchandisers of consumer durables.

To support its coverage, USAA maintains records not only of replacement goods but also of original household possessions. That gives it unique insights into the contents of millions of American homes, as well as into risk profiles, driving records, incident reports, and loss histories. Such rich segment-of-one information would make USAA a powerful player in the emerging infomediary business.

Other firms that could aspire to an infomediary role are AT&T as the world's leading telecommunications brand and Disney in family entertainment.

In theory, fiduciaries, as entrenched players, are ideally positioned to establish themselves as powerful infomediaries. Yet their scale and history also make them the least likely pretenders to the infomediary marketspace. Just as IBM unwittingly created Microsoft's first market opportunity by licensing its original PC operating system, DOS, fiduciaries are more likely to outsource the role of infomediary than to take it up themselves.

Mature players are seldom capable of creating divisions or subsidiaries that can operate effectively in new markets with rapidly evolving competitive dynamics. Notwithstanding their established brands, they suffer various handicaps: often slow to move, they possess limited capabilities in network-based operations, and their brands may not translate readily to new media. In particular, such players should take a long, hard look at the degree of trust their brand engenders among both existing customers and the broader market. Brands can easily be tarnished or constrained by the images and associations evoked by past actions.

Retailers

One type of established player that might have an easier time playing the role of infomediary is major retailers. Their success has always depended on acting as an intermediary between vendors and consumers. Becoming an infomediary would represent a less radical departure for them than for fiduciaries. But few retailers possess the necessary brand breadth or transaction intensity. Those that do may find the infomediary business a natural extension of their existing customer loyalty programs, which already gather detailed transaction histories to build rich customer profiles.

Firms that might qualify include Wal-Mart, Kmart, and Sears in general merchandising, the UK grocery chain Tesco, and Nordstrom in upmarket apparel. General merchandisers enjoy strong links with families or households, and can track long-term buying patterns across numerous consumer segments. Moreover, their stock covers thousands of everyday products, from branded packaged goods to consumer durables. Similarly, grocery chains, with stores boasting an average 35,000 SKUs, are able to use their customers' food choices to gain insights into family size, members' ages and needs, price sensitivity, brand loyalty by category, and possible future health risks, to name but a few. Such insights can be powerful, especially when linked to a loyalty program like Tesco's that rewards regular shoppers in appropriate ways, such as by giving them vouchers for money off frequently purchased goods.

Companies whose high-quality merchandise and outstanding service help them form intense, long-standing relationships with loyal customers are likely to possess the depth of trust to become infomediaries for their target markets. An obvious example is Nordstrom, which has become something of a legend for putting its customers' interests before its own, even "taking back" products purchased from other stores. Indeed, so high is Nordstrom's credibility in its customers' eyes that it might even be thought to represent their interests better than they could themselves. What position could be better for a firm seeking to act as a proxy in the infomediary world?

Retailers do, however, come with the same baggage as fiduciaries. It is difficult for firms that have earned their spurs in the world of retail sites and supply chain management to compete in the market for pure information. But if they can overcome their historical bias, the rich consumer relationships they command would provide the right foundation for the infomediary business.

Purchasing Brokers

Firms that exist primarily to aggregate consumer demand as power buyers or brokers are in an even better position to become infomediaries, since they already earn their living by gathering, processing, and exploiting segment-of-one customer information.

One example is CUC International, which offers members of its purchasing service the lowest possible prices on a broad range of goods by selling at or just above cost in exchange for membership fees billed annually. With its claimed 350,000 SKUs of general merchandise inventory, CUC has already amassed a huge database of consumer buying histories, supplemented by its apartment rental, grocery delivery, and travel services.

HFS, the firm with which CUC has agreed to merge, has played a similar game in hospitality and travel services. With its millions of customer profiles, the new firm, Cendant Corporation, will represent a treasure trove of consumer insights. Were the new firm to expand beyond membership fees to collect other types of infomediary commission, it might come to dominate an even larger segment of the US population.

Similarly, the TV home shopping channel QVC could pursue an infomediary strategy. Its databases comprise 5.3 million active customer records. With its 45 percent market share in the $4 billion TV home shopping industry and its broad selection of merchandise, it would have enormous potential as an infomediary if it could devise a strategy to exploit its vast databases without arousing privacy concerns.

Database Players

Firms that possess core skills in managing customer information for risk management, payment processing, and other financial purposes are natural contenders in the infomediary marketspace.

Companies such as Equifax and Experian (a merger between CCN Group and TRW Information Systems & Services) have collected decades' worth of consumer credit histories to supply to the retail and banking sectors for credit card purchase approvals, loan authorizations, and mortgage applications. Their records of how much customers spend on what give them an inherent advantage in entering the infomediary fray.

Database marketing consultants such as Epsilon, until recently a subsidiary of American Express, and Omnicom's Rapp Collins Worldwide also have access to substantial cross-category purchase data in their customer records. Rapp operates one of the largest customer information systems in the world for Loyalty Management Group's AIR MILES Canada; its database contains more than 600 million items of data for a customer population numbering millions. Similarly, AT&T's True Rewards loyalty program, administered by the direct marketing agency Bronner Schlosberg Humphrey through its Strategic Interactive Group, claims more than 30 million active customer accounts.

Data warehousing firms such as Acxiom enjoy similar advantages. Having recently acquired mailing list market leader Direct and electronic phone directory start-up ProCD, Acxiom possesses a wealth of raw data and has begun to mine it strenuously to serve marketers in a variety of industries.

Firms like these would, however, come up against one distinct disadvantage in the infomediary role. Though they have access to masses of transaction data pertaining to numerous products and services, they have limited brand presence in consumer markets—sometimes none at all. Where they are known, consumers normally have the opposite of an emotional bond with them; many loathe credit reporting agencies and are deeply suspicious of database marketers.

With such a reputation, database players are unlikely to be able to establish infomediary businesses on their own. Instead, they would have to form partnerships with companies that could bring consumer-friendly brands to "front" relationships with customers. Whether such a strategy is viable remains to be seen.

Media Players

Last but not least are the media companies that aggregate audiences around content categories to market them to vendors for advertising purposes. Firms such as Time Warner, News Corporation, and General Electric's NBC in traditional media, as well as America Online, Yahoo!, and clnet in new media, could in theory develop their existing mass audience relationships into individual customer preference profiles. This would clearly represent less of a stretch for AOL than for Time Warner. Nonetheless, such an approach would mean shifting the focus of the business from content origination and packaging to customer analysis and insight, so it is unlikely to come about other than through strategic alliances.

Among existing media players, the most probable winners are firms that combine several sets of characteristics: the brand presence of the fiduciaries, the emotional bond and transaction intensity of the retailers, and the customer information, access to transactions, and analytical methodologies of the purchasing brokers and database players. Companies such as Intuit, maker of Quicken software, and Charles Schwab, with its online extension eSchwab, might be excellent candidates. Such firms have substantial brand equity; customers view them as reliable and trust them with sensitive financial information.

What is likely to happen is that existing players will form alliances to operate infomediary businesses. Joint ventures could bring together the assets of established players with the organizational capabilities of network-based traffic aggregators. An early example is the recently announced tie-up between Intuit and Yahoo!; one might speculate on similar pairings such as Amex and clnet, Nordstrom and MSN, or Cendant (CUC/HFS) and AOL.

Whether firms lacking well-established brand franchises can play this game is a moot point. New entrants capable of developing strong in-category brand recognition could conceivably build levels of trust that are transferable to a broader infomediary role.

The business opportunities and challenges implied by the infomediary role go to the core of a firm's existing businesses. Today's corporate world is far too cavalier about customer information. While the transformation we describe may take years to come about, companies seeking to turn it to their advantage must act now. Building new skills and mindsets takes time, and raising levels of trust among consumers is a slow process.

Senior executives who wish to alert their management teams to these issues can find out where their company currently stands by asking two critical questions:

- Would my customers trust me to act as a custodian of their most sensitive information?

- Is my company able to extract the maximum economic value from the customer information available today?

Unless the answer to both questions is a resounding "yes," there is no time to waste in developing a plan of action. If senior management does not get personally involved in understanding the possible implications of the rise of infomediaries and move smartly to reposition the business, the information and profits that are flowing freely today will almost certainly be at risk tomorrow.

The McKinsey Quarterly, 1997 Number 4, pp. 54–70. Reprinted with permission of McKinsey & Company.

Note

1. This point is argued in more detail in "The coming battle for customer information," *Harvard Business Review*, January–February 1997; reprinted in *The McKinsey Quarterly*, 1997 Number 3, pp. 64–76.

15

Theory in Action

Price Strategy: Time to Choose Your Weapons

ROBERT G. DOCTERS

When it comes to battling new competitors and protecting their margins, large, established companies tend to use the same arsenal of strategies. They cut costs, introduce new products, diversify their offerings, and accelerate their speed to market. But all too often, corporate strategists overlook one of their best weapons: improved pricing strategies.

Although most companies view price decisions as important, requiring senior-level attention or approval, they often make these decisions purely on a tactical basis or in response to competitor initiatives. The typical response is, "Let's reduce the price of Product X by 15% to meet competition, but let's see if we can make it up with an increase in Product Y."

This response is sometimes sufficient, but on other occasions may not be enough to deter the competitor and often results in lower sales of Product Y. For instance, one U.S. airline with an east-west route structure found itself under attack on a key route from Delta Airlines, which has a north-south route structure. The defending east-west airline found reactive price reductions useless because Delta was using spare capacity on the contested route and so could lower its prices much further. It took a counterattack of price reductions on some of Delta's north-south routes to ward off further price drops.

Instead, price strategy for leading firms should be more than a rapid response to market conditions. It should reflect fundamental pricing strategy, market segmentation and elasticities, costs, competitor understanding, and executional capabilities.

Companies' abilities to make the best price decisions and to execute them—their pricing capabilities—often fall short of best practice.

To achieve the kind of pricing sophistication exhibited by such veteran competitors as airlines, commodity chemical manufacturers, or office equipment vendors you

Robert G. Docters is a principal at the New York office of Booz, Allen & Hamilton, Inc., management consultants. He focuses on price, segmentation, product, and new market development, with emphasis on telecommunications new entrants and incumbent carriers.

must have the requisite management skills, knowledge base, and information technology support. Managers with pricing responsibility in increasingly competitive markets need to consider whether they have in place the analysis and the corporate capabilities required to face new competition and preserve shareholder value. If not, now is the time to develop a pricing strategy and choose your pricing "weapons."

Fundamental Pricing Strategy

Pricing strategy is a crucial choice in deciding how to seize or defend market share. But price strategies differ markedly between entrants—whether start-ups, from related industries, or from overseas—and incumbents. That is because their objectives, economics, perceived customer value, competition, price history, regulatory/legal constraints, and customer ties are fundamentally different.

Of course, the choice of price level and structure are specific to each company, but there are some fairly typical pricing behaviors. Entrants and incumbents classically choose different pricing levels and structures (Figure 1).

Entrants can be start-ups such as Internet bookseller Amazon.com and catalogue florist Calyx & Corolla. They can come from related industries, such as local telephone exchange companies GTE and SNET entering the long distance telephone market. Or they can be from overseas, such as Taiwanese manufacturer Formosa muscling its way into the commodity plastics business.

Entrants face the problem of changing customer buying habits. Price level relates to the perceived value of a product or service, so entrants typically will set a superior price/performance offer before potential customers. Depending on the quality of the product or service, this price may be above or below that of the incumbent. With

---

FIGURE 1   **CLASSIC PRICE STRATEGIES**

Entrant price strategies	Incumbent price strategies
• Underprice incumbent • Target most attractive segments with low prices and loss-leaders • Simple pricing • Bundle with attacker's core products • Use of agent and 3rd party channels and price structures • Partnerships • Innovative product at appropriate price	• Make clear willingness to compete on price • Avoid price transparency • Retaliate against attacker's core market (e.g. Long Distance) • Leverage channels • Lock up customers with contracts • Bundling of services • Two-part price schemes • Loyalty programs • Free services to compensate for attacker's volume discount • Link price strategy to attacker's investment plan

THE MARKET

multiple competitors in a market, companies are likely to resort repeatedly to lower pricing as a way of gaining share. This is why, to no one's surprise, more competitors generally means lower prices.

To send the message, "I am offering you a lower price," entrants tend to favor a relatively simple, "transparent" price. Underpricing the incumbent works best when customers can compare product or service prices easily. But it becomes less effective the more complex the purchase. Complexity and hidden price elements are usually not good tactics because they force customers to work to understand the entrant's price advantage.

For instance, in the long-distance telephone service market, larger corporate users' service tariffs run hundreds of pages and depend on dozens of elements such as usage, geography, installations, and features. Consequently, direct "apples to apples" price comparison is difficult. This is one reason why price is a less effective tool for capturing large business customers than for winning smaller business and consumer accounts. That is why MCI and Sprint offer greater price discounts, relative to AT&T, for long distance service in the small business market than they do for heavier users.

In contrast, customer inertia and conservatism help incumbents. To avoid the effort and perceived risk in changing suppliers, or to avoid a proliferation of suppliers, customers will often allow incumbent suppliers a material price premium. For example, as part of its quality programs, at one point, a leading office equipment manufacturer explicitly allowed AT&T up to a 15% price premium over MCI and others before it would switch telecommunications provider.

When customers are not willing to grant incumbent vendors a price premium explicitly, the real price level is often masked through a complex price structure. Unless they have a monopoly, incumbents have a strong incentive to make it difficult for customers to compare prices directly. For instance, consumer electronics manufacturers such as Sony vary their model numbers among retailers so that consumers cannot be sure they are comparing the same model. Similarly, in the commodity chemicals business, buyers are highly sensitive to price. As a result, companies make sure that list prices have very little to do with actual net prices paid, reducing price transparency.

Beside avoiding price transparency, market leaders have strong economic incentives to favor more complex, two-part pricing. The economist Walter Oi pointed this out in his classic analysis of pricing at Disneyland, which charges both a significant entrance fee *and* a small charge for rides once inside. Oi demonstrated that by charging marginal costs for rides and a material entrance fee, Disney (or any entity with substantial market share) ends up with greater profitability than charging only the usage fees for rides.

This is because a two-part charge effectively taps the "consumer surplus," that is, the amount of money *greater than the market price* that high-need segments would pay for a good *if* they did not benefit from sellers' desire to capture lower-need consumers also (generally shown on supply and demand charts as the triangle above the market price). In other words: You can get more revenue with two-part tariffs than with a single price if you have market power.

Market leaders can and do make use of this economic principle by charging two-part fees. For instance, local telephone companies charge a significant fixed monthly charge and per-minute charges, in addition. Car rental companies obtain mileage charges plus daily rental rates. Warehouse clubs such as SAM's charge membership fees, plus the discounted price.

The less market power a company has, the less it can obstruct the process of price comparisons—and so must typically offer simpler pricing. Most retailers cannot afford to seek membership fees. In the highly competitive residential long-distance market there are relatively few fixed monthly charges. Hence Sprint's 10-cents-a-minute pricing advertisements.

Finally, even the strongest incumbents in some markets are entrants in others. No company is uniformly strong in all regions in which it operates. Differences in market share and power across geographies is an obstacle to effective global pricing strategy. Therefore the price structure should vary to reflect these differences—in some cases an incumbent strategy is appropriate, in others the company should view itself as an entrant.

Market Segmentation and Elasticities

Companies also segment markets to earn better margins. The best segmentation comes from an understanding of what drives the differences within a market. These differences usually have an impact on customers' sense of value, purchase behavior, and willingness to pay.

Take the data communications market and specifically the multiplexer, a device for combining and separating data streams. One study by Booz, Allen & Hamilton showed that there were five major customer segments in this market during 1990–1995. The selling environment, preferred price structures, and appropriate price tools also differed among customer segments. Most important, these segments paid up to 30% more or less for the same product.

One reason that prices varied stemmed from differences in customers' missions. In some cases, the mission was to reduce costs, so they were very sensitive to price tags. In other cases, their mission was to improve computer support to business units, so they were less focused on the price and more on the operational capabilities being created. Thus it was highly profitable for multiplexer manufacturers to price (and package) their products differently for these segments. Any attempt to price uniformly could only mean losing share or forgoing profits.

Over time, many industries will see segmentation become increasingly important as competition heats up. For instance, in the airline industry, pricing has undergone significant evolution from 1978 to the present. Airlines have become masters of segmentation. Pricing, which was once uniform, now varies by city, route, time of day, and by passenger.

To fully capture the value their markets have to offer, companies must understand price elasticities either in aggregate or, better yet, by segment. Then they must trace through what price offers the best total margin. Numerous case studies in consumer goods, capital equipment, and services have shown that higher prices often do not maximize margins. For instance, at various times, lower prices in long distance telephone charges and lower prices for computer memory have resulted in increased total margins for industry participants, as volume increases far offset margin reductions. Often, it's easier to understand price elasticities and determine the optimum price by segment, because you can better understand the price dynamics and potential discontinuities in the segment.

Costs

Costs should not single-handedly determine prices, but they do play a role. Depending on the industry, different levels of cost detail are needed. For instance:

- In utilities, where regulations limit pricing flexibility, knowing overall cost levels may be enough.

- In more competitive industries (e.g., consumer non-durables), costs must be known at the product level.

- In the most competitive industries, costs must be known *by customer and by deal.*

For industrial goods and services, many sales will be at incremental cost ("mill fill"), with only the rush-order or the best customers providing real profits. For example, in the commodity plastics business—Styrofoam plates, shopping bags, and wraps—most large orders are at cost, with only geographically desirable deliverables or innovative products offering solid margins.

Competitor Understanding

Competitors' costs structures, timing, and objectives must be understood and exploited. New entrants have different vulnerabilities than incumbents. The stock market, for instance, has evaluated new telecommunications ventures by market share rather than immediate profitability. On the other hand, incumbents typically must deliver quarterly earnings per share or their share price suffers. This means that new entrants such as Netscape can sacrifice margin for volume and be rewarded, while incumbents such as Digital Equipment/Alta Vista must deliver quarterly earnings.

Understanding this difference is key to considering how to price products or services. For instance, in the New York City area, the alternative data carrier Teleport Communications Group found financing based on its ability to undercut New York Telephone's high rates for service within distances of five miles or less. After Teleport built its network, New York Telephone lowered its prices for these distances, but then raised prices for distances beyond five miles to compensate. Although this was not good news for Teleport, it was not enough to deter the company from its growth objectives. Teleport moved to capture a share of the beyond-five miles market by extending its network to capitalize on the new New York Telephone rates. Eventually, New York Telephone reluctantly lowered its overall rates, but by then it was too late: A competitor had gained a foothold in the market. Preventative action had come too late.

Executional Capabilities

Finally, managers must become familiar with the wide suite of pricing options. (A partial list of pricing tactics is shown in Figure 2.) That means not just understanding which option is ideally suited for the objective but also the *operational risks* of each tool.

Discounts carry risks. For instance, a few years ago a major cigarette manufacturer offered a significant price break to its wholesalers. But it failed to structure the new price to pass savings to end users. As a result, the wholesalers got a one-time windfall, end users saw no change in price, and the manufacturer failed to win any new market share.

Information technology capabilities are crucial in some markets. The right I/T capabilities cannot only help improve the quality of customer service that supports premium pricing, but also help generate segmentation and price changes. But for a company to push its pricing strategy beyond its I/T capabilities can be counterproductive. For instance, a leading long distance company unintentionally sent almost one million checks, designed to induce long distance users to change vendors, to its *own* customers—needlessly costing it $30 million.

FIGURE 2	EXAMPLES OF PRICING TACTICS

TOOL	OBJECTIVE	PRICE STRUCTURE
• Cumulative discounts • Cross-product discounts	• Decrease customer shopping around/churn • Induce trial for existing customer base	• Change your volume discounts into cumulative discounts • Create discounts for new products when bought with existing ones
• Resale price levels	• Reduce price negotiation at the point of sale (e.g. cars, tires)	• Reduce the spread between manufacturer's suggested retail price and wholesale price
• Distributor exclusivity	• Increase distribution attention to your product (e.g. building products, wholesalers)	• Explicitly tie wholesale discounts to specific activities such as exclusive distribution
• Wholesaler discounts	• Reduce harmful product brokerage	• Narrow the quantity discount and increase functional discounts for specific activities (such as providing a showroom)
• Segment-based pricing	• Realize higher price in a non-price sensitive segment	• Design discount structure as customers self-select based on segment requirements
• Loss leaders	• Avoid new entrants in your markets	• Price to pre-empt up-front profits (loss leaders)
• Signaling	• Discourage competitors from discounts	• Signal that you will retaliate after XX% discount below your price.
• Bundling	• Leverage existing market position or channels	• Price multiple products together perhaps with bundle discounts

In summary, when handled correctly, price is a powerful tool to help combat new competitors and preserve margins. But price level must reflect the relative position of the product or service being priced—a key distinction being that between new entrants and incumbents. Prices will vary dramatically by segment; if not, you probably don't have a good segmentation in place. Price structure must reflect your objectives and capability to execute a price strategy. To ignore the power of improved pricing is to forgo one of the most powerful tools available to management.

16

Good-Bye to Fixed Pricing?

*How electronic commerce could create
the most efficient market of them all*

AMY E. CORTESE, WITH MARCIA STEPANEK

*There is a revolution brewing in pricing that promises to profoundly alter the way goods
are marketed and sold. In the future, marketers will offer special deals—tailored specifically for the consumer, just for the moment—on everything from theater to tickets to
blank loans to camcorders. The Internet, corporate networks, and wireless setups are
linking people, machines, and companies around the globe. This is enabling buyers to
quick and easily compare products and prices, putting them in a better bargaining position. At the same time, the technology allows seller to collect detailed data about customers' buying habits so they can tailor their products and prices. As buyers and sellers
do battle in the electornic world, the struggle should result in price that more closely collect their true market value.*

Coca-Cola Co. has a bold idea: Why should the price of a can of Coke be the same
all the time? Would people pay more for a cola fix on a sweltering summer day
than they would on a cold, rainy one? The beverage giant may soon find out when it
begins experimenting with "smart" vending machines that hook up to Coke's internal
computer network, letting the company monitor inventory in distant locales—and
change prices on the fly.

Sure, consumers might balk if Coke's prices were suddenly raised. But they also
might be persuaded to buy a cold soda on a chilly day if the vending machine flashed a
special promotion, say 20 cents off—the digital equivalent of the blue-light special.
Says Sameer Dholarka, director of pricing solutions for Austin-based software maker
Trilogy Systems: "List pricing is basically irrelevant."

Forget sticker prices. Forget sales clerks, too. There's a revolution brewing in
pricing that promises to profoundly alter the way goods are marketed and sold. In the
future, marketers will offer special deals—tailored just for you, just for the moment—
on everything from theater tickets to bank loans to camcorders.

Business Week; *New York, May 4, 1998*

Behind this sweeping change is the wiring of the economy. The Internet, corporate networks, and wireless setups are linking people, machines, and companies around the globe—and connecting sellers and buyers as never before. This is enabling buyers to quickly and easily compare products and prices, putting them in a better bargaining position. At the same time, the technology allows sellers to collect detailed data about customers' buying habits, preferences—even spending limits—so they can tailor their products and prices. This raises hopes of a more efficient marketplace.

Today, the first signs of this new fluid pricing can be found mostly on the Internet. Online auctions allow cybershoppers to bid on everything from collectibles to treadmills. Electronic exchanges, on the other hand, act as middlemen, representing a group of sellers of one type of product or service—say, long-distance service—that is matched with buyers.

The pricing revolution, though, goes beyond the Net. Companies also are creating private networks, or "extranets," that link them with their suppliers and customers. These systems make it possible to get a precise handle on inventory, costs, and demand at any given moment—and adjust prices instantly. In the past, there was a significant cost associated with changing prices, known as the "menu cost." For a company with a large product line, it could take months for price adjustments to filter down to distributors, retailers, and salespeople. Streamlined networks reduce menu cost and time to near zero.

This will clearly benefit consumers. Already, many are finding bargains at the hundreds of online auction sites that have cropped up. And on the Net, it's a cinch to check out product information and compare prices—thanks to a growing army of shopping helpers called "bots." That, says Erik Brynjolfsson, a management-science professor at Massachusetts Institute of Technology, "shifts bargaining power to consumers."

But that doesn't mean sellers get a raw deal. Businesses can gather more detailed information than ever before about their customers and run it through powerful database systems to glean insights into buying behavior. While the concept of point-of-sale promotions, such as Coke's, is not new, in a wired world, it takes on a whole new dimension. Suddenly, marketers can communicate directly with prospective buyers, offering them targeted promotions on an individual basis. Says Yanni Bakos, a visiting professor at MIT's Sloan School of Management: "It's like an arms race, where you give a more powerful weapon to both sides."

As buyers and sellers do battle in the electronic world, the struggle should result in prices that more closely reflect their true market value. "The future of electronic commerce is an implicit one-to-one negotiation between buyer and seller," says Jerry Kaplan, founder of Onsale Inc., a Net auction site. "You will get an individual spot price on everything."

The notion of fixed costs is a relatively recent development. A couple of hundred years ago, when a person went to the cobbler to order a pair of shoes, they negotiated the price face-to-face. It wasn't until the arrival of railroads and canal systems, which allowed products to be distributed widely, that uniform prices came into being.

The Net brings us full circle. "We've suddenly made the interaction cost so cheap, there's no pragmatic reason not to have competitive bidding on everything," says Stuart I. Feldman, director of IBM's Institute for Advanced Commerce based in

Hawthorne, N.Y. Someday, you might haggle over the price of just about anything, the way you would negotiate the price of a carpet in a Turkish bazaar. Except it's likely to take place on an electronic exchange, and it may be a computer bidding against another computer on your behalf.

Win-Win. For a preview of what's to come, just look to the financial markets. Take the NASDAQ stock market, or Instinet's even more automated system, after which many Net entrepreneurs are modeling their businesses. NASDAQ, for example, uses a system of dealers, or market makers, who trade shares of stock for brokers or individuals. The dealers are linked by an electronic network that matches buy orders with sell orders, arriving at the value of a stock for that moment in time.

Like NASDAQ dealers, the new Internet market makers must set up mechanisms for clearing transactions and for making sure that both buyers and sellers are satisfied. As electronic exchanges are established to trade everything from advertising space to spare parts, the true market value of products will emerge. "All of this brings you closer and closer to the efficient market," says Robert MacAvoy, president of Eastman Consulting in Stamford, Conn.

The most widely used form of this today is online auctions. In the world of virtual gavels, Kaplan's Onsale is the kingpin. The Web site runs seven live auctions a week where people outbid one another for computer gear, electronics equipment, even steaks. Onsale buys surplus or distressed goods from companies at fire-sale prices so they can weather low bids. And customers love it. Grant Crowley, president of Crowley's Yacht Yard Inc. in Chicago, bought 14 old-model desktop PCs for his business via Onsale. He figures he saved 40% over what he would have paid in a store. "It's a great deal for people in small businesses like mine," Crowley says.

So far, the lure of a bargain has proved powerful: More than 4 million bids have been placed since Onsale opened its doors three years ago. It sold $115 million worth of goods last year, up nearly 300% from 1996. "Suddenly, consumers are active participants in price-setting," says Onsale founder Kaplan. "It's infinite economic democracy."

For every couple dozen online auctions, though, there is an entrepreneur applying the new Net economics in ways that will ultimately transform entire industries—from telecommunications to energy. These companies are setting up exchanges for trading things such as phone minutes, gas supplies, and electronic components, a market Forrester Research projects will grow to $52 billion by 2002. Their approach is such a departure from the past that analyst Vernon Keenan of Zona Research Inc. says they represent the "third wave" of commerce on the Net—companies that are moving beyond simple marketing and online order-taking to creating entirely new electronic marketplaces.

Equal Footing. Who are these trailblazers? Some are established companies, while others are born of the Net. But they all share a radical new vision of electronic commerce. "This is the model of the future," says Eric Baty, business-information manager at Southern California Gas Co.

You might not think of a stodgy utility as being in the vanguard of cyberspace, but that's exactly where Southern California Gas is. A couple of years ago, it saw an opportunity in the dovetailing of two sweeping trends—the deregulation of the energy industry, which lets customers shop for energy suppliers the way they shop for long-distance phone service, and the rise of the Web. So, last fall, it launched Energy Marketplace, a Web-based exchange that lets customers shop for the best gas prices.

The system has something for everyone. Small and midsize gas providers list their prices on the exchange. That lowers their marketing costs and gives them access to a broader market—putting them on equal footing with big energy suppliers. Customers, mostly businesses, save money by shopping for the best price, or locking in long-term deals when prices are low. And Southern California Gas, as a distributor, increases its volume of business and collects a subscription fee from gas providers that use the exchange. In coming months, SoCalGas will offer residential customers the same opportunity and expand the service to include electricity.

Does it work? Using Energy Marketplace, Sumiden Wire Products Corp. in Stockton, Calif., found a new supplier, Intermarket Trading Co., and now saves $500 a month—about 20% of its $3,000 a month energy bill. "They're cheaper than the other guys," says Wayne Manna, plant manager at Sumiden. "It's much simpler and easier than before."

Energy Marketplace is typical of the early electronic bazaars. Like the pork bellies or wheat traded in the financial markets, the first goods to be bartered in the new electronic markets are commodities. Whether No. 2 steel or No. 2 pencils, price—not features or how something looks, feels, or fits—is the determining factor in a sale. And if the commodity happens to be perishable—such as airline seats, oranges, or electricity—the Net is even more compelling: Suppliers have to get rid of their inventory fast or lose the sale.

Alex Mashinsky sees similar qualities in long-distance phone minutes. A former commodities trader, Mashinsky's New York-based ArbiNet (short for Arbitrage Networks) is building an exchange for routing phone calls over the lowest-cost networks—on the fly.

Most telecommunications carriers have built massive networks to handle peak loads. The problem is, much of the capacity goes unused. AT&T, for example, typically uses just 20% of its global network capacity. In a fiercely competitive market that has seen margins erode, "that excess capacity is becoming extremely sensitive," says Mashinsky. "It can be the difference between making money and losing money." ArbiNet's exchange lets carriers optimize their capacity by accepting lower-cost calls over their networks during off-peak hours. There are other companies that broker long-distance minutes. But ArbiNet is the only one attempting it in real time.

The ArbiNet Clearing Network works this way: Network carriers, such as AT&T, supply information about their network availability and price at a given time. Carrier customers send calls through ArbiNet's clearinghouse—say, a phone call from New York to Hong Kong that must travel over secure lines. ArbiNet's powerful computers and phone switches match the request with the lowest-cost carrier for that particular call, check to make sure the capacity is in fact available, and route the call—all in a millisecond. "We arbitrage the capacity available at any given time," says Mashinsky.

ArbiNet's focus today is on the wholesale, or carrier-to-carrier, business. But Mashinsky thinks that two years from now, the market will be ripe for consumers. A "smart" phone, for example, could automatically check for the lowest carrier on each call that is placed. Such a scenario could be unnerving to the giant phone companies.

PLAYING THE PRICE IS RIGHT

Internet bidding exchanges are flourishing for a wide array of products—and more are sure to come

Aucnet (aucnet.com)

Wholesalers flock to this used-car auction. A big draw: AucNet's rating system, which helps buyers judge the quality of the cars

Narrowline.Com (narrowline.com)

An electronic exchange for Net advertising that brings together media buyers with Web sites looking to sell available ad space

Eworldauction (eworldauction.com)

This site holds monthly online auctions of old books, maps, and medieval manuscripts

Netmarket (netmarket.com)

For $69 a year, subscribers to Cendant's Web site can shop for a wide range of products—autos, books, music, and more—at the guaranteed lowest price. If Netmarket's search agent finds a lower price elsewhere, it will instantly drop its price

Energymarket (energymarket.com)

This exchange, launched last fall by Southern California Gas, lets suppliers of natural gas-and soon, electricity-compete for the business of big corporate energy users

Priceline (priceline.com)

Mortgages, cars, and airline tickets: Name your price and terms—and Priceline, a new Web service, will try to find you a willing seller

"The big carriers don't want to do this," says Mashinsky. "It would undercut their prices."

Indeed, big businesses are sensitive about falling prices. Some entrenched companies already are fighting the idea of electronic markets that make it easy for customers to compare products and prices. Houston-based energy giant Enron Corp., for example, last month filed suit against SoCalGas and its Energy Marketplace. Enron, which plans to enter the California market, alleges that Energy Marketplace unfairly favors local suppliers that are better known. SoCalGas calls the suit a blocking tactic.

Beyond Surplus.   Other big players are embracing the Net, but half-heartedly—using it to dispose of surplus goods while protecting margins on their core products. Not that surplus inventory is anything to sneeze at. Chicago-based FastParts Inc. and FairMarket Inc. in Woburn, Mass., operate thriving exchanges where computer electronics companies swap excess parts. All told, U.S. industries generate some $18 billion in excess inventory a year—around 10% of all finished goods, says Anne Perlman, CEO of Moai Technologies Inc., a Net startup that makes software for creating online bartering sites. "Excess and obsolete equipment is a big and painful problem," she says.

Or a huge opportunity. Perlman knows firsthand about surplus goods. Before joining Moai, she ran Tandem Computer Inc.'s personal computer business. When Intel Corp.'s 386 microprocessor came out, she found herself with a boatload of earlier-generation 286 chips that were instantly obsolete. Afraid that she might have to write off the inventory as a loss, Perlman made some calls and found a customer willing to buy the stock—though she was left with the nagging feeling that she could have gotten a better price. Now, at Moai, along with co-founders Deva Hazarika and Frank Kang, she sells a $100,000-plus package to companies that want to run their own auctions to generate revenue from aging merchandise.

Most of the Net pioneers had to build their own systems—a time-consuming and costly task. The availability of off-the-shelf software packages from Moai and others should help jump-start more electronic exchanges.

"Third Wave."   That could pave the way for fluid pricing to reach beyond commodity products and surplus goods to popular, even premium-priced items. Electronic markets could be just as effective selling unique items, such as a Van Gogh painting or a company's core product line. "The move away from surplus goods to primary goods will be the real thrust of the third wave," says Zona's Keenan.

There's just one snag: When anyone on the Net can easily compare prices and features, some high-margin products could fall in price. And a strong brand name alone may not be enough to make a premium price tag stick. Some branded products may even prove to be interchangeable. You might not trust your phone service to an outfit you have never heard of on the basis of price alone. But you might be willing to swap among AT&T, MCI, or Sprint for a better deal. And do you really care if your credit card is from MasterCard or Visa? "There's a commoditization at the top level of brands," contends Jay Walker, CEO of Priceline, a new Web service that lets consumers name their price.

One way companies can respond is by cooking up creative ploys to distinguish their products. That could include personalizing products or offering loyalty programs that reward frequent customers. "Inventiveness in marketing is going to be very important in this world where people can go out and compete on price," says IBM's Feldman. That's happening in online brokerage services, a cutthroat market. Thanks to Internet brokers, trading fees are already rock-bottom. Now, companies such as E*trade are mulling loyalty programs that reward frequent traders.

There are other ways to sidestep the effects of the ultra-efficient Net market. Just look at the airline industry. It was one of the first industries to go online, starting with American Airlines Inc.'s Sabre automated-reservation system in the 1960s. When other airlines followed suit, American introduced the frequent-flier program to keep customers loyal.

Three decades after Sabre, airlines still manage to get many passengers to pay rich fares. The secret: knowing whom to gouge—in this case, the business customer who has to get somewhere and is less price-sensitive. Airlines also have perfected the science of yield management, concocting complicated pricing schemes that defy comparison. The price for an airline seat can change several times an hour, making it virtually certain that the person sitting next to you paid a different fare. "Airlines are using the Internet to raise the average price of a fare," says Ken Orton, CEO of Preview Travel, an online ticketing site.

Now, airlines are tapping into the Net—but mainly as a way to sell unfilled seats. They routinely send out E-mail alerts of last-minute fare specials. And several major

DIARY OF A DIGITAL SALE

FastParts matches buyers and sellers of computer electronics

1. A COMPUTER MAKER finds itself with a shortage of a memory chip needed to assemble a circuit board. It needs to buy 20,000 chips—fast.

2. A PURCHASING EXEC logs on to FastParts, an Internet trading exchange, and enters information about the chip he's seeking. The system returns a list of available lots, with price, quantity, and other details. One lot looks like it fits the bill: 20,000 of the needed chips are available at 36 cents a piece.

3. THE BUYER puts in a lower bid: 29 cents apiece. The supplier and other buyers interested in the same part are notified of the bid by E-mail.

4. THE SELLER lowers the price to 33 cents. The computer maker is alerted by E-mail. It's a good price, and he accepts.

5. FASTPARTS confirms the details of the sale, and the payment is held in a special escrow bank account. Once the buyer receives the chips, he has five days to inspect and accept them. After five days, the payment is released to the seller.

---

airlines have signed up with Priceline, which lets consumers specify when and where they want to travel, and name their price. Priceline then forwards the bids to participating airlines, which can choose to accept the request or not. The company makes its money on the spread between the bid and the lower airline price. "It empowers the buyer," says Walker, "but also the seller. They can plug in demand to empty flights."

As long as Priceline is clearly targeted at the leisure—not the business—traveler, airlines are willing to go along. "It's not for frequent fliers but to get people out of cars without affecting the airlines' retail price structure," says Walker.

In the end, such tactics may simply delay the inevitable march of the Internet. And the truth is, Net-based markets may not be such a bad thing for sellers. They produce a price that fairly reflects demand. Some companies may be surprised by the results.

Look at AucNet, an online auction for used cars. Dealers and wholesalers flock to AucNet's Web site to buy and sell some 6,000 cars a month. Surprisingly, sellers fetch more for their used cars than they might on a physical lot. That's partly because of the larger audience they get on the Net. But dealers also have come to trust the quality ratings that AucNet inspectors assign to each car after physically examining them, and they are willing to pay more for that seal of approval. Moai's Perlman has seen similar results in other online marketplaces. Most of the time, she says, "the market will bid a better price than the vendor was expecting."

Or at least, the right price. So why fight the perfect market?

17

The Real Impact of Internet Advertising

CAROLINE CARTELLIERI
ANDREW J. PARSONS
VARSHA RAO
MICHAEL P. ZEISSER

Will the Internet have as big an impact on advertising as radio and television did? Most marketing executives say no. Here's why they are wrong.

How much impact is the Internet really having on advertising and marketing? Is it just another emerging niche medium with some peculiar creative capabilities and constraints? Or might it transform consumer marketing in the same way that network television revolutionized consumer culture and commercial practice four or five decades ago?

Interviews with marketers reveal that few believe the Internet will change their approach to advertising. Most see it as little more than a complement to traditional marketing practices, and don't expect it to reduce expenditure on broadcast and print media or change the form, pricing, or delivery of advertisements. Their view is probably a reaction to the early hype about the Internet and the World Wide Web, which created unrealistic short-term expectations among marketers and frustration with the inadequacies of the delivery technologies among consumers.

We take a contrary view. We believe that Internet advertising will account for a growing proportion of overall advertising expenditure. Moreover, advertising—and marketing in general—will adopt practices first developed or deployed on the Internet. As the technology improves, the impact of Internet advertising will increase and become easier to measure, and the gap between this new precise, interactive marketing capability and conventional "fuzzy" passive media will widen. Over the next few

Caroline Cartellieri and **Varsha Rao** are consultants, **Andrew Parsons** is a director, and **Michael Zeisser** is a principal in McKinsey's New York office. Copyright© 1997 McKinsey & Company. All rights reserved.

We would like to acknowledge the contributions of Eric Simonson, Inder Soni, and John Leibovitz to this article.

years, advertising agencies and consumer marketers will be under pressure to change their whole approach to marketing communications.

Marketers will become more accountable for their results, and they will pay more attention to building a total customer relationship. Offering consumers value in return for information will become vital in eliciting their preferences, which in turn will be critical to customizing advertising.[1] And companies' entire marketing organizations will be progressively redesigned to reflect interactions with consumers on the Internet.

For ad agencies, fees based on results will become standard. The economics of Internet advertising are likely to make current business models obsolete. New capabilities will be required as creative production speeds up and becomes more closely integrated with marketing activity. A deep understanding of enabling technologies will become a prerequisite for fresh forms of advertising.

Our views on the evolution of Internet advertising and its impact on traditional marketing may seem provocative to some, premature to others. But the intriguing marketing experiments taking place on and off the Internet suggest it is time for consumer marketers to begin looking to networks for new ways of thinking about the marketing theories and approaches on which they have long relied—and to begin capturing the lessons Internet advertising holds for all their advertising practices, online and conventional.

Caution: Changes Ahead

Looking at today's Internet advertising to predict what tomorrow will bring is about as helpful as using a rear-view mirror to watch the road ahead. But a point of view about what online advertising will look like in three to five years' time can and should influence current management decisions about how to invest marketing communication dollars on the Internet. A number of fundamental forces are currently reshaping Internet advertising: the near-daily emergence of new technologies that improve measurement, targeting, and data interpretation; the strenuous efforts of primarily entrepreneurial marketers to make business use of the Web; and the establishment of patterns in consumers' use of these new interactive networks. Thanks to the impact of these forces, tomorrow's ads will differ from today's in the **shape** they take, in the **metrics** available for gauging their effectiveness, and in the **pricing** structure that governs their purchase and sale.

New Shapes

The first and most obvious change in advertising will be in what consumers see on their screens. Ads are likely to change in terms of their **content,** the type of **customization** they employ, and their **delivery** to the consumer.

Content.　Aspirations to transcend today's form of Internet advertising will first be realized in the content of ads. The development of new technologies such as virtual reality and chat, coupled with consumers' growing preference for material that is directly valuable to them, is driving the emergence of new forms of content. Three main types are on the horizon: **experiential, transaction-oriented,** and **sponsored content.**

Experiential content will allow consumers to "experience" the ownership of a product, service, or brand. The best current examples let the user test out a product. Sharp's Web site offers a personal tour of the Zaurus personal digital assistant in which consumers can input calendar or address information exactly as they would if they used the product in real life. At The Gap's site, customers can "try on" outfits and mix and match separates from the current range. In the future, technologies such as virtual reality will make ads even more experiential: customers will feel as though they are test-driving a new car, or walking down the aisles of a grocery store.

Transaction-oriented content will invite consumers to make a purchase directly from an ad. Advertising content will become increasingly oriented toward transactions. Indeed, the Internet may already be changing consumers' buying behavior, particularly for considered purchases such as cars. Prospective car buyers who are looking for product information before making a decision can obtain more information more quickly through the Internet than by any other means currently available. Having done their research in advance, they are more ready to buy at the point when they actually encounter a manufacturer or seller.

The implication for marketers is simple: they need to make it possible for consumers to carry out transactions easily and seamlessly, or risk losing sales to competitors. Consider Casio, which uses Virtual Tag technology developed by First Virtual to enable customers to make purchases from an Internet banner ad. An Internet user can learn about Casio products, purchase a watch on line, and select the means of delivery without ever leaving the banner.

Sponsored content will blur the line between editorial matter and advertising. A lot of sponsored content already exists on the Internet—for example, Nissan sponsors weekly soccer tips on Parent Soup in association with the American Youth Soccer Association—but by and large it tends to resemble the "brought to you by ABC" model familiar from traditional media. The emergence of advanced forms of hybrid commercial—editorial content will be driven by consumers' ability to "tune out" straightforward commercial messages, be they banners, interstitials (ads that pop up while users wait for a requested Web page to appear), or standard forms of sponsorship, and by advertisers' desire to influence attitudes in more subtle ways.

By way of analogy, consider the growing use of product placement in films and television (James Bond drives a BMW Z3 in his latest movie) as marketers seek to make their offerings stand out from the clutter of ads and break through the cognitive filters that allow consumers to discount ordinary commercials. The network environment offers ample scope for hybrid content: entire sites can be funded and co-managed by advertisers (as with Procter & Gamble and ParentTime), while avatar technologies[2] bring advertisers into chat rooms. However, the issue of editorial independence and the possibility of consumer rejection or backlash may ultimately set limits on the pursuit of this approach.

Customization. Anyone who has been offered a credit card they already hold can appreciate the need for greater customization or "addressability" in mass-market advertising, and even in direct mail. Indeed, the level of response that advertisers receive largely depends on the accurate and timely targeting of messages, as do the number of transactions and the degree of loyalty that are generated.

The Internet is supposed to enable marketers at last to target their offers to that elusive "segment of one." Yet advertising on the Internet has so far been targeted mainly on the basis of editorial content, just as it is in traditional media. Part of the reason is technical, though the development of tracking software that allows ads to be delivered only to target audiences is overcoming this obstacle. Consumers' reticence has been a further barrier, but as Internet users grow more willing to provide information about themselves, two types of customized content will emerge.

First, content will be customized by means of **information inferred about users.** The Ultramatch technology recently launched by Infoseek, to take one example, makes it possible to target those Web users who are most likely to respond to a given ad. Based on neural networking technology, Ultramatch observes users' behavior when they put out queries and explore subjects, collecting the results in its database. Advertisers using the service can select individuals according to their interests and thus pitch their campaign to a receptive audience. Ultramatch also allows them to ascertain which individuals are responding to ads, and to move the ads to places where they will attract similar users.

Second, ads will be customized on the basis of **information voluntarily provided by users.** The key to making this approach work will be to overcome consumers' desire for privacy or anonymity by offering them rewards for personal details in the form of special information, discounts, or promotions. On ParentTime, for example, users who enter the ages of their children receive relevant care information as well as Pampers ads geared to those age groups. Experience suggests that consumers are willing to release information about themselves as long as they are the prime beneficiaries. Organizations such as etrust (an initiative sponsored by leading companies to develop electronic commerce) and the Internet Marketing Council take a similar view. The IMC requires marketers to provide a "giveaway" or discount before they can gain certification. This scheme is specifically designed to prevent information provided by consumers from being misused in e-mail.

Delivery.   The recent hype about "push" technology on the Internet might suggest that this will be the dominant vehicle for delivering advertising on the Web. We believe the reality will be more integrated, combining today's "pull" format Web sites with "push" technology such as PointCast to deliver ads to people according to their interests. Triggered banners (ads that appear when certain key words are mentioned) and interstitials are early examples that point the way. Consider how one automaker's ads are pushed to chatroom participants when the topic of cars comes up, or how a user waiting for content to be downloaded is sent an ad related to that content. Marketers must ask themselves a number of questions: What is the right balance? Where can push technology be exploited most effectively? How much push are users willing to take before they begin to tune out?

As online advertising develops, advertisers will discover that the Internet is the only medium that can deliver certain types of message, such as multisensory and interactive ads. These new forms will allow advertisers to achieve several objectives—some of them unattainable via conventional media—simultaneously (Figure 1). They are likely to make Internet advertising more important in the overall marketing mix as marketers capitalize on their unique capabilities. At the same time, our glimpse of the emerging future casts doubt on the merit of current heavy investments in big brand sites that require content to be "pulled," or in banner ads that—like most on the Internet today—merely replicate the forms of advertising that exist in the physical world.

FIGURE 1	INTERNET ADVERTISING OBJECTIVES

Shaping attitudes	One-way communication
	Build brand or product awareness
Delivering content	Detailed product or service information
	Communication is typically "pulled" by recipient
Soliciting response	Two-way communication
	Response can vary from click-through to information exchange to actual purchase
Enabling transaction	Two-way interaction
	Online sale
Encouraging retention	Continuous two-way interaction
	Customized for recipient

WHY THE INTERNET IS A BETTER AD VEHICLE THAN YOU THINK

The Internet has already become an important standalone advertising medium; moreover, many of the missing links it needs in order to achieve scale are now being forged.

It's already important . . .

The Web presents great advertising opportunities for marketers because of its continuing growth, its user demographics, its effectiveness, and its cost-competitiveness.

Growth in usage. The overall Web population is reaching critical mass. Recent surveys show there are 25 to 40 million adult Web users in the United States—between one-eighth and one-fifth of the population. Twenty-five million Americans use the Web at least once a week according to one source, and 8.4 million are daily users. The average user spends 8.6 hours a month on line.

Audience profile. The demographics of Internet users are broadening, but remain attractive. More women are now using the Internet: one survey puts the figure at 47 percent, another at 38 percent. In financial terms, 91 percent of those who used the Web in the past six months have household incomes above $60,000—almost double the average US household income of $31,000.

Marketers pursuing certain segments of the population are finding the Internet increasingly useful. For those interested in, say, American men aged 35 to 44 with incomes over $75,000, the Web can provide access to about 2 million—over 40 percent of the target demographic segment, and a critical mass in itself (Figure A).

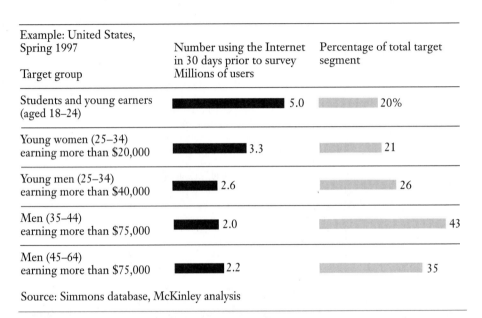

| FIGURE A | PENETRATION APPROACHES CRITICAL MASS |

Example: United States, Spring 1997 Target group	Number using the Internet in 30 days prior to survey Millions of users	Percentage of total target segment
Students and young earners (aged 18–24)	5.0	20%
Young women (25–34) earning more than $20,000	3.3	21
Young men (25–34) earning more than $40,000	2.6	26
Men (35–44) earning more than $75,000	2.0	43
Men (45–64) earning more than $75,000	2.2	35

Source: Simmons database, McKinley analysis

Higher effectiveness. Studies have shown that the Internet is reasonably good at achieving standard advertising objectives such as shaping attitudes. However, it also has capabilities that traditional media cannot match. Features that make the Internet a superior medium include its addressability, its interactivity, and its scope for customization. Advertisers can do things on the Internet that are impossible in traditional media: identify individual users, target and talk to them one at a time, and engage in a genuine two-way dialogue.

Competitive efficiency. In terms of advertising economics, the Internet can already compete with existing media, both in response as measured by click-throughs and in exposure as measured by CPM (Figure B).

Moreover, the Internet's economics look better and better the more precisely a target consumer segment is defined. The cost to an Internet advertiser of reaching families that earn over $70,000 and own a foreign car, for instance, can be less than a quarter the cost of using a specialty magazine such as *Car and Driver* (Figure C).

. . . and it's still improving

The major factors limiting the growth of Internet advertising are being addressed.

Measurement. Like traditional media, the Internet needs consistent metrics and auditing in order to gain broad acceptance from marketers. Both are emerging slowly, driven by old players such as Nielsen and new ones such as WebTrack.

FIGURE B   COMPETITIVENESS IN COST PER THOUSAND

	5	10	15	20	50	100	500+
Direct marketing							—
Web	————————————————						
Niche magazine				————————			
Newspaper			————————				
General magazine		———					
Network TV	———————						
Cable TV	———————————						
Radio	——						
Billboard	——						

FIGURE C   COMPETITIVENESS IN REACHING TARGET SEGMENT

Cost per thousand, $	Base cost	By demographic	
		Income above $70,000 with children ...	... and a foreign car
Car and Driver	79	440	720
New York Times	65	287	458
NBC Network News	8	117	217
Pathfinder (Internet)	22	133	176

Source: Interviews; Simmons database; Paul Kagan Associates; McKinley analysis

Pricing and placement standards. Advertisers and agencies cannot afford to produce a different ad and negotiate a different price for every site. Standards for size, position, content, and pricing are badly needed and are now being developed; an example is CASIE, the Coalition for Advertising Supported Information and Entertainment, a joint project of the Association of National Advertisers and the American Association of Advertising Agencies.

Emergence of placement networks. Unless they place their ads on one of the few highly trafficked sites, advertisers find it difficult to ensure that sufficient people see them. Responding to advertisers' need for scale, placement networks such as DoubleClick do the aggregating for them, making sure that a specified number of people will be exposed to their ads.

New Metrics

The Internet affords marketers an unprecedented opportunity to measure the effectiveness of their advertising and learn about their viewers. The capacity to measure impact sets the Internet apart from other media. Measurements available for television, for example, estimate the total size of an audience; what they don't do is tell an advertiser how many people actually saw an ad, or what impact it had. On the Internet, by contrast, marketers are able to track click-throughs, page views, and leads generated in close to real time. The result: measurements that are more precise and meaningful than anything available in traditional media.

The emergence of these new metrics will affect not only ads themselves, but also the way that marketers and agencies develop them. First, more precise measurements will yield better insights into the effectiveness of advertising spend. It will be easier to identify ads that don't work, and to find out why. Advertisers will also start to expect the content of ads to be renewed more frequently in response to audience reaction. A new product from Infoseek offers a hint of things to come. Copy Testing in a Box is a tool that combines the immediate feedback of the Internet with sophisticated targeting technology to allow marketers to refocus their Internet campaigns to the most responsive customer segments within a matter of days.

Second, advertisers will be able to assess the impact of their ads earlier in the spending cycle. As a result, they will have the flexibility to launch and roll out a campaign in such a way that it can be changed before most of the money is committed. This will affect the very process of creating Internet ads, and perhaps spur advertisers and agencies to devise new ways of organizing around it.

New Pricing

Whereas marketers tend to have fairly uniform objectives in traditional media, such as shaping attitudes in television or obtaining responses in direct mail, the Internet, as we have seen, allows them to pursue several different goals simultaneously. In the same way, the standard types of pricing used in traditional media, such as CPM (the cost of exposing a message to a thousand viewers of TV or readers of print), will give way on the Internet to pricing that varies as widely as the objectives of the ads themselves. Indeed, the technology can support several pricing mechanisms at once: pay per click-through, lead, transaction, dollar spend, or conventional CPM. This kind of variegated pricing is already appearing in the marketplace: P&G has pushed for pricing per click-through; CD Now pays Web sites commissions on the transactions they generate; and Destination Florida pays according to leads generated. Similarly, DoubleClick is introducing an advertising network, DoubleClick Direct, whose rates are based on results, and has already signed up clients including Alta Vista and GTE's Internet service.

Because of these factors, pricing for Internet advertising is likely to be multitiered, based on results, and tied to marketers' objectives. At least three pricing mechanisms will coexist: pricing by **exposure, response,** and **action** (Figure 2).

Pricing per exposure—for instance, via a rate card based on CPM—will prevail for ads placed on the Internet to generate awareness of a product or brand. Over time,

| FIGURE 2 | EMERGING INTERNET PRICING MODELS |

	Metrics
Pricing per exposure	Impression
	Unit of time spent
Pricing per response	Click-through
Pricing per action	Download
	Information exchange
	Transactions

this form of pricing should become more refined. As measurability and metering improve, advertisers will want to pay only for impressions on their target customers, while publishers will eagerly search for ways to extract premium exposure rates. The result is likely to be the establishment of an additional tier of "effective" CPM rates.

Pricing per response will establish itself as the standard for simple consumer responses such as click-through. Prices will vary according to the types of user a site attracts and how much advertisers are willing to pay for access to them.

Pricing per action is similar, but more elaborate. A site publisher might charge an advertiser more for a consumer who downloads a piece of software or provides some demographic information, say, than for one who merely clicks on a banner. We believe that the ability of Web publishers to charge advertisers for the true value they receive is likely to make the difference between profit and loss. The price for a lead generated, for instance, could reflect the prospect's potential lifetime value; if it did, sites would charge automotive OEMs and white goods manufacturers different prices for prospect leads. As a result, a fee per action or sales commission is likely to emerge as a major pricing mechanism for Internet advertising over time.

How quickly and how far these models take hold in the near term will depend on how risk is shared between marketers, agencies, and sites. Results-based pricing gives marketers the opportunity to shift some of the risk of failure to sites or agencies. Publishers and broadcasters in traditional media have usually been loath to take on this kind of risk. However, Internet publishers should find risk sharing attractive if it is appropriately priced, as it could boost the advertising revenues on which their success depends.

Pricing in general is fraught with issues. Will site publishers demand a degree of control over the creative execution of ads to ensure quality, for instance? We believe that the sharing of risk in Internet advertising will ultimately be determined by the prevailing balance of power, which will vary from advertiser to advertiser and site to site, and shift over time. Large, well-known, "safe" advertisers may be able to secure results-based pricing more easily than others, particularly at times when site publishers are struggling to make their economics work.

It will be in the best interests of marketers, site publishers, and even agencies to prevent the lowest common denominator from setting the industry's pricing standard. To settle for a simplistic, unsophisticated, "one size fits all" pricing scheme would mean leaving a lot of money on the table. The widespread acceptance of multi-tiered, performance-based pricing will make the Internet both distinctive and highly lucrative as an advertising medium.

The Spillover Effect

The changes now taking place in the shape, measurement, and pricing of advertising on the Internet may seem dramatic enough in themselves, but we believe they will have a much broader impact on marketing practices in general. This spillover effect will occur for four reasons.

First, new ways of advertising on line will inspire new creative approaches elsewhere. Second, the Internet will prompt marketers to reevaluate their use of traditional media. Third, Internet advertising will help marketers to improve their understanding of consumers' needs, preferences, and product usage. Finally, once marketers get a taste for the measurability of Internet ads and the tailored pricing it enables, their expectations of the effectiveness and measurability of other media will rise.

New Creative Approaches

The timeliness and direct tone of advertising on the Internet will increasingly inspire marketers operating in other media. Seeing the daily updates of information that the Web makes possible and the lengths to which online advertisers must go in order to keep users' interest (for instance, renewing banners weekly) may sharpen their appetite for replicating Internet practices on TV and in print.

The notion that creative approaches pioneered on the Web will spill over to more traditional media should surprise few. Historically, the emergence of new media has always prompted content changes in existing media. Consider how print changed after radio, and later television, arrived on the scene.

Fidelity Investments recently attempted to mimic the immediacy of the Internet in its television advertising. It refreshed its ads on a daily basis by incorporating current news headlines. However, the campaign met with mixed success, perhaps because it lacked a distinctive point of view.

Marketers' adoption of creative techniques pioneered on the Internet will grow as technologies like broadband, Web TV, and virtual reality begin to influence traditional media. Wink and Worldgate are developing technologies that allow viewers to "save" a commercial to watch later, or to obtain more detailed information. These technologies are in their early test stages on television.

The enormous creative flexibility offered by the Internet will increase pressure for more choices of delivery in traditional media. The (probably apocryphal) story of Helena Rubenstein asking to buy an extra three seconds for a 30-second spot to realize her creative vision suggests how we may start to question accepted standards and constraints in traditional media.

Marketers may also need to reexamine the theories that underpin their advertising practices. As we noted, online advertisers have found that banners must be renewed frequently if consumers are to keep clicking. Their experience defies the conventional wisdom in advertising that any ad must be seen at least four times to make an impression. On the Internet, greater impact can be achieved by showing a wider range of ads that are repeated less often. Insights like this cast doubt on the effectiveness of current television campaigns, most of which are still based on old ideas of frequency.

Reevaluating Media Investments

Everyone has heard the advertiser's lament: "I know 50 percent of my advertising is working; I just don't know which 50 percent." The greater measurability of Internet advertising will prompt marketers to reevaluate all their investments in media, especially in the addressable categories of print and direct marketing. Not only are response rates often higher in Internet advertising, but the cost of reaching target customers can be lower, with better information received in return. As a result, we may well see a migration of targeted marketing spending from direct mail and other traditional media to the Internet.

Consider a recent example. AT&T used the Internet to generate awareness of and shape attitudes toward its toll-free collect-call service, which is mainly targeted at 16- to 24-year-olds. The company had previously found this audience difficult to reach cost-effectively through print or broadcast media. The results of the online effort were excellent. Top-of-mind awareness increased by over 30 percent, and AT&T opted to replace its print advertising with an Internet campaign.

The traditional approach to customer response and lead generation has been to use ads in trade magazines and customer response or "bingo" cards. However, findings announced by one large publisher of trade titles indicate that more than two-thirds of bingo cards either go unanswered or are not responded to promptly because of the time it takes to qualify and manage leads. The study suggests that the Web is an excellent tool for generating quality leads and may even supersede bingo cards in time.

Migration of this kind will reallocate the slices of the advertising pie. Interviews we conducted with marketers reveal that most believe their initial spending on the Internet did not come at the expense of other media (in other words, their overall advertising budget grew). But many expect that future increases in their Internet expenditure will be taken from other areas, probably print and/or direct marketing. They also see their Internet advertising budgets growing much faster than their traditional media budgets.

Migration may also take place in non-addressable media spending. Striking levels of media displacement are already evident among Internet users. Most notably, TV viewing has declined among a third of adult Internet users (Figure 3). Similarly, in a

FIGURE 3   DECLINE IN USAGE OF TRADITIONAL MEDIA

Percentage of adult Internet users surveyed who
say their usage of traditional media has declined

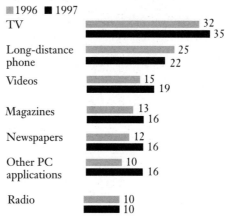

■1996 ■ 1997

TV — 32 / 35
Long-distance phone — 25 / 22
Videos — 15 / 19
Magazines — 13 / 16
Newspapers — 12 / 16
Other PC applications — 10 / 16
Radio — 10 / 10

Source: PINCYSVP 1997 American Internet User Survey

recent *Wall Street Journal* poll, 21 percent of respondents cited spending more time on their computer or in using online services as a reason for watching the major TV networks less than they did five years earlier. When marketers accept the idea that brand building can be accomplished on line, some spending on TV, radio, billboards, and other non-addressable media may migrate to the Internet.

Getting Closer to the Consumer

We believe marketers will soon start to use the Internet as a kind of testbed for campaigns planned for print, TV, or radio. One leading-edge marketer, London International, the maker of Durex condoms, is already trying out advertising concepts on its Web site before transferring them to other media where their effectiveness is harder to track. It is testing three concepts ultimately destined for conventional media: "Online Lovers," "Dr Dilemma," and "The Nurse." By monitoring pages selected, clickthroughs, responses generated, and other indicators, the company is able to discover which parts of a prospective campaign work and which don't, thereby reducing the risk of launching the equivalent of a box-office flop.

Conducting market research and obtaining feedback from consumers can be expensive and difficult. The Internet offers cost-effective alternatives to conventional methods, and may yield more revealing information. Several of the marketers we interviewed said that their presence on the Web had taught them a tremendous amount about their customers' views of their products and services. They maintain that the Web offers a non-judgmental way of providing feedback and ideas, and is less intimidating for consumers to use than standard toll-free numbers.

Marketers at Fidelity, London International, and Coors found that users of toll-free numbers mainly called to ask questions about products. On the other hand, Internet users, even when given answers to the most frequently asked questions, would often provide feedback about the quality of a product, new variations on it, and ways that it might be changed. To be sure, some of the additional interaction may be down to the different demographic profile of Internet users, but gathering information of this kind is becoming an increasingly important way to use the Web.

To gather deeper feedback, marketers are experimenting with Internet focus groups. LiveWorld has already hosted several sessions for NFO, a company specializing in this area. The advantage of conducting a focus group on line is that participants are anonymous and can speak their mind without worrying what others in the group think. In addition, geographically dispersed participants can be assembled at a fraction of the usual cost. London International is planning to conduct an online focus group to assess the effectiveness of its Web efforts in the near future.

Finally, the opportunities for testing new product ideas on the Internet are legion, particularly for electronic or intangible items such as magazine covers, entertainment concepts, and personal financial services. The possibilities are just beginning to be exploited.

Rising Expectations

Two features of Internet advertising—the measurability of its impact and the probability of some form of results-based pricing emerging—are likely to raise marketers' expectations of traditional media. If they do, pressure may build for a more accurate measurement system or a shorter measurement cycle. The demand for greater accuracy in measurement is already coming from the broadcast networks in any case. The coding technology tests being carried out by SMART (the emerging competitor to Nielsen), by Nielsen itself, and by its joint effort with Lucent to develop Media TraX indicate that improvements are technically feasible.

In fact, it would not be surprising if new measurement tools and techniques originally designed for the Internet were to spill over and be applied to traditional media in the not so distant future. Moreover, in those traditional media that are already more measurable, such as print, we foresee increasing pressure from advertisers for results-based or tiered pricing like that offered on the Internet.

The developments we have described are necessarily speculative, and may not materialize as broadly or as quickly as we suggest. All the same, they are worth watching out for because of their implications. Most of the media industry is affected by the billions of dollars spent every year on consumer marketing. If key advertisers were to reallocate their media budgets, the impact on traditional media could be profound.

As the aspirations, techniques, and expectations associated with Internet advertising spill over into traditional media, both marketers and advertising agencies will have to rethink the capabilities they bring to bear on selling products and services.

Implications for Marketers

The growing importance of Internet advertising and its effect on conventional marketing will have profound implications for practitioners. First, the Internet model will set new standards for building relationships in the physical world, challenging many current practices and expectations. Second, a new concept, value exchange, will emerge as a core marketing capability. Finally, the move toward organizational structures and processes designed around consumers' experiences with specific products or services will accelerate further.

New Standards in Relationship Management

The Internet will set new standards for total relationship management in both breadth and depth. "Breadth" means that a relationship will increasingly last for the entire ownership experience, including the time before and after the purchase of the product or service. Consider Coors, which used consumer feedback received via the Web during both the development and promotion of its beverage Zima—thus involving customers at all stages in the product life cycle.

"Depth" reflects the degree of interaction with consumers at any given point in their experience of a product. The book retailer Amazon.com, for instance, is beginning to use the information it gleans from customers to create value-added services such as suggestions about books that a particular reader might enjoy. This raises the bar for competitors on the Internet and in the physical world, posing a challenge that other players must meet if they are to retain customers' loyalty.

The Internet's role in consumer relationship management has important consequences for marketers. Network-based interactions must be integrated into the rest of a business, with all that this entails.

If car purchasers make fewer trips to the showroom, say, doing their own online research into different models instead of talking to salespeople, dealers will need to rethink the way they manage the whole consumer relationship. Eventually, customers may go to them only to place an order; at this point, the role dealerships play may no longer justify their cost, and they will have to find new ways to offer buyers value if they are not to disappear. Moreover, as consumers' behavior changes, so will the skills that salespeople need. And how are those salespeople going to be compensated when consumers make their purchases through channels other than dealerships?

Design and funding is another key area. If the Internet's role is to grow beyond advertising, the design of online activities should probably not be constrained by the priorities of a single functional area such as marketing, or by the limitations of the marketing communications budget.

Value Exchange as a Core Capability

Much of the Internet's potential relies on the creation of a dialogue between consumer and marketer in which information is exchanged for value. Marketers need to develop the new skill of rewarding consumers for giving them access to personal information such as who they are, what they like, and what they buy. This reward may take the form of discounts toward future purchases, or benefits such as valuable information or a personalized product or service.

This process of value exchange will become critical as new standards are created to protect consumers' privacy. The proposal announced by Netscape in May 1997 to capture information on consumers' hard drives rather than on marketers' computers marks a step in a new direction with its implicit acknowledgement that consumers will "own" information about themselves and control the release of that information to marketers. The demand for value among consumers is likely to grow as they become aware of how highly marketers prize their demographic profiles, product preferences, and transaction histories.

A few marketers are beginning to manage this process effectively. In exchange for basic information such as name, address, age, and income, *Vogue* provides readers with discounts, special offers, and previews of forthcoming articles. Saturn's approach is to offer convenient access to information. Consumers who reveal a small amount of information about themselves are able to use Saturn's interactive pricing center to research new cars, saving them trips to a showroom.

Organizations Centered on Consumers

As the Web merges marketing with other business processes such as customer service, it will put more pressure on the organization of most marketers. The coming of age of interactive networks will accelerate the move toward new organizational models in which marketers will structure their various functional capabilities around an integrated customer front end.

For a real-life example, take the insurance company USAA. Its customer center receives and manages all communications with consumers, whether direct via telephone, mail, and the Internet, or indirect via intermediaries. The rest of the organization revolves around the customer center. Sophisticated information systems help the company to process interactions and maximize their value.

The benefits are many. Customers feel that USAA knows them better, and the company is quick to respond to a complaint or learn about important market changes such as a cut in a competitor's price in a particular territory.

As more and more companies reorganize themselves around their customers, intranets linked to the Internet will become crucial. They will make it economically feasible for managers within an organization to have more information about consumers—and more interactions with them—than ever before.

Implications for Agencies

The rise of Internet advertising, with its unique economics, may well call the validity of current business models and processes into question. It will also compel agencies to rethink the way they create and develop campaigns, and the skills and capabilities they need to survive.

New Business Model

So different are the revenues generated by conventional and Internet advertisements that traditional agencies will have to think carefully about their approach to online advertising if they are to pursue it profitably. At present, most agencies incur high fixed costs in developing campaigns. Big creative teams and the like were fine in the days when agencies could rely on the commissions they earned from large media buys associated with a small number of creative executions. On the Internet, however, this cost structure is inverted: the creative element of the total advertising cost is much larger in relation to the media element. The resulting commissions will no longer be sufficient to cover agencies' high operating costs.

We believe that traditional agency business models simply will not work for Internet advertising. A trend toward retainer compensation is already emerging. Agencies may well seek to enhance their revenue streams by taking a cut of the results of their efforts in the shape of a commission on leads or sales generated. In future, agencies will increasingly share in the risk of their advertising instead of—as they do today—leaving all of it to be borne by marketers.

Compensation models will be transformed. The measurability of Internet advertising makes results-based pricing more feasible than in any other media, as we have seen. Some examples are already in evidence. Site Specific is using performance-based contracts for clients including Duracell, CUC International, and Intuit's TurboTax division. Though these arrangements are not yet making it any money, they are expected to do so as advertising effectiveness increases. In time, results-based compensation will probably spill over into traditional media as the measurement of advertising impact improves. It will then have its most profound impact, affecting agencies' core business and revenue source.

New Capabilities

This vision of the future calls agencies' current capabilities into question. Many have seen themselves as the guardian angel of the brands they represent. But agencies have a patchy record of orchestrating brand-building activities across the full range of marketing disciplines: media advertising, direct mail, promotions, and so on. The emergence of interactive media means that agencies must not only manage a broader and more complex mix of marketing tools, but also master radically different skills. Three main gaps will need to be filled:

- **Inform creative execution with a deeper understanding of enabling interactive technologies.** Such an understanding scarcely exists in agencies today, except in some of the more specialized enterprises such as Site Specific and AGENCY.COM. Traditional agencies may find their technological and creative skills are not sufficiently integrated to compete with the specialist Internet ad agencies, which enjoy a higher profile and more confidence among marketers in this area of work.

- **Integrate one-way and response-oriented campaign design skills.** Interactive advertising blurs the boundaries between traditional advertising, direct marketing, and customer services—normally separate preserves run by different individuals. Agencies will need to learn to integrate these skills in their design efforts.

- **Increase the speed and responsiveness of creative production.** The immediacy of interactive networks will make growing demands on the pace and frequency of creative production. Agencies are currently organized around work processes with relatively generous cycle times. Today, it is acceptable to take three to six months to design one campaign, and to run it for up to two years. Tomorrow, a campaign with 300 one-on-one executions will have to be designed in two to three months, and adapted continuously in response to real-time consumer feedback.

In summary, the future holds many challenges for agencies. The emergence of new business models and the need for new capabilities are likely to shake up an industry that has been under pressure for some time. Some agencies have shown that they can customize their processes and economics to specific industry needs like those of grocery retailers or auto dealers. Now they must learn to institutionalize these capabilities within their organizations or spin off a cluster of flexible, technology-savvy boutiques with low fixed costs. Viewed another way, the emergence of Internet advertising may represent an opportunity for renewal—a chance for agencies to reclaim the high ground of brand stewardship that some marketers argue they have let slip away in the past two decades.

The emergence of Internet advertising is likely to have wider implications for business than many imagine. Its effects will not be confined to the online world, but will extend to traditional marketing activities and processes. For those who look closely, Internet advertising holds many more opportunities and risks than is commonly assumed. And the payoff waiting for those who rise to the challenge will more than justify the efforts required.

Reprinted with permission of McKinsey & Company, The McKinsey Quarterly, *1997 Number 3, pp. 44–62.*

Notes

1. For more on this subject, *see* Andrew V. Abela and A. M. Sacconaghi, Jr., *"Value exchange: The secret of building customer relationships on line,"* The McKinsey Quarterly, 1997 Number 2, pp. 216–19, and John Hagel III and Jeffrey F. Rayport, "The coming battle for customer information," pp. 64–76.
2. An avatar is a virtual character that can graphically represent a user on the computer screen.

18

Advertising on the Web:
Is There Response before Click-Through?

REX BRIGGS
Millward Brown Interactive

NIGEL HOLLIS
Millward Brown International

A study of Web banner advertising that measured attitudes and behavior found important attitudinal shifts even without click-through. By using Millward Brown's BrandDynamics™ system, along with other copytesting measures, the authors have documented increases in advertising awareness and in brand perceptions to Web banner ads for apparel as well as technology goods.

This is the full report of the research conducted jointly between HotWired and Millward Brown international to assess the effectiveness of advertising on the World Wide Web. It was first presented December 2, 1996 to an audience of over 100 representatives of on-line ad agencies, web sites, and the press at the Jupiter Online conference in New York. A summary version of the report was issued at that time, but this represents the full report which includes more details of all the findings touched on in the presentation

Rex Briggs is vice president of MBinteractive, a division of Millward Brown International. Formerly, Mr. Briggs was director of research for HotWired. Mr. Briggs began analyzing the impact of the Internet on marketing in 1993. San Francisco-based MBinteractive is a full service research practice dedicated to helping clients measure and understand interactive marketing.

Nigel S. Hollis is the Group Research and Development Director at Millward Brown International. In his current role he has global responsibility for all projects related to improving Millward Brown's current services or developing new ones. Over the last two years he has worked on projects related to brand equity, and interactive and on-line research.

Mr. Hollis started work in market research at Cadbury Schweppes in the United Kingdom. After gaining a broad experience of different research methodologies at Cadbury, he joined Millward Brown in 1983. There he had a key role in the development of Millward Brown's successful TV Link pretest. In 1988 transferred to the United States and, until moving to his current role, worked on a variety of client business, mostly related to the analysis of tracking research.

He has had papers published in the *Journal of Advertising Research*, *Admap*, *plunung und analyse*, and the *Journal of the Market Research Society*.

Since advertising on the World Wide Web began in 1994, marketers have asked the same question they ask of all advertising in any media: Does it work? More specifically, do banner ads (those small, hyperlinked pixel displays popping up on public Web sites) actually provide a vehicle for effective commercial communication? As marketers are projected to spend billions of dollars on Web advertising in the next few years, this question becomes increasingly important.

Until now, the only available answer has been partial at best. The accepted wisdom suggests that, yes, ad banners *do* work as direct marketing vehicles—but only when viewers click on them for transport to the advertiser's own Web site, where a wide range of customized marketing processes begins.

The problem is that only a fraction of all viewers click on the banners they see. As a consequence, a few marketers have elected to pay only for proven click-throughs, while the rest of the marketing community, which pays for ad placements according to CPM (cost per 1,000 impressions), is left to wonder whether the millions of impressions its banner ads generate without click-through are simply wasted.

Are advertisers throwing away money on byte-sized electronic billboards which go unnoticed and un-noted in an environment unfriendly to advertising? Or do Web banners, even without the benefit of click-through, stimulate brand awareness, brand affinity, and purchase interest as effectively as more traditional advertising does?

To answer these questions, two research teams collaborated in an on-line experiment. The researchers came from the research department of HotWired, Inc., the Internet publisher that innovated the ad banner, and Millward Brown International, a recognized leader in advertising effectiveness research. The experiment was the first significant research study on Web advertising effectiveness, a study which dealt successfully with the unique research challenges posed by the Internet environment. This article describes the methodology of this important study and details its findings.

What to Measure

Many people have argued that the best measure of advertising response on the Web is the click-through rate. The advantages of this metric are that it is a behavioral response and easy to observe, and that it indicates an immediate interest in the advertised brand. But many other factors are also likely to influence the click-through response, and these factors may have more to do with the original predisposition of the audience than with the advertising itself. Thus the practice of evaluating Web advertising on the basis of click-through is like evaluating television ads for automobiles on the basis of how many people visit a showroom the next day. A showroom visit is an ideal response, but hardly the most likely one, since relatively few people will be in the market for a new car on a particular day.

Because most advertising does not evoke an immediate behavioral response, we designed our study to observe and measure both the attitudinal and the behavioral responses to a Web banner. In particular, our objective was to measure whether or not banners themselves have the potential to build brands, by creating awareness and image. We divided the population of our experiment into two cells: an exposed cell, which saw a banner for a tested brand on HotWired's homepage, and a control cell, which did not. Using these two groups, we sought to assess the impact on an advertised brand of one single incremental banner exposure.

How We Measured the Response

The question we then faced was how to define and measure the "impact" of one Web banner exposure. Traditionally, researchers have relied upon measures of awareness, recall, and reported response to indicate whether or not advertising has had an impact. These measures allow us to assess the degree to which an ad has been noticed (a necessary precursor to any more fundamental effect) and the degree to which the advertisement is likely to lead to a purchase. We adapted Millward Brown's proprietary measurement systems to the Web environment to assess the awareness of, and reaction to, the ad banners themselves. However, we sought to go beyond measures of awareness, recall, and reported purchase probability. We sought to determine the contribution the ad banner makes to building the brand. To do this, we adapted Millward Brown's BrandDynamics™ System to work in the context of an online interview (Dyson, Farr, and Hollis, 1996).

The BrandDynamics™ System

The BrandDyanics™ System is composed of two modules: the Consumer Value Model and the BrandDynamics™ Pyramid.

The Consumer Value Model.   The Consumer Value Model allows us to identify the probability that an individual will choose a particular brand for their next purchase. We call this measure *Consumer Loyalty*. The prediction of Consumer Loyalty is based on:

- consumers' claimed brand consideration

- a measure of brand size

- the price of the brand relative to others in the category

The Consumer Value Model has been validated against behavioral data and market share in many different categories in both North America and Europe. A higher average Consumer Loyalty in the exposed cell than the control would suggest that the banner exposure had positively affected the likelihood that people would buy the advertised brand.

The BrandDynamics™ Pyramid.   Based on a consistent set of survey measures that can be applied across different brands, categories, and countries, the BrandDynamics™ Pyramid allows us to explain the variation we observe in respondents' Consumer Loyalty scores. Each level of the Pyramid is a composite of awareness and imagery measures. We use these levels as building blocks to define an individual's relationship with a brand, as shown in Figure 1.

FIGURE 1   BRANDDYNAMICS™ PYRAMID

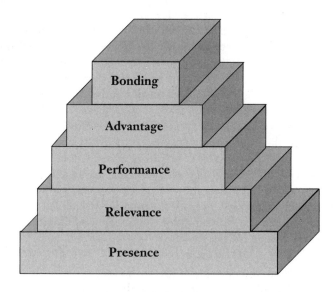

As we move up the levels of the Pyramid we describe a deepening attitudinal involvement with the brand. The brand relationship moves from consciousness of the brand (*Presence*), through acquaintance and examination (*Relevance and Performance*), to experience (*Advantage*), and then, finally, to the point where the consumer finds it difficult to consider alternative choices (*Bonded*). By comparing the percentage of people in the control and exposed cells who attain each level of the BrandDynamics™ Pyramid, we explain any observed changes in Consumer Loyalty.

Immediate vs. Delayed Effects

An important point to note is that the findings reported in this document relate to consumers' reactions a day or so after exposure. Tracking advertising response in traditional media suggests that the observed increases would erode over time without the reinforcement of further exposure. A positive response to advertising, while obviously desirable, is of little benefit to a brand unless it positively influences the consumer's choice on the next purchase occasion. Therefore, a key function of advertising is not only to establish but to *maintain* key brand associations in long-term memory so that they come to mind the next time the person encounters the brand. Unfortunately, it is beyond the scope of this project to evaluate the advertising in this respect. The objective of our study was to identify the immediate effect of one additional banner exposure. However, since exposure is rarely limited to one occasion, we assume there would be additional effect with repeated exposure (and the results of this study suggest as much).

The Study Design

We designed our research to address the particular concerns of both the advertiser and the researcher. Advertisers need to accurately measure the impact of advertising. Therefore, we measured the communication value of the advertising banner (i.e., its impact on consumers' attitudes), as well as its ability to elicit an immediate behavioral response (the click-through). We controlled exposure carefully to ensure that observed differences were due to the advertising and not extraneous variables. And we tested ads which had varying levels of preexisting advertising "weight" in order to gauge diminishing returns.

The research objective was to execute a rigorous and carefully controlled study which avoided the bias sometimes encountered in on-line research. We represented the "real world" as precisely as possible, by ensuring that the true nature of the research was not immediately apparent to participants. Our recruitment methodology guaranteed us a true cross-section of users, and our ability to record the Web site behavior of both Responders and Nonresponders enabled us to look for significant differences between Responders/Nonresponders and Control/Test Cells. No significant differences were observed.

First Day. From the universe of users who accessed HotWired between September 9 and September 16, 1996, a random sample was solicited for participation in a short research study, "To Help HotWired Better Understand Their Audience." Thirty-eight percent of those solicited participated. Respondents completed a seven-minute survey covering demographics and webographics. The survey avoided any indication of the true purpose of the research. Upon submission of the survey, respondents were returned to HotWired's homepage. Respondents were randomly assigned to Control or Exposed (test) cells. One of three test ads, or a control ad, was randomly placed in the designated advertising space on HotWired's homepage.

Second Day. Respondents were sent an email thanking them for their participation and inviting them to participate in a second survey (with the added incentive of a chance to win $100). Respondents were provided a URL (Web address) in the email and directed to link to the Web page in order to participate in the survey. Sixty-one percent of the original respondents participated in the second survey.

Respondents from the test cells were served one of three category-specific surveys based on their exposure to the advertisement on the first day. Respondents from the control cell were randomly directed to one of the three exposure surveys. The resulting final base sizes for each cell are shown in Table 1.

There was no special selection process for the creative used in the experiment. We believe it is possible for advertisers to create banners that compare favorably to the ones tested in this study. What was significant about the ad banners used was that each one represented a brand at a different stage of developing a "presence" on the Web.

Men's Apparel Brand. For reasons of client confidentiality we have used de-branded data in this paper. At the time of this study, the men's apparel brand was preparing to launch their Web site. In fact, the very first Web advertising impressions

	Total	Exposed	Control
TABLE 1			
Total sample	1,232	910	293
Men's apparel brand	397	301	82
Telecommunication company ISP	422	312	95
Web browser	413	297	116

that were seen for this brand occurred as part of this study. Thus we expected the banner exposure to increase *Presence* (consciousness of the brand) and *Relevance* (perception that the brand might suit their clothing needs). We expected the advertising to sway individuals who identified with the Web toward purchasing the brand that had recently become "wired." Seeing the advertising might also cause people in this target audience who had previously rejected the brand to reevaluate their opinion, perhaps even to perceive an *Advantage* and then *Bond* with it. This could result in an increase in their likelihood to purchase the brand, as measured by the difference in Consumer Loyalty scores between the exposed and control cells.

A Telecommunication Company's Internet Service Provider Brand. While the telecommunication company helped pioneer Web advertising, the ISP brand had not been advertised on the Web prior to our study. Given the telecommunication company's strong over-arching brand name, we expected that the ad banner might reinforce the parent company's generic presence rather than generate significant awareness for the ISP brand specifically. And because the telecommunication company's objective was to create an immediate behavioral response (a click-through), we wondered whether we would observe an attitudinal response at all.

Web Browser. The latest version of this Web browser was released with a significant Web advertising campaign. The browser was a new product but with pervasive presence and a well-known parent company; therefore, we were prepared to see little response at all to just one more banner exposure. If, however, users did show a measurable response to one additional exposure to the ad banner, then we would conclude that Web advertising has the potential to impact consumers even at higher levels of frequency.

Did the Advertising Affect Attitudes?

To answer this question, we will start by considering the overall impact of an additional ad banner exposure on the various brands tested using the Consumer Loyalty score. We will then explore the factors that may have caused the observed differences on a brand-by-brand basis.

Consumer Loyalty

The Consumer Loyalty score, which measures the likelihood that the consumer will purchase the product on the next purchase occasion, has been shown to be highly predictive of consumer purchase behavior. In each of our three test cells, the Consumer Loyalty score is higher than that for the control cell, suggesting that the extra exposure did have an effect. (When considering the implications of these scores, it is important to bear in mind how they are derived. The basic component of the Consumer Loyalty score is a consideration scale. Another key component is the relative price of the different brands within their category. For the men's apparel and ISP brands we calculated a *perceived* relative price from the brand image data. The men's apparel brand indexes 10 percent higher than the average khaki pants, and the ISP 30 percent higher than the average Internet service provider. To the extent that this perception-based measure differs from the actual relative prices in the market, the absolute Consumer Loyalty will be biased up or down. However, any bias will be consistent between the two cells. (In the case of the Web browser, the price index is set to nearly zero, given that it could be downloaded for free.) The difference is most significant in the case of the men's apparel brand, reflecting the fact that the exposure was the first time the brand had ever advertised on the Web. The impact of a single Web banner exposure on the Consumer Loyalty score ranged from a 5 percent increase for the Web browser to an increase of over 50 percent for the men's apparel brand as shown in Figure 2.

Why does the Consumer Loyalty score increase so strongly for the men's apparel brand? Do those who are exposed to the advertising banner suddenly say that this brand is the only brand they will buy? Though the impact of the advertising is not this dramatic, Figure 3 shows how the advertising makes some people a bit more likely to consider this brand compared to other brands. The differences noted are statistically

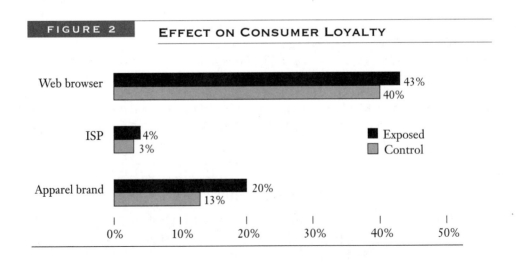

FIGURE 2   **EFFECT ON CONSUMER LOYALTY**

Web browser — 43% Exposed, 40% Control

ISP — 4% Exposed, 3% Control

Apparel brand — 20% Exposed, 13% Control

FIGURE 3   CONSIDERATION OF APPAREL BRAND

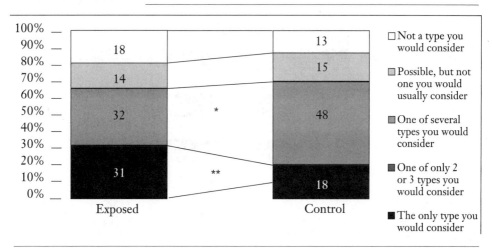

significant. (Statistically significant differences have been marked as follows: 95 percent confidence level denoted with **, 90 percent confidence level denoted with *.)

The first appearance of a banner for the men's apparel brand seemed to cause some people to move the brand higher up in their consideration hierarchy. A complementary question, designed to determine if the brand might fulfill a specific role in relation to other brands people might consider, demonstrates that exposure to the men's apparel brand ad banner increased the likelihood that the brand will be bought for a purpose that other competing brands don't fulfill (exposed: 14 percent versus control: 5 percent).

The ISP and Web browser brands show a different pattern of response, perhaps indicating a degree of diminishing returns associated with increased advertising weight on this particular measurement. Neither brand shows statistically significant increases in the consideration hierarchy. However, those exposed to the ISP banner clearly demonstrate an increased propensity to "buy" the service for a purpose that other competing brands don't fulfill (exposed: 26 percent versus control: 14 percent).

It is important to note that the differences reported refer to future purchase consideration. There is no difference between the exposed and control cells in terms of prior brand experience or ownership for any of the three brands, confirming that exposure to a single additional advertising banner has the potential to increase purchases.

Name Recognition

Given that a basic function of all advertising is to increase the presence of the advertised brand in the marketplace, and that the men's apparel brand had never advertised in this medium before, it is not surprising that awareness of the men's apparel brand is higher in the exposed cell than the control, as shown in Figure 4. This result is also

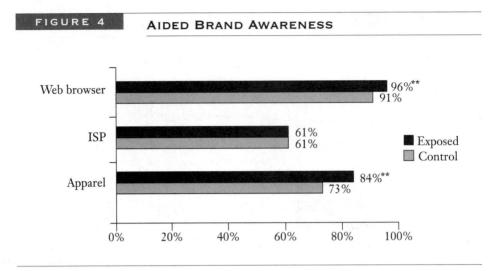

FIGURE 4   **AIDED BRAND AWARENESS**

observed with the Web browser, despite the fact that the level of awareness of that brand is already extremely high.

It appears that, in addition to increasing the Consumer Loyalty scores, the advertising increases passive name recognition as well. So, how does the advertising appear to affect the levels of the BrandDynamics™ Pyramid for each brand?

The BrandDynamics™ Pyramid: Men's Apparel Brand

All levels of the pyramid increased from the Control to the Exposed cell, with the largest effect observed at the *Presence* level (see Figure 5). The score at each of the Pyramid levels is a composite of awareness and image measures. By looking at the individual measures which comprise each level, we can further diagnose the effects of the advertising. This increase in *Presence* is driven entirely by an increase in just one of the measures used to define *Presence*—endorsement of the statement, "Comes readily to mind when you think about (clothes)." (Fifty percent of the exposed agree with this statement, compared to thirty-two percent of those in the control cell.) The increase of the *Presence* dimension then fuels the majority of the increase at higher levels of the Pyramid, suggesting that many people held latent good opinions of the men's apparel brand which emerge upon exposure to the advertising banner. There are also some modest increases observed for attributes that affect the higher levels of the Pyramid. These are shown in Figure 6.

As can be seen from the chart, the largest difference is in the attribute "just the same as other brands." While not expressly used to build the Pyramid, this attribute contrasts "offers something different," which is used, in part, to derive *Advantage* and *Bonding*. This finding suggests that the advertising has a positive affect on perceptions as well as *Presence*, by creating a distinctiveness for this brand among the Web audience.

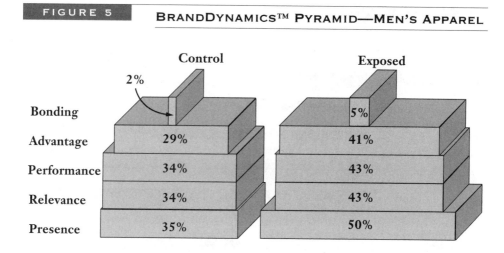

FIGURE 5   BRANDDYNAMICS™ PYRAMID—MEN'S APPAREL

The hypothesis that Web advertising can positively impact perceptions is confirmed by the fact that other diagnostic measures also exhibit a difference between the exposed and control cells. Out of 18 adjectives which might describe the men's apparel brand with which people can agree or disagree, 5 are higher in the exposed cell compared to the control (see Figure 7).

For this brand, the findings appear conclusive. The effect of its first exposure on the Web has a strong immediate effect on the brand. Consumer Loyalty and brand *Presence* increase, perceptions of the brand's personality are positively impacted, and

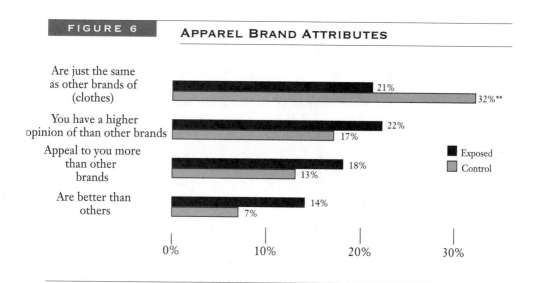

FIGURE 6   APPAREL BRAND ATTRIBUTES

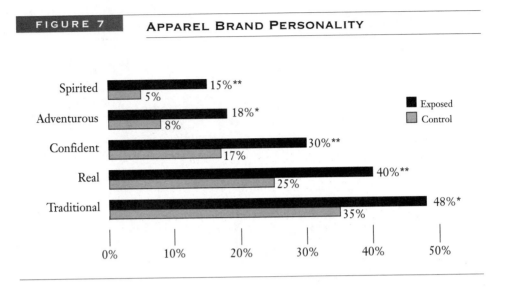

| FIGURE 7 | APPAREL BRAND PERSONALITY |

the advertising helped to differentiate the brand from its competition. We attribute these effects both to the context in which exposure takes place and the power of the banner on the target audience. The Web and the HotWired site have strong positive images for these people; HotWired delivers content they find relevant through a medium—the Web—which they find exciting. Advertising on the Web transferred some of this excitement and relevance on to the men's apparel brand itself.

The BrandDynamics™ Pyramid: ISP

As might be expected from the Consumer Loyalty results, we do not see quite the same degree of impact resulting from the first exposure to the ISP banner (see Figure 8).

The results for this brand may suggest that increasing brand awareness for new products and services (especially when branded under a strong parent name) may take more than a single banner impression to have a dramatic impact on consumers' perceptions and purchase intentions. While there is little change in the overall Pyramid, there are two individual attributes that exhibited a significant difference.

One measure, "is growing more popular," helps define perceptions of *Advantage* and *Bonding* (38 percent of the exposed cell agreed with this statement compared to 26 percent of the control). The other attribute, "is a good Internet service provider," helps to define the *Performance* level of the pyramid but only among those who have first achieved the level of *Relevance*. Overall, 43 percent of the exposed cell agrees that this ISP would be a good Internet service provider versus 31 percent among the control. The increase we observed in these two measures occurred among people who had failed to qualify for either the *Presence* or *Relevance* levels of the Pyramid.

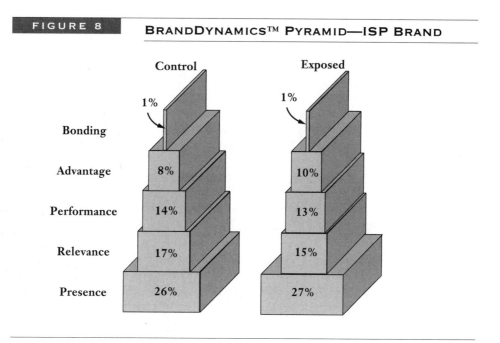

FIGURE 8   BRANDDYNAMICS™ PYRAMID—ISP BRAND

The BrandDynamics™ Pyramid: The Web Browser

The overall Pyramid and its underlying attributes provide intriguing insight into consumer perception of the parent brand, as well as the advertising for this particular product (see Figure 9).

Even with ubiquitous advertising levels, there is a modest positive increase in *Presence* as a result of one more exposure to the Web browser's ad banner on HotWired's homepage. We also see some marginal increase at the levels of *Performance* and *Advantage*. The *Bonding* score, however, declined. This decline may have been caused by the negative press surrounding the brand during the time of the advertising effectiveness test.

To a similar point, the *Presence* level comprises not just an active awareness of the brand, but an active awareness of the brand promise (defined by an acceptance or rejection of the notion that the brand is relevant to the individual's needs). In the case of the Web browser brand, the awareness component for the exposed cell is higher than the control cell (47 percent versus 41 percent). However, active rejection is also 5 percentage points higher (12 percent in the exposed cell versus 7 percent in the control cell). Similarly, when we turn to the higher levels of the Pyramid, "have a higher opinion of than other Web browsers" is lower among the exposed cell (6 percent versus 12 percent among the control). This increase in active rejection, in part, accounts for the reduced score at the *Bonding* level.

| FIGURE 9 | BRANDDYNAMICS™ PYRAMID—WEB BROWSER |

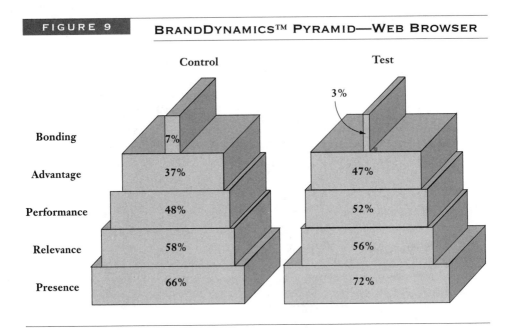

Control   Test

	Control	Test
Bonding	7%	3%
Advantage	37%	47%
Performance	48%	52%
Relevance	58%	56%
Presence	66%	72%

Overall, it would appear that the single additional advertising exposure increased the awareness and *Presence* of the brand among some viewers; however, it also reminded a few of their negative views of the parent company, which may have been generated by the intense scrutiny focused on the security provisions within the product.

These findings suggest that exposure to an ad banner on HotWired's homepage can have an immediate impact on consumer perceptions of the advertised brand. We now turn to the advertising-specific data to better understand these reactions.

Remembered Exposure: Brand-Linked Ad Awareness

We know that all those in the exposed cell had one more opportunity to see the ad banner than those in the control cell. This additional exposure should result in those exposed having both a higher level of brand awareness, in general, and a higher level of ad banner awareness specifically.

We will now assess the results for specific brand-linked ad awareness, a measure that has been found to have a strong predictive relationship with sales in traditional media (Hollis, 1994). Figure 10 confirms that the proportion of people who claimed to remember seeing the tested brand advertised on the World Wide Web in the past seven days was higher in all cases. The chart shows that the increase in ad awareness varies by brand. This variance is a function of the overall power of the banners, diminishing returns related to the individual brands' Web advertising weights, and the original level, the "base," from which ad awareness had been increased.

To properly understand the last factor, we need to consider the fact that it must be incrementally more difficult to raise awareness from a base level of 73 percent than

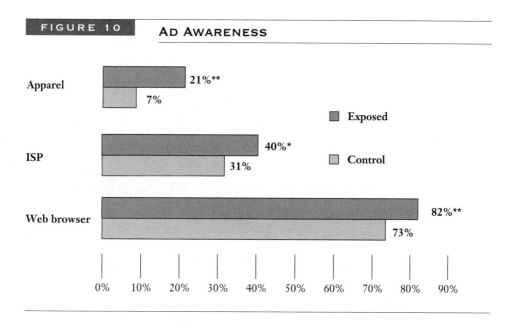

FIGURE 10   **AD AWARENESS**

from 7 percent. Millward Brown's FORCE score (the *First Opportunity to see Response Created by the Execution*) (Dyson and Farr, 1995) accounts for the effects of diminishing returns and consequently allows a like-for-like comparison of the three banners ability to create brand-linked ad awareness.

Millward Brown utilizes the FORCE score in traditional media such as television and print. As the FORCE score models out the effects of time, exposure weight, diminishing returns, and base level, FORCE scores can be directly compared across media types. While time-series modeling is normally employed to calculate the FORCE measure, in this case it was not necessary. The aspects of time, exposure weight, and base level were all controlled for by the test design and a simple calculation can be used to allow for the diminishing returns effect.

As the median FORCE score for television advertisements is only 10 percent the scores reported in Figure 11 (an average score of 20) suggest that the Web banners we tested compare very favorably to most TV ads in terms of creating brand-linked ad awareness.

Though this finding may seem surprising at first glance, previous work done by Millward Brown in the United Kingdom suggests that print also compares very favorably to TV in its ability to create brand-linked awareness of advertising (Farr, 1994). The median FORCE score for print ads is 18 percent, as can be seen in Figure 12.

While TV has the advantage of being more intrusive (moving visuals, sound, etc.), it is nonetheless a passive medium. The content is displayed to the viewer irrespective of whether they are actually attending to it. Conversely, Web- and print-based media both have the advantage of active reader involvement. The consumer actively engages with the content as they peruse it and search for items of interest.

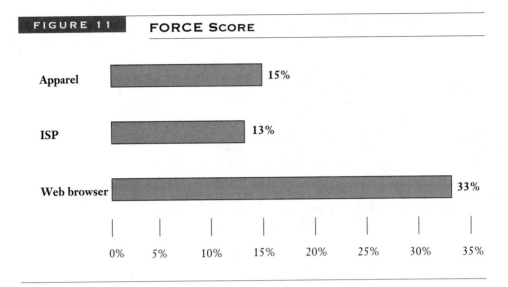

FIGURE 11   FORCE SCORE

This engaged state, that the nature of the Web encourages, seems to result in higher initial recall of advertising than might otherwise be expected.

We have now observed that, overall, Web advertising can create strong increases in brand-linked ad awareness, the necessary precursor to the changes in brand-related measures. But how do the individual banners compare?

As the men's apparel brand banner had not run anywhere else on the Web prior to the study, we are able to see a true picture of the effect of one exposure. Seven percent

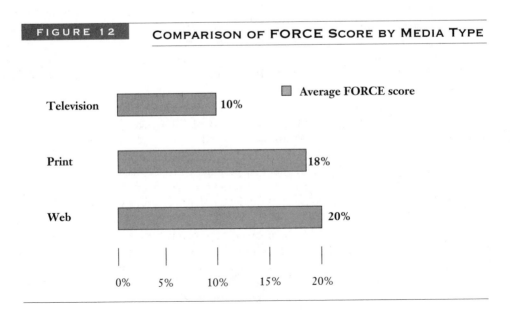

FIGURE 12   COMPARISON OF FORCE SCORE BY MEDIA TYPE

of the respondents in the control cell claim to have seen an ad for the brand in the past seven days. While we know this to be contrary to fact, this level of base awareness is not unusual; in fact, it is to be expected from an established and relatively well-known brand like the one tested. The increase of 200 percent for the exposed cell is considerable, even by the standards of television and print advertising. The resulting FORCE score, however, is only marginally higher than the observed increase in ad awareness. This is due to the fact that the effects of diminishing returns and exposure weight (which negatively impact the absolute increase observed for the other brands) are minimal in the case of the men's apparel brand, since it started with a low level of awareness.

The telecommunication company's banner generated a 29 percent increase in general awareness of advertising for the brand on the Web. The higher base level and the increased impact of diminishing returns account for the difference in the size of this increase relative to the one observed for the men's apparel brand.

The results for the Web browser's FORCE score stand out from the others. Though the base awareness level in the control cell is extremely high in comparison to any point-in-time measure for traditional media, it is clear that an extra exposure on HotWired's homepage is capable of improving even on *that* high level of awareness. The FORCE score indicates that the browser's banner created a high level of brand-linked memorability—a level far higher, in fact, than the averages for television and print. The publicity and other marketing activity surrounding the browser's introduction may well have played a part in the increased attention that people paid to this ad, but the score is dramatic nonetheless.

The Effect of Diminishing Returns

What is the incremental value of the additional ad banner exposure? Analysis of Web server-log files by one Web media company suggests that diminishing returns on the behavioral click-through begin immediately and that, at a frequency of three exposures, little to no additional click-through benefit is garnered. If this suggestion is correct, does the brand communication value generated from the exposure of the banner exhibit a similar pattern?

To fully analyze the diminishing returns function requires a tightly controlled experiment which measures the effect at multiple levels of exposure for each banner ad. While this type of measurement is beyond the scope of this study, the following analysis does provide some insight into the incremental benefit one might expect to find at different levels of frequency. The analysis is based on a comparison of the single exposure for the three different ads tested. On average, these brands have different levels of weight ranging from the men's apparel brand (no previous exposure) to the Web browser (significant exposure on average).

For instance, specific banner awareness (elicited by showing people the actual ad banner) displays a classic diminishing-returns function consistent with findings from traditional media. Initial banner awareness is highest for the Web Browser (see Figure 13), since many of these people are likely to have been exposed to this banner, or one like it, elsewhere, but the incremental benefit of one additional exposure is the lowest

FIGURE 13

BASELINE SPECIFIC BRAND-LINKED AWARENESS

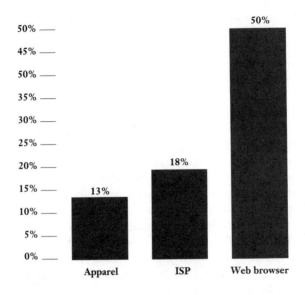

of the three (see Figure 14). The converse can be seen for the apparel brand. Initial awareness is lowest, but one additional exposure results in the strongest increase. The suggestion that there may be diminishing returns does not preclude the fact that there is likely to be (as in the cases tested) measurable incremental effects at higher levels of frequency. Whether the incremental benefit warrants the cost of exposure is a question that can only be answered on a brand-by-brand basis.

A key finding is that the benefits are likely to be derived even after multiple exposures. In addition, findings for the men's apparel brand seemed to indicate that the communication power was partially a function of the surrounding program context.

Ad Reaction

The questions employed to understand consumer reaction to the advertising banners themselves were adapted from Millward Brown's Link copy test. The results reinforce the notion that the Web is a unique medium. It resembles traditional print media in some respects but exhibits some similarities with outdoor advertising in the way people describe their reaction to the content.

The main finding in this area is the lack of variation in response to the ad banners. It tends to confirm that part of the ad awareness increase observed for the Web browser's banner could be due to synergy with other marketing activity and exposure.

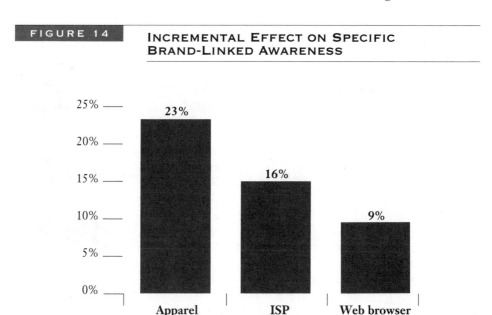

FIGURE 14 — INCREMENTAL EFFECT ON SPECIFIC BRAND-LINKED AWARENESS

While the lack of variation in this diagnostic data might be a function of the banners tested, it does suggest that the high-involvement, prominent placement aspects of advertising on the Web dominate the differences in creative impact.

An example of this uniformity of response can be seen in how the banners exhibit little difference in the degree to which people thought they were "eye catching," as shown in Figure 15. The similar results are especially noteworthy given that the men's apparel brand and ISP were animated banner ads, while the Web browser was not. The power of an advertisement to hold a consumer's attention and be remembered at a later date varies widely in other forms of media, even given a constant level of exposure. The main causes of the variation differ by medium. In print, category interest is key, since people are actively searching for items of interest; the creative power of an ad plays a supporting role. For TV advertising, creative power dominates and viewer involvement is key. (Viewer involvement is a function of enjoyability and the degree to which attention involves active processing rather than passive) (Hollis, 1995). Our results from this study suggest that the Web is far more similar to print than TV in this respect.

Determining Factors of Click-Through

A focus of the Web advertising debate has centered on the value of click-through. Click-through on ad banners transports readers from content focused Web sites to advertiser sites where direct marketing can occur. From this point of view, ad banners

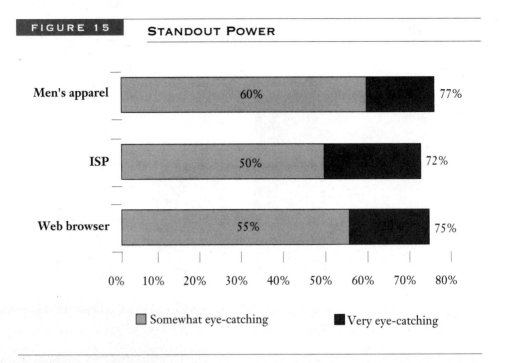

FIGURE 15 — STANDOUT POWER

| | Somewhat eye-catching | Very eye-catching |

are similar to direct mail envelopes, enticing the recipient to open it up, browse further, and take action. Using this logic, many people have argued in favor of the click-through rate as the best measure of advertising response on the Web. However, we believe that the click-through response is determined by five basic factors, three of which relate to the predisposition of the audience, not the advertising itself.

Audience-related factors are:

- innate tendency to click on advertisements
- immediate relevance of the product to the audience
- preexisting appeal of the brand or company

Advertising-related factors are:

- immediate relevance of the message to the audience
- involvement or intrigue created by the ad

The results of this experiment indicate that those who click through had, as might be expected, actual recall of the ad banner (which they may have seen in locations other than HotWired). More importantly the brand had immediate personal relevance to the user. People who remembered the ad and who said the product category was of interest to them were three times more likely than the average to claim to have clicked-through. The fact that we observe little difference between the reported click-through rates for any of the banners tested indicates that click-through in itself may not predict the level of brand building likely to be realized.

While more extensive studies need to be conducted to fully understand other factors that might drive click-through, these findings suggest that ad agencies and content providers who agree to be remunerated solely on the basis of click-through rates are tying their revenues to current levels of interest in the advertised brands of their clients. Since our study has proven that advertising on the Web has sizable effects on brand loyalty and attitudes which are not reflected in click-through, the use of click-through rates alone are likely to undervalue the Web as an advertising medium.

If this finding proves to be a general one, then tactics designed to generate click-through may also underutilize the power of Web advertising. The practice of running "unbranded" banners, which has been reported to yield high click-through rates, surely runs counter to the concept of brand building through ad banner exposure. In short, click-through certainly has value (especially if the goal is to create an immediate behavioral response such as downloading software), but the click-through rate itself is unlikely to be indicative of the overall value of a banner exposure.

Conclusions

So what do our findings tell us about Web banner advertising? Our results tell us, simply and unequivocally, that it works. Moreover, it works with or without the added benefit of click-through. One single banner exposure generated increases in Consumer Loyalty scores ranging from 5 percent for the Web Browser to 50 percent for the men's apparel brand. Advertising awareness increased from a low of 12 percent (for the brand with the highest base of ad awareness) to a high of 200 percent for the previously unadvertised men's apparel brand. The FORCE scores we calculated for the three banner ads suggest that Web banners may rival or surpass TV and print advertising in producing brand-linked ad awareness. We observed, as expected, a diminishing returns factor associated with levels of advertising weight. This factor dampened but did not extinguish the advertising effects.

In addition, our findings to date suggest that the high-involvement nature of the Web and the prominence of the advertising seemed to play a larger role in defining ad effectiveness than did consumer reaction to any particular execution we tested. In this respect advertising on the Web appears to work similarly to print rather than TV. A combination of factors appear to generate click-through, the primary one being the nature of the audience and the inherent interest the product category holds for them. The appeal of the creative plays a secondary role at best.

The Web offers unique and undeniable advantages over other media in terms of targeting and direct marketing. One such advantage is the ability of advertising banners to serve as gateways to an advertiser's own Web site. But our results suggest that the ad banner is a legitimate advertising vehicle in its own right. This experiment shows that banner ads on the HotWired Network have a significant impact on their viewers, an impact that demonstrably builds the advertised brand. Banner ads remind people of a brand's existence, stimulate latent or dormant brand associations, and can cause people to change their attitudes toward the brand, thus increasing their likelihood to purchase. The unique marketing power of the on-line environment and the established communication benefits of traditional advertising combine to make the Web a powerful new advertising medium with real potential for brand building.

References

Dyson, P., A. Farr, and N. Hollis. "Understanding, Measuring, and Using Brand Equity." *Journal of Advertising Research* 36, 6 (1996): 9–21.

———, and A. Farr. "Effective Frequency, New Evidence on an Old Debate." In the Proceedings of the 1995 Market Research Society Conference.

Farr, A. "Ad Track 94." A study of magazine advertising effectiveness, available from IPC Magazines or Millward Brown International.

Hollis, N. "The Link Between TV Ad Awareness and Sales." *Journal of the Market Research Society*, January 1994.

———. "Like It or Not, Liking Is Not Enough." *Journal of Advertising Research* 35, 5 (1995): 7–16.

19

The Changing Role of the Sales Force

Now it's urgent. Companies must take some steps to redesign their selling strategies.

DAVID W. CRAVENS

Pressures for reshaping traditional sales strategies are mounting as executives respond to diverse customer requirements, intense competition, and rapid change in the marketplace. Having learned that complacency kills, cutting-edge companies are aggressively reinventing their sales organizations. Examining the role of the sales force starts with a candid look at how the sales strategy measures up to what is being done in other organizations in several important areas. This should be followed by an agenda for taking action on eight key success indicators.

Intense global competition, slow growth in many markets, and demanding customers are forcing many companies to change their sales strategies and structures. Reinventing the sales organization is becoming a critical item on the agenda as companies restructure to lower costs and leverage their capabilities to build customer satisfaction.

Examples of the changes under way include developing a customer-orientation throughout the organization, building strong internal and external relationships, creating multi-functional teams to manage key business processes, and reshaping the traditional pyramid structure of the organization (see Figure 1).

There is perhaps no better illustration of these changes than American Express Financial Advisors AEFA), an AMEX unit selling financial products such as mutual

David W. Cravens holds the Eunice and James L. West Chair of American Enterprise Studies and is Professor of Marketing, M.J. Neeley School of Business, Texas Christian University. Prior to his faculty appointments, he held sales and marketing management positions with International Systems and Controls and was Director of Operations of the Aerospace Research Applications Center at Indiana University. Dave is the author of *Strategic Marketing* (Homeswood, IL: Richard D. Irwin Inc., 1994), editor of the *Journal of the Academy of Marketing Science,* and chair of the AMA's Marketing Strategy, Special Interest Group. Dave conducts seminars on sales management and marketing strategy for companies in the United States and several other countries. He holds an engineering degree from MIT and MBA and DBA degrees from Indiana University.

FIGURE 1	SETTING AN AGENDA FOR REINVENTING THE SALES ORGANIZATION

Do any of the following need management attention?	Major problem area	Definitely needs attention	Uncertain — evalution is needed	Okay, but could be improved	Very satisified
			(Check one of the above for each of the eight areas)		
1. Building long-term relationships with customers					
2. Fostering organizational change					
3. Gaining commitment to customer satisfaction					
4. Coaching rather than commanding					
5. Measuring salesperson performance (keeping score)					
6. Taking different avenues (channels) to customers					
7. Removing performance hurdles for salespeople					
8. Leveraging information technology					

funds and insurance. AEFA's financial performance has been good but management's long-term vision about the financial services market is guiding major changes in the company's sales strategy.

As part of this vision. AEFA's 8,000 planners are building long-term relationships with clients. The company gives planners special training to help them shift into relationship building and provides software to increase productivity and reduce response time. The old commission pay structure has been scrapped in favor of bonuses used to reward planners and managers for scoring well on customer satisfaction. Sales teams now have responsibility for managing processes like client satisfaction and account relations. AEFA's performance targets include 95% client retention, 80% planner retention after four years, and annual sales growth of 18%. (Planner retention under the commission plan was only 30%.)

AEFA's experience previews several changes under way in many sales organizations. The reforming process requires redesigning the traditional sales organization, leveraging information technology to lower costs and provide quick response, designing the sales strategy to meet different customer needs, and building long-term relationships with customers and business partners. The sales force continues to be a key contributor in organizations like AEFA, but salespeople are being asked to assume new responsibilities, and the methods for keeping score are changing.

The contribution of the sales force to the sales, profit, and customer satisfaction performance of many companies highlights the urgency of designing selling strategies to match the demands and uncertainties of the rapidly changing marketplace.

Building Relationships

Building customer relationships is the core sales strategy of Marriott International Inc.'s business travel sales organization. The travel manager is the target for the selling activities of the 2,500 person sales organization. The key features of the major account sales strategy are to:

- Choose customers wisely (Marriott follows a comprehensive customer evaluation process).

- Build customer research into the value proposition (understanding what drives customer value and satisfaction).

- Lead with learning by following a step-by-step sales process.

- Invest in the customer's goal-setting process, rather than Marriott's.

- Develop a relationship strategy with a sense of purpose, trust, open access, shared leadership, and continuous learning.

Marriott's management recognizes that customers who regularly purchase the company's services are valuable assets who demand continuous attention by high-performance teams. Rapidly changing markets and customer diversity add to the importance of developing strong ties with valuable customers.

Setting Priorities

Relationship marketing means getting and keeping customers through cooperation, trust, commitment, and sharing of information. Executives in many companies are making long-term customer relationships the core focus of their sales strategies. Firms pursuing these strategies besides Marriott include American Express, AT&T, Electronic Data Systems, Motorola, and Owens-Corning.

A 1991 study conducted by Stamford-Conn.-based Learning International revealed that 96% of the 300 sales executives surveyed consider "building long-term relationships with customers" to be the most important activity affecting sales productivity. Surprisingly, only 39% saw incentive programs as an important driver of sales productivity.

Salespeople and managers are the front line contacts with customers, and relationship marketing is altering the salesperson's traditional role. Perhaps the most sweeping change is that the entire organization is responsible for customer satisfaction. The era of the "lone wolf" salesperson is giving way to building customer relationships involving all business functions. Importantly, a commitment to relationship marketing increases the sales organization's opportunity to gain internal support for its sales strategy. Greater involvement of other business functions in the customer relationship also changes selling from an individual to a team responsibility.

Assessing Customer Value

Relationship strategies take into account differences in the value of customers to the seller and differences in the requirements of customers. Marriott's emphasis on the wise choice of customers with whom to partner indicates the need to segment accounts for corporate influence and profit.

Relationship building is often a good strategy when there are large differences in the value of customers. The high-value customers might want close collaboration from suppliers in product design, inventory planning, and order processing. Some customers might proactively pursue collaboration. And buyer/seller collaboration is an essential aspect of total quality management programs. The objective is to focus buyer and seller efforts on relationships where both partners can benefit from a close collaborative relationship.

Implementing the Relationship Strategy

Gainsco Inc., a successful property casualty insurance company selling through more than 150 independent agents, decided that more collaborative relationships were needed with these agents. Management launched a customer-driven strategy to shift from a transaction to a collaborative relationship with the agents. Using information from customer satisfaction surveys (conducted on a continuing basis), the company developed software to help the agents prepare sales quotes and process orders. The company also offers seminars at regional locations to help the agents improve their operations.

Relationship building places new demands on all those involved in the process. The issues to be considered include:

- Deciding what criteria to use in partner selection.

- Recognizing that both partners must be willing to collaborate if the relationship is to be successful.

- Developing and implementing operating guidelines (such as Marriott's) for the relationship strategy.

Relationship building requires careful planning and implementation. It is a long-term proposition built on the foundations of trust and commitment. Deciding the value and feasibility of relationship building is the starting point.

Fostering Change

Complacency in the rapidly changing business environment can have dire consequences, as illustrated by the experience of Encyclopedia Britannica Corp. First published 225 years ago in Edinburgh, Scotland, peak sales for *Encyclopedia Britannica* were $650 million in 1990, with profits of $40 million. During the early 1990s, CD-ROM technology gained acceptance in the encyclopedia market but Britannica's management did not respond to the threat and continued to market through a direct sales force of 2,300 people.

By 1994, Britannica's sales force was less than half its former size. Competitors had entered the market with CD-ROM encyclopedia packages available at prices ranging from $99–$395 to an estimated 7 million U.S. households. The typical $1,500 *Encyclopedia Britannica* sale pays the salesperson a commission of $300, but it's tough to sell against a high-tech version priced far below that. Sales drastically declined and the company now is in severe financial trouble.

Competing against the CD-ROM threat would have required Britannica's management to offer buyers the new technology and alter its traditional direct selling strategy, reaching computer users through retail outlets, direct mail, and telemarketing. Or the company could have collaborated with CD-ROM manufacturers who bundle software with hardware. Britannica's direct sales force is too costly for selling the CD-ROM packages to households. Moreover, computer households are difficult for the direct sales force to identify but could be accessed easily via database marketing and computer retailers.

Removing Barriers to Change

During the 1990s, managers aggressively reduced the size and altered the structures of their sales organizations. Flexible, adaptable organizational structures are essential for competing today. Popular terms such as the virtual, horizontal, and boundaryless organization describe the corporate architectures being shaped to compete in the future.

One unique aspect of these new organizations is that they are complex networks of independent companies and units linked to share competencies and buffer risk and uncertainty. These changes are altering how sales organizations are designed and used to implement strategies.

International Business Machines' search for the perfect organizational design highlights the profound changes taking place in many sales organizations. There is perhaps no other company that has restructured so many times in recent years (17 revampings by one count).

The company announced another reorganization in 1994, implemented by IBM's new CEO, Louis V. Gerstner Jr. The new design involves major changes in IBM's country chiefs. The actions will eliminate one or more layers of management and simplify the previous hierarchical network of sales branches, trading area managers, and regional sales managers. The objective is to transform IBM account executives from mere order takers into teams of business consultants in their respective industries.

How Organizations Are Changing

Three major trends are changing the structures of traditional sales organizations and affecting the job responsibilities and careers of sales managers and salespeople.

First, organizations are becoming flatter and focused on the management of core processes, such as customer service. Multi-functional teams are responsible for client relationships and new product planning. Sales managers and salespeople need to develop new skills such as multi-functional collaboration and teamwork, and they will assume different responsibilities. The selling process today is shifting away from a short-term sales focus to problem solving aimed at customer satisfaction.

Second, specific customers and customer groups (market segments) are increasingly the basis for designing the sales organization and deploying salespeople. This means that sales managers will be responsible for managing multiple sales strategies directed at target segments.

Consider, for example, how sales organizations in the pharmaceutical industry are being redesigned to target customers in different market segments. The industry giant, Merck & Co., and its strategic partner, Sweden-based Astra AB, formed Astra/Merck to sell drugs. The new sales organization has a much smaller sales force than does the typical pharmaceutical company. By reducing the levels between salespeople and the CEO to only three and using information technology, Astra/Merck lowers selling costs and fosters close ties with customers.

Small powerful laptop computers help salespeople access information relevant to each customer's needs. For example, a doctor concerned about drug costs gets research data on treatment costs. Other market segments targeted by Astra/Merck are managed health care organizations concerned about economic factors, traditional physicians seeking the right drugs for the treatment of different diseases, and medical thought leaders interested in the newest therapies.

Third, companies are examining the logic of specialized sales forces, each responsible for certain products. Previously separate sales forces are being merged to reduce duplication in customer coverage and enhance customer coordination. These changes create different responsibilities for salespeople and could result in layoffs because multiple sales calls from specialized sales forces are eliminated.

The changes being made at Kraft Foods Inc. are illustrative. This new food division of the Philip Morris Co. combines Kraft, General Foods, Oscar Mayer Foods, and Maxwell House products. The 3,500 people from the specialized sales forces are now one unit, organized into 300 marketing support teams, each assigned to a chain of stores. The salesperson, formerly a specialist, is now responsible for a wide range of grocery products. Kraft has account-service teams and other support personnel to help manage the various food categories.

Making It Happen

Several guidelines for organizing the sales force are available, and new configurations will likely appear in the future. The effectiveness of the new designs such as Kraft Foods' cannot be fully evaluated until the companies gain additional experience. The following organizational design issues need to be considered by sales managers:

- The typical pyramid organization of the 1970s and 1980s—with a chief sales executive, regional managers each directing several district managers, and 8 or 10 salespeople assigned to each district—is being redesigned to improve customer satisfaction and reduce costs.

- Red flags signaling the need to rethink the sales structure include high expense-to-sales ratios, loss of customers, large sales variations across territories, merging sales forces, and salesperson turnover. Benchmarking successful sales organizations can provide useful comparisons.

- The use of process management by companies is calling for greater participation of other business functions in the sales process, and for new ways to organize salespeople.

- Employing multiple sales channels to customers requires changing the sales structure and the method of customer coverage to leverage the advantages of each channel.

The revamping of traditional sales structures promises to be an exciting, though demanding, experience for sales managers and salespeople. Finding a viable sales organization design promises much trial and evaluation. Sales structures are more likely to change more frequently in the future, creating new challenges for managers and salespeople, making agility and flexibility essential success requirements.

Gaining Commitment

The popularity of teams comprising people from different business functions escalated in the 1990s. The objective is to get people from the different functions to work together rather than each person and department performing a task and then passing it on to the next function. Deciding how to form and use sales teams in customer relationships, and how sales managers and salespeople are to participate in other team relationships such as new product planning and brand management, are important sales management issues.

The Value of Teams

Teams can produce some impressive results. Publishing Image Inc., a small newsletter publisher, uses self-managed work teams to improve organizational effectiveness. The company doubled its 1993 sales and increased its profit margin from 3% to 20%. The CEO of the 26-employee company credits the success to the firm's four teams, each responsible for a group of customers.

Each team includes an account executive (salesperson), editorial specialists, and production workers. A team member has unique skills but also performs other members' functions when necessary to meet deadlines. For example, an account executive might do research for writers, proofread copy, and assist in layout. The experience gives each member a view of the entire business operation. The team becomes involved in the sales process when client contact is initiated. Publishing Image's teams have increased efficiency, curtailed employee turnover, and improved customer satisfaction.

DuPont, the giant chemical company, uses teams made up of employees from research, manufacturing, and sales for planning new products. Ideas are identified, evaluated, and developed. The teams are encouraged to compress the time needed for new product development. One team moved a new auto safety product from idea to prototype in just 60 days. DuPont also forms joint teams with customers to help them solve problems.

Removing Functional Barriers

Though the team concept is compelling, making it work is another thing. The functionally organized company presents major obstacles. The restructuring of Corporate America successfully removed some of these functional barriers, but also required major changes in corporate culture, traditional priorities, attitudes, work processes, and incentives.

Decisions must be made concerning the selection of team members, reporting relationships (and authority), job responsibilities, performance assessment, and incentive compensation. The company can't respond to these issues without establishing a culture conducive to team relationships and providing training for leaders and members.

For example, the leaders of IBM's client teams spend three weeks at the Harvard Business School learning about business operations, consulting, and the client's industry. During the rest of the year, the consultants work on case studies and write a thesis on the customer. Harvard professors grade the papers and the students who pass are certified. Attending the training program is not mandatory.

Interestingly, the IBM sales teams have the flexibility to recommend the products that best meet the customer's requirements, and this includes competitors' products. The objective is helping the customer solve problems rather than selling IBM's products.

Leveraging Team Experience

Sales managers and salespeople who have been involved in major account management programs have valuable experience and skills in team building. Working with both customer buying center participants and people from various internal functions, major account people have been in the middle of turf battles and learned how to develop a consensus.

Sales managers face several challenges in organizations that are working to build multi-functional relationships. These are some of the more important questions that need to be answered:

- Is there a shared vision in the organization about the value of teams?
- Should client teams be formed and, if so, what will be their responsibilities?
- What is the role of the salesperson on both internal teams and customer-linked teams?
- What guidelines are needed for team member selection and team operations?

The reality is that many corporations are committed to employing teams as the basis of organizing work activities. When used in situations where their capabilities are needed and properly implemented, teams can produce impressive results. They work best in a corporate culture where strong functional hurdles are not present.

Coaching Vs. Commanding

Evidence is mounting that sales managers are coaching rather than commanding their salespeople. Discussions with chief sales executives and sales managers in many companies indicate that managers are coaching salespeople, directing their activities, and monitoring what they do. Although the tight command and control management style is losing favor, the responses indicate that sales managers believe some amount of monitoring and directing is essential.

Shifting Styles

A major survey of managers points to several shifts in management practices: (1) collaboration rather than control, (2) coaching instead of criticizing, (3) employee empowerment rather than domination, (4) sharing information instead of withholding it, and (5) adapting to individual salespeople rather than treating everyone the same.

Some managers sense the changing business environment and adjust their management processes to account for the change requirements. But not all managers recognize these demands and not all corporate cultures accommodate the change requirements. Shifting from commanding to coaching is a major challenge for both managers and salespeople. And some managers might be unwilling or unable to make the transition.

Companies planning to change their sales management practices should first review their recruiting, selection, and training of managers and salespeople. Not surprisingly, it's easier to create a coaching culture in a new organization than to transform an existing command-and-control organization. Coaching calls for a specific type of leadership style, and substantial investment in manager development and training might be necessary.

Keeping Score

For decades, sales volume has been the sales manager's way of keeping score. The salesperson or sales manager who meets and exceeds the sales objective (quota) is considered to be performing well. Nonetheless, scorekeeping in the sales organization also is undergoing change. Managers continue to track sales but now use additional measures such as customer satisfaction, profit contribution, share of customer (share of product category sales), and customer retention to evaluate salespeople and managers.

The Rules Are Changing

The changes in performance evaluation are driven by three factors. First, total quality management and customer relationship building encourage a long-term orientation. Sales results are important, but so are the activities that influence long-term sales results, such as building relationships. Second, primary emphasis on sales volume might lead to overselling customers and excessive inventory problems, causing customer dissatisfaction. Third, in sales organizations where pay is closely tied to sales, it's tough to encourage salespeople to develop new accounts, provide customer service, and emphasize all the products that are important to the company's marketing strategy. Ironically, compensation schemes encourage salespeople to put forth the most effort where they can generate sales today.

Customer satisfaction is being used by a small but growing number of companies to help track performance with the customer. Eastman Chemical Co., winner of a 1993 Malcolm Baldrige National Quality Award, has several ways of tracking customer satisfaction. The company's complaint process and its customer satisfaction survey were cited by the selection committee as the most useful ways of monitoring satisfaction.

Eastman produces eight versions of its survey for major customer groups. The survey covers 25 performance items and is printed in nine languages. Example items include on-time and correct delivery, product quality, pricing practice, and sharing of market information. Responsibility for each item is assigned to the function(s) in the organization that can affect the customer satisfaction problem. The survey is managed by the sales organization, and salespeople discuss the results with customers, indicating actions being taken by the company to overcome problems.

Activity or Outcome?

Performance evaluation is driven by the sales force control system the organization uses. The options range from primary emphasis on what the salesperson does (e.g., building effective relationships with customers) to emphasis on outcomes (e.g., sales). Either system is effective when matched to the right selling situation.

For example, emphasis on activities works best when the sales strategy is to build long-term collaborative relationships with customers. Many companies, such as American Airlines, Caterpillar, IBM, and Procter & Gamble, employ a blend of activity and outcome control. Direct selling organizations like Avon, Mary Kay, and Tupperware base compensation primarily on commissions.

Two salesperson performance issues require evaluation by sales managers. First, teams shift the management focus to group rather than individual performance. In this situation determining individual commissions becomes very complex and may not even be feasible. However, salespeople who have earned incentive compensation based on individual performance are not likely to favor group incentives. Thus, an issue in keeping score for teams is deciding how to allocate incentive rewards. Moreover, team effectiveness evaluation usually includes consideration of more than short-term sales results.

The second issue is deciding the amount of salary compared to incentive pay. Sales managers who want to encourage relationship strategies and form multi-functional teams will undoubtedly have to modify how they keep score and compensate salespeople.

Taking Different Avenues

The conventional wisdom that the salesperson handles all contacts with customers face-to-face is under severe assault. Consider, for example, Wal-Mart's satellite information system linking its retail stores, distribution centers, headquarters, and suppliers.

Inventory replacement orders for the retail stores are transmitted to distribution centers and suppliers. Many routine activities traditionally handled by salespeople are now accomplished electronically. Recording is triggered by the information system based on reorder guidelines.

This system gave Wal-Mart the competitive edge in the 1980s to leap ahead of Kmart and other discounters. Suppliers' salespeople concentrate on providing information on new products, merchandising support, and other supporting services.

Value/Cost Assessment

The widespread sales force reductions by companies in the 1990s indicate that managers are concerned about the cost and effectiveness of personal selling as the primary way of customer contact. They are employing a combination of methods to perform functions previously handled by salespeople.

Today, customers can be contacted less expensively through telemarketing, direct marketing, computer networks, part-time salespeople, and selling partnerships (alliances). Dell Computer, founded in 1984, will have more than $4 billion in sales in 1995. This incredible growth record was achieved primarily by telemarketing coupled with supporting services (via a contract organization) provided at the customer's location.

Personal selling is an important avenue to the customer in many selling situations but will increasingly be coupled with other selling channels. These alternatives should be used when their value and cost are favorable compared to contact by salespeople. Downsizing of sales forces, escalating selling costs, competitive pressures, the use of client teams, powerful information technology, and demanding customers all point to the importance of finding the most effective channels to customers.

Choosing the Best Channel

Too often we assume that field salespeople are essential in many lines of business. Yet, managers in an increasing number of companies are challenging this premise. American Family Life Assurance Co. (AFLAC) sells its cancer insurance to Japanese consumers through partnerships with Japanese business firms. The companies encourage employees to buy the insurance, and buyers can have the premiums deducted from their paychecks. Over 90% of Japanese companies participate, and 28 million people in Japan are insured by AFLAC.

AFLAC highlights the important issue of finding the best channel to the customer. The process starts by studying customer requirements, identifying available avenues to the customer, and looking at the capabilities and costs of each sales channel. To adopt a multiple sales channel strategy, managers must decide what is the best channel to each customer group, define the role of the field sales force, and decide how to coordinate the activities of the different channels.

A company that has used only field sales is likely to encounter major internal resistance when shifting to the use of multiple avenues to the customer. Nonetheless, following this strategy can yield substantial benefits.

Xerox's approach to supplying customers with toner refills is a striking example of how rethinking sales channels to customers can yield impressive results. The old way was to move all supplies through the producer to customers. Instead, Xerox shifted the sales and distribution responsibility to the toner cartridge supplier. The supplier formed a direct relationship with Xerox's end-user customers, eliminating the need for Xerox to purchase, stock, and process toner orders. Since making this change three years ago, Xerox's estimated savings exceed $1 billion.

Removing Performance Hurdles

Sales managers know that competent salespeople who work hard should perform well. Nonetheless, studies examining sales management practices and results in a wide range of companies point up another key influence: performance hurdles.

Assigning a salesperson to a territory or group of accounts with low market potential, intense competition, or too many accounts reduces the salesperson's opportunity to perform well. A performance hurdle means that the opportunity to perform is constrained (or enhanced) by factors not controlled by the salesperson. As a result, two equally competent and highly motivated salespeople will perform differently. The huge differences found in the sales results in a business unit of a *Fortune 500* services company show the importance of removing performance hurdles. Annual sales for 24 salespeople ranged from less than $300,000 to over $60 million! The unit had 24 service centers with one salesperson assigned to each location. The problem was that the low-sales areas did not have enough potential to justify assigning a full-time salesperson there. Similarly, in the high-sales areas, salespeople had an impossible sales coverage situation.

Both the high- and low-sales areas created performance hurdles for the salespeople. Importantly, the experience, skills, and effort of the salespeople did not account for the large differences in sales. An account analysis was used to reallocate selling effort. The high-potential locations were assigned to more than one salesperson, whereas the very low-sales areas were served by telemarketing and by routing field salespeople into the area to call on the customers less frequently than the past coverage. As a result of this reallocation, the company was able to cut the sales force by five and lower sales expenses while retaining prior sales levels.

If hurdles are not removed, two problems often occur. First, because pay is tied to sales performance through incentives and salary increases, salespeople might leave the company. Even if they stay, the hurdle is likely to affect their morale and commitment to the organization. Second, faulty assignment of accounts and prospects (e.g., too high or not enough market potential) constrain salespeople from using their selling effort in the most effective manner.

When deciding whether or not the salesperson's assigned customers and prospects provide a reasonable opportunity to perform well, sales managers should look at several factors: sales productivity (e.g., sales per salesperson), number and purchasing power of accounts, customer requirements, customer loyalty, geographical area, calls per salesperson, travel requirements, market potential, intensity of competition, and workload equity across salespeople.

Poor allocation of selling effort affects the productivity of the sales organization. When all or most of the salespeople's work assignments are in balance, the overall effectiveness of the sales organization will be higher than when several hurdles exist.

Leveraging Technology

Not surprisingly, early efforts to apply information technology in sales organizations met a lot of resistance. Nonetheless, sales force automation is changing both the effectiveness of selling and how it is done in many companies. Computers, telecommunications, and software give sales managers and salespeople a powerful array of capabilities. Information technology is becoming indispensable in many companies.

For example, Godiva Chocolates' salespeople use their portable computers to process orders, plan time allocations, forecast sales, and communicate with internal personnel and customers. While in the department store candy buyer's office, the salesperson calculates the order cost (and discount), transmits the order, and obtains a delivery date. She uses the customer's phone and her computer to communicate with the order processing center.

The investment in applying these technologies is substantial, but well-designed and implemented systems give valuable capabilities to the sales force. The equipment, software, and training costs for automating the sales force ranges from $2,500–$5,000 or more per person. One company, which spent $2.5 million to equip its 300-person sales staff with computers and software, considers the investment worthwhile because of increased sales and reduced costs.

Sales force automation applications include account analysis, time management, order processing and status, sales presentation, proposal generation, and product training. Some companies are using information technology to eliminate the need for field offices. These systems reduce office costs and provide flexibility in deciding where salespeople and managers will be located. They also change how managers and salespeople communicate because they do not operate out of the same office.

Using information technology, salespeople are able to analyze sales history much better and much faster than in the past. On the road or in the customer's office, information is at their fingertips to answer questions and solve problems. Visual displays portray products, applications, and performance information. Motorola salespeople, for example, are able to design phone pagers in the customer's office by combining various design modules from the computer.

Deciding How to Use Technology

Many companies have not yet implemented sales force automation. Hewlett-Packard is just beginning to automate its sales force by conducting a test with 100 salespeople using laptop computers. A standard set of software tools is available to check order status, obtain product information, and retrieve sample presentations that can be modified to fit the salesperson's selling situation. Plans include providing all salespeople access to the network to obtain the information they need on demand.

Two issues are of central importance in considering how to use information technology in an organization. First, companies not currently involved in sales force automation need to be looking at what is available and how it can be used to improve the effectiveness of their sales organizations. These capabilities are available to small as well as large companies. The issue is deciding how automation fits the requirements of a particular company. Management needs to evaluate the potential value provided by the technology against the cost of implementation.

Second, applying information technology involves far more than giving each salesperson a laptop computer and software. It also involves substantial training. Hewlett-Packard is not only training its salespeople how to use the computer system, but also providing a hotline for them to call about problems.

Information technology such as interactive video also offers potentially powerful training capabilities for salespeople. The technology can be used to provide product knowledge and other training needs. In the future, the traditional classroom could become obsolete. Both new and experienced salespeople can tap these resources to improve their selling skills and product knowledge.

An Action Agenda

Some companies are aggressively reinventing their sales organizations, others are beginning to recognize the need to develop action plans, and some remain complacent. Nonetheless, the changes occurring in many sales organizations underscore the importance of deciding which trends need management attention in your sales organization.

Not all sales organizations need to be reinvented to follow the guidelines in this article. By using Exhibit 1 as a checklist, managers can evaluate their own needs; some actions may be imperative, whereas others may not fit a company's selling environment and strategy. Each executive must consider how his or her particular sales organization will be affected by change.

My objective here is to offer a framework for management analysis and action rather than to propose a particular sales management strategy. Nonetheless, there is a compelling base of evidence pointing to the urgency to decide if and how a company's sales organization should be reinvented.

Reprinted with permission from the Fall 1995 issue of Marketing, Management, *published by the American Marketing Association, Cravens, David., Fall 1995/Vol. 4, pp. 48–57.*

Additional Reading

Fierman, Jaclyn (1994), "The Death and Rebirth of the Salesman," *Fortune,* (July 25), 80–91.

Harnar, George (1994), "Pills 'n Pads No More," *Forbes ASAP,* (June 6), 36–41.

Jacob, Rahul (1995), "The Struggle to Create an Organization for the 21st Century," *Fortune,* (April 3) 90–9.

Levine, Daniel S. (1995) "Justice Served," *Sales & Marketing Management,* (May), 53–61.

McKenna, Regis (1991), *Relationship Marketing,* Reading, MA: Addison-Wesley Publishing Co.

Samuels, Gary (1994), "CD-ROM's First Big Victim," *Forbes,* (Feb. 28), 42–4.

Selz, Michael (1994), "Testing Self-Managed Teams, Entrepreneur Hopes to Lose Job," *The Wall Street Journal,* (Jan. 11), B1–B2.

20

Technology's Effect on Customer Service: Building Meaningful Relationships through Dialogue

JENNIFER FREEDMAN
RUBY SUDOYO

Most companies today recognize the importance of good customer service and the effect it has on their bottom line. But as businesses, they also have to take into consideration the resources necessary to provide good customer service. Can they afford the manpower? How do they provide good customer service in a cost-effective way? Many companies turn to technology because they think it will solve both problems. They buy Automated Voice Response (AVR) systems and/or Internet sites because they believe technology is the key to providing cost-effective customer service. However, the real key to good customer service is not technology, but dialogue. According to Terry Vavra:

> Engaging in dialogue with customers tells them that they are important. It assures customers that their opinions are sought and that the company is interested in serving their needs. Dialogue also can ease a wary customer's mind, soothe an angry customer's temper, or reaffirm a satisfied customer's purchase decision.[1]

Technology is not a bad thing. It can be used effectively to facilitate meaningful dialogues and create better relationships with customers, but most often it falls short of these goals. Technology can actually get in the way of meaningful dialogue. It might even destroy a brand's relationship with its customers.

A recent study conducted at the University of Colorado explores the effective use of technology in customer service. For the past two years, graduate students in the

---

Data-Driven Communication Team Members: Ed Chambliss, Carlos Chaves, Jennifer Freedman, Julie Funasaki, Dana Hamilton, Anne Heilemann, Kristen Kammerer, Jooyoung Kim, Rich Khleif, Laurel Lane, Matt Marriott, Kris McInerney, Jennifer Montague, Suzie Moore, Adrian Nicol, Jessica Schneider, Ruby Sudoyo; Tom Duncan, Professor.

Integrated Marketing Communications (IMC) program at the university have conducted an annual customer service study of selected organizations. The objective of the class project was to evaluate communication technology application and use in the customer service arena.

Methodology

Over a period of five weeks, 19 researchers each contacted at last 10 for-profit and non-profit organizations. The researchers were asked to initiate at least five telephone contacts and five Internet contacts. They also were also asked to contact both business-to-business and consumer product companies—not as students, but as customers. Of particular interest was how communications companies handled their own communications, so every researcher contacted at least one communications company.

During the study, the researchers recorded the following:

Ease or difficulty of the initial contact

Nature of the reply

Friendliness of the interaction

Thoroughness of the reply

Company follow-up

Their rating of the entire experience

Researchers were asked to rate their experience with each company, based on their own perceptions, according to the following criteria:

Good—customer inquiry satisfied easily and thoroughly

Fair—customer inquiry answered, but the interaction involved one or more shortcomings, such as an unenthusiastic representative, a canned, barely on-target response, or long hold or response time.

Unacceptable—non-response, rude representative, excessive hold or response time, unfriendly phone system, off-target response, and other items producing customer inconvenience or dissatisfaction.

There were 200 total contacts to 174 different companies. This represents a convenient ethnographic sample rather than a random projectable sample; researchers chose organizations that were convenient to contact and were of "real life" interest. Of those companies, 136 were nationally known and 38 were regional or niche companies. The following organization classifications were used during the study and for analysis:

Service/Goods

Communications/Non-profit/Other

Business-to-business/Consumer

The organizations contacted in last year's study are not necessarily the same as those contacted this year. This year's research was not meant to be a follow-up study, but a new study in the same genre.

Findings

Out of 200 contacts, 78 contacts (39%) were rated Unacceptable. However, it is interesting to note that of the 78 Unacceptable contacts in our study, 28 were from companies that did not respond at all. In addition to the Unacceptable responses in our study, 39 companies provided only Fair service.

Internet inquiries generated more Unacceptable responses (45%) than phone inquiries (33%). Fair responses were almost equal at 20% for Internet contacts and 19% for phone contacts. (See Figure 1 for an overview of 1998 ratings by medium.)

The performance ratings of nationally known organizations showed little difference compared to those of regional/niche organizations. This indicates that there is no correlation between the size of a company, the depth of their pockets and the degree of customer service offered. (See Figure 2 for an overview of ratings by company profile.)

One aspect studied was how the customer service of organizations that provided services compared to organizations that provided goods. The expectation was that service companies would be very service-oriented, thus outperforming goods companies when it came to customer service. After the results were tabulated, however, service companies had a higher Unacceptable rating in both Phone and Internet contacts. (See Figure 3 for ratings by product category)

To ascertain if there were any differences from industry to industry, the organizations were divided into the following classifications:

Communications—Twenty-eight contacts were made with various telecommunication companies, Internet service providers and cable service providers. Of those

| FIGURE 1 | RATINGS BY MEDIUM |

	Rating			
	Good	*Fair*	*Unacceptable*	*Total*
Internet	35	20	45	100
Phone	48	19	33	100
Total	83	39	78	200
Contacts	41.5%	19.5%	39%	100%

FIGURE 2

RATINGS BY PROFILE

	Rating			
	Good	*Fair*	*Unacceptable*	*Total*
National	64	33	61	158
	40.5%	21%	38.5%	100%
Regional/ Niche	19	6	17	42
	45%	14%	41%	100%
Total	83	39	78	200
Contacts	41.5%	19.5%	39%	100%

FIGURE 3

RATINGS BY PRODUCT CATEGORY— PHONE CONTACTS

	Rating			
	Good	*Fair*	*Unacceptable*	*Total*
Service	33	11	27	71
	46.5%	15.5%	38%	100%
Goods	15	7	4	26
	57.7%	26.9%	15.4%	100%
Both Goods and Services	0	1	2	3
		33.3%	66.7%	100%

RATINGS BY PRODUCT CATEGORY— INTERNET CONTACTS

	Rating			
	Good	*Fair*	*Unacceptable*	*Total*
Service	13	10	18	41
	31.7%	24.4%	43.9%	100%
Goods	21	10	19	50
	42%	20%	38%	100%
Both Goods and Services	1		8	9
	11.1%	0	88.9%	100%

contacts, 43% were Unacceptable, an unbelievable fact considering that these companies are, ostensibly, on the cutting edge of communication technology. Yet, there seems to be a major disconnect between possessing cutting-edge technology and applying it to satisfying customers. One company put a researcher on hold for eight minutes. Technology may make communicating more efficient for the company, but what kind of message does a long hold time send to a customer?

Non-profit—There is a dichotomy among non-profits. Out of 27 contacts to non-profit organizations, 44% achieved a Good rating, the highest of all three classifications. However they also achieved an Unacceptable rating of 41%. So, their customer service ranged dramatically from very good to very bad.

All other industries—because of the variety of organizations contacted, we were unable to break out any other significant classifications. In this group, which includes airlines, banking, retail, auto, health care, computers, etc., 41.5% achieved Good ratings and 38% received Unacceptable ratings. It is interesting to note that of all these different industries, 145 contacts in all, only the auto industry had zero Unacceptable ratings.

One final exercise was to compare business-to-business and consumer organizations to determine any significant differences in their level of customer service. The business-to-business classification applies to firms that serve other businesses. The consumer classification includes organizations that provide goods and services to individuals. The research showed that there was no discernable difference in level of customer service between these two classifications.

The Human Element

It seems so obvious, yet critical to state, that customers *are* human. There is a higher level of satisfaction when they are treated as individuals, with individual needs and problems. An organization needs to facilitate a dialogue with its customers. According to Terry Vavra:

> The two-way dialogue between customer and company generates goodwill and goodwill leads to satisfaction and satisfaction leads to customer loyalty.[2]

The research showed that, when a human element was introduced, such as a real person answering the phone or a personalized Internet response, there were a greater number of Good ratings.

Phone inquiries that were answered immediately by a Customer Service Representative (CSR) generated a higher level of customer satisfaction. Humans answered 34% of the phone contacts, and of that group, 59% received Good ratings. AVR systems answered 66% of the phone contacts, but, of that group, only 42% received Good ratings.

The human element in these Internet contacts was measured by the degree of the personalization of the response. If a response was directed specifically to the person by name, and the response was tailored to address the question or problem, we classified it as "totally personalized." Of the 31 Internet responses that were totally personalized, 64% received Good ratings. Of the 22 responses that were somewhat personalized,

50% received Good ratings. Of the 20 responses that were not personalized at all, only 20% received Good ratings. Twenty-seven Internet contacts did not respond at all, which automatically earned them an Unacceptable rating. (See Figure 4 for Internet ratings by level of personalization.)

The human element was a factor in overall satisfaction even when phone contacts were answered by AVR. There were some instances that even when a caller had to go through multiple levels of an AVR system before reaching a human, the quality of that human interaction determined overall satisfaction. As one researcher pointed out:

> I found the attentiveness and efficiency of a CSR out weighed the frustration caused by the multi-level AVR.

People like to be treated as individuals, and they really like to know that they are important enough for a company to make a special effort to satisfy them. The human element is a big factor in customer satisfaction.

Recognizing Key Problems

The data revealed that many organizations shared common problems that seriously affected the quality of their customer service. These problems are discussed below.

Customer Service Systems in General

Message Consistency. In many cases, there was a lack of message consistency on the part of the company. In some cases, one person calling a company several times had a different response each time.

FIGURE 4   **RATINGS BY LEVEL OF PERSONALIZATION— INTERNET CONTACTS**

Level of Personalization	Rating			
	Good	*Fair*	*Unacceptable*	*Total*
Totally	20 64%	8 26%	3 10%	31 100%
Somewhat	11 50%	6 27%	5 23%	22 100%
Not at all	4 20%	6 30%	10 50%	20 100%
No response	0	0	27 100%	27 100%

In other cases, several researchers called the same company and experienced totally different responses. Out of sixteen organizations that were contacted multiple times, only two, Saturn and Amazon.com, received consistent ratings—and all those ratings were Good. Six organizations were rated both Good and Unacceptable by different researchers.

Opportunities Lost.   Very few companies took the opportunity of customer contact to gather information about their customers. Even though the questionnaires were not designed to specifically record this data, researchers' comments indicated only 14 organizations attempted to elicit additional information from them. According to Terry G. Vavra:

> The benefits a company can reap from toll-free telephone information go beyond solving complaints and making sales. Callers' opinions can identify up-to-the-minute changes in trends, fads, and consumer tastes. Companies spend thousand of dollars on marketing research studies to collect many of the same opinions that consumers voluntarily offer during their calls to the companies.[3]

Researchers also indicated that there were very few organizations contacted that capitalized on the customer contact by cross-selling other products. Most of the organizations are missing the opportunity to inform a customer about their other products.

Telephone Customer Service Systems

Technology.   Some AVR systems are just not user-friendly. They often have too many levels that can be confusing and frustrating, especially if there is no option to either speak to a human or return to the beginning of a menu. It is not always clear to customers which menu choice is appropriate for their needs.

The quality of an AVR system can affect customer service. Substandard phone lines cause static and inhibit communication. A poorly designed system can hang up on customers. One researcher had to call one company three times because the AVR system disconnected her twice.

Human Resources.   The person who answers the phone is of paramount importance. Unpleasant, surly or condescending attitudes will affect a customer's perception of the brand, regardless of whether the question is answered adequately. Also, a CSR who does not have the knowledge to answer specific questions, or have access to that knowledge, is giving poor customer service.

Time is very important to customers, and they resent having their time wasted. A customer on hold gets frustrated easily. Keep in mind that even a minute on hold can be perceived as a very long time. One researcher was on hold for a full 15 minutes with an airline company and found it extremely aggravating.

Response.   Customers contact organizations because they want something. They have a question, a complaint or a need for information. Their opinion of the brand could rest on how well the organization responds. The research pointed out the following response problems:

- Scripted or canned message—a form letter is sent that does not address the question.

- Promises not kept—a CSR promises to call back or send material and does not do it.

- Answer is off-target—the question is not answered fully; the answer lacks necessary details or includes information that does not pertain to the question at all.

Internet Customer Service Systems

Technology.   The relative ease of use of a web site can affect how the customers find information or contact the company through the web site. Some common problems were:

- Site hard to find—different search engines had to be used before a site could be found.

- Site hard to navigate—not easy to find the information that is wanted—not user-friendly.

- No clear channels of communication—difficult to find an appropriate e-mail address, if any. Some sites had no e-mail connection, but gave only a phone number to call.

- Level of technology—hardware and software systems are not adequate to support the site.

Response.   Responding to customers' inquiries is as important on the Internet as in any other medium. The study found the following problems:

- No response—the company neither acknowledges an inquiry nor responds to it.

- Long response time—most Internet users expect real-time communication. Our research showed that 66% of e-mail contacts were *not* responded to within 24 hours.

- No apparent response—several companies responded to researchers' questions by mailing information. However, they did not e-mail the researchers to tell them that they had done so. The perception, at first, was that their inquiry had been ignored.

- Scripted or canned message—a form e-mail is sent that does not address the question. Answer is not personalized; it is not directed to the specific person.

- Answer is off-target—the question is not answered fully; the answer lacks necessary details or includes information that does not pertain to the question at all.

- Promises not kept—an e-mail response promises further action and does not deliver.

Look for "How Does Your Customer Service System Stack Up?" (following this article), for a list of Customer Service Audit Questions that can help any organization evaluate its own customer service system.

Conclusion.   The results of this study directly mirror the results of the study conducted by the 1997 IMC class,[4] especially in overall ratings.

Both the 1997 and the 1998 customer service studies showed that many organizations have a long way to go when it comes to building effective relationships with customers. There are some rays of hope—41.5% of our contacts were rated Good.

However, many of the organizations have not realized that customer service is not about technology; it is about dialogue. It's about having REAL people available, with the right answer and the right attitude, even if technology initiates the first contact.

These companies need to learn that technology is only a tool that must be used effectively to establish meaningful dialogue with the customer. As Ernan Roman stated:

> We must never forget that the technology is simply the facilitator; it cannot form the relationship that business must establish with the customers.[5]

How Does Your Customer Service System Stack Up?
It's All About Relationships . . .

The kind of relationship you hold with your customer, whether it is good, bad or neutral, is based solely on the customer's perception of your company. It doesn't matter if you think you have a good relationship. It doesn't matter if you think you have great customer service. If you want to maintain a good relationship with your customer, it only matters what the customer thinks as he or she interacts with your company. A satisfied customer, a good relationship and continued profits can rest on that interaction.

Below is a list of Customer Service Audit Questions that are designed to help you evaluate your customer service systems.

Customer Service Audit Questions

The following list of audit questions was first compiled by Steere and Weiss' and subsequently revised by Freedman and Sudoyo.

Telephone Customer Service System

User-Friendliness
- Have you tested your system with a broad cross-section of customers to make sure features are easy to use and provide the functionality they expect?

- Can customers easily access a live person if they have difficulty with interfaces or cannot find the answers they need?

- If the customer wants to hear instructions or information again, or if a customer "goofs," does the voice response system allow the customer to re-listen or re-key, or does it require the customer to hang up and dial again?

Time Sensitivity
- Do you regularly place customers on hold for more than 60 seconds?

- Does your system provide a choice between holding and leaving a message? How quickly do you reply to those messages?

- Does your system state anticipated wait time to help callers decide whether to stay on the line or call back later?

- Does your system ask for the same information more than once?

- Do you state, up front, any topics that your system cannot handle and refer customers to the appropriate resource for assistance?

- During non-business hours, does your voice response system immediately indicate that you are closed or only after the customer goes through several layers of options? Do you offer customers the opportunity to leave a message or call an emergency number to reach a live person?

Response Time
- Is your voice response system staffed during all business hours? What happens during staff meetings, lunches, breaks, times of heavy call volume and phone/computer/power outages? Do you let customers know when to expect a return call? Do you provide them with a way to reach someone faster in the event of an emergency?

- Do you have someone to step in and handle phone calls in cases of vacation or illness?

Accuracy and Proper Functioning
- Is the voice response recording clear, without background noise? Is it functioning properly?

- Are all customer service phone numbers, web site addresses and e-mail addresses on packaging, stationery, advertising and promotional materials reviewed for accuracy at least once a month?

Customer Service Representatives
- Are your CSRs well trained, both in attitude and knowledge, to provide superior customer service?

- When promises are made by CSRs to follow up in some manner, is that promise kept, and is it done in a timely manner?

Miscellaneous

- What do customers hear while they are waiting on hold? Music? Product information? Is there auditory variety? Do you give a choice of different things the customer can listen to?

- If the voice response system permits changes of address or other information, does the system read the changes back to the customer for confirmation or correction?

- Is your message consistent? Does every phone call give the same quality of customer service? Are your CSRs always courteous, knowledgeable and helpful? Is your customer always satisfied that he or she got the best answer possible?

- When a customer contacts you, do you take the opportunity to gather information about your customer for your customer database or to cross-sell other products?

Internet Customer Service System

User-friendliness

- Have you tested your web site interfaces with a broad cross-section of customers to make sure features are easy to use and provide the functionality customers expect?

- Is it easy for a customer to communicate with you through your web site? Do you have different channels of communication for different questions? Is it clear how the customer should use these channels of communication?

- Does your site contain so many technological gadgets that it takes forever to load?

- Will your web site work smoothly with older computers and modems slower than 14,400? If not, do you offer customers an alternate way to reach you?

- Is your web site registered with all major search engines so that customers can find it easily?

- Do you state, up front, any topics that your interface cannot handle and refer customers to the appropriate resource for assistance?

Response Time

- If a customer e-mails you, do you respond with a personal reply or a form letter? If the latter, do you indicate how customers should contact you again if they need more details?

- Do you have a customer response form? Is it possible for your customers to ask any questions that they want to, or must they address a specific subject matter?

- If your web site generates automatic e-mail acknowledgments (such as "we received your e-mail and you'll hear from us by phone tomorrow"), does your company have a system for determining that follow-ups occur as promised?

- If you do not have an automatic e-mail reply system, do you respond to all e-mails within 24 hours? If not, do you acknowledge their inquiry immediately and inform them of the action you will take? Do you keep your promises?

- Does your company respond to e-mail via regular mail? If yes, does your web site state this? Or, do you send an acknowledgment e-mail stating the response will be mailed?

- If you cannot respond to e-mail inquiries, does your web site provide a different way for customers to get an immediate response, such as a telephone number to call?

- Do you have someone to step in and handle e-mail and web problems in cases of vacation or illness?

Accuracy and Proper Functioning

- Does your web site come up properly in searches? Is it easy to find? Is it registered on all search engines? When you click on your site description, do you end up in your site or somewhere else?

- Are all contact names, phone numbers and e-mail addresses on the web site reviewed for accuracy weekly or at least monthly?

- Is your web address correct on all product packaging, stationery, advertising and promotional materials? Do you check at least once a month?

- What procedures have you established for responding to web site malfunctions?

Miscellaneous

- Does your web site ask how customers would prefer to receive responses—by e-mail, work phone, home phone, etc? Can you/do you honor each customer's preference?

- Do you force your customer to give information before they can ask their questions (e.g. Can they bypass your questionnaire if they want to)?

- Are you consistent in the messages you send to your customers and the manner and efficiency with which you send them?

- When a customer contacts you, do you take the opportunity to gather information about your customer for your customer database or to cross-sell other products?

MC Research Journal, Spring 1999, pp. 3–8 by Freedman, Jennifer and Ruby Sudoyo.

Notes

1. Terry G. Vavra, *After-marketing—How to Keep Customers for Life through Relationship Marketing* (New York: McGraw-Hill, 1995), p. 124.
2. Ibid., p. 128.

3. Ibid., p. 124.

4. Leigh Ann Steere & Timothy J. Weiss, "Is Technology Damaging Your Brand Image?" *Integrated Marketing Communication Research Journal.* (Boulder, CO: University of Colorado, 1998), pp. 17–25.

5. Ernan Roman, *Integrated Direct Marketing—The Cutting-Edge Strategy for Synchronizing Advertising, Direct Mail, Telemarketing and Field Sales.* (Chicago: NTC Business Books, 1995), p. 62.

6. Leigh Ann Steere & Timothy J. Weiss, op. cit., pp. 20–25.

IV

Ethical, Legal and Societal Impact

Menzel, Donald C. (1998), "www.ethics.gov: Issues and Challenges Facing Public Managers," *Public Administration Review*, 58 (September/October), 445–452.

Introna, Lucas D. and Athanasia Pouloudi (1999), "Privacy in the Information Age: Stakeholders, Interests and Values," *Journal of Business Ethics*, 22, 27–38.

Perry, Barlow (1994), "The Economy of Ideas: A Framework for Patents and Copyrights in the Digital Age," *Wired Magazine*, 2, (March), http://www.wired.com/wired/archive/2.03/economy.ideas_pr.html

IV

Ethical, Legal, and Social Impact

Part IV of the textbook focuses on issues of ethics, law, and societal impact. Just as other technologies since the Industrial Revolution have made enormous impact on society with respect to its culture, structure, processes and behaviors, it is likely that the Internet will also impact society. Just think of the impact of railroads, automobiles and airplanes on society's mobility; and the impact of the printing press, radio and television on society's values, culture and information.

The fundamental effects of technologies in general, and the Internet in particular, are the democratization of information, wealth, and power. Prior to the Industrial Revolution, wealth was created through inheritance only. You had to be born into monarchy or nobility. Private wealth is a direct consequence of the industrial revolution. It created many millionaires in steel, shipping, railroads, oil, and automobiles. Today, the Internet is creating not only many millionaires but also billionaires! Similarly, today it is possible for virtually anyone in any place of the world to access information. Just as radio and television transgressed national boundaries and ideologies (witness the MTV generation across all cultures), videocassettes and cameras, e-mail and Web content are creating even more democratization of information and influence. As the Internet access expands through television, car radio, and cell phones in addition to the personal computers, it is likely to become universal just as the transistor radio become universal in the forties and the fifties.

Unlike other media, however, the Internet is an interactive medium enabling and empowering instant feedback, interaction, and co-creation. This will inevitably reduce the gap between the elite and the masses. In other words, the fear of the "digital divide" or the information rich and poor gap is more a present reality anchored to personal computer as the Internet access appliance. It is not likely to be the case in the future as Internet access becomes universal through other communication media and especially the wireless mobile phones. Indeed, it is impressive to see a rural villager in an emerging country in Africa, Asia or Latin America using the digital cell phone to communicate!

As democratization of wealth, information, and power or influence take place, it is likely to make everyone aware of more diversity of opinions and beliefs in the cyberspace. Web sites just like the preachers of ideology in the old age will be utilized for propaganda and influence. The societal benefits of the Internet will be also matched by increasing personal deviancy and the dark side of the human being as manifested in the marketplace. This includes hackers, white-collar crimes, invasion of privacy, and stealing of intellectual assets. This is because the traditional gatekeepers who did not permit manifestation of the dark side of human beings (priests, professors, journalists, censors, and institutions in general) will have lesser role to play in a fully market-driven unregulated Internet-age economy.

Three readings illuminate the ethical and societal challenges facing marketing professionals in the Internet age. In the first article titled, *www.ethics.gov: Issues and Challenges Facing Public Managers*, Menzele discusses the ethical and management challenges facing public managers are identified and speculates about what the consequences may be for the public when government agencies in the United States go online. The meaning of cyber management as a prelude to developing organizational strategies for promoting Internet use and discouraging Internet abuse is discussed. The article concludes with questions that must be answered in order for public managers to become effective cyber-age managers.

In the second reading, *Privacy in the Information Age: Stakeholders, Interests and Values*, Introna and Pouloudi offer a systematic discussion of potentially different notions of privacy. They maintain that privacy as the freedom or immunity from the judgment of others is an extremely useful concept to develop and understand. To this end, a framework of principles is developed that explores the interrelations of interests and values for various stakeholders where privacy concerns have risen or are expected to rise. It is argued that conflicts between the interests and values of different stakeholders may result in legitimate claims of privacy being ignored and underrepresented.

The final article in this section is by Barlow, *The Economy of Ideas: A Framework for Patents and Copyrights in the Digital Age*, and emphasizes the fact that most copyright laws legislated for the physical world will not apply in the digital world. Barlow maintains that protection of thoughts and ideas are more likely to occur by encryption and promotion of ethical use of the Internet rather than the legal system. Moreover, the author points out that mere possession of an idea in itself does not generate value. It is the execution or implementation that determines the value creation potential of the idea. Using the new economic theories, Barlow concludes that in the Internet age the value of ideas increases with supply rather than through scarcity, as is the case in the physical world.

21

www.ethics.gov:
Issues and Challenges Facing Public Managers

DONALD C. MENZEL
Northern Illinois University

This article identifies ethical and management challenges facing public managers and speculates about what the consequences may be for the public when government agencies in the United States go on line (i.e., access the Internet and establish Web sites). The article is organized into five sections. The first section discusses the meaning of cyber management as a prelude to developing organizational strategies for promoting Internet use and discouraging Internet abuse. Section 2 draws the reader's attention to the specific content of acceptable use policies for the Internet. Section 3 then explores the challenges facing public managers to understand and abate the undesirable and sometimes unethical consequences that Internet usage may have for social or group life in public organizations. This discussion is followed by an examination of government use and abuse of the Internet. The final section highlights questions that must be answered in order for public managers to become effective cyber-age managers.

It is no secret that governments worldwide are going "online" (i.e., accessing the Internet and establishing Web sites) at a very rapid rate. Tracking statistics recorded in 1997 show there are 1,915 national level government agencies worldwide with Web sites (*http://w3.arizona.edul-CyPRG/*). The United States leads all countries with 205 agencies online. Canada with 153 agencies and Australia with 151 online agencies follow the United States. The French national government has 104 agencies online, the Netherlands 74, the United Kingdom 73, Germany 38, and Russia has only five agencies with Web sites. In the Middle East, Israel leads other nations with 75 sites, and Egypt has seven sites. In South America, Argentina and Brazil have 35 and 34 sites,

Donald C. Menzel is professor of public administration and director of the Division of Public Administration at Northern Illinois University. He is a former member of the faculties at the University of South Florida and West Virginia University. He is currently working on a book, *Ethics Management in Government,* and conducting research on the ethical environment of public administration graduate education.

respectively. In the Far East, Malaysia leads other nations with 59 sites, Japan has 33 sites, and one site has been documented for China.

At the subnational level in the United States, more than 2,500 state government agencies have established Web sites. Texas state government leads all states with 134 agencies online. Utah and California are second and third, respectively, with 122 Utah online agencies and 115 California agencies online. Cities and countries have also been going online at a rapid rate. Statistics show, for example, that in Florida 26 of the state's 67 counties (39 percent) have established Web sites and 10 percent of Florida's 395 municipalities are online (*http://www.piperinfo.com*). A similar pattern exists for New York where 36 percent of the state's 58 counties are online and 7 percent of its municipalities are online. In California, the most populated state in the nation, 48 percent of the counties and 30 percent of the municipalities have established Web sites.

These statistics document the rapid diffusion of a new information technology and, perhaps most importantly, signal what many believe are profound changes taking place in the social and governmental fabrics of many countries. "We are moving rapidly," writes one scholar (Gregorian, 1997, 597), "to the dawn of an information revolution that may well parallel the Industrial Revolution in its impact and far-reaching consequences."

Transformations in education, commerce, industry, entertainment, politics, government, and even church and family are taking place. While the magnitude of change in these many sectors appears to be substantial, there is very little knowledge or understanding of the consequences in any sector.

This paper takes a step toward exploring what the consequences may be for public managers and the public when governments go online. More specifically, the paper examines the ethical and managerial issues and challenges facing public managers when their governments go online (i.e., access the Internet and establish Web sites). The paper is organized into five sections. The first section discusses the meaning of cyber management as a prelude to developing organizational strategies for promoting Internet use and discouraging Internet abuse. Section 2 draws the reader's attention to the specific content of acceptable use policies for the Internet. Section 3 then explores the challenges facing public managers to understand and abate the undesirable and sometimes unethical consequences that Internet usage may have for social or group life in public organizations. This discussion is followed by the fourth section, an examination of government use and abuse of the Internet. The final section highlights questions that must be answered in order for public managers to become effective cyber-age managers.

Cyber Management

Public organizations and private-sector firms are reorganizing and realigning themselves to take full advantage of new information technology and the promise of Internet as a medium for rapid communication and information retrieval and dissemination. Indeed, a new occupational speciality has been created for just this purpose, the Webmaster. Nearly every organization, except perhaps those that have outsourced their Internet services, has a Webmaster. This person is expected to know the technical ins and outs of creating and maintaining sites (sometimes referred to as pages) on the World Wide Web. Moreover, he or she must monitor traffic through the site and make sure that the Web server hardware and software are operating properly. The Webmaster is also likely to know how to write common gateway interface scripts using computer languages such as Java, Perl, C++, and others.

A Webmaster could be considered a cyber manager but cyber management encompasses much more. The more has to do with understanding and dealing with the internal and external dynamics of the rapidly expanding use of information technologies, especially Internet-based technologies, in public organizations. Those dynamics include possible changes in how employees relate to one another and their organizational superiors, and how the organization itself may experience horizontal and vertical shifts in communication and authority patterns. Traditional top-down management styles, for example, may not be particularly effective in cyber workplaces. Nor may traditional authority patterns based on the organizational hierarchy retain as much meaning or presence in cyber-driven organizations.

The organizational imperative—that is, to get ahead one must swear allegiance and fealty to the company line—is likely to become blurred and pushed aside in favor of a more open, participative, and even a democratic workplace. As Sclove (1995, 232) maintains, "personal computers and telecommunications harbor the potential for allowing more democratic, decentralized, and debureaucratized social coordination, but much remains to be learned about effective strategies for realizing that potential." Sclove is correct. There is much to learn. Current efforts to apply effective strategies for debureaucratizing organizations, public and private, are mostly trial-and-error experiences.

Similarly, very little is known or understood about what might be the ethical or unethical implications of this brave new world. Effective cyber managers must be able to anticipate and respond to new ethical issues and challenges wrought by the information revolution. But what are some of these issues? And, what can or should managers do to resolve them? One issue is Internet use and—abuse.

When an agency decides to go online to establish a Web site and access the Internet—among the very first decisions that must be made is: "Who in the organization should be granted access privileges?" This question is usually followed by: "Who needs access and who doesn't?" And the third question is: "How might the privilege be abused?" Might there be undesirable if not unethical use of the Internet? The answer to this last question is clearly yes. But, what constitutes abuse and what might done to discourage it? Consider, the following behaviors: surfing the Web for ~rtainment; downloading or viewing obscene or sexually oriented material; adver- or soliciting for personal financial gain; making political statements or promot- ~ididates for public office; posting or downloading derogatory racial, ethnic, or ~material; waging, betting, or selling chances; using pseudonyms or pen transmitting electronic messages. Most public managers would probably ehaviors as undesirable, if not unethical, and perhaps even illegal. Thus be considerable incentive to put rules or policies into place that pre- ~s and punish those who violate the rules.

~ptable use policy for the Internet in place, however, can be a ~cts from the presumed benefits of accessing the Internet in the ~ple, many public managers believe that access to the Internet can stimulate and empower employees. This change can, in turn, result in more innovative and responsive government. Thus there is a substantial incentive to support employees' access to and experimentation with the vast storehouse of data and information on the World Wide Web, electronic bulletin boards, listservs, and chat rooms. Finding the balance point between Internet use and abuse is, however, a major challenge for public managers.

Nonetheless, the challenge must be met and many government managers are attempting to do so, although not all acknowledge the potential for abuse. Some government officials believe that once the novelty of the Internet diminishes there will be little to worry about. After all, one might argue, the Internet is really like any other new information technology such as the telephone, fax machine, and the copy machine. In time, it will be treated as a routine part of the workplace.

Finding the balance point for many public managers means developing, implementing, and enforcing an acceptable use policy for the Internet. But what are the key components of such a policy? How and why do the components vary from organization to organization?

Acceptable Use Policies for the Internet

What have public agencies done to prevent Internet abuse and yet encourage Internet use? To answer this question, a survey was conducted in the spring of 1997 of state and local government agencies with Web sites. The tracking study cited earlier contains information on the electronic mail addresses of the Webmasters at many state sites. Thus a number of agencies could be contacted to retrieve information about their acceptable use policies. Additionally, the author used the Web to locate government sites and communicate directly with many Webmasters. In total, over 60 acceptable use policies were retrieved from special districts, cities, counties, and 34 state agencies in 31 states. (See Appendix A for a list of government organizations that have put their policies online.) These policies do not constitute a random sample, but they do provide first-cut information about these important policies and emerging practices in government.

What do these policies emphasize? How comprehensive are they? What kind of guidance do they give? Before these questions are addressed, it may be helpful to identify the kinds of Internet usage that a public employee might pursue. There are four primary categories of Internet usage: sending and receiving electronic mail (known as e-mail), accessing and posting documents on the World Wide Web, sending and retrieving computer files (known as file transfer protocol or FTP), and joining electronic discussion groups (such as news groups, listservs, and Internet relay chat groups). E-mail is the most widely used Internet service, although many users are active in all categories.

A review of the acceptable use policies indicates that most place some type of restriction on who can access the Internet. This is usually couched in terms of "need" or job relevance. Accounts and passwords must be requested by a user and approved by a higher authority. Open access, giving nearly anyone in the organization an account, is uncommon. The village of Downers Grove, Illinois, is one exception.

two-page acceptable use policy offers employees trial subscriptions to the Internet. Employees may use the account for three months at no cost but are required to contribute three dollars per pay period once their trial subscription expires.

It is also uncommon for public organizations to allow employees to use Internet accounts for personal purposes. The vast majority of public organizations among those surveyed limit Internet use to official business. There are, however, some exceptions. Washington County, Minnesota, for example, allows its employees to use computers, networks, and electronic mail for "incidental and occasional personal business use" provided that such use is (1) done on the employee's personal time, (2) does not interfere with the employee's or other employees' job activities, and (3) does not result in incremental expense for the county. The state of Oregon has a similar policy which states that "limited personal uses are allowed." Such use must be "at virtually no cost to the state" and "be trivial compared to use for assigned work." The state of Washington also permits employees limited personal use of state resources (e.g., local telephone calls and Internet messages) so long as it does not result in additional costs to the state. Another state agency, the New York State Office of Real Property Services, has deliberately refrained from prohibiting personal use of the Internet because "we want to get folks thinking about how they can use it to do their jobs better" (message posted on the GOVPUB listserv by Fran Pinto, Internet Coordinator, September 6, 1996).

Nearly every acceptable use policy for the Internet contains a statement of purpose, although most use generic language like "to advance the mission" of the city, county, or state or "for conducting official state business." The New Jersey policy asserts that the state's public presence on the Internet presents opportunities to improve communications and public service, extend government service hours, and enhance the image of government.

Perhaps the most thoughtful statement of purpose among the acceptable use policies reviewed for this article is contained in the acceptable use policy of the city of Fort Collins, Colorado. According to Fort Collins's document, the dissemination of information over the Internet is expected (1) to contribute to the economic development of the city by providing favorable information via the World Wide Web to current and potential visitors and residents, (2) to aid in policy development and decision making by giving employees immediate access to research material and other technical and professional information, (3) to conserve resources that would otherwise be consumed by the use of paper and fossil fuels and by employee attendance at conferences, (4) to ʾter participatory democracy by encouraging citizen involvement in and under-ʾling of local issues, and (5) to improve service delivery by promoting and facilitat-ʾiciency and innovation.

ʾrding the use and abuse of Internet privileges, the policy documents ʾhere generally reflect one of three approaches. The most *generic* approach is ʾe user that the Internet is no different from any other information tech-ʾone, fax machine, copying machine, etc.) and the user is subject to the ʾl legal standards. There may also be a brief enumeration of forbidden ʾ"don't harass or threaten" anyone. Some agencies cite city or county ʾstatutes regarding the illegal uses of communication technologies. ʾh is to develop a more detailed statement of acceptable and ʾiors. This approach might be labeled *formalistic*. The California

Housing Finance Agency is an example. The agency lists the following as acceptable activities:

- General communications with state, federal, or local government personnel, vendors, contractors, consultants or other business partners on bona fide agency business matters.

- Electronic mail with business associates outside the agency on matters that directly relate to the user's job duties.

- World Wide Web access for bona fide agency-related and specific job-related reasons.

Unacceptable activities, those that do not conform to the purpose, goals, and mission of the agency include:

- Activities for private or personal profit, for example: consulting for pay, selling goods for companies such as Avon and Amway, and providing tax preparation services.

- Use for personal gain in any form.

- Access to Web sites that have no direct relevance to agency business (e.g., sports scores, games, hobbies, etc.).

- Use for any illegal purpose.

- The transmission of threatening, obscene, or harassing messages or the use of inappropriate language for which the agency could be held liable.

- The access or downloading of obscene, sexually explicit, or tasteless and offensive materials in any form including multimedia photos, video, or audio.

- The downloading of software or data without authorization.

- Excessive use of e-mail for personal communication or any purpose not related to business.

- The intentional seeking of information about others unless expressly authorized to do so in writing. This includes obtaining copies of such information, modifying data, and obtaining passwords.

- Interference with or disrupting network operations including the distribution of unsolicited advertising, propagation of computer viruses, or using the network to gain unauthorized entry to another computer.

- The divulging of passwords, phone numbers, or other network access information to any unauthorized persons.

The formalistic approach typically requires the user to sign a statement that he or she has read, understands, and agrees to abide by the agency's acceptable use policy. Failure to abide by the policy can result in disciplinary action including, but not limited to, termination of access privileges or, in serious cases, termination of employment.

A third approach can be labeled a *guidelines* approach. This type of acceptable use policy is long on guidelines, brief on do's and don'ts, and comes across as nonpunitive. One example is the policy of the Greene County, Ohio, library. The Greene County policy informs the user that he or she must use the Internet in a responsible, efficient, ethical, and legal manner. It then proceeds to describe acceptable and unacceptable uses. Finally, two pages are devoted to describing online etiquette.

The adoption of an acceptable use policy by a public organization may constitute an important first step in discouraging the more overt forms of undesirable behavior in the workplace; however, more subtle yet equally important changes may take place in the agency's group life as a result of going online. The next section examines several of these possible changes.

The Internet and Group Life in the Workplace

The technical aspects of accessing the Internet, while challenging, may pale alongside the challenge faced by managers to understand and prevent the undesirable and sometimes unethical consequences that the use of this technology may have on social or group life in public agencies. For example, a study by Markus (1994, 119) on the effects of e-mail on social life in the corporate workplace found that negative effects, such as making the workplace less personal, were a product of two factors—the technology itself (e.g., the depersonalization of social relations due to a reduction in the need for face-to-face interaction) and choices by users or employees "to avoid unwanted social interactions." In other words, e-mail technology itself is not solely responsible for "negative" social effects in the workplace. Employees can and do make choices about who they want to communicate with and who they do not. Managers committed to promoting a strong ethical climate in their organizations are likely to find this type of situation especially challenging, particularly in light of the nearly total lack of knowledge of such behavior.

Another example of a possibly undesirable outcome of information-sharing technology in the workplace is provided by Orlikowski's (1997) study of the introduction of groupware (Lotus Notes) into one office of a large corporation. She was interested in finding out how this technology with its emphasis on information sharing and cooperation would be received. Would it, she asked, act as a "counterculture to an organization's structural properties (competitive and individualistic culture, rigid hierarchy)?" (Kling, 1997, 174). Orlikowski found that top-level managers and front-line employees were not reluctant to share information that presumably benefitted the company at large. However, this spirit of team work and sharing did not extend to mid-career managers, who believed that by sharing their knowledge with others they would lose a competitive advantage over their peers. In other words, information ownership was viewed by mid-career professionals as an essential ingredient in advancing their careers. Under these circumstances, why would one want to use information-sharing technology to its fullest extent? It would be contrary to the individual's self-interest to do so. Although Orlikowski's study was exploratory, it certainly suggests a downside to information-sharing technologies (electronic mail, listservs, and bulletin boards.) Even if an agency establishes an *Intranet* (an internal information technology that uses Internet protocols and is accessible by members of the organization), it cannot be assumed that information will be widely shared or free flowing.

There are other consequences for an organization's group life as a result of going online. On the negative side, a diminished ethical environment could result if the "frontier" character of the Internet with its stress on individualism and the depersonalization of relationships encourages employees to engage each other and the agency's clientele in a manner that demeans human dignity and diminishes respect for others. Several studies of online behavior suggest that some users are more direct, and even abrasive with others in the absence of face-to-face exchanges (Kiesler, Siegel, and McGuire, 1984). Are employees likely to treat each other or the public differently, perhaps rudely? This is an empirical question that can and should be answered.

On the positive side, the ethical environment of the workplace could be enhanced if electronic communication enabled members of the organization to obtain greater knowledge of the internal and external workings of the organization and therefore a better understanding of their own role in and contribution to the success of the agency. Insofar as members of an organization are able to reach out to peers in other organizations throughout the nation and world, they are likely to obtain an even broader understanding of their work.

The complexity of modern organizations often results in a tunnel vision that can lead to confusion, apathy, and even alienation on the part of some employees—circumstances hardly consistent with a strong ethical workplace. Internet usage may enable employees to sort through complexity and therefore become more productive and ethical. Indeed, there is some limited evidence supporting this proposition. In a study of municipal employees' use of electronic mail, it was found that greater e-mail use resulted in employees' becoming more committed to their employer and developing a stronger bond with their city government (Huff, Sproull, and Kiesler, 1989). This finding is especially suggestive because the study compared computer communication with more traditional forms of communication—telephone exchanges and written memos—and found no relationship between employee commitment to the organization and the extent to which the employee communicated with others via telephone or written memorandum.

Government Use and Abuse of the Internet

Other ethical and perhaps legal challenges go beyond employee access and use of the Internet and have to do with the posture of government itself. Presumably in a democracy, online governments and their leaders should promote democratic practices such as easier and greater citizen access to public information while at the same preventing the disclosure of sensitive information stored in governmental data bases. It is one thing to post information about neighborhood crime rates or AIDS statistics and another to allow public access to names or addresses of victims. Likewise, the question might be asked: Is a public service being provided when a property appraiser's office creates a searchable data base containing the names and addresses of owners and the property values of residential and commercial real estate? Or is this merely making it easier for scam artists, thieves, and other criminals to employ the same technology to target would-be victims?

The possibility of the misuse of government data bases raises the very important issue of how to prevent it. Consider the case of drivers license and automobile registration in Texas. This information has been public for some time and has been drawn upon primarily by insurance companies, private investigators, and even family members looking for missing relatives. Recently, a private firm in Dallas placed drivers license and automobile registration information in a searchable data base on the Internet (*http://www.publiclink.com/*). This site enables anyone who possesses a Texas drivers license, owns a personal computer, and has an Internet connection to look up any other Texan and any Texas license plate number. The site developers inform visitors that the data base will be expanded in the future. Is it likely that an expanded data base might include information about arrest and conviction records, marriage records, or voter registration?

Many governments are also facing tight budgets and could be motivated to be entrepreneurial by selling advertising space on their official home pages or charging for hypertext links to business firms. Very entrepreneurial governments might even go so far as to endorse a product as the "official" product of its city, country, or state! Would these practices be ethical? Legal? Is the endorsement of a product or charging for Web links any different from placing commercial ads on municipally owned buses or city subways? The commercialization of the Internet is, of course, well underway. But how far should we go in commercializing government?

Finally, there is the matter of electronic communication between public officials (elected and appointed) and citizens. Few (small d) democrats would object to e-mail replacing fax messages between citizens and public officials, but it may be an entirely different matter when the communication path is between officeholders or between public employees and their elected bosses. Although some small communities such as Downers Grove, Illinois, encourage employees who hold Internet accounts to "communicate information to elected officials, as needed," this position is more likely to be the exception than the rule. Direct electronic communication between elected officials in the same city, county, or state government, especially if it deals with the public's business, may undermine the public's preference for government in the sunshine. Will the information (r)age, especially in its electronic form, cast a cloud over government in the sunshine? Or, will public officials exercise due care, diligence, and caution before jumping on the keyboard and sending important messages to elected peers or top managers in their government?

Questions and Some Answers

This article raises many questions that need to be answered if public managers are going to be able to meet the growing and formidable management and ethical challenges of the cyber age. This section, therefore, attempts to draw together a number of questions raised above and puts forward some answers in the form of hypotheses.

Going Online

Why are so many public organizations in the United States going online? And why are some agencies going online faster than others? While the answer to the first question might appear straightforward—to improve service delivery, disseminate information, and increase organizational responsiveness—there may be other less obvious reasons. Studies of the diffusion of social and technological innovations conducted in many fields suggest that the adoption of an innovation such as setting up a Web site can be a result of many factors. For example, it may be that larger, more affluent, and professionally oriented agencies are more likely to go online faster than smaller, less affluent, and less professionally oriented agencies. It may also be the case that there is a cueing effect. That is, smaller agencies may be taking cues from larger agencies that have already developed a Web site. Additionally, the rapid rate of the adoption and use of Internet technology by federal agencies may have spurred state and local government agencies to do the same. Finally, there is always the possibility that professional competition to be on the leading edge of technology motivates some adopters to take action faster than other adopters.

Managing Behavior with Acceptable Use Policies

Are public employees abusing their Internet privileges? Moreover, insofar as abuse, occurs, how serious is it? And, what are the consequences for their organization? The public? Is it costly to their organization in terms of lost productivity or diminished service quality? Does Internet abuse diminish the ethical environment of an agency? These questions can and should be answered by careful, systematic empirical research. At the moment, however, one can only speculate about what might be happening, although a few abuse stories (mostly dealing with business firms) have been reported in the popular press.

How are acceptable use policies working out? Are they making a positive difference? If not, why not? Do acceptable use policies foster a strong ethical environment, or are they largely innocuous? Moreover, do some acceptable use policies stifle employee creativity and problem solving effectiveness? It is most likely that the policy developed by an organization will mirror the prevailing values or culture of the organization. In other words, a heavily rule-oriented organization is likely to put together a heavily rule-oriented acceptable use policy. Similarly, an organization that is more trusting, (i.e., where employees are accorded greater discretion, trust, and respect) is more likely to develop an acceptable use policy that relies on self-policing to promote acceptable (and hopefully ethical) Internet behaviors and discourage unethical acts.

It is, of course, possible that the Internet is sufficiently different from other workplace technologies to require prevailing management practices, including the organization's culture itself, to change significantly in order to accommodate new ways of doing things. Consider the implications for altering group life in the workplace.

Group Life in the Workplace

Earlier it was noted that some research shows that electronic communication can have negative consequences for group life in an organization. That is, employees can use e-mail to engage in selective communication with other members of the organization.

Thus, it is conceivable that instead of facilitating communication and encouraging team work, the technology may foster just the opposite. It is also possible to imagine a workplace that is less civil and ethical insofar as employees treat each other with less respect and consideration.

On the other hand, could the reverse occur? Might the ethical environment of a public organization actually be strengthened when its government goes online? It could be hypothesized that the ethical environment will be strengthened because as organizational members access and use the Internet, they will become more trusting and respectful of others, including their organizational superiors. This could occur because information would become less scarce and would therefore reduce status differences between employees and managers. The flattening of the status or authority structure could motivate workers and managers to treat each other with greater respect and could engender trust. Previous research has shown that high levels of organizational trust and respect go hand in hand with a strong ethical environment (Menzel, 1993; 1996).

Group life in the workplace might also be altered if Internet access and use fosters the democratization of information and communication. Widespread use of the Internet could result in a more democratic workplace—one in which employees feel a sense of participation, ownership, empowerment, and self-management. Could the idea and ideal of a democratic workplace be realized?

Government (Mis)use of the Internet

Are government agencies opening their data banks too quickly and too widely? What safeguards are in place to prevent government data from being used improperly by private-sector organizations? Are public agencies becoming too entrepreneurial with regard to selling government data or charging business firms for links placed on an agency's home page? Is the Internet a catalyst for the commercialization of government? If so, are there undesirable side effects? For example, a municipality that charges local businesses for links to the city's home page could put itself at a competitive disadvantage with other cities that provide this service free of charge.

Given the exploratory nature of this article, the most appropriate conclusion is to challenge future investigators to pursue some of the leads highlighted in the previous pages. It seems abundantly evident that there is a substantial need for systematic study of the interplay between Internet use and organizational behavior and performance. Indeed serious work in this area is in its infancy. As Kling (1996, 53) poignantly remarks about organizational worklife: "There is little research that examines the relationships between work online and life in the organization off line." "We need," he concludes, "a strong research program that examines how the social design/organization of electronic forums strengthens or weakens group life in workplaces and communities." The time to begin this important work is at hand.

Reprinted with permission from Public Administration Review *by the American Society for Public Administration (ASPA), 1120 G Street, NW, Suite 700, Washington, DC 20005. All rights reserved.*

References

Gregorian, Vartan (1997). "Technology, Scholarship, and the Humanities: The Implications of Electronic Information." In Rob Kling, ed., *Computerization and Controversy*. San Diego: Academic Press.

Huff, C., L. Sproull, and S. Kiesler (1989). "Computer Communications and Organizational Commitment: Tracing the Relationship in a City Government." *Journal of Applied Social Psychology* 19: 1371–1391.

Kiesler, Sara, Jane Siegel, and Timothy W. McGuire (1984). "Social Psychological Aspects of Computer-Mediated Communication." *American Psychologist* 39 (October): 1123–1134.

Kling, Rob, ed. (1996). *Computerization and Controversy.* San Diego: Academic Press.

Markus, M. L. (1994). "Finding a Happy Medium: Explaining the Negative Effects of Electronic Communication on Social Life at Work." *ACM Transactions on Information Systems* 12 (April): 119–149.

Menzel, Donald C. (1993). "The Ethics Factor in Local Government: An Empirical Analysis." In H. George Frederickson, ed., *Ethics and Public Administration.* New York: M. E. Sharpe.

———— (1996). "Ethics Stress in Public Organizations." *Public Productivity & Management Review* 20 (September): 70–83.

Orlikowski, Wanda J. (1997). "Learning from Notes: Organizational Issues in Groupware Implementation." In Rob Kling ed., *Computerization and Controversy.* San Diego: Academic Press.

Sclove, Richard E. (1995). *Democracy and Technology.* New York: Guliford

APPENDIX A: GOVERNMENT WEB SITES WITH ACCEPTABLE USE POLICIES AND DOCUMENTS ON-LINE

Alabama
AL Research and Education Network
www.asc.edu/html/accusepol.html

Alaska
www.gov.state.ak.us//ltgov/tic/offhtm/html
Dept. of Environmental Conservation
www.state.ak.us/local/akpages/
ENV.CONSERV/das/is/webcord/
interpol.htm

Arizona
www.state.az.us/isd/forms/inetagre.htm

California
Department of Information Technology
www.doit.ca.gov/simm/internet.asp

Connecticut
www.state.ct.us/cmac/statpoli.htm

Delaware
www.otm.state.de.us/otm/sitnlaw.htm

Indiana
www.state.in.us/dpoc/dpoc.html

Kansas
www.ink.org/public/itask/policy/policy.htm

Kentucky
www.state.ky.us/kirm/docs.htm

Louisiana
www.doa.state.la.us/otm/accept.htm

Maine
www.state.me.us/ispb/interpol.htm

Minnesota
www.state.mn.us/ebranch/admin/ipo/
hb/document/seltop1.html#table
or
www.state.mn.us/ebranch/admin/
internet-usage.html

Missouri
www.state.mo.us/comofc/policy.htm

Nebraska
www.das.state.ne.us/das_doc/doc/aup.htm

New Jersey
www.state.nj.us/infobank/circular/
cir9701s.htm

New York
www.irm.state.ny.us/policy/tp_968.htm

North Carolina
www.osc.state.nc.us/irmc/documents/
approvals/irmcinet.html

North Dakota
www.state.nd.us/isd/external.html

APPENDIX A: CONTINUED

Ohio
www.state.oh.us/dis/direct/97-23.html
or
www.ohio.gov/opp/opp-pol.htm

Oregon
www.state.or.us/IRMD/policies/03
-13net.htm
or
www.state.or.us/IRMD/policies.htm

Seattle, Washington
www.ci.seattle.wa.us/pan/iau5-2.htm

South Carolina
www.state.sc.us/nis_itg/em_guidelines.html
or
www.state.sc.us/nis_itg/index.html

South Dakota
www.state.sd.us/bit/is/document/
internet.htm

Tennessee
www.state.tn.us/finance/oir/
int-aup.html

Texas
State Lib. and Archives Com.
www.tsl.state.tx.us/IRT/netpol_rev3.htm

U.S. Department of Agriculture
National Agricultural Library
www.nal.usda.gov/general_info/
webpolicy.html

Utah
www.gvnfo.state.ut.us/sitc/aup.htm

Washington
www.wa.gov/dis/tsd/tutorial/policy.htm

22

Privacy in the Information Age:
Stakeholders, Interests and Values

LUCAS D. INTRONA
ATHANASIA POULOUDI

Privacy is a relational and relative concept that has been defined in a variety of ways. In this paper we offer a systematic discussion of potentially different notions of privacy. We conclude that privacy as the freedom or immunity from the judgement of others is an extremely useful concept to develop ways in which to understand privacy claims and associated risk. To this end, we develop a framework of principles that explores the inter-relations of interests and values for various stakeholders where privacy concerns have risen or are expected to rise. We argue that conflicts between the interests and values of different stakeholders may result in legitimate claims of privacy/transparency being ignored or underrepresented. Central to this analysis is the notion of a stakeholder. We argue that stakeholders are persons or groups with legitimate interests, of intrinsic value, in the procedural and/or substantive aspects of the privacy/transparency claim and subsequent judgements in that basis. Using the principles of access, representation and power, which flow from our framework of analysis, we show how they can facilitate the identification of potential privacy/transparency risks using examples from the British National Health Service.

Lucas D. Introna is a Lecturer in Information Systems at the London School of Economics and Political Science and Visiting Professor of Information Systems at the University of Pretoria. His research interest is the social dimension of information technology and its consequences for society. In particular he is concerned with the way information technology transforms and mediates social interaction. He is associate editor of *Information Technology & People* and co-editor *Ethics and Information Technology*. His practical and consulting experience includes design and implementation of information systems for various large corporations as well as strategic management consulting. He is an active member of IFIP WG 8.2, The Society of Philosophy in Contemporary World (SPCW), International Sociological Association WG01 on Sociocybernetics, and a number of other academic and professional societies. His most recent work includes a book *Management, Information and Power* published by Macmillan, and more than 40 academic papers in journals and conference proceedings on a variety of topics such as theories of information, information technology and ethics, autopoiesis and social systems, and virtual organizations. He holds degrees in management, information systems and philosophy.

1. Introduction

Respect for privacy is one of the primary concerns of ethical computing. However, privacy is not a straightforward concept; it can be interpreted from many different perspectives. One reason for this is that privacy is a relational and a relative concept. Often, there is a thin line between the need to disclose information for the benefit of some individuals and the need to safeguard the privacy of some individuals by not disclosing this information—the privacy/transparency claim. Following a systematic discussion of potentially different notions of privacy we will discuss how conflicts between the interests and values of different stakeholders may result in different perceptions of privacy.

Part of this analysis is based on different elements of stakeholder theory, namely the descriptive, instrumental and normative elements. These elements can facilitate a more comprehensive view of the stakeholders that may affect or be affected by a certain attitude to privacy. In particular they highlight who the *stakeholders* are and what their *perspectives* concerning privacy issues are (descriptive element), what *interests* underlie these perspectives (instrumental element) and what *values* affect their attitudes (normative element).

The information age makes it particularly important to explore the perspectives of privacy as well as the interests and values of stakeholders. Indeed, the possibility to speed up information exchange and to aggregate information items may substantially alter what were previously understood as privacy interests; it may also generate new interests. Moreover, there is an element of power associated with the interests and values of stakeholders. Certain stakeholders are in a better position to serve their interests and satisfy their internal values than others are. This asymmetry of power may raise risks for the privacy of the weaker stakeholders.

The information systems literature provides ample evidence of the broad implications that the use of information technology can have on power and also on how power can affect the use of information technology. As a result, information systems may change the context of stakeholder relations and pose a systematic threat to privacy. The paper uses examples from the healthcare context to illustrate how this may occur in practice and how the theoretical framework can help in understanding the phenomenon and preventing inappropriate judgments in the context of privacy conflicts.

The next section introduces different notions of privacy and focuses on the notion of privacy as freedom from the judgment of others. Section 3 gives an overview of different aspects to stakeholder theory and explores their ethical implications. In section 4 we present our framework of analysis from which we derive a number of principles that support the intrinsic value of the privacy/transparency claims of stakeholders. Section 5 applies this framework to examples in the healthcare domain and illustrates

Athanasia Pouloudi is a Lecturer in Information Systems in the Department of Information Systems and Computing at Brunel University since 1997. Her research and publications focus on social issues in information systems development and implementation, organizational change and electronic commerce. She is a member of the ACM, AIS, UK AIS, and the UK OR Society. She has worked as an evaluator of research projects for the Secretariat of Research and Technology in Greece and as a referee in various international journals and conferences in the area of information systems.

how it can inform our understanding of privacy situations and identify further privacy risks.

2. Privacy as the Freedom from the Judgement of Others

Privacy, or the lack thereof, for most at least, is easy to identify when experienced but difficult to define. It seems for every definition proposed by jurists and philosophers alike a counterexample could be found. This may be the reason for some of the severe critique raised against the very notion of privacy. Despite the fairly intense debate since the late 1960s there are still no universally accepted definition of privacy. There have been various attempts to create a synthesis of existing literature such as the work by Parent (1983) and Schoeman (1984). What remains clear is that there is no simple or elegant solution. Nevertheless, we want to argue that it may be very useful, when considering decisions about the appropriateness of the public/private divide, to use the notion of privacy as *the freedom from the judgements of others.* This definition allows one to critically investigate the self/other relationship in a particular context (Introna, 1997b). Such an analysis, as we will show, provides the context for understanding the particular privacy claims of all the different stakeholders in a particular context. Before discussing the framework for such an analysis it may be useful to review some of the ways in which privacy has been defined.

Brandeis and Warren (1890, p. 205) defined privacy as the "the right to be let alone." It is easy to see that there are various grounds upon which one can fault this definition. If I, for example, use an extremely strong telescope to watch your every move, I am in the strict sense of the word leaving you alone. However, one can hardly call this a condition of privacy. There are also certain institutions or individuals that have a legitimate right not to leave you alone such as the tax service or your creditors. As is clear this is a too limited definition that does not take enough cognisance of the subtle and complex social context where privacy is at stake. For Van Den Haag (1971, p. 149) "privacy is the exclusive access of a person to a realm of his own. The right to privacy entitles one to exclude others from (a) watching, (b) utilising, (c) invading his private [personal] realm." In this (rather circular) definition the issue of private or a personal realm comes to the fore. It implies that there is a certain realm, here expressed as personal or private, that one may legitimately limit access to. The obvious problem in this case is the definition of what is private or personal. For some cultures the bare torso or breasts are extremely personal. For some African tribes it is in the public domain. Most scholars agree that to a large extent the exact demarcation of the personal realm is culturally defined; there is no ontologically defined personal realm. Nevertheless, from a legal and communicative perspective personal information can be defined as "those facts, communications or opinions which relate to the individual and which it would be reasonable to expect him to regard as intimate or confidential and therefore to want to withhold or at least to restrict their circulation" (Wacks, 1980, p. 89). Gross (1967) is in agreement with this notion of privacy as "the condition of human life in which acquaintance with a person or with affairs of his life which are personal to him is limited." He also refers to "intellectual" access by using the word "acquaintance".

Fried (1968) defines privacy as "control over knowledge about oneself." This notion of control of personal information is also captured in the definition by Westin (1967) by defining privacy as "the claim of individuals, groups or institutions to determine for themselves when, how and to what extent information about them is communicated to others" (pp. 7 and 42). Or in a more general sense by Parker (1974) as the "control over when and whom the various parts of us can be sensed by others." This idea of the control over the distribution of personal information (given that personal is culturally defined) is very powerful in situations where it is important to determine whether or not an individual's right to privacy has been violated. On the other hand someone can at his own discretion divulge personal information to whoever cares to listen thus, not having lost control yet cannot be said to have any privacy. Gavison (1980, p. 434) defines a loss of privacy occurring when "others obtain information about an individual, pay attention to him, or gain access to him." In this definition and the previous group the need for privacy is implicitly assumed. There is also no mention of the "other" in the relationship given that privacy is a relational notion. This is where the notion of judgement-by-others becomes explicit.

We want to argue with Johnson (1989, p. 157) that the fundamental issue at stake in privacy is the judgement of *others*. He expresses it as follows:

> Privacy is a conventional concept. What is considered private is socially or culturally defined. It varies from context to context, it is dynamic, and it is quite possible that no single example can be found of something which is considered private in every culture. Nevertheless, all examples of privacy have a single common feature. They are aspects of a person's life which are culturally recognised as *being immune from the judgement of others*. (emphasis added)

It is the knowledge that others would judge us in a particular way, perhaps based on preconceived or inappropriate ideas, norms, and values that makes the individuals desire a personal or private space of immunity. It is the inevitable loss of control over the decontextualisation and recontextualisation of the data obtained, and subsequent judgement thereof that motivates the individual to "hide" it. This desire to "hide" does not imply deceit. It is rather an acknowledgement of the fact that values and interests may in many cases differ (even radically). Furthermore, that we do not neatly isolate, in appropriate ways, values and interests when faced with particular judgements. We are always already enmeshed in our values and interests. This is exactly where the whole argument of Posner (1978) fails.

Posner argues that personal information can be divided into discrediting or non-discrediting information. If the personal information is accurate and discrediting then, we have a social incentive to make this information available to others that may have dealings with this person. To fail to do this is, according to Posner, the same as failing to reveal a fraudulent scheme. If the information is false or non-discrediting, there is no social value in such information and it could be kept privately. The begging question, of course, is whose values are used to make the judgement of discrediting or non-discrediting information. Posner assumes that there is a set of self-evident, universally accepted values that can unequivocally separate discrediting information from non-discrediting information. The so-called discrediting judgement is obviously context dependent. For example, the fact that a person hides his positive HIV status from a potential sexual partner may be discrediting and deceitful but it should not necessarily be "discrediting" when applying for a job as a taxi driver. The whole point of Johnson is that the person may be unfairly judged as "not suitable" as a taxi driver as a result of his medical condition due to the personal values held by the owner of the Cab Company.

Such, very real, possibilities surely create significant grounds to grant an individual some form of immunity of judgement within a particular domain. The problem of diverging values and interests are compounded by the exponential increase in electronic data capturing in all walks of society. These database records, as we know, can become "mobile" and be reinterpreted in different contexts in wholly inappropriate ways, interpretations that apply values and interests in ways incommensurable with the original capturing criteria and purpose. It is within this context of abundantly accessible information that the freedom from the inappropriate judgement of others becomes the central source for legitimate privacy/transparency claims. This judgement-by-others issue is well captured by DeCew (1986, p. 171) in stating that "an interest in privacy is at stake when intrusion by others is not legitimate *because* it jeopardises or prohibits protection of a realm free from scrutiny, judgement, and the pressure, distress, or losses they can cause." It seems to us that this perspective of judgement-by-others in a particular context provides a particularly useful basis for exploring privacy/transparency claims in the Information Society. Before exploring these claims it may be useful to reflect on who or what the "other", in any claim, may imply. Generally the "other" are the stakeholders in a particular context. In the next section we will explore the notion of a stakeholder before discussing the framework for analysing privacy/transparency claims.

3. Stakeholders and the Interests of the "Other"

Although the stakeholder concept has been used extensively and in a variety of contexts, it is within the area of strategic management where most development has occurred. Within this field, the concept has been applied in a many different ways. Donaldson and Preston (1995) have captured this variability in a framework that distinguishes between a descriptive, an instrumental and a normative aspect to stakeholder theory. More specifically, the stakeholder theory is *descriptive* in the sense that "it describes the corporation [social unit] as a constellation of cooperative and competitive interests possessing intrinsic value" (p. 66). It is *instrumental* because "it establishes a framework for examining the connections, if any, between the practice of stakeholder management and the achievement of various corporate [social unit] performance goals" (pp. 66–67). Finally, "the fundamental basis" of stakeholder theory is *normative* and involves acceptance of the following ideas: "stakeholders are persons or groups with legitimate interests in procedural and/or substantive aspects of corporate [social] activity" and "the interests of all stakeholders are of intrinsic value" (p. 67). They further argue that the normative aspect is at the *core* of stakeholder theory (this point is also supported by Freeman (1994)), so that the three aspects could be viewed as nested circles.

It is worth noting that most stakeholder theory can generally be characterised by a managerial focus, reflecting the priorities of the strategic management theory within which it has been developed. Moreover, over the years there has been a notable shift towards a normative argument to support the use of stakeholder theories. This normative argument reflects the managerial perspective and has been summarised as follows:

> [T]he ultimate managerial implication of the stakeholder theory is that managers should acknowledge the validity of diverse stakeholder interests and should attempt to respond to them within a mutually supportive framework because that is a moral requirement for the legitimacy of the management function (Donaldson and Preston, 1995 p. 87).

If we accept their argument of a normative core, the shift of attention towards the more normative aspect of the theory could be explained as a result of the central role of ethics in stakeholder theory. Another perspective would be to see this shift only as a change in the rhetoric used in stakeholder theory, whereas its purpose remains instrumental. This latter view can be supported by the fact that many proponents of what we may call "ethical stakeholding" have used instrumental arguments to defend the benefits of their normative approach. Such an instrumental rhetoric can be traced back to Freeman's 1984 book where he argued that "to be an effective strategist you must deal with those groups that can affect you, while to be responsive (and effective in the long run) you must deal with those groups that you can affect" (Freeman, 1984 p. 46). For some, this way of thinking implies that an instrumental core underpins the normative rhetoric, rather than the other way round:

> There is also a deliberate ambiguity about the pronouncements of stakeholder theorists. Such theorists say that managements should look beyond the bottom line and mere financial return. On the other hand, they are quick to tell their opponents and companies which adopt the practices of which they approve will also be more prosperous. It is like the old Welsh preacher who waxed eloquent about the moral virtues of honesty, adding just before he left the pulpit that it also paid. (Sir Samuel Brittan in the *Financial Times*, 1 February 1996, quoted in (Willetts, 1997); see also (Goodpaster, 1993 p. 87).)

The implications for the use of stakeholder theory in the future are multiple. First, the normative core of the theory is questioned and attention is drawn to the preconditions that are necessary for the realisation of the normative potential of stakeholder theory. For example, Phillips (1997) discusses some problems with the application of ethical stakeholding (lack of a coherent justification framework; problems of identifying who is and who is not a stakeholder in the moral sense) and proposes the use of a principle of fairness. Burton and Dunn (1996) argue that stakeholder theory lacks moral grounding and suggest the use of feminist ethics, which can provide such grounding by focusing on relations between stakeholders and notions of "care". This approach, they argue, can also assist managers to resolve problems of conflicting responsibilities to stakeholders: decision making should ensure that the most vulnerable stakeholders are not harmed and those stakeholders with whom the organisation maintains the closest relations are given preference. Calton and Kurland (1996), based on a similar "affirmative post-modern epistemology" (p. 164), advocate enabling participation and giving "voice" (cf. Hirschman, 1970) to stakeholders.

A key point in Calton and Kurland's thesis for promoting a postmodern praxis of organisational discourse and in order to "reinforce the normative promise of stakeholder theory" (p. 163) is to do away with the managerial character of the theory (which Donaldson and Preston (1995) emphasise). Some implications of "decentering" stakeholder theory from management correspond to the characteristics that a modern stakeholder theory is trying to achieve and which have been outlined previously. More specifically, responsibility is shared by all parties and all parties seek win-win solutions to conflict situations:

> Ontology in a theory of stakeholder enabling involves a way of being that evokes postbureaucratic, network, interactive organizations. There is no clear center of power; rather, power is located in multiple stakeholders and not exclusively in an institutionalized, managerial hierarchy. Stakeholders engage in interactive dialogue for the purposes of achieving shared goals and mutual growth. A metadecision process for achieving consensual legitimation consists of three essential elements: (a) bringing together stakeholders, (b) creating a dialogue, and (c) achieving consensus on a path forward. (Calton and Kurland, 1996, p. 170)

In short, by not limiting the use of the stakeholder concept within a managerial perspective the situation at hand can be considered from multiple perspectives, without privileging *a priori* any of the viewpoints. For our discussion the following aspects of stakeholder theory are fundamental:

- Stakeholders are persons or groups with legitimate interests in procedural and/or substantive aspects of the privacy/transparency claim and subsequent judgments on that basis. Furthermore the interests of all stakeholders in the domain under consideration are of *intrinsic* value.

- Stakeholder analysis provides a way to make explicit, or give a voice to, the legitimate privacy/transparency claims of all those involved in the domain of activity and judgement.

- The ability, or influence, that the different stakeholders have to make their claims "stick" are rarely, if ever, equal.

With this understanding of stakeholders in hand we now want to discuss a framework for analysing the privacy/transparency claims within a particular domain of activity and judgement.

4. Framework for the Analysis of Privacy Claims and Risks

When making judgments we are always already enmeshed, or situated, *in* our values and interests. We can not un-entangle ourselves from an existing web of interests and values (Introna, 1997a). They are the very horizon from which we speak and judge when we speak and judge (Gadamer, 1989). There is no neutral ground, no absolute horizon, from which we can make rational and informed judgements. Our values and interests become sedimented as tacit knowledge that function as extensions of our body (Polanyi, 1973; Merleau-Ponty, 1962). To try and "suspend", or direct, our values and interests, *in making* our judgements, is like trying to do something without engaging our bodies—it is unthinkable. Furthermore, in a similar way that we are completely and utterly unaware which particular muscles participate in any action, so we are unaware which values and interests participate in any judgement. To make the discussion more specific, let us consider the following example. Let us imagine a promotion committee considering the application for promotion by a professor. Lets imagine that on the morning before the meeting it was reported in the local papers that the professor was charged for beating his wife. Lets imagine that the chairperson of the committee reminds the members, after reviewing all the material before them, that the judgement they have to make is about the competence of the professor as an academic (his research, teaching, and so forth). Also, that although they may think it appalling that he beats his wife they should not allow this to "cloud" their judgement of him *as an academic*. Now it is our argument, outlined above, that it is impossible, when *actually* raising their hands in approval or disapproval for the members to say whether their judgement was or was not, and to what degree, affected by the fact that they already knew (and most probably disapproved) of his conduct in beating his wife. They may, of course, argue at length about how they did not allow their judgement to be "clouded". However, in doing this they can only discuss their judgements analytically as observers of themselves in a way an athlete may analytically describe which muscles are used in jumping over the hurdle. Similarly, as the athlete can not run *and* simultaneously attend to the particular muscles she uses, so they cannot judge *and* simultaneously attend to the particular causal relationships when applying their interests, values and information *in* the act of judging. This is the point: we are always already entangled in our interests and values when making judgements in ways that are obscure and inaccessible to us *in making those judgements*. Furthermore, since values are implicit part of our "bodies" it is impossible to explicitly take up, or consider, *in actual* judgements, the values—and to some degree the interests—of others.

If this is true, then it has two levels at which it affects our discussion. First, since it is impossible for an individual, or groups of individuals, to neatly separate information, values and interests *in making* judgements about others, they ought to have access only to that information which is appropriate in that particular context of judgement (such as considering the application for promotion). For example, if the professor was appearing in front of a disciplinary hearing for assaulting a student then it could be argued that the information in the paper ought to become part of the judgement. Let us call this the *access principle*. Second, when claims of privacy/transparency are considered all stakeholders ought to be "present" as such. When we say "present" we mean actually present or represented by some-*body* that embody their values and interests. Stakeholders can only function as stakeholders if they are present. Let us call this the *representation principle*.

It is in this context of present stakeholders with already present values and interest that the claims of privacy/transparency should be evaluated. A privacy/transparency claim always implies an "other". When a privacy/transparency claim is raised there are always a number of stakeholders involved; each with their already present bodies of values and interests. Now if all the stakeholders made their claims in an ideal speech situation (Habermas, 1984; Habermas, 1987) then one could foresee the possibility where the "force of reason" could prevail over what ought to be private, and what public, in a particular context. However, the participants do not only enter with their values and interests, they also enter within an already there set of relations of power, influence, and discipline. Like values power cannot merely be suspended by an act of rational choice. This means that there is no way in which stakeholders can make privacy/transparency claims as "equals"—not even in a court of law.[1] Let us return to our example. Let us assume that the chairperson of the committee is also a very influential figure in the university. Lets assume that the chairperson indicates that although the fact that the professor beats his wife has nothing to do with his competence as an academic he nevertheless feels that it does go against the spirit of the institution. Such a judgement by the chairperson may implicitly receive more "weight" than the details of the CV or the interview with the candidate. It would be difficult, if not impossible, for the members of the committee *in making* their judgements to make explicit, or separate out, that the chairperson is just one of the members of the committee and that there may be many others who implicitly or explicitly still feel that it does not have any bearing on the candidates competence as an academic. It would be impossible for them to suspend, or separate out, *in the making* of the judgements, the already present relations of power influence, and discipline. Nevertheless, all stakeholders ought to be able to have equal power to make their claims of privacy/transparency stick. Let us call this the *power principle*.

Any context where claims of privacy/transparency are made which ignore the normative principles outlined above will lead to a risk that stakeholder claims will go unacknowledged or be underrepresented. Such a risk would lead to an inappropriate judgement that violates the intrinsic claims of a stakeholder in the particular context or domain (such as the professor being refused promotion because of a local newspaper report). It is our contention that we could therefore use these principles to analyse potential claims of privacy/transparency so as to *identify and make explicit privacy/transparency risks*. Only when claims are honoured do stakeholders function as stakeholders. In the next section we will use these principles to analyse various claims in a case study of the British National Health Service (NHS) below.

5. Privacy Claims and Risks in the British NHS

One of the most recent and important debates on privacy matters in the British NHS concerns the use and exchange of patient data over the *NHSnet*, a network that has recently been established to improve electronic communication between healthcare professionals in Britain (NHS Executive, 1994). However, doctors have not been satisfied that the network can be used securely, especially for transferring patient data.

The main concern is that both NHS members and external parties can misuse data. This situation has resulted in an explicit conflict between the NHS Executive who are responsible for the implementation of the network on the one hand and the doctors and their representatives (the British Medical Association and their security consultants) on the other. However, the stakeholders of the network and those that will be affected by the outcome of this conflict are multiple (Pouloudi, 1997; Pouloudi and Whitley, 1996). For the purposes of this paper we will look at two specific privacy concerns that derive from the implementation of NHSnet and where our framework can be used to study privacy/transparency risks.

Confidentiality of Patient Data

First, it is worth considering that the confidentiality of patient data is at the heart of the conflict. Evidently, the stakeholders that will be most severely affected by breeches of confidentiality will be the patients. And yet, these stakeholders are absent from the debate. Instead, their interests are carried forward by the organisation representing the medical profession at a national level, the British Medical Association and by the Data Protection Registrar, who is responsible for the application of the Data Protection Act (currently under revision following a European Union Directive on the matter).

In terms of our framework, the *representation principle* needs to be considered here. As the patients are not present themselves, we would expect them to be represented by somebody that clearly embodies their values and interests. One could argue that doctors, because of their Hippocratic oath and their professional responsibility to respect the confidentiality of patient data, could claim that they could stand in for the patients. However, it may well be that doctors could also have values and interests that are different to those of the patients. On the one hand these may overlap and support the confidentiality claim such as when primary care doctors safeguard their "gate-keeper" role to secondary care by remaining responsible for scrutinising which patient data will be forwarded to whom. On the other hand, it may not, such as when doctors have an interest in easier and faster exchange of patient information, which could be facilitated if electronic means are used. Clearly it is fairly easy to imagine many instances where doctors as representatives of patient claims and interests, and doctors as health professional can conflict. We would therefore argue, using the representation principle, that there is a significant risk that stakeholder's claims would go unacknowledged or underrepresented.

It is interesting to note the layering of levels of representation. This complex web of representation is brought about by the *power principle* that indicates that stakeholders ought to have access to equal power and influence to make their claims hold. This leads to the patients being represented by the doctors who are represented by the BMA. It seems as if the doctors (on behalf of the patients) realised that they would have a better chance to make their claims heard it they utilised the institutional infrastructure of the BMA to oppose the NHS Executive. This conflict was mainly expressed through two individuals: Ray Rogers (the then director of the Information Management Group of the NHSE) and Ross Anderson (security consultant of the BMA and also an academic). From this analysis it seems that there may be a certain amount of tension between the representation principle and the power principle. One may have to sacrifice a degree of representation to gain access to an appropriate level of power. In this case, however, it seems as if both principles are disregarded simultaneously which leads to a significant risk for the legitimate claims of the patients.

One could argue that the interests of the patients are also represented by the Data Protection Registrar, but her role has been restricted by the limited provisions of the Data Protection Act of 1984 (some of these limitations have made its amendment imperative in the recent years). Also, in the case of the NHSnet the Registrar has supported the BMA concerns without becoming explicitly involved in the conflict over the network's use. Her stance can be explained in part by the lack of resources or institutional power in relation to the NHSE. Consequently, the NHSnet case seems to indicate that since neither effective representation nor appropriate access to power can be secured the confidentiality of patient data still poses a risk for the major stakeholder, the patients.

The NHSE have defended their position by arguing that the NHSnet is likely to be more secure and consistent than previous systems of information exchange (both computerised and manual). The NHSnet may, however, make certain aspects appear more efficient whilst these may inadvertently compromise the confidentiality of patient data and consequently patient privacy. More specifically, it has been considered that in cases of emergency all patient data may be accessible by doctors at a national level. Whilst this is expected to have important benefits for the delivery of health care, it will be less evident to determine in which cases such data could be accessed and by whom. Any attempt to fix specific rules would "remove the context" of professional judgement (and that could have severe implications as discussed in the previous sections). On the other hand, absence of rules would leave the system open to interpretation and possibly abuse of access rights, particularly if those accessing the information are not subject to rigorous professional obligations (Barber, 1998).

Access, Patient Consent and Insurance Companies

Another important case where the storage, processing and exchange of information may create privacy/transparency problems in the healthcare domain concerns the notion of patients consenting to the sharing of their data within the NHS. Much of the recent discussions on data protection have stemmed from the recent EU Directive on, amongst others, the matter of consent (which may also require that the Data Protection Act of 1984 be updated). The provisions that deal with consent of any data protection act within the health care context poses a number of sensitive issues. Barber (1998) summarises some important implications:

- Some patients may be physically or legally incapable of giving consent, for example as a consequence of mental illness.

- Patient data are not only accessed and handled by health professionals but also by other support staff. Those who are not part of the health profession do not face as severe consequences in case of a confidentiality breach.

Since specific guidelines on consent arrangements are not available, doctors often rely on a notion of *implied consent* by the patient which means they can share their data with other health professionals when appropriate. In other words, it is assumed that the patients rely on the professional *judgement* of their doctor in a given *context*. However, if this data is exchanged through an electronic network, and particularly if patient information is held centrally where healthcare professionals can access it, the notion of patient consent becomes extremely problematic. More importantly, the healthcare professionals (and support staff) accessing the information may be unable to view this information in relation to the context in which the patient disclosed the information. Thus, the relevance, or not, of some information may be difficult to judge. The *principle of access* discussed above indicates that this may compromise the privacy claims of the patients.

These problems can become critical if those accessing the information are not healthcare professionals (and associated support staff) but other stakeholders such as insurance companies. The latter have a clear interest to know of any medical conditions that may affect future health of the patient. However, the access of insurance companies to medical information is often determined by the doctor rather than the patient (which obviously defies the access and representation principles above). Although the doctors may wish to comply with their professional guidelines there may be cases where such guidance is vague or cannot be readily applied to the situation at hand. Indeed, there is evidence of similar issues being raised often in *gp-uk*, an electronic mailing list where GPs seek the advice of their peers in relation to their obligations and responsibilities for disclosing information on medical cases.

Let us look into the access of insurance companies to personal health data in more detail. First, it is worth noting that insurance companies are obviously entitled to have access to information on general health trends so that they can set realistic premiums. This condition, however, does not necessarily entitle them to access to individual health information, at least not *before* a contract has been signed. Such access would imply that they would tend only to cover a healthy person, which removes the fundamental purpose of insurance in the first place. Current legislature seems unable to safeguard the rights of the patient in this respect. Turner (1998) reports that the guidelines of the Department of Health on the protection and use of patient information in primary care state that:

> [P]atients have a right to keep personal health information confidential between themselves and the doctor if they ask for this, except when disclosure is specifically required by law. Life insurance companies etc will not be sent information unless the patient consents, but if the patient refuses they will be informed of this (which could be a double-edged sword).

We would like to agree on this last point. This is a clear indication that the Department of Health does not recognise the patient as a stakeholder with an intrinsic claim. The patient is in fact implicitly obliged to make private information available. Not only this, the patient does not have any control over the way the user may judge this information. For example, in cases such as HIV testing the patient may feel trapped in a no-win situation. Insurance companies often consider HIV testing as a sign of someone leading a "dangerous" lifestyle—someone that would have "reasons" to be tested (regardless of the result of the HIV test or for the reasons leading a person to such action). On the other hand, they may also interpret someone's refusal to take an HIV test not as a means of safeguarding private information but as an attempt to hide a positive result. This situation may even discourage responsible behaviour; an individual may opt for not being tested and thus posing risk for his/her partners if such test is likely to affect future insurance policies. In this case both the access principle and the power principle are disregarded.

6. Conclusion

The analysis in this paper has presented the access, representation and power principles and has clearly highlighted how these principles could be used to identify situations in which stakeholder claims could go unacknowledged or underrepresented. It seems that in the healthcare context the underrepresented interests would typically be those of the patients. It is our contention that the framework of principles can provide legislators and professionals with an analytical ability to proactively identify and understand privacy/transparency risks. The framework may also be used to evaluate the appropriateness of existing mechanisms to ensure that claims are acknowledged and represented. As the electronic capturing of data rapidly expands so will the risks. It is this concern that continually motivates us to make stakeholder's claims as explicit as possible. It is our moral duty.

Note

1. For example, the wealthy defendant can enrol more expert witnesses to raise reasonable doubt in the mind of the jury.

References

Andre, J.: 1986, 'Privacy as a Value and as a Right', *The Journal of Value Inquiry* **20**, 309–312.

Barber, B.: 1998, 'Towards a Measure of Privacy', *British Journal of Healthcare Computing and Information Management* **15**(1), 23–26.

Brandeis, L. and S. D. Warren: 1890, 'The Right to Privacy', *The Harvard Law Review* **4**(5), 193–220.

Burton, B. K. and C. P. Dunn: 1996, 'Feminist Ethics as Moral Grounding for Stakeholder Theory', *Business Ethics Quarterly* **6**(2), 133–147.

Calton, J. M. and N. B. Kurland: 1996, 'A Theory of Stakeholder Enabling: Giving Voice to an Emerging Postmodern Praxis of Organizational Discourse', in D. M. Boje, R. P. Gephart and T. J. Thatchenkery (eds.), *Postmodern Management and Organization Theory* (Sage, Thousand Oaks), pp. 154–177.

Campbell, D. and S. Connor: 1987, 'Surveillance, Computers and Privacy', in R. Finnegan et al. (eds.), *Information Technology: Social Issues* (Hodder & Stoughton, London), pp. 134–144.

Clarke, R. C.: 1988, 'Information Technology and Dataveillance', *Communications of the ACM* **31**(5), 498–512.

DeCew, J. W.: 1986, 'The Scope of Privacy in Law and Ethics', *Law and Philosophy* **5**, 145–173.

Donaldson, T. and L. E. Preston: 1995, 'The Stakeholder Theory of the Corporation: Concepts, Evidence, and Implications', *Academy of Management Review* **20**(1), 65–91.

Dunlop, C. and R. Kling: 1991, *Computerization and Controversy* (Academic Press, Boston), pp. 410–419.

Forester, T. and P. Morrison: 1994, *Computer Ethics: Cautionary Tales and Ethical Dilemmas in Computing*, Second Edition (The MIT Press, Cambridge).

Foucault, M.: 1980, *The History of Sexuality; Volume I: An Introduction*, Translated by Robert Hurley (Vintage Books, New York).

Freeman, R. E.: 1984, *Strategic Management: A Stakeholder Approach* (Ballinger, Cambridge, MA).

Freeman, R. E.: 1994, 'The Politics of Stakeholder Theory: Some Future Directions', *Business Ethics Quarterly* **4**(4), 409–421.

Fried, C.: 1968, 'Privacy', *Yale Law Journal* **77**, 475–493.

Gadamer, H. G.: 1989, *Truth and Method* (Weinsheimer, Joel Marshall, Donald G, Trans.), (Sheed and Ward, London).

Gavison, R.: 1984, 'Privacy and the Limits of the Law', in F. Schoeman (ed.), *Philosophical Dimensions of Privacy* (Cambridge University Press, Cambridge), pp. 365–371.

Gavison, R.: 1980, 'Privacy and the Limits of the Law', *The Yale Law Journal* **89**(3), 421–471.

Gerstein, R. S.: 1984, 'Intimacy and Privacy', in F. Schoeman (ed.), *Philosophical Dimensions of Privacy* (Cambridge University Press, Cambridge), pp. 265–271.

Goffman, E.: 1959, *The Presentation of Self in Everyday Life* (Doubleday & Co., Garden City).

Goodpaster, K. E.: 1993, 'Business Ethics and Stakeholder Analysis', in T. L. Beauchamp and N. E. Bowie (eds.), *Ethical Theory and Business* (Prentice Hall, Englewood Cliffs, NJ).

Gross, H.: 1967, 'The Concept of Privacy', *New York University Law Review* **42**, 35–36.

Habermas, J.: 1984, *The Theory of Communicative Action* (Heinemann Education, London).

Habermas, J.: 1987, *The Theory of Communicative Action* (Polity, Cambridge).

Hirschman, A. O.: 1970, *Exit, Voice, and Loyalty: Responses to Decline in Firms, Organizations, and the States* (Harvard University Press, Cambridge, MA).

Introna, L. D.: 1997a, *Management, Information and Power* (Macmillan, Basingstoke).

Introna, L. D.: 1997b, 'Privacy and the Computer: Why we Need Privacy in the Information Society', *Metaphilosophy* **28**(3), 259–275.

Johnson, J. L.: 1989, 'Privacy and the Judgement of Others', *The Journal of Value Inquiry* **23**, 157–168.

Kling, R. and S. Iacono: 1984, 'Computing as an Occasion for Social Control', *Journal of Social Issues* **40**(3), 77–96.

Kupfer, J.: 1987, 'Privacy, Autonomy, and Self-Concept', *American Philosophical Quarterly* **24**(1), 81–82.

Merleau-Ponty, M.: 1962, *Phenomenology of Perception* (Routledge & Kegan Paul, London).

NHS Executive: 1994, *A Strategy for NHS-wide Networking* (No. E5155), Information Management Group.

Parent, W. A.: 1983, 'Recent Work on the Concept of Privacy', *American Philosophical Quarterly* **20**(4), 341–355.

Parker, R. B.: 1974, 'A Definition of Privacy', *Rutgers Law Review* **27**(1), 275–296.

Posner, R. (1978), 'The Right to Privacy', *Georgia Law Review* **12**, 393–422.

Pouloudi, A.: 1997, 'Conflicting Concerns over the Privacy of Electronic Medical Records in the NHSnet', *Business Ethics: A European Review* **6**(2), 94–101.

Pouloudi, A. and E. A. Whitley: 1996, 'Privacy of Electronic Medical Records: Understanding Conflicting Concerns in an Interorganizational System', in P. Barroso, T. W. Bynum, S. Rogerson and L. Joyanes (eds.), *ETHICOMP96—III International Conference: Values and Social Responsibilities of the Computer Science* (Pontifical University of Salamanca in Madrid, Spain), pp. 307–327.

Phillips, R. A.: 1997, 'Stakeholder Theory and a Principle of Fairness', *Business Ethics Quarterly* **7**(1), 51–66.

Prosser, W. L.: 1960, 'Privacy', *The California Law Review* **48**, 383–422.

Rachels, J.: 1975, 'Why Privacy is Important', *Philosophy & Public Affairs* **4**(4), 328.

Reiman, J. H.: 1976, 'Privacy, Intimacy, and Personhood', *Philosophy & Public Affairs* **6**(1), 26–44.

Schoeman, F.: 1984, 'Privacy: Philosophical Dimensions', *American Philosophical Quarterly* **21**(3), 199–213.

Schoeman, F.: 1984, 'Privacy and Intimate Information', in F. Schoeman (ed.), *Philosophical Dimensions of Privacy* (Cambridge University Press, Cambridge), pp. 403–417.

Shattuck, J.: 1984, 'Computer Matching is a Serious Threat to Individual Rights', *Communications of the ACM* **27**(6), 538–541.

Turner, R.: 1998, 'The Caldicott Committee Reports', *British Journal of Healthcare Computing and Information Management* **15**(1), 23–26.

Van Den Haag, E.: 1971, 'On Privacy', *Nomos* **13**, 147–153.

Wacks, R. (1980), 'The Poverty of "Privacy"', *The Law Quarterly Review* **96**, 73–95.

Westin, A.: 1967, *Privacy and Freedom* (Ateneum, New York).

Willetts, D.: 1997, 'The Poverty of Stakeholding', in G. Kelly, D. Kelly and A. Gamble (eds.), *Stakeholder Capitalism* (Macmillan, Basingstoke), pp. 20–28.

23

The Economy of Ideas

*A framework for patents and copyrights
in the Digital Age.
(Everything you know about
intellectual property is wrong.)*

JOHN PERRY BARLOW

"If nature has made any one thing less susceptible than all others of exclusive property, it is the action of the thinking power called an idea, which an individual may exclusively possess as long as he keeps it to himself; but the moment it is divulged, it forces itself into the possession of everyone, and the receiver cannot dispossess himself of it. Its peculiar character, too, is that no one possesses the less, because every other possesses the whole of it. He who receives an idea from me, receives instruction himself without lessening mine; as he who lights his taper at mine, receives light without darkening me. That ideas should freely spread from one to another over the globe, for the moral and mutual instruction of man, and improvement of his condition, seems to have been peculiarly and benevolently designed by nature, when she made them, like fire, expansible over all space, without lessening their density at any point, and like the air in which we breathe, move, and have our physical being, incapable of confinement or exclusive appropriation. Inventions then cannot, in nature, be a subject of property." —Thomas Jefferson

Throughout the time I've been groping around cyberspace, an immense, unsolved conundrum has remained at the root of nearly every legal, ethical, governmental, and social vexation to be found in the Virtual World. I refer to the problem of digitized property. The enigma is this: If our property can be infinitely reproduced and instantaneously distributed all over the planet without cost, without our knowledge, without its even leaving our possession, how can we protect it? How are we going to get paid for the work we do with our minds? And, if we can't get paid, what will assure the continued creation and distribution of such work?

John Perry Barlow (barlow@eff.org) is a retired cattle rancher, a lyricist for the Grateful Dead, and co-founder and executive chair of the Electronic Frontier Foundation.

Since we don't have a solution to what is a profoundly new kind of challenge, and are apparently unable to delay the galloping digitization of everything not obstinately physical, we are sailing into the future on a sinking ship.

This vessel, the accumulated canon of copyright and patent law, was developed to convey forms and methods of expression entirely different from the vaporous cargo it is now being asked to carry. It is leaking as much from within as from without.

Legal efforts to keep the old boat floating are taking three forms: a frenzy of deck chair rearrangement, stern warnings to the passengers that if she goes down, they will face harsh criminal penalties, and serene, glassy-eyed denial.

Intellectual property law cannot be patched, retrofitted, or expanded to contain digitized expression any more than real estate law might be revised to cover the allocation of broadcasting spectrum (which, in fact, rather resembles what is being attempted here). We will need to develop an entirely new set of methods as befits this entirely new set of circumstances.

Most of the people who actually create soft property—the programmers, hackers, and Net surfers—already know this. Unfortunately, neither the companies they work for nor the lawyers these companies hire have enough direct experience with nonmaterial goods to understand why they are so problematic. They are proceeding as though the old laws can somehow be made to work, either by grotesque expansion or by force. They are wrong.

The source of this conundrum is as simple as its solution is complex. Digital technology is detaching information from the physical plane, where property law of all sorts has always found definition.

Throughout the history of copyrights and patents, the proprietary assertions of thinkers have been focused not on their ideas but on the expression of those ideas. The ideas themselves, as well as facts about the phenomena of the world, were considered to be the collective property of humanity. One could claim franchise, in the case of copyright, on the precise turn of phrase used to convey a particular idea or the order in which facts were presented.

The point at which this franchise was imposed was that moment when the "word became flesh" by departing the mind of its originator and entering some physical object, whether book or widget. The subsequent arrival of other commercial media besides books didn't alter the legal importance of this moment. Law protected expression and, with few (and recent) exceptions, to express was to make physical.

Protecting physical expression had the force of convenience on its side. Copyright worked well because, Gutenberg notwithstanding, it was hard to make a book. Furthermore, books froze their contents into a condition which was as challenging to alter as it was to reproduce. Counterfeiting and distributing counterfeit volumes were obvious and visible activities—it was easy enough to catch somebody in the act of doing. Finally, unlike unbounded words or images, books had material surfaces to which one could attach copyright notices, publisher's marques, and price tags.

Mental-to-physical conversion was even more central to patent. A patent, until recently, was either a description of the form into which materials were to be rendered in the service of some purpose, or a description of the process by which rendition occurred. In either case, the conceptual heart of patent was the material result. If no purposeful object could be rendered because of some material limitation, the patent was rejected. Neither a Klein bottle nor a shovel made of silk could be patented. It had to be a thing, and the thing had to work.

Thus, the rights of invention and authorship adhered to activities in the physical world. One didn't get paid for ideas, but for the ability to deliver them into reality. For all practical purposes, the value was in the conveyance and not in the thought conveyed.

In other words, the bottle was protected, not the wine.

Now, as information enters cyberspace, the native home of Mind, these bottles are vanishing. With the advent of digitization, it is now possible to replace all previous information storage forms with one metabottle: complex and highly liquid patterns of ones and zeros.

Even the physical/digital bottles to which we've become accustomed—floppy disks, CD-ROMs, and other discrete, shrink-wrappable bit-packages—will disappear as all computers jack-in to the global Net. While the Internet may never include every CPU on the planet, it is more than doubling every year and can be expected to become the principal medium of information conveyance, and perhaps eventually, the only one.

Once that has happened, all the goods of the Information Age—all of the expressions once contained in books or film strips or newsletters—will exist either as pure thought or something very much like thought: voltage conditions darting around the Net at the speed of light, in conditions that one might behold in effect, as glowing pixels or transmitted sounds, but never touch or claim to "own" in the old sense of the word.

Some might argue that information will still require some physical manifestation, such as its magnetic existence on the titanic hard disks of distant servers, but these are bottles which have no macroscopically discrete or personally meaningful form.

Some will also argue that we have been dealing with unbottled expression since the advent of radio, and they would be right. But for most of the history of broadcast, there was no convenient way to capture soft goods from the electromagnetic ether and reproduce them with quality available in commercial packages. Only recently has this changed, and little has been done legally or technically to address the change.

Generally, the issue of consumer payment for broadcast products was irrelevant. The consumers themselves were the product. Broadcast media were supported either by the sale of the attention of their audience to advertisers, by government assessing payment through taxes, or by the whining mendicancy of annual donor drives.

All of the broadcast-support models are flawed. Support either by advertisers or government has almost invariably tainted the purity of the goods delivered. Besides, direct marketing is gradually killing the advertiser-support model anyway.

Broadcast media gave us another payment method for a virtual product: the royalties that broadcasters pay songwriters through such organizations as ASCAP and BMI. But, as a member of ASCAP, I can assure you this is not a model that we should emulate. The monitoring methods are wildly approximate. There is no parallel system of accounting in the revenue stream. It doesn't really work. Honest.

In any case, without our old methods, based on physically defining the expression of ideal, and in the absence of successful new models for nonphysical transaction, we simply don't know how to assure reliable payment for mental works. To make matters worse, this comes at a time when the human mind is replacing sunlight and mineral deposits as the principal source of new wealth.

Furthermore, the increasing difficulty of enforcing existing copyright and patent laws is already placing in peril the ultimate source of intellectual property—the free exchange of ideas.

That is, when the primary articles of commerce in a society look so much like speech as to be indistinguishable from it, and when the traditional methods of protecting their ownership have become ineffectual, attempting to fix the problem with broader and more vigorous enforcement will inevitably threaten freedom of speech. The greatest constraint on your future liberties may come not from government but from corporate legal departments laboring to protect by force what can no longer be protected by practical efficiency or general social consent.

Furthermore, when Jefferson and his fellow creatures of the Enlightenment designed the system that became American copyright law, their primary objective was assuring the widespread distribution of thought, not profit. Profit was the fuel that would carry ideas into the libraries and minds of their new republic. Libraries would purchase books, thus rewarding the authors for their work in assembling ideas; these ideas, otherwise "incapable of confinement," would then become freely available to the public. But what is the role of libraries in the absence of books? How does society now pay for the distribution of ideas if not by charging for the ideas themselves?

Additionally complicating the matter is the fact that along with the disappearance of the physical bottles in which intellectual property protection has resided, digital technology is also erasing the legal jurisdictions of the physical world and replacing them with the unbounded and perhaps permanently lawless waves of cyberspace.

In cyberspace, no national or local boundaries contain the scene of a crime and determine the method of its prosecution; worse, no clear cultural agreements define what a crime might be. Unresolved and basic differences between Western and Asian cultural assumptions about intellectual property can only be exacerbated when many transactions are taking place in both hemispheres and yet, somehow, in neither.

Even in the most local of digital conditions, jurisdiction and responsibility are hard to assess. A group of music publishers filed suit against CompuServe this fall because it allowed its users to upload musical compositions into areas where other users might access them. But since CompuServe cannot practically exercise much control over the flood of bits that passes between its subscribers, it probably shouldn't be held responsible for unlawfully "publishing" these works.

Notions of property, value, ownership, and the nature of wealth itself are changing more fundamentally than at any time since the Sumerians first poked cuneiform into wet clay and called it stored grain. Only a very few people are aware of the enormity of this shift, and fewer of them are lawyers or public officials.

Those who do see these changes must prepare responses for the legal and social confusion that will erupt as efforts to protect new forms of property with old methods become more obviously futile, and, as a consequence, more adamant.

From Swords to Writs to Bits

Humanity now seems bent on creating a world economy primarily based on goods that take no material form. In doing so, we may be eliminating any predictable connection between creators and a fair reward for the utility or pleasure others may find in their works.

Without that connection, and without a fundamental change in consciousness to accommodate its loss, we are building our future on furor, litigation, and institutionalized evasion of payment except in response to raw force. We may return to the Bad Old Days of property.

Throughout the darker parts of human history, the possession and distribution of property was a largely military matter. "Ownership" was assured those with the nastiest tools, whether fists or armies, and the most resolute will to use them. Property was the divine right of thugs.

By the turn of the First Millennium AD, the emergence of merchant classes and landed gentry forced the development of ethical understandings for the resolution of property disputes. In the Middle Ages, enlightened rulers like England's Henry II began to codify this unwritten "common law" into recorded canons. These laws were local, which didn't matter much as they were primarily directed at real estate, a form of property that is local by definition. And, as the name implied, was very real.

This continued to be the case as long as the origin of wealth was agricultural, but with that dawning of the Industrial Revolution, humanity began to focus as much on means as ends. Tools acquired a new social value and, thanks to their development, it became possible to duplicate and distribute them in quantity.

To encourage their invention, copyright and patent law were developed in most Western countries. These laws were devoted to the delicate task of getting mental creations into the world where they could be used—and could enter the minds of others—while assuring their inventors compensation for the value of their use. And, as previously stated, the systems of both law and practice which grew up around that task were based on physical expression.

Since it is now possible to convey ideas from one mind to another without ever making them physical, we are now claiming to own ideas themselves and not merely their expression. And since it is likewise now possible to create useful tools that never take physical form, we have taken to patenting abstractions, sequences of virtual events, and mathematical formulae—the most unreal estate imaginable.

In certain areas, this leaves rights of ownership in such an ambiguous condition that property again adheres to those who can muster the largest armies. The only difference is that this time the armies consist of lawyers.

Threatening their opponents with the endless purgatory of litigation, over which some might prefer death itself, they assert claim to any thought which might have entered another cranium within the collective body of the corporations they serve. They act as though these ideas appeared in splendid detachment from all previous human thought. And they pretend that thinking about a product is somehow as good as manufacturing, distributing, and selling it.

What was previously considered a common human resource, distributed among the minds and libraries of the world, as well as the phenomena of nature herself, is now being fenced and deeded. It is as though a new class of enterprise had arisen that claimed to own the air.

What is to be done? While there is a certain grim fun to be had in it, dancing on the grave of copyright and patent will solve little, especially when so few are willing to admit that the occupant of this grave is even deceased, and so many are trying to uphold by force what can no longer be upheld by popular consent.

The legalists, desperate over their slipping grip, are vigorously trying to extend their reach. Indeed, the United States and other proponents of GATT are making adherence to our moribund systems of intellectual property protection a condition of membership in the marketplace of nations. For example, China will be denied Most Favored Nation trading status unless they agree to uphold a set of culturally alien principles that are no longer even sensibly applicable in their country of origin.

In a more perfect world, we'd be wise to declare a moratorium on litigation, legislation, and international treaties in this area until we had a clearer sense of the terms and conditions of enterprise in cyberspace. Ideally, laws ratify already developed social consensus. They are less the Social Contract itself than a series of memoranda expressing a collective intent that has emerged out of many millions of human interactions.

Humans have not inhabited cyberspace long enough or in sufficient diversity to have developed a Social Contract which conforms to the strange new conditions of that world. Laws developed prior to consensus usually favor the already established few who can get them passed and not society as a whole.

To the extent that law and established social practice exists in this area, they are already in dangerous disagreement. The laws regarding unlicensed reproduction of commercial software are clear and stern . . . and rarely observed. Software piracy laws are so practically unenforceable and breaking them has become so socially acceptable that only a thin minority appears compelled, either by fear or conscience, to obey them. When I give speeches on this subject, I always ask how many people in the audience can honestly claim to have no unauthorized software on their hard disks. I've never seen more than 10 percent of the hands go up.

Whenever there is such profound divergence between law and social practice, it is not society that adapts. Against the swift tide of custom, the software publishers' current practice of hanging a few visible scapegoats is so obviously capricious as to only further diminish respect for the law.

Part of the widespread disregard for commercial software copyrights stems from a legislative failure to understand the conditions into which it was inserted. To assume that systems of law based in the physical world will serve in an environment as fundamentally different as cyberspace is a folly for which everyone doing business in the future will pay.

As I will soon discuss in detail, unbounded intellectual property is very different from physical property and can no longer be protected as though these differences did not exist. For example, if we continue to assume that value is based on scarcity, as it is with regard to physical objects, we will create laws that are precisely contrary to the nature of information, which may, in many cases, increase in value with distribution.

The large, legally risk-averse institutions most likely to play by the old rules will suffer for their compliance. As more lawyers, guns, and money are invested in either protecting their rights or subverting those of their opponents, their ability to produce new technology will simply grind to a halt as every move they make drives them deeper into a tar pit of courtroom warfare.

Faith in law will not be an effective strategy for high-tech companies. Law adapts by continuous increments and at a pace second only to geology. Technology advances in lunging jerks, like the punctuation of biological evolution grotesquely accelerated. Real-world conditions will continue to change at a blinding pace, and the law will lag further behind, more profoundly confused. This mismatch may prove impossible to overcome.

Promising economies based on purely digital products will either be born in a state of paralysis, as appears to be the case with multimedia, or continue in a brave and willful refusal by their owners to play the ownership game at all.

In the United States one can already see a parallel economy developing, mostly among small, fast moving enterprises who protect their ideas by getting into the marketplace quicker then their larger competitors who base their protection on fear and litigation.

Perhaps those who are part of the problem will simply quarantine themselves in court, while those who are part of the solution will create a new society based, at first, on piracy and freebooting. It may well be that when the current system of intellectual property law has collapsed, as seems inevitable, that no new legal structure will arise in its place.

But something will happen. After all, people do business. When a currency becomes meaningless, business is done in barter. When societies develop outside the law, they develop their own unwritten codes, practices, and ethical systems. While technology may undo law, technology offers methods for restoring creative rights.

A Taxonomy of Information

It seems to me that the most productive thing to do now is to look into the true nature of what we're trying to protect. How much do we really know about information and its natural behaviors?

What are the essential characteristics of unbounded creation? How does it differ from previous forms of property? How many of our assumptions about it have actually been about its containers rather than their mysterious contents? What are its different species and how does each of them lend itself to control? What technologies will be useful in creating new virtual bottles to replace the old physical ones?

Of course, information is, by nature, intangible and hard to define. Like other such deep phenomena as light or matter, it is a natural host to paradox. It is most helpful to understand light as being both a particle and a wave, an understanding of information may emerge in the abstract congruence of its several different properties which might be described by the following three statements:

Information is an activity.
Information is a life form.
Information is a relationship.

In the following section, I will examine each of these.

I.   Information is an Activity

Information Is a Verb, Not a Noun

Freed of its containers, information is obviously not a thing. In fact, it is something that happens in the field of interaction between minds or objects or other pieces of information.

Gregory Bateson, expanding on the information theory of Claude Shannon, said, "Information is a difference which makes a difference." Thus, information only really exists in the Delta. The making of that difference is an activity within a relationship. Information is an action which occupies time rather than a state of being which occupies physical space, as is the case with hard goods. It is the pitch, not the baseball, the dance, not the dancer.

Information Is Experienced, Not Possessed

Even when it has been encapsulated in some static form like a book or a hard disk, information is still something that happens to you as you mentally decompress it from its storage code. But, whether it's running at gigabits per second or words per minute, the actual decoding is a process that must be performed by and upon a mind, a process that must take place in time.

There was a cartoon in the Bulletin of Atomic Scientists a few years ago that illustrated this point beautifully. In the drawing, a holdup man trains his gun on the sort of bespectacled fellow you'd figure might have a lot of information stored in his head. "Quick," orders the bandit, "give me all your ideas."

Information Has to Move

Sharks are said to die of suffocation if they stop swimming, and the same is nearly true of information. Information that isn't moving ceases to exist as anything but potential . . . at least until it is allowed to move again. For this reason, the practice of information hoarding, common in bureaucracies, is an especially wrong-headed artifact of physically based value systems.

Information Is Conveyed by Propagation, Not Distribution

The way in which information spreads is also very different from the distribution of physical goods. It moves more like something from nature than from a factory. It can concatenate like falling dominos or grow in the usual fractal lattice, like frost spreading on a window, but it cannot be shipped around like widgets, except to the extent that it can be contained in them. It doesn't simply move on; it leaves a trail everywhere it's been.

The central economic distinction between information and physical property is that information can be transferred without leaving the possession of the original owner. If I sell you my horse, I can't ride him after that. If I sell you what I know, we both know it.

II. Information is a Life Form

Information Wants to Be Free

Stewart Brand is generally credited with this elegant statement of the obvious, which recognizes both the natural desire of secrets to be told and the fact that they might be capable of possessing something like a "desire" in the first place.

English biologist and philosopher Richard Dawkins proposed the idea of "memes," self-replicating patterns of information that propagate themselves across the ecologies of mind, a pattern of reproduction much like that of life forms.

I believe they are life forms in every respect but their freedom from the carbon atom. They self-reproduce, they interact with their surroundings and adapt to them, they mutate, they persist. They evolve to fill the empty niches of their local environments, which are, in this case the surrounding belief systems and cultures of their hosts, namely, us.

Indeed, sociobiologists like Dawkins make a plausible case that carbon-based life forms are information as well, that, as the chicken is an egg's way of making another egg, the entire biological spectacle is just the DNA molecule's means of copying out more information strings exactly like itself.

Information Replicates into the Cracks of Possibility

Like DNA helices, ideas are relentless expansionists, always seeking new opportunities for Lebensraum. And, as in carbon-based nature, the more robust organisms are extremely adept at finding new places to live. Thus, just as the common housefly has insinuated itself into practically every ecosystem on the planet, so has the meme of "life after death" found a niche in most minds, or psycho-ecologies.

The more universally resonant an idea or image or song, the more minds it will enter and remain within. Trying to stop the spread of a really robust piece of information is about as easy as keeping killer bees south of the border.

Information Wants to Change

If ideas and other interactive patterns of information are indeed life forms, they can be expected to evolve constantly into forms which will be more perfectly adapted to their surroundings. And, as we see, they are doing this all the time.

But for a long time, our static media, whether carvings in stone, ink on paper, or dye on celluloid, have strongly resisted the evolutionary impulse, exalting as a consequence the author's ability to determine the finished product. But, as in an oral tradition, digitized information has no "final cut."

Digital information, unconstrained by packaging, is a continuing process more like the metamorphosing tales of prehistory than anything that will fit in shrink-wrap. From the Neolithic to Gutenberg (monks aside), information was passed on, mouth to ear, changing with every retelling (or resinging). The stories which once shaped our sense of the world didn't have authoritative versions. They adapted to each culture in which they found themselves being told.

Because there was never a moment when the story was frozen in print, the so-called "moral" right of storytellers to own the tale was neither protected nor recognized. The story simply passed through each of them on its way to the next, where it would assume a different form. As we return to continuous information, we can expect the importance of authorship to diminish. Creative people may have to renew their acquaintance with humility.

But our system of copyright makes no accommodation whatever for expressions which don't become fixed at some point nor for cultural expressions which lack a specific author or inventor.

Jazz improvisations, stand-up comedy routines, mime performances, developing monologues, and unrecorded broadcast transmissions all lack the Constitutional requirement of fixation as a "writing." Without being fixed by a point of publication the liquid works of the future will all look more like these continuously adapting and changing forms and will therefore exist beyond the reach of copyright.

Copyright expert Pamela Samuelson tells of having attended a conference last year convened around the fact that Western countries may legally appropriate the music, designs, and biomedical lore of aboriginal people without compensation to their tribes of origin since those tribes are not an "author" or "inventors."

But soon most information will be generated collaboratively by the cyber-tribal hunter-gatherers of cyberspace. Our arrogant legal dismissal of the rights of "primitives" will be soon return to haunt us.

Information Is Perishable

With the exception of the rare classic, most information is like farm produce. Its quality degrades rapidly both over time and in distance from the source of production. But even here, value is highly subjective and conditional. Yesterday's papers are quite valuable to the historian. In fact, the older they are, the more valuable they become. On the other hand, a commodities broker might consider news of an event that occurred more than an hour ago to have lost any relevance.

III. Information is a Relationship

Meaning Has Value and Is Unique to Each Case

In most cases, we assign value to information based on its meaningfulness. The place where information dwells, the holy moment where transmission becomes reception, is a region which has many shifting characteristics and flavors depending on the relationship of sender and receiver, the depth of their interactivity.

Each such relationship is unique. Even in cases where the sender is a broadcast medium, and no response is returned, the receiver is hardly passive. Receiving information is often as creative an act as generating it.

The value of what is sent depends entirely on the extent to which each individual receiver has the receptors-shared terminology, attention, interest, language, paradigm-necessary to render what is received meaningful.

Understanding is a critical element increasingly overlooked in the effort to turn information into a commodity. Data may be any set of facts, useful or not, intelligible or inscrutable, germane or irrelevant. Computers can crank out new data all night long without human help, and the results may be offered for sale as information. They may or may not actually be so. Only a human being can recognize the meaning that separates information from data.

In fact, information, in the economic sense of the word, consists of data which have been passed through a particular human mind and found meaningful within that mental context. One fella's information is all just data to someone else. If you're an anthropologist, my detailed charts of Tasaday kinship patterns might be critical information to you. If you're a banker from Hong Kong, they might barely seem to be data.

Familiarity Has More Value than Scarcity

With physical goods, there is a direct correlation between scarcity and value. Gold is more valuable than wheat, even though you can't eat it. While this is not always the case, the situation with information is often precisely the reverse. Most soft goods increase in value as they become more common. Familiarity is an important asset in the world of information. It may often be true that the best way to raise demand for your product is to give it away.

While this has not always worked with shareware, it could be argued that there is a connection between the extent to which commercial software is pirated and the amount which gets sold. Broadly pirated software, such as Lotus 1-2-3 or WordPerfect, becomes a standard and benefits from Law of Increasing Returns based on familiarity.

In regard to my own soft product, rock 'n' roll songs, there is no question that the band I write them for, the Grateful Dead, has increased its popularity enormously by giving them away. We have been letting people tape our concerts since the early seventies, but instead of reducing the demand for our product, we are now the largest concert draw in America, a fact that is at least in part attributable to the popularity generated by those tapes.

True, I don't get any royalties on the millions of copies of my songs which have been extracted from concerts, but I see no reason to complain. The fact is, no one but the Grateful Dead can perform a Grateful Dead song, so if you want the experience and not its thin projection, you have to buy a ticket from us. In other words, our intellectual property protection derives from our being the only real-time source of it.

Exclusivity Has Value

The problem with a model that turns the physical scarcity/value ratio on its head is that sometimes the value of information is very much based on its scarcity. Exclusive possession of certain facts makes them more useful. If everyone knows about conditions which might drive a stock price up, the information is valueless.

But again, the critical factor is usually time. It doesn't matter if this kind of information eventually becomes ubiquitous. What matters is being among the first who possess it and act on it. While potent secrets usually don't stay secret, they may remain so long enough to advance the cause of their original holders.

Point of View and Authority Have Value

In a world of floating realities and contradictory maps, rewards will accrue to those commentators whose maps seem to fit their territory snugly, based on their ability to yield predictable results for those who use them.

In aesthetic information, whether poetry or rock 'n' roll, people are willing to buy the new product of an artist, sight-unseen, based on their having been delivered a pleasurable experience by previous work.

Reality is an edit. People are willing to pay for the authority of those editors whose point of view seems to fit best. And again, point of view is an asset which cannot be stolen or duplicated. No one sees the world as Esther Dyson does, and the handsome fee she charges for her newsletter is actually payment for the privilege of looking at the world through her unique eyes.

Time Replaces Space

In the physical world, value depends heavily on possession or proximity in space. One owns the material that falls inside certain dimensional boundaries. The ability to act directly, exclusively, and as one wishes upon what falls inside those boundaries is the principal right of ownership. The relationship between value and scarcity is a limitation in space.

In the virtual world, proximity in time is a value determinant. An informational product is generally more valuable the closer purchaser can place themselves to the moment of its expression, a limitation in time. Many kinds of information degrade rapidly with either time or reproduction. Relevance fades as the territory they map changes. Noise is introduced and bandwidth lost with passage away from the point where the information is first produced.

Thus, listening to a Grateful Dead tape is hardly the same experience as attending a Grateful Dead concert. The closer one can get to the headwaters of an informational stream, the better one's chances of finding an accurate picture of reality in it. In an era of easy reproduction, the informational abstractions of popular experiences will propagate out from their source moments to reach anyone who's interested. But it's easy enough to restrict the real experience of the desirable event, whether knock-out punch or guitar lick, to those willing to pay for being there.

The Protection of Execution

In the hick town I come from, they don't give you much credit for just having ideas. You are judged by what you can make of them. As things continue to speed up, I think we see that execution is the best protection for those designs which become physical products. Or, as Steve Jobs once put it, "Real artists ship." The big winner is usually the one who gets to the market first (and with enough organizational force to keep the lead).

But, as we become fixated upon information commerce, many of us seem to think that originality alone is sufficient to convey value, deserving, with the right legal assurances, of a steady wage. In fact, the best way to protect intellectual property is to act on it. It's not enough to invent and patent; one has to innovate as well. Someone claims to have patented the microprocessor before Intel. Maybe so. If he'd actually started shipping microprocessors before Intel, his claim would seem far less spurious.

Information as Its Own Reward

It is now a commonplace to say that money is information. With the exception of Krugerrands, crumpled cab fare, and the contents of those suitcases that drug lords are reputed to carry, most of the money in the informatized world is in ones and zeros. The global money supply sloshes around the Net, as fluid as weather. It is also obvious, that information has become as fundamental to the creation of modern wealth as land and sunlight once were.

What is less obvious is the extent to which information is acquiring intrinsic value, not as a means to acquisition but as the object to be acquired. I suppose this has always been less explicitly the case. In politics and academia, potency and information have always been closely related.

However, as we increasingly buy information with money, we begin to see that buying information with other information is simple economic exchange without the necessity of converting the product into and out of currency. This is somewhat challenging for those who like clean accounting, since, information theory aside, informational exchange rates are too squishy to quantify to the decimal point.

Nevertheless, most of what a middle-class American purchases has little to do with survival. We buy beauty, prestige, experience, education, and all the obscure pleasures of owning. Many of these things can not only be expressed in nonmaterial terms, they can be acquired by nonmaterial means.

And then there are the inexplicable pleasures of information itself, the joys of learning, knowing, and teaching; the strange good feeling of information coming into and out of oneself. Playing with ideas is a recreation which people are willing to pay a lot for, given the market for books and elective seminars. We'd likely spend even more money for such pleasures if we didn't have so many opportunities to pay for ideas with other ideas. This explains much of the collective "volunteer" work which fills the archives, newsgroups, and databases of the Internet. Its denizens are not working for "nothing," as is widely believed. Rather they are getting paid in something besides money. It is an economy which consists almost entirely of information.

This may become the dominant form of human trade, and if we persist in modeling economics on a strictly monetary basis, we may be gravely misled.

Getting Paid in Cyberspace

How all the foregoing relates to solutions to the crisis in intellectual property is something I've barely started to wrap my mind around. It's fairly paradigm warping to look at information through fresh eyes-to see how very little it is like pig iron or pork bellies, and to imagine the tottering travesties of case law we will stack up if we go on legally treating it as though it were.

As I've said, I believe these towers of outmoded boilerplate will be a smoking heap sometime in the next decade, and we mind miners will have no choice but to cast our lot with new systems that work.

I'm not really so gloomy about our prospects as readers of this jeremiad so far might conclude. Solutions will emerge. Nature abhors a vacuum and so does commerce.

Indeed, one of the aspects of the electronic frontier which I have always found most appealing-and the reason Mitch Kapor and I used that phrase in naming our foundation-is the degree to which it resembles the 19th-century American West in its natural preference for social devices that emerge from its conditions rather than those that are imposed from the outside.

Until the West was fully settled and "civilized" in this century, order was established according to an unwritten Code of the West, which had the fluidity of common law rather than the rigidity of statutes. Ethics were more important than rules. Understandings were preferred over laws, which were, in any event, largely unenforceable.

I believe that law, as we understand it, was developed to protect the interests which arose in the two economic "waves" which Alvin Toffler accurately identified in The Third Wave. The First Wave was agriculturally based and required law to order ownership of the principal source of production, land. In the Second Wave, manufacturing became the economic mainspring, and the structure of modern law grew around the centralized institutions that needed protection for their reserves of capital, labor, and hardware.

Both of these economic systems required stability. Their laws were designed to resist change and to assure some equability of distribution within a fairly static social framework. The empty niches had to be constrained to preserve the predictability necessary to either land stewardship or capital formation.

In the Third Wave we have now entered, information to a large extent replaces land, capital, and hardware, and information is most at home in a much more fluid and adaptable environment. The Third Wave is likely to bring a fundamental shift in the purposes and methods of law which will affect far more than simply those statutes which govern intellectual property.

The "terrain" itself-the architecture of the Net-may come to serve many of the purposes which could only be maintained in the past by legal imposition. For example, it may be unnecessary to constitutionally assure freedom of expression in an environment which, in the words of my fellow EFF co-founder John Gilmore, "treats censorship as a malfunction" and reroutes proscribed ideas around it.

Similar natural balancing mechanisms may arise to smooth over the social discontinuities which previously required legal intercession to set right. On the Net, these differences are more likely to be spanned by a continuous spectrum that connects as much as it separates.

And, despite their fierce grip on the old legal structure, companies that trade in information are likely to find that their increasing inability to deal sensibly with technological issues will not be remedied in the courts, which won't be capable of producing verdicts predictable enough to be supportive of long-term enterprise. Every litigation will become like a game of Russian roulette, depending on the depth of the presiding judge's clue-impairment.

Uncodified or adaptive "law," while as "fast, loose, and out of control" as other emergent forms, is probably more likely to yield something like justice at this point. In fact, one can already see in development new practices to suit the conditions of virtual commerce. The life forms of information are evolving methods to protect their continued reproduction.

For example, while all the tiny print on a commercial diskette envelope punctiliously requires a great deal of those who would open it, few who read those provisos follow them to the letter. And yet, the software business remains a very healthy sector of the American economy.

Why is this? Because people seem to eventually buy the software they really use. Once a program becomes central to your work, you want the latest version of it, the best support, the actual manuals, all privileges attached to ownership. Such practical considerations will, in the absence of working law, become more and more important in getting paid for what might easily be obtained for nothing.

I do think that some software is being purchased in the service of ethics or the abstract awareness that the failure to buy it will result in its not being produced any longer, but I'm going to leave those motivators aside. While I believe that the failure of law will almost certainly result in a compensating re-emergence of ethics as the ordering template of society, this is a belief I don't have room to support here.

Instead, I think that, as in the case cited above, compensation for soft products will be driven primarily by practical considerations, all of them consistent with the true properties of digital information, where the value lies in it, and how it can be both manipulated and protected by technology.

While the conundrum remains a conundrum, I can begin to see the directions from which solutions may emerge, based in part on broadening those practical solutions which are already in practice.

Relationship and Its Tools

I believe one idea is central to understanding liquid commerce: Information economics, in the absence of objects, will be based more on relationship than possession.

One existing model for the future conveyance of intellectual property is real-time performance, a medium currently used only in theater, music, lectures, stand-up comedy, and pedagogy. I believe the concept of performance will expand to include most of the information economy, from multicasted soap operas to stock analysis. In these instances, commercial exchange will be more like ticket sales to a continuous show than the purchase of discrete bundles of that which is being shown.

The other existing, model, of course, is service. The entire professional class-doctors, lawyers, consultants, architects, and so on are already being paid directly for their intellectual property. Who needs copyright when you're on a retainer?

In fact, until the late 18th century this model was applied to much of what is now copyrighted. Before the industrialization of creation, writers, composers, artists, and the like produced their products in the private service of patrons. Without objects to distribute in a mass market, creative people will return to a condition somewhat like this, except that they will serve many patrons, rather than one.

We can already see the emergence of companies which base their existence on supporting and enhancing the soft property they create rather than selling it by the shrink-wrapped piece or embedding it in widgets.

Trip Hawkins's new company for creating and licensing multimedia tools, 3DO, is an example of what I'm talking about. 3DO doesn't intend to produce any commercial software or consumer devices. Instead, it will act as a kind of private standards setting body, mediating among software and device creators who will be their licensees. It will provide a point of commonality for relationships between a broad spectrum of entities.

In any case, whether you think of yourself as a service provider or a performer, the future protection of your intellectual property will depend on your ability to control your relationship to the market—a relationship which will most likely live and grow over a period of time.

The value of that relationship will reside in the quality of performance, the uniqueness of your point of view, the validity of your expertise, its relevance to your market, and, underlying everything, the ability of that market to access your creative services swiftly, conveniently, and interactively.

Interaction and Protection

Direct interaction will provide a lot of intellectual property protection in the future, and, indeed, already has. No one knows how many software pirates have bought legitimate copies of a program after calling its publisher for technical support and offering some proof of purchase, but I would guess the number is very high.

The same kind of controls will be applicable to "question and answer" relationships between authorities (or artists) and those who seek their expertise. Newsletters, magazines, and books will be supplemented by the ability of their subscribers to ask direct questions of authors.

Interactivity will be a billable commodity even in the absence of authorship. As people move into the Net and increasingly get their information directly from its point of production, unfiltered by centralized media, they will attempt to develop the same interactive ability to probe reality that only experience has provided them in the past. Live access to these distant "eyes and ears" will be much easier to cordon than access to static bundles of stored but easily reproducible information.

In most cases, control will be based on restricting access to the freshest, highest bandwidth information. It will be a matter of defining the ticket, the venue, the performer, and the identity of the ticket holder, definitions which I believe will take their forms from technology, not law. In most cases, the defining technology will be cryptography.

Crypto Bottling

Cryptography, as I've said perhaps too many times, is the "material" from which the walls, boundaries—and bottles—of cyberspace will be fashioned.

Of course there are problems with cryptography or any other purely technical method of property protection. It has always appeared to me that the more security you hide your goods behind, the more likely you are to turn your sanctuary into a target. Having come from a place where people leave their keys in their cars and don't even have keys to their houses, I remain convinced that the best obstacle to crime is a society with its ethics intact.

While I admit that this is not the kind of society most of us live in, I also believe that a social over reliance on protection by barricades rather than conscience will eventually wither the latter by turning intrusion and theft into a sport, rather than a crime. This is already occurring in the digital domain as is evident in the activities of computer crackers.

Furthermore, I would argue that initial efforts to protect digital copyright by copy protection contributed to the current condition in which most otherwise ethical computer users seem morally untroubled by their possession of pirated software.

Instead of cultivating among the newly computerized a sense of respect for the work of their fellows, early reliance on copy protection led to the subliminal notion that cracking into a software package somehow "earned" one the right to use it. Limited not by conscience but by technical skill, many soon felt free to do whatever they could get away with. This will continue to be a potential liability of the encryption of digitized commerce.

Furthermore, it's cautionary to remember that copy protection was rejected by the market in most areas. Many of the upcoming efforts to use cryptography-based protection schemes will probably suffer the same fate. People are not going to tolerate much that makes computers harder to use than they already are without any benefit to the user.

Nevertheless, encryption has already demonstrated a certain blunt utility. New subscriptions to various commercial satellite TV services skyrocketed recently after their deployment of more robust encryption of their feeds. This, despite a booming backwoods trade in black decoder chips, conducted by folks who'd look more at home running moonshine than cracking code.

Another obvious problem with encryption as a global solution is that once something has been unscrambled by a legitimate licensee, it may be available to massive reproduction.

In some instances, reproduction following decryption may not be a problem. Many soft products degrade sharply in value with time. It may be that the only real interest in such products will be among those who have purchased the keys to immediacy.

Furthermore, as software becomes more modular and distribution moves online, it will begin to metamorphose in direct interaction with its user base. Discontinuous upgrades will smooth into a constant process of incremental improvement and adaptation, some of it manmade and some of it arising through genetic algorithms. Pirated copies of software may become too static to have much value to anyone.

Even in cases such as images, where the information is expected to remain fixed, the unencrypted file could still be interwoven with code which could continue to protect it by a wide variety of means.

In most of the schemes I can project, the file would be "alive" with permanently embedded software that could "sense" the surrounding conditions and interact with them. For example, it might contain code that could detect the process of duplication and cause it to self-destruct.

Other methods might give the file the ability to "phone home" through the Net to its original owner. The continued integrity of some files might require periodic "feeding" with digital cash from their host, which they would then relay back to their authors.

Of course files that possess the independent ability to communicate upstream sound uncomfortably like the Morris Internet Worm. "Live" files do have a certain viral quality. And serious privacy issues would arise if everyone's computer were packed with digital spies.

The point is that cryptography will enable protection technologies that will develop rapidly in the obsessive competition that has always existed between lock-makers and lock-breakers.

But cryptography will not be used simply for making locks. It is also at the heart of both digital signatures and the aforementioned digital cash, both of which I believe will be central to the future protection of intellectual property.

I believe that the generally acknowledged failure of the shareware model in software had less to do with dishonesty than with the simple inconvenience of paying for shareware. If the payment process can be automated, as digital cash and signature will make possible, I believe that soft product creators will reap a much higher return from the bread they cast upon the waters of cyberspace.

Moreover, they will be spared much of the overhead presently attached to the marketing, manufacture, sales, and distribution of information products, whether those products are computer programs, books, CDs, or motion pictures. This will reduce prices and further increase the likelihood of noncompulsory payment.

But of course there is a fundamental problem with a system that requires, through technology, payment for every access to a particular expression. It defeats the original Jeffersonian purpose of seeing that ideas were available to everyone regardless of their economic station. I am not comfortable with a model that will restrict inquiry to the wealthy.

An Economy of Verbs

The future forms and protections of intellectual property are densely obscured at this entrance to the Virtual Age. Nevertheless, I can make (or reiterate) a few flat statements that I earnestly believe won't look too silly in 50 years.

- In the absence of the old containers, almost everything we think we know about intellectual property is wrong. We're going to have to unlearn it. We're going to have to look at information as though we'd never seen the stuff before.

- The protections that we will develop will rely far more on ethics and technology than on law.

- Encryption will be the technical basis for most intellectual property protection. (And should, for many reasons, be made more widely available.)

- The economy of the future will be based on relationship rather than possession. It will be continuous rather than sequential.

- And finally, in the years to come, most human exchange will be virtual rather than physical, consisting not of stuff but the stuff of which dreams are made. Our future business will be conducted in a world made more of verbs than nouns.

INDEX